FRANCE

Irún St. Jean de Luz
Hendaye Pau
an Sebastián
GUIPÚZCOA
Pamplona
NAVARRE Jaca
stella
Tafalla

Pyrenees
Val d'Aran ANDORRA
Perpignan
Seo de Urgel Figueras
Puigcerdá

Huesca Tremp
Barbastro R. Segre Vich Gerona
ARAGON
R. Ebro Balaguer Manresa
Saragossa Lérida Artesa de Segre
CATALONIA
Bujaraloz Fraga Borjas Blancas Barcelona
Calatayud
Montblanch
Belchite Caspe Tarragona
Alcañiz Gandesa
Maestrazgo Sierra de Pandols
Montalban Tortosa
Amposta
Sierra de Palomera Vinaroz

Teruel
Cuenca Castellón

Minorca
Port Mahon

Sagunto
Palma
Valencia Mallorca

Albacete Gandía

Alcoy Ibiza Ibiza
Elda Formentera
este Alicante

Murcia

Cartagena

ría

THE SPANISH CIVIL WAR

THE SPANISH CIVIL WAR

ANTONY BEEVOR

PETER BEDRICK BOOKS
NEW YORK

Distributed in the USA by Harper & Row
and in Canada by Book Center, Montreal

PICTURE ACKNOWLEDGMENTS

The publishers would like to thank Editorial Planeta S.A., Barcelona, and Editions Ruedo Ibérico, Paris, for supplying most of the illustrations for this book. Other illustrations were kindly provided by the following sources: Associated Press, Bundesarchiv, René Dazy, Mary Evans Picture Library, Robert Hunt Library, Illustrated London News Picture Library, Imperial War Museum, John Topham Picture Library, Roger Viollet.

First American edition published in 1983 by Peter Bedrick Books. Published by agreement with Orbis Publishing Limited, London.

© 1982 by Antony Beevor

ISBN 0-911745-11-4
LC 83-71475
Printed in Great Britain

CONTENTS

INTRODUCTION

A Spanish proverb says that history is a common meadow in which everyone can make hay. It is particularly appropriate for a civil war which became the subject of such international propaganda at a time when the regimes of Hitler and Stalin were consolidating themselves. These two extremes, which yet had so much in common, exploited their enmity shamelessly. Their apparently implacable antipathy created artificial alternatives through gross simplification. They set out to persuade their audiences that the individual was redundant; the great enemy could only be defeated with mass organization, discipline and a supra-human ideology.

Such total mobilization required artists, writers and intellectuals to subordinate their talents and beliefs to political necessity. This of course had a profound, almost traumatic effect on the intellectual life of a generation. On the left most withdrew their support from the Communist Party as a result of events in Republican Spain and the Nazi-Soviet pact in August 1939, five months after General Franco's victory. The utter disillusionment which so many of them faced probably explains in part the comparatively restrained commitment of intellectuals thirty years later during the war in Vietnam.

The civil war in Spain has almost certainly provoked more books in more languages than any other, although there have been remarkably few general histories. It is perhaps the best example of a subject which becomes more confusing when it is simplified. If the war is only unfolded along a single dimension of class struggle, events and motives become unnecessarily hard to understand. This book therefore sets out to explain the enmities and alliances in terms of the three basic forces of conflict: right against left, centralist against regionalist, and authoritarian against libertarian. The tensions and shifts within the Republican camp leading to 'a civil war within the civil war' make this clarification even more essential.

The account of events in Nationalist Spain is hardly in dispute except for the level of civilian slaughter. In contrast, the struggle within the Republican alliance has provoked major arguments, of which the most famous was Noam Chomsky's critique in *American Power and the New Mandarins* of Gabriel Jackson's history of the war. Chomsky attacked the book for its assumption of the 'official' standpoint and its reliance on the testimony of Republican ministers and army officers, who may have felt a need to justify their support of communist power.

The effects of Communist Party propaganda persisted for a remarkably long time after the war. In the last five years several historians have moved further away from the almost unconditional respect originally accorded to Juan Negrín, the social democrat prime minister whom the communists advanced to achieve their aims. The most durable part of communist propaganda, however, has been the professional image which they used to justify their covert control and to impress foreigners like Hemingway. This book also sets out to re-examine their conduct of the war and the argument that there was no alternative strategy.

The Spanish civil war is probably the most convincing reminder that the last word on history is impossible. The absolute truth about such a politically passionate subject can never be known, because nobody can discard prejudice sufficiently.

THEIR MOST CATHOLIC MAJESTIES

Recent events indicate that the Spanish civil war is not yet entirely finished. On the evening of 23 February 1981 a greater number of Spaniards than usual were watching the debate in the Cortes on their television sets. Adolfo Suárez, the first elected prime minister since before the civil war, had resigned on 29 January. And Leopoldo Calvo Sotelo, his successor from the conservative UCD (Union of the Democratic Centre), was unlikely to achieve confirmation by a large margin.

Despite the odd rumours of another military conspiracy, few amongst the television audience expected the scenes which occurred shortly before 6.30 pm. In mid-debate some 220 civil guards armed with automatic weapons charged into the Cortes led by Lt-Colonel Antonio Tejero. Deputies and ministers dived for cover as they fired bursts at the ceiling. Some were hit by falling plaster. The television cameras were shot out or smashed, making screens go blank across the country. The young socialist leader Felipe González was led off to a small room where at gunpoint he was made to sit facing the wall.

Most left-wing deputies had immediately assumed they would be executed. In 1936 the military rebels and their allies hunted down and killed 34 of their predecessors. It appears that lists for execution had also been prepared on this occasion. Later, without any trace of self-consciousness, Lt-Colonel Tejero began to lecture his hostages on how the army would save Spain from terrorism.

At 7 pm Tejero rang one of the chief conspirators, General Milans del Bosch, a defender of the Alcázar of Toledo in 1936 when a lieutenant, a veteran of the Spanish Blue Division which fought for the Germans on the Russian front, and now the captain-general in Valencia commanding III Military Region. Tejero reported that all was in order, '*sin novedad*', which had also been the codeword for the 1936 rising. The general then ordered his tanks to move out into the streets.

The most vital formation for a coup, however, was the Brunete Armoured Division, whose barracks lay just beyond the suburbs of Madrid. Its senior staff officer, one of the coup planners, sent sub-units to seize various points including the government television and radio station. Some of the troops involved were told that they were going to prevent ETA

Basque guerrillas from attacking the Cortes, just as in 1936 garrison troops in Barcelona were told they were marching out to pre-empt an anarchist rising.

Even if few officers were actively implicated in Tejero's operation, his subsequent treatment as a hero would indicate that a considerable proportion of the regular army sympathized. The government received no warning of the coup from military intelligence or any other source, and only three of the ten most important army commanders at the time could have been counted as definitely loyal to the constitution.

Nevertheless the attempted coup faltered within a few hours largely through inadequate preparation. The conspirators had advanced their plans in order to take advantage of the uncertainty between Suárez's resignation and Calvo Sotelo's confirmation. The rebels' hasty action meant that, instead of securing the firm commitment of other officers beforehand, they counted on their example triggering the sympathetic into action. This left the moment of decision too late. Potential supporters were thus tempted to hang back until the outcome was easier to predict. So, by starting without that critical minimum of guaranteed support, the conspirators jeopardized the elements essential to a coup's success: initiative, momentum and decisiveness.

Doubtful officers were most concerned by the possible reaction of King Juan Carlos. Unlike even conservative politicians, the king carried a considerable influence as a result of his years in the army. He had stated his commitment to the constitution in unequivocal terms, yet many regulars seemed to regard this as no more than a necessary gesture. Only a couple of hours before the storming of the Cortes, the former head of his military household, General Alfonso Armada, approached the king without revealing himself as the proposed head of a military government, in order to gauge his reaction discreetly.

The king's exact role that night is of course disputed. The conspirators with the exception of General Armada claim that they acted on his orders, but only the wishful on the extreme right take this seriously. Many more assert, however, that he too hung back, waiting to see how events developed before committing himself. But if he did, it would have been a reversal of his policy for the previous five years.

Juan Carlos had made it clear that he did not want to fulfil the opposition's prophecy on General Franco's death in 1975 that he would only be remembered as Juan the Brief. He had decided that a monarchy in modern Europe was unlikely to last if it associated itself with a military dictatorship. His grandfather Alfonso XIII abdicated in 1931 on realizing his unpopularity after the rule of General Primo de Rivera. In June 1946 the Italians voted for a republic after their royal family's earlier tolerance of Fascism. And in more recent times his brother-in-law Constantine left revolt against the Greek Colonels too late to convince the electorate of his democratic credentials. In contrast, Juan Carlos's strategy since the death of Franco had been devoted to introducing the parliamentary system and to persuading the diehard elements from the old regime not to fight gradual reform.

Once the king began to order in loyal units and contact other officers within the Brunete Armoured Division, Generals Armada and Milans del

Bosch backed down while all those on the edge of joining hurried to cover their tracks. Lt-Colonel Tejero's daughter then rang her father in the Cortes and the revolt was over in under eight hours.

Many foreign newspapers described the whole affair in comic opera terms. Tejero was portrayed as a quixotic character with his Zapata moustache and civil guard bicorn hat. And on the surface it was tempting to think of Marx's aphorism about history repeating itself, the first time as tragedy, the second as farce. But farce is not always far removed from tragedy. The farce of General Sanjurjo's revolt in 1932 was followed by the tragedy of July 1936. Many Spaniards now fear that Tejero's performance may be followed by a much better organized attempt once the conservative UCD loses power. And for politicians to underestimate the threat from the army is as dangerous now as in 1936

If one cannot yet define a clear end to the Spanish civil war, not even the tidy-minded could say that the conflict simply began in July 1936 with the rising of the 'Nationalist' generals against the Republican government. That event merely signalled the greatest clash in the conflict of forces which had dominated Spanish history. One of those antagonisms was evidently between class interests, but the other two were no less important: authoritarian rule against libertarian instinct and central government against regionalist aspirations. These pairs of conflict often mingled or overlapped and strange alliances were sometimes formed. But, when the war started in 1936, the Nationalist generals and their supporters represented three coherent poles: they were authoritarian, they upheld the interests of landowner and industrialist and they believed in centralized government. The Catholic church, the oldest and most powerful political force in Spain, was to provide them with a rallying banner and an emotive ideology to justify the rising. The opposing coalition, usually called Republican, was an incompatible alliance since, within its ranks, it contained all three axes of conflict of which the most far-reaching was the clash between the authoritarian communists and the libertarian anarchists. In fact the only name to be universally accepted was 'anti-fascist', which underlined what a disparate and defensive association it was.

The genesis of the three strains of conflict lay in the way the *Reconquista* of Spain from the Moors had shaped the social structure of the country and formed the attitudes of the Castilian conquerors. The intermittent warring against the Moors, begun by Visigoth warlords in the eighth century, finally ended in 1492 with the triumphal entry of Isabella and Ferdinand into Granada. For the Spanish traditionalist the event marked both the culmination of a long crusade and the beginning of the country's civilization. This idea permeated the Nationalist alliance of 1936, which continually invoked the glory of Ferdinand and Isabella, the Catholic monarchs, and referred to their own struggle as the second *Reconquista*, with liberals, 'reds' and separatists allotted the role of contemporary heathen.

With a feudal army forming the prototype of state power, the monarchy and warrior aristocracy took possession of the land during the fight against the Moors. In order to continue the *Reconquista*, the aristocracy needed money, not food. The cash crop which could provide it was Merino wool.

The peasants' land was seized for sheep grazing, which not only had a catastrophic effect on the peasants' food supply, but also led to soil erosion, ruining what had once been the 'granary of the Roman empire'. Few people were needed to tend the sheep and the only alternative to starvation was the army and, later, the empire. In the Middle Ages Spain was estimated to have a population of about 14 million. At the end of the eighteenth century it was a little over seven million.

Castilian authoritarianism developed from a feudal–military emphasis to one of political control by the church. During the seven centuries of the *Reconquista*'s uneven course, the church's role had been mainly that of propagandist for military action, and even of participant. Then, in Isabella's reign the warrior archbishop was superseded by the cardinal statesman. Nevertheless, the connection between church and army remained fundamental during the rapid growth of Spain's empire when the crucifix was the shadow of the sword over half the world. The army conquered, then the church integrated the new territories into the Castilian state.

The power which was exerted over the population was an irresistible force, backed by the threat of hell and its earthly foretaste in the form of the Inquisition. A single denouncer, an anonymous whisper from a jealous enemy, was often enough for the Holy Office, and the public confessions extracted before *autos da fé* provided a striking foretaste of the totalitarian state. In addition the church controlled every aspect of education and placed the entire population in a protective custody of the mind by burning books and enforcing a *cordon sanitaire* to keep out religious and political heresy. It was also the church which vaunted the Castilian qualities like endurance of suffering and equanimity in the face of death. It encouraged the idea that it was better to be a starving *caballero* than a fat merchant. (In October 1936, after the philosopher Unamuno's attack on the 'necrophiliac' mentality of Nationalist Spain, the propaganda department of Franco's GHQ stated that 'the supreme dignity of man, of Spanish man, is not the search for the happiness of comfort, nor material progress, but a difficult life and the tragic sense of existence where the words "pain" and "war" hold an affirmative and beautiful quality'.)

This Spanish Catholic puritanism had been guided by Cardinal Ximénez de Cisneros, the ascetic friar promoted by Isabella to be the most powerful statesman of the age. It was basically an internal reformation. The papacy was being rejected because of its corruption, so Spain had to save Europe from heresy and Catholicism from its own weakness. As a result the clergy practised what it preached, with the exception of forgiveness and brotherly love, and sometimes issued pronouncements on property which were almost as subversive as the original teaching. Nevertheless, the church provided spiritual justification for the Castilian social structure and was the most authoritarian force in its consolidation.

The third strain of conflict, centralism against regionalism, also developed in the fifteenth and sixteenth centuries. The first major revolt against the united kingdoms had a distinctly regionalist element. The rising of the *comuneros* in 1520 against Isabella's grandson, the Emperor Charles V, was provoked not only by his use of the country as the treasury of his empire and by the arrogance of his Flemish courtiers but also by his disregard for local rights and customs. Much of the country had been assimilated into the Castilian kingdom through royal marriage, and the Spanish Habsburgs until Philip IV preferred to let the church act as the binding force of the realm. Particular regions were allowed to keep their old laws and traditions (*fueros*), which the monarch swore to respect and defend (as with the Basques under the oak tree of Guernica). In return they usually paid an agreed sum rather than suffer the imposition of direct taxes from Castile. There were, however, clashes of interest, of which the most important were basically economic.

These three determining attributes of the Castilian state, feudal, authoritarian and centralist, were strongly interlinked. This was particularly true when it came to the regional question. Castile had established a central authority in Spain and built the empire, but its administration rigidly refused to acknowledge that feudal economic relationships were growing out of date. The wars in northern Europe, the fight against the French in Italy and the destruction of the Armada meant that the imperial power, developed in less than two generations, had started to decline almost immediately. Castile had the unbending pride of a newly inpoverished nobleman, who refuses to see the cobwebs and decay in his great house and resolutely continues to visualize the grandeur of his youth. This capacity for seeing only what it wanted to see made the Castilian ruling order introverted. It did not accept that the treasures in the churches fed nobody, and that the vast quantities of precious but useless metal only undermined the country's economic infrastructure.

Catalonia, which had been absorbed into the kingdom of Aragon during the Middle Ages, was very different from the rest of the peninsula and it was inevitable that a major dispute would develop between Madrid and Barcelona. The Catalans had enjoyed a considerable amount of power in the Mediterranean. Their empire had included the Balearics, Corsica, Sardinia, Sicily and the Duchy of Athens. But as it had been the Castilian Isabella, not Ferdinand of Aragon, who financed Columbus, they did not have direct trading access to the Americas.

In 1640 Catalonia and Portugal rose against Philip IV of Spain and his minister, the Count-Duke of Olivares. Portugal won its independence but Catalonia acknowledged Louis XIII of France as its king, until Barcelona fell to Philip IV in 1652. Then, after the death of the last Spanish Habsburg in 1700, the War of the Spanish Succession started and Catalonia sided with England against Louis XIV's grandson, Philip of Anjou. The Catalans were betrayed by the English in the Treaty of Utrecht, and the Bourbon Philip V abolished Barcelona's rights, after it was reduced in 1714. The castle of Montjuich was built to dominate the city and remind the Catalans that they were ruled from Madrid. With this beginning Philip proceeded to implement the centralist idea of his Sun King grandfather. The unifying force of the church had waned, so a new centripetal strength was needed if the monarchy was to control non-Castilians. The twentieth-century Basque philosopher, Unamuno, who was no separatist, stated that 'the aim was unity and nothing else; unity stifling the slightest individuality and difference ... It is the dogma of the ruler's infallibility.' But toughness did not solve the problem; it only stored up trouble for the future.

The backwardness of Spanish commercial activity during the seventeenth and eighteenth centuries was mainly due to the way that Spanish

Catholicism had maintained an anti-capitalist line by clinging to medieval teaching on usury. The code of the *hidalgo* (Spanish gentleman) forced him to despise money in general and the earning of it in particular. The census of 1788 showed that almost 50 per cent of the adult male population was not involved in any form of productive work. The army, the church and, above all, the vast nobility were a dead weight on the rest of the population. It was perhaps this statistic which provoked the famous saying that 'one half of Spain eats but does not work, while the other half works but does not eat'.

In reaction against the commercial backwardness and rigidity of the ruling order, Spain was to experience a middle-class revolution in advance of most of Europe. The country enjoyed a brief easing of the chains in the mid-eighteenth century, during Charles III's reign, when the influence of the Enlightenment was felt. Reforms severely reduced the church's influence over the army, while many officers were attracted to freemasonry. This anti-clerical and, therefore, political movement, was inextricably linked with the development of liberalism among Spain's very small, professional middle class.

Liberalism became a recognizable force early in the nineteenth century as a result of the 'War of Independence' against Napoleon's armies. The mentally deficient Charles IV was deposed by a popular mutiny because he tolerated French control. Napoleon refused to recognize Ferdinand VII and much of the Spanish aristocracy sided with the occupying power. Then Murat's executions in Madrid provoked a spontaneous rising by the people on the famous Second of May, 1808, when they ferociously attacked the emperor's Mameluke cavalry with knives. 'Napoleon's ulcer', as the rising was called, was the first large-scale guerrilla war of modern times and 60,000 Spaniards died in the defence of Saragossa. The bitter resistance came from a popular movement, though some liberal army officers played a major role, especially within the local juntas of defence.

The traditional ruling structure of 'Old Spain' suffered its first formal upset in 1812, when the central junta of defence proclaimed the Constitution of Cádiz, which was based upon middle-class liberal principles. This opportunity of dispensing with the stifling restrictions of monarchy and church led to many towns and provinces declaring themselves as self-governing cantons within a Spanish federation. These changes did not last, for, although Ferdinand VII was allowed to return on condition that he accepted the constitution, he later broke his word and invoked the Holy Alliance, under which in 1823 the French King Louis XVIII sent an army, called 'The Hundred Thousand Sons of St Louis', to crush Spanish liberalism. Ferdinand dismantled the liberal army and reintroduced the Inquisition to destroy 'the disastrous mania of thinking'.

Spain in the nineteenth century continued to suffer from the clash between liberalism and traditionalism. After Ferdinand's death in 1833 the traditionalist forces grouped themselves round his brother, Don Carlos (and thus became known as Carlists). The main Carlist strength lay among the smallholders of the Pyrenees, especially in Navarre, and his supporters became famous for their religious fanaticism and ferocious rejection of modernity. Ferdinand's heir was the young Queen Isabella II; the liberal army supported her succession (and later provided most of her lovers).

The free-thinking liberalism which permeated the increasingly middle-class officer corps in the early years of the century declined as its supporters profited from the sale of church lands and developed into a reactionary *grande bourgeoisie*. The governments in Madrid were corrupt and the generals acquired a taste for overthrowing them. This was the age of the *pronunciamiento*, when generals would form up their troops and make long speeches appointing themselves saviour and dictator of the country. Between 1814 and 1874 there were 37 attempted coups, of which 12 were successful. The country lurched along, becoming poorer and poorer, while Queen Isabella exercised her guards officers. She was finally deposed in 1868 after choosing a lover of whom the army did not approve. Two years later Amadeo of Savoy was chosen as her successor, but his earnest goodwill was not enough to win support from a population exasperated with the monarchy. His abdication in February 1873 was followed by a vote in the Cortes establishing a republic.

The First Republic was brought down by military intervention, even though its federalist programme had enjoyed strong support. This had included the abolition of military conscription, but within a few weeks of the first election held by the new republic, sporadic Carlist revolts became a full-scale civil war and the government was forced to break this important promise. The Carlist pretender's most effective troops were the staunchly Catholic Basques, who were primarily motivated by separatist ambitions of throwing off rule from Madrid. Spanish monarchs were only lords of the Basque provinces, which constituted a *señorío* and which had never been subjected to central rule like other parts of the peninsula.

The generals saw the army's main role as enforcing Spanish unity, especially after the loss of the South American empire in the 1820s. As Castilian centralists, they were appalled by the prospect of separatist Basque and Catalan nations occupying the Pyrenean frontier. They were also implacably opposed to federalism, so, when self-governing cantons were proclaimed in other areas, they did not hesitate to crush this movement against government from Madrid as well as the Carlists and Basques. The First Republic lasted only a few months.

The conservative politician, Cánovas del Castillo, had been planning the re-establishment of the Bourbons since the fall of Isabella. He also wanted to institute stable government while returning the army to barracks. This was achieved when General Martínez Campos proclaimed Alfonso XII king at the end of 1874. Alfonso was Isabella's son (and therefore presumably of good military stock), but he was still only a Sandhurst cadet.

Under Cánovas' constitution, which was to last half a century, church and landowner were back in strength. They had every intention of keeping it that way and elections were unashamedly manipulated. Peasants and tenants had to vote as their landlord told them or face eviction and starvation. Canvassing consisted of the political bosses, the *caciques*, sending out armed gangs known as *El Partido de la Porra* (the Bludgeon Party) and if that did not look like working, then ballot papers were destroyed or substituted. Political and economic corruption spread from Madrid in a way that far exceeded anything known in previous centuries. The courts were rigged right down to the village tribunals, so no poor person ever expected to have his case heard, let alone obtain justice. Meanwhile, although there may have often been a vicious rivalry between liberals and conservatives in the provinces, there was virtually a gentleman's agreement between their leaders in the capital. Whenever there was an unpopular measure to carry out, the conservatives retired and the liberals, who had now become almost indistinguishable from their opponents, came in. The two parties resembled those little wooden men who appear alternately out of their houses to indicate the weather. But any high-minded figure, however aristocratic, who denounced the corruption was regarded as a traitor and shunned. The trinity of church, army and monarchy, which had originally made the empire, was also to preside over its final collapse. In 1898 the Spanish-American war saw the pathetic rout of the armed forces and the loss of Cuba, the Philippines and Puerto Rico. Most of the soldiers' food and equipment had been sold by the officers.

Karl Marx observed that, with the exception of Turkey, Spain was the most misunderstood nation in Europe. The misunderstanding arose principally because the Moorish invasion had thrown the country out of synchronization with the rest of Europe. As a result feudalism was imposed later than in the rest of western Europe, whereas the process of national unification began much earlier than in Germany or Italy. In addition, the extended *Reconquista* developed an integrated state and empire well in advance of France. Yet the notions of the Spanish governing class never wavered. Cervantes brilliantly illustrated the gap between the Castilian self-image (represented by Don Quixote, the knight of the Sad Countenance) and reality (the knight of the Mirrors). Even the tawdry end of the *Reconquista* vision in Cuba in 1898 did not rouse the rulers of Spain from their armoured complacency. They could not admit that the obsession with empire had ruined the country. To admit that would have been to undermine the institutions of aristocracy, church and army. This refusal to face reality started to come up against new political forces, which were growing rapidly and which, unlike the liberalism of the early nineteenth century, could not be absorbed into the governing structure. The incompatibility of 'Eternal Spain' with these new political movements developed into the clash which later tore the country apart.

II

ROYAL EXIT

Spain began the twentieth century with very little industry and an agricultural system which kept almost half of its four-and-a-half million agricultural workers on the edge of starvation. It had an army with one general to every hundred ragged soldiers and a vast surplus of incompetent officers whose only successes consisted of crushing unarmed rural revolts. The navy, meanwhile, had almost ceased to exist after its defeat in the Spanish-American war. Corruption, financial scandals and speculations in public life were so common that they aroused little interest. The treasury still reneged on its bonds, a practice which had provoked the English traveller Richard Ford to comment in the mid-nineteenth century that 'no country stands lower in financial discredit'.

The tax system was a farce. More than a third of government income went into the pockets of the collectors and even more disappeared in the speculations of ministers and their subordinates. Remarkably few taxes were imposed on the rich in the first place and yet fiscal fraud deprived the government of between 50 and 80 per cent of the total due. According to an observer in 1909, small landowners paid between 30 and 40 pesetas per acre, while the large landowners paid virtually nothing.

A budgetary deficit had been usual for nearly two centuries. In anticlerical times it had been made up by plundering religious establishments, but this expedient was now unthinkable. The church had once again achieved a dominant position within the royal family, in politics and in education. Its new strength was business despite its previous teaching, and the stock exchange gazette was now the only liberal paper which it was not a mortal sin to read. Thirty years after the restoration of the Bourbons, the Spanish church was said to have owned up to one-third of the total wealth of Spain. This development gave it all the more reason to defend the *status quo* with every means at its disposal. A Jesuit priest who preached a thought-provoking sermon on private property to a wealthy Madrid congregation was dismissed by his bishop for offending them.

The other elements of Spain's traditional ruling group fitted together like mutually defensive chess pieces. The *caciques*, usually large landowners, who organized the elections for the government, obtained in return the complete co-operation of the civil governor, the bureaucracy, the police

17

and even the judiciary. They spawned their own neo-feudal hierarchy, with sub-agents right down to village level making sure that the machine ran smoothly.

The great landowners of the centre and especially the south (the northern belt was mainly an area of smallholdings) had a power out of proportion even to their wealth. In Estremadura, La Mancha and Andalucia, 7,000 landowners owned 15 million acres, the three richest grandees accounting for about 600,000 of them. Many landlords visited their estates only once a year to check accounts or enjoy the partridge shooting. One duke kept 56,000 acres uncultivated for this purpose alone. As has often been pointed out, the landowners' attitude towards their estates was that of foreign owners to colonial properties; their peasants were treated almost as a subject race. The far more numerous landowners of the *grande bourgeoisie*, who had profited from the sale of church and common land in the first half of the nineteenth century, were no better. The rural lower-middle class of smallholders, meanwhile, was under the sway of the clergy and provided the basis of all anti-progressive movements.

After the Cuban disaster of 1898, which provoked a remarkable intellectual renaissance, the liberal army drew closer to the arch-conservatism it had challenged during the nineteenth century. The strength of freemasonry, and thus of anti-clericalism and even republicanism, diminished within the officer corps. This monarchist revival was helped by the passion of the young King Alfonso XIII for uniforms and all things military.

The one section of the 'ruling 20 per cent', which did not like the interlocking defence of established privilege, was the business community. Spain's late industrial development cannot be equated to a similar stage in other European countries, for so much of it was the result of British and French investment. The only two major manufacturing centres were Catalan Barcelona and Basque Bilbao. Both were constricted by the Castilian aristocracy's attitude to commerce, and local industrialists were supporting a resurgence of their own culture.

The development of Spain's middle class had been restricted by the combination of church and aristocracy. At the beginning of the nineteenth century the country had experienced a short-lived bourgeois revolution, but its effect was almost totally negated when the new *grande bourgeoisie* became an integral part of the *ancien régime* restored after 1875.

Meanwhile, in the third quarter of the nineteenth century, the lower middle class of mainly urban artisans (in marked contrast to their rural counterparts) emerged as a revolutionary force eager to throw off the corruption of Madrid rule. In the last quarter of the century this *petite bourgeoisie* joined with lawyers, teachers and doctors (an alliance which formed liberal republicanism), when the rise of socialism displaced it as the vanguard of change. With the development of this far more threatening level of opposition, the monarchy, together with its supporters of church, aristocracy and *grande bourgeoisie*, became even more inflexible. Any protest or disorder was repressed with heavy loss of life by the army and the civil guard.

The first attempt to organize some form of trade union had occurred as early as the 1830s, and there were small non-political associations in existence at the middle of the century. Twenty years later new political ideas arrived across the Pyrenees and began to take root among the million industrial workers and three million landless peasants.

The anarchist, or libertarian, form of socialism arrived first, and its fundamental disagreement with Marxist socialism was to have great repercussions. Proudhon had already been translated by Pi y Margall, the president of the First Republic, when Giuseppe Fanelli arrived in Spain in 1868. Fanelli was an admirer of Bakunin, Marx's great opponent in the First International. He came to Madrid without speaking any Spanish and with no money, but the Idea, as it became known, found a very enthusiastic audience. Within four years there were around 50,000 Bakuninists in Spain, of whom the majority were to be found in Andalucia.

Mikhail Bakunin was a Russian prince who had devoted his enormous energies to the overthrow of autocracies since witnessing the suppression of the Polish revolt as an artillery officer in the Imperial Guard. He could perhaps be best described as the prime moving force of anarchism while others, such as Kropotkin and Malatesta, were more important as theorists.

The natures and ideas of Marx and Bakunin were totally incompatible. 'He called me a sentimental idealist,' Bakunin wrote later, 'and he was right. I called him a vain man, perfidious and crafty, and I was right.' Bakunin utterly distrusted Marx's character and predicted that the philosophy of such a man could only lead to dictatorship and deceit. As Isaiah Berlin emphasizes, 'an alliance built on an almost complete absence of common aims could not last long: the orderly, rigid, unimpressionable Marx regarded Bakunin as half charlatan, half madman, and his views as absurd and barbarian.' In return Bakunin issued a warning in 1870, nearly half a century before the Russian revolution: 'Take the most radical revolutionary and place him on the throne of all the Russias and give him dictatorial power and within a year he will have become worse than the Tsar himself.' The anarchists did not only reject the communist idea of a worker-state; they believed that the domination of one human by another was the root source of all violence and evil. It was an analysis which had far more radical implications than Marx's mainly economic critique of capitalism.

There were several reasons why anarchism became the largest force within the Spanish working class and exceeded the influence it achieved in countries such as Italy, Russia, France and Switzerland. Its proposed structure of co-operative communities, associating freely, corresponded to deep-rooted traditions of mutual aid, and the federalist organization appealed to anti-centralist feelings. It also offered a strong moral alternative to a cynically corrupt political system and hypocritical church. Many observers have pointed to the often naive optimism which anarchism inspired amongst the landless peasants of Andalucia. Much has also been made of the way in which the word was spread by ascetic, almost saint-like characters and how the converts gave up tobacco, alcohol and infidelity (while rejecting official marriage). As a result it has often been inaccurately described as a secular religion. Even so, the optimistic intensity of this early anarchism led converts to believe that everybody else must see that freedom and mutual aid were the only foundation of a naturally ordered society. An uprising was all that was needed to open people's eyes, unfetter the vast potential of goodwill and set off what Bakunin called the 'spontaneous creativity of the masses'. The anarchists tended to underrate the influence which habit and the fear of change can exercise on people's minds. Their frustration at being unable to 'unlock the mechanism of history', as the Russian writer, Victor Serge, described it, led to individual acts of political violence in the 1890s. The *tigres solitarios*, as their fellow anarchists called them, acted either in the hope of stirring up others to emulate them or in reprisal for the indiscriminate brutality of the Brigada Social, the secret police. The most famous example was the torturing to death in 1892 of several anarchists in the castle of Montjuich in Barcelona. This led to an international outcry and to the assassination of Cánovas del Castillo, the organizer of the restoration. A vicious circle of repression and revenge was to follow.

After the Barcelona upheaval of 1909, known as the *Semana Trágica*, or 'Tragic Week' (see below), a majority in the libertarian movement evolved a new strategy. This new direction was mainly influenced by the French syndicalist movement, with a union-based policy, the ultimate objective of which was a general strike followed by the reorganization of society based on self-managed industry and agriculture. This led to the setting up of the anarcho-syndicalist National Confederation of Labour (CNT), whose component unions were to be organized by industry, not by craft. The Spanish libertarian movement thus consisted basically of anarchist purists and anarcho-syndicalists.

During the last quarter of the nineteenth century the Marxist wing of socialism, *los autoritarios*, as their opponents called them, developed much less rapidly. In late 1871 Karl Marx's son-in-law Paul Lafargue arrived after the fall of the Paris Commune and within a year the basis of Spanish Marxist socialism was laid in Madrid. The Marxists' lack of success, in comparison to the anarchists, was partly due to the emphasis which they placed on the central state. The idea of a 'parliamentary road to socialism' was unthinkable in such a blatantly crooked electoral system as Spain's. Marx wrote to Engels that they would 'have to leave Spain to him [Bakunin] for the time being'.

The socialists under Pablo Iglesias, a typesetter who emerged as the leading Spanish Marxist, proceeded cautiously and concentrated on building an organization. They obviously hoped that they were going to be the tortoise to the anarchist hare. Eventually in 1879 they founded the Spanish Socialist Workers' Party (PSOE) and formed their General Union of Labour (UGT). Iglesias still insisted that the class struggle should be waged in a moderate and evolutionary manner (it was not until 1914 that the PSOE formally repudiated the monarchy). The socialists accused their anarchist rivals of 'irresponsibility' and 'frivolity', but they were themselves seen as heavy and uninspired and were nicknamed the 'Spanish Prussians'. The workers also preferred the anarchist idea that no official should be paid or gain power from his position. The socialists were not suspected of corruption in any way, but their undemocratic and middle-class central committee was unpopular.

Another reason for the socialists' tiny size in comparison to the anarchists was Marx's contempt of the peasantry and what he called 'the idiocy of rural life'. He believed that capitalism would be overthrown only by its

20

own creation, the industrial proletariat. However, in Spain, the major part of industry was concentrated in Catalonia, which had become the stronghold of anarchism. As a result the 'Castilian' socialists had to look to Bilbao for support among industrial workers. The central mass of Spain and the northern coast were to be their main spheres of influence, while the anarchist following was greatest down the Mediterranean belt. At the beginning of the century the socialists had some 15,000 followers, while the anarchists were approaching 100,000. By the time of the Russian revolution, the socialists had some 200,000 followers to the anarchists' 800,000. They were to overtake them only during Primo de Rivera's dictatorship in the 1920s, when all libertarian organizations were banned. Government figures in 1934 put UGT membership at 1.44 million and CNT membership at 1.58 million.

The rigid attitudes of the Spanish *ancien régime* helped ensure that the Spanish urban workers and landless peasantry became one of the most politically aware working classes in the world during the early years of the twentieth century. From the 1890s until the early 1920s Spain experienced many turbulent years, especially those which coincided with the Russian and German revolutions at the end of the First World War. The main areas of strife were the large landed estates, the *latifundia*, of Andalucia and Estremadura, the mining valleys of Asturias and Vizcaya, and industrial Catalonia. In *fin de siècle* Barcelona, *nouveaux riches* factory owners indulged in triumphant ostentation, both architecturally and socially. Their self-satisfaction created a suffocating atmosphere in addition to the appalling conditions of work in the factories and, as several historians have pointed out, much of the early violence was an urge to shock and shake their complacency. Also, in the years following the incidents of 1892, the Brigada Social was to interpret its role as the guardian of public order in a manner which often strained belief. Gangsters were hired or black-mailed into implementing what would now be called a strategy of tension in order to provoke the imposition of martial law on a permanent basis and thus crush working-class power. In many cases the police gangs also worked for the Employers' Federation, which had a close liaison with the Brigada Social. In one year there was an extraordinary spate of bomb attacks against property belonging to Catalan industrialists. Investigations revealed that the vast majority, if not all, of the 2,000 explosions were the work of a police gang under a convicted criminal, Juan Rull, who was acting on the orders of the Duke of Bivona, the governor of Barcelona.

The *Semana Trágica* at the end of July 1909 was the first urban explosion of unrest. These events were not caused by industrial dispute, but came as a result of the colonial war in Morocco. Riffian tribesmen had wiped out a column of soldiers on its way to secure mining concessions bought by the Count of Romanones, one of Alfonso XIII's advisers. The government called up the reserves; the poor could not afford to buy themselves out of military service and married workers were the most affected. A strong anti-militarist mood had grown up in the years following the Cuban disaster, and the spontaneous reaction in Barcelona to the Morocco crisis was sudden and overwhelming. The 'young barbarians' who supported the Radical party leader, Lerroux, went wild. There was an explosion of violence against property, which mainly consisted of church-burning and

21

forms of desecration such as the famous incident of a worker dancing with a disinterred nun. Such symbolic violence against the church, together with the burning of religious buildings, was the reaction of a people traumatized by the intense superstition which had been inflicted upon them over previous centuries. Much of the teaching of the Spanish Catholic church sounded appropriate to the Dark Ages and this mental repression, together with the political role played by ecclesiastical authorities, made the church rank with the civil guard as the first target of an uprising. Some half a dozen people were killed during this disturbance, but when the army arrived to restore order there was a massacre. Hundreds were arrested including Francisco Ferrer, the founder of the libertarian Modern School. Although it was evident that Ferrer could have had nothing to do with the rioting, the Catholic hierarchy put heavy pressure on the government to convict their educational opponent. He was sentened to death on the basis of obviously false testimony and his execution led to a wave of protest in Spain and abroad.

The First World War had important effects on the country. Spain enjoyed the greatest export boom in its history. Vast new areas of land came under cultivation to take advantage of foreign buying, while industry expanded at a rapid rate, drawing in manpower from depressed rural areas. The country's gold reserves nearly quadrupled and business profits soared, but prices rose faster than wages. The year 1917 was to see some curious developments. Business leaders had begun to chafe even more at the heavy control of Madrid. They resented the fact that taxation from the industrial areas subsidized the rest of the country and lined the pockets of officials. Both Basque and Catalan separatism had a strong economic base and it was no coincidence that their cultural revival coincided with their financial development. At the same time, it looked as if the army was reacting against the corruption and inefficiency of Madrid government. Juntas of defence, which seemed akin to military trade unions, were being organized by both officers and non-commissioned officers. Many were thus led to believe that the army was becoming a progressive force again in the early nineteenth-century tradition: but in fact the officers were only interested in better pay and enhanced status.

Despite the reformist caution of its leadership at this time, the socialist UGT was provoked by the government's sudden repudiation of a railway workers' pay agreement. It called a general strike on 10 August. The anarcho-syndicalist CNT was persuaded to join it, despite misgivings. But in Barcelona the alliance between Catalan businessmen, workers and the army against the government was shown to be an illusion. The army reverted to its authoritarian and centralist role and turned its machine-guns on the strikers.

With the end of the war the export boom slackened, but the workers, finding themselves worse off at a time of vast business profits, had become more militant. Also, the news from Russia brought hope, and there was talk of Europe blazing with revolution at both ends. The period of 1918–1920, with uprisings in Andalucia and strife in Barcelona, was known as the 'three years of Bolshevism'. The Catalan employers replied with lockouts and resorted to blackleg labour from depressed areas. They also hired *pistoleros* to shoot down union leaders. The police, too, had their squads of hired criminals, organized by Bravo Portillo, a former German agent who had just come out of prison. Portillo's successor was 'Baron Koenig', another former German agent, who supplemented his salary from the captain-general (regional governor) of Catalonia for shooting union leaders by blackmailing and kidnapping industrialists. CNT members fought back and their unions hired gunmen as well. To restore order Alfonso XIII then appointed General Martínez Anido as captain-general. His chief-of-police, General Arleguí, reorganized the police *pistoleros*, and 21 union leaders were shot down either at home or in the street in less than 48 hours. But such actions, together with a terrorist attack which the captain-general staged against himself in order to justify his actions, made the new government of Sánchez Guerra remove him from his post.

The political system of Old Spain was incapable of adapting. Its attitude remained that of Ferdinand VII, who revealed the aptitude of Spanish rulers for confusing cause and effect in vivid metaphors. 'Spain is a bottle', he had declared solemnly not long before dying of gout, 'and I am the cork, and when the cork is no longer there the champagne gushes over.' A new cork was tried in September 1923, when General Primo de Rivera seized power.

Primo's dictatorship, which lasted for six years, came about because of outrage in the country against the army. Apart from the extraordinary events in Barcelona, the army also suffered the most ignominious defeat in its history when a division commanded by General Silvestre was ambushed at Annual on 20 July 1921 by Moroccan tribesmen under Abd-el-Krim. For reasons of personal vanity, King Alfonso was said to have wanted an outstanding victory to announce on the feast of St James (the Spanish army's patron saint) and to have gone behind the minister of war's back to encourage Silvestre in this venture. It was a classic example of military incompetence: 10,000 soldiers were killed, 4,000 were taken prisoner and Silvestre committed suicide. A week later another major position was lost, another 7,000 soldiers were massacred and all the officers were led away in chains. The reaction throughout Spain was so bitter that a commission of inquiry was formed. The king was severely censured in its findings, but a few days before the report was due to be published the new captain-general of Catalonia, Miguel Primo de Rivera, made a *pronunciamiento*, appointing himself dictator with Alfonso remaining as head of state. The other generals gave him tacit support to prevent this public condemnation of the army and the king.

Primo de Rivera was not a typical dictator of the inter-war period. He was in many ways an Andalucian version of those hard-living, hard-riding squires of Regency England. As a young officer he had been sickened by corrupt practices within the army such as the selling of the soldiers' food and equipment and in 1893 he shot General Margallo, the commander-in-chief in Morocco, for selling rifles to the tribesmen they were fighting. (To stop the scandal, Margallo was reported killed in action and given a hero's funeral.)

Primo's assumption of power was also accepted by the liberal middle classes, who felt that nothing could be worse than the recent years of chaos and bloodshed. They hoped that the dictator, even though a member of the aristocracy, might be able to implement agrarian reforms which no

23

landowning government would consider. But, although Primo sympathized with the peasants in a patriarchal fashion, any serious attempt to
tackle the agrarian problem would have required measures that were too
radical for him and unthinkable for those on whom he depended. He did,
however, attempt to end the industrial warfare in Catalonia. Workers'
organizations had to be involved, he decided, and the employers controlled. The centralist socialists were the obvious choice for Primo, and he
brought the secretary of the UGT, Francisco Largo Caballero, into his
government to set up industrial arbitration boards.

The anarchists accused Largo Caballero of opportunism when their
organizations and publications were banned. Personally honest, Largo
was much less scrupulous when the UGT had a chance of growing at the
expense of the CNT. But opposition to collaborating with Primo grew
within socialist ranks and by 1929 Largo was forced to realize his mistake.
When in 1930 the socialists opposed the monarchy and the dictatorship,
UGT membership began to rise rapidly. From 211,000 members in 1923 it
increased to 277,000 in 1930 and just over half a million in 1932.

The Catalan employers, meanwhile, hated the new government's control
over their methods of dealing with union leaders. Primo also took a spiteful
pleasure in attacking their nationalism through attempts to suppress Catalan language and culture. Like all patriarchs, he was convinced of his
own good intentions. He made grand gestures, took petty measures and
was unpredictable. His biggest success was to end the war in Morocco
through a joint operation with the French. However, his plans to moder-
nize Spain included ambitious engineering projects which resulted in enormous waste as a result of bad planning. The deficit doubled between
1925 and 1929, so the country's accounting system was changed to wipe
out the national debt with a stroke of the pen. Primo was so pleased that
he ordered mattresses to be redeemed from pawnshops by the government
so that the people could share in his pleasure. Primo had a completely
arbitrary approach to justice, trying often to play Solomon with a sense of
humour which fell flat. But there was no police-state brutality.

Under Primo's rule a claustrophobic irritation built up and the middle
classes started to react when he interfered with the universities. As a
flamboyant product of his profession and background, the well-meaning
patriarch became a vastly tempting coconut shy for the intellectuals whom
he detested. Like a stern, insensitive father whose authority is challenged,
Primo tried to enforce his will more and more. Hurt and confused at not
being appreciated, he appealed to the army to reassure himself of their
support. It was not forthcoming, so Primo resigned on 28 January 1930.
He died in Paris a few weeks later.

After Primo's departure the king needed to maintain the dictatorship
and General Berenguer was placed at the head of the government. But the
day of judgement for the monarchy was thereby only delayed. Alfonso,
who had often seemed to treat the ruling of Spain as little more than a
fascinating hobby, realized by the end of 1930 that he must start to restore
the constitution. Berenguer offered his resignation on 13 February 1931
and four days later Admiral Aznar formed a government to organize
municipal elections on 12 April. At those elections the monarchists held
the countryside, thanks mainly to the loyalty of the conservative small-

holders of the northern belt and electoral intimidation where the *caciques* remained powerful. But every large town except Cádiz went to anti-monarchical candidates. The king was shocked by the proof of his unpopularity. His chief minister, Aznar, spoke of a 'country which we believed to be monarchist turning republican in twenty-four hours'. When the army failed to declare its support and General Sanjurjo, the commander of the civil guard, made it clear that he could not maintain the king in power, Alfonso realized that he had no alternative but to abdicate.

The supposed sportsmanship of Alfonso's departure was to influence later events. Its chief effect was on conservative opinion in England, which was to play such an important role during the civil war. The damage which Alfonso's vanity had caused Spain was ignored, along with his resulting unpopularity. Winston Churchill demonstrated this when he wrote that 'the articulate forces in France, Britain and, we doubt not, in the United States, were more attracted by the character and personality of King Alfonso than by the character and personality of the Spanish people'. Alfonso had all the qualifications which appealed to British connoisseurs of foreign royalty. He was married to a Battenberg princess, was colonel-in-chief of a British lancer regiment, played polo and showed a cool head in a tight situation. He personified the sort of monarch for whom the fictional heroes of the period would risk life and limb. But then the only foreigners the English establishment liked were those who imitated their customs, tailoring and values.

Alfonso possessed a disastrous combination of being both imperceptive and having a taste for intrigue. It had led to the disaster of Annual; then it led him to believe that he could continue after the dictatorship as if nothing had happened. The most striking example of his insensitivity to public opinion was the confirmation of the death sentences imposed on two anti-monarchist officers who had attempted an unsuccessful rising at Jaca. It was a move which contributed much to his downfall.

The fluidity of the transfer from monarchy to republic during the afternoon of 14 April 1931 stemmed from a meeting in San Sebastián the previous summer. There nine conservative and liberal republicans as well as Indalecio Prieto, the moderate socialist, concluded what came to be called the pact of San Sebastián. This set out to provide the framework for a centre government once the monarchy fell.

Several of these men were of the *grande bourgeoisie*, which had traditionally sided with the monarchy. They now joined the intellectuals, such as the novelist, Pérez de Ayala, and the philosopher, Ortega y Gasset, who represented the liberal movement of revolt against the asphyxiating complacency of the monarchy. This movement was rather different from a middle-class revolution encouraged by economic motives. Miguel Maura, a former monarchist and future minister of the interior, stated later that he had joined the liberal republicans 'so as to defend conservative principles from within' because 'the monarchy had committed suicide'.

The rising in December 1930, which followed the San Sebastián manifesto, had been a fiasco. However, the imprisonment of the signatories guaranteed their popularity and Alfonso's execution of Captain Galán and Lieutenant Hernández provided the anti-monarchist movement with martyrs. Thus, when the king departed that evening of 14 April 1931, the leading figures of the new government were ready. They drove through the cheering crowds on their way to form an administration. The new prime minister was Niceto Alcalá Zamora, an Andalucian lawyer and landowner as well as a former monarchist minister. Lerroux, the former radical demagogue of Barcelona and leader of the Young Barbarians who had now become conservative and notoriously corrupt, was made foreign minister. Other members of the cabinet included Prieto, Largo Caballero, Fernando de los Ríos (a moderate socialist and professor from Granada), Casares Quiroga (a liberal Galician lawyer) and Manuel Azaña. Azaña was soon to take over as prime minister and in 1936 he became president of the Republic, a post which he held without great enthusiasm throughout the civil war.

Even though the Second Spanish Republic had arrived without violence, after the collapse of a discredited institution, it was automatically an object of dislike for what Churchill termed 'the articulate forces'. But the euphoric crowds were congratulating themselves, for they felt sure that the 'immaculate' Republic could not fail to be respected by other countries, as well as within Spain, and that there could be no pretence for intervention to restore the *ancien régime* as had happened in the past.

III

THE SECOND REPUBLIC

The middle-class government stepped in to replace the king's men, who mustered superficial good grace in accepting the situation until they had time to reorganize. The workers, meanwhile, were encouraged by the direction of events, especially in the latifundist regions of the south-west, where the monarchy symbolized the great landowners. Yet it soon became evident that the Republican centre was to be caught between the forces of traditional Spain, which only regarded its defeat as a temporary setback, and the expectations of a desperately underprivileged mass. The Republic was to be involved in deep conflict over the questions of land reform, the power of the church and the army, and regional devolution. The centralist and authoritarian representatives of old Spain regarded any attempt to tamper with the traditional structure of the nation as treason. They believed themselves to be justified in fighting back with any means. In reply, the new government of the centre was to adopt an approach which was like knocking over an opponent without disarming him. When the loyalty of the army and the civil guard was so uncertain it was most incautious to emphasize the political defeat which the old order had suffered. The trial *in absentia* of Alfonso, for example, infuriated its enemies while achieving little.

General elections were held in June 1931. The PSOE socialists won 117 seats, the radical socialists 59, Azaña's Republican Action 27, the Esquerra (the Catalan left republicans of Luis Companys) 33, the Galician republicans of Casares Quiroga 16, Lerroux's Radical Party 89 and Alcalá Zamora's right republicans 27. The non-Republican right won only 57 seats. The socialists were for once united with unusual harmony between Largo Caballero and Indalecio Prieto, the moderate from Bilbao who was a strenuous advocate of a centre-left alliance with liberal republicans. Largo Caballero agreed on socialist participation in the government because he felt it was in the best interests of the UGT, his overriding concern. Even though his union was growing rapidly, the CNT was outstripping it, since becoming legal again the previous year. Socialist membership was consolidated with their development of *casas del pueblo*, which were centres for meeting and education and the equivalent of the anarchist *ateneos libertarios*. The only dissident voice against PSOE policy at that time belonged to Julián Besteiro, the president of the party and a philosophy professor who, although a moderate, insisted from his theoretical Marxist viewpoint, that the Republicans must be left to carry out the middle-class revolution on their own.

Manuel Azaña, the most prominent liberal republican, was a strongly anti-clerical intellectual of brilliant wit and lugubrious pessimism. He came to regard himself as the strong man of the Republic, but he lacked consistency and stamina for such a role. His support came mainly from the progressive middle class, such as teachers and doctors, as well as from the lower middle-class artisans and clerks. The right republicans, dominated by Lerroux's radicals, were supported by the conservative and business elements who had disliked Alfonso, but had no deep-rooted opposition to the principle of monarchy.

Of the main difficulties which the Republic was to face, the question of church power came to the fore barely a fortnight after Alcalá Zamora's government had taken office in mid-April. Cardinal Segura, the archbishop of Toledo and primate of the Catholic Church in Spain, issued a pastoral which heaped praise on Alfonso (to whom he owed his rapid advancement) and represented a trumpet-blast of defiance against change in any form. Segura was no indolent prince of the church and he may well have pictured himself as a second Ximénez de Cisneros, the protégé of Isabella who had helped save the Spanish crown for the Emperor Charles with the words 'aut Caesar, aut nihil' during the revolt of the Comuneros in 1520. Less than 20 per cent of Spain's total population went to mass. In most areas south of the Guadarrama mountains the figure was under 5 per cent. Church attendance in Spain was the lowest of any Christian country, yet Segura was to declare that in Spain one was 'either a Catholic, or nothing at all'. It was a phrase with a familiar ring. His provocative pastoral marked the beginning of a struggle in which an unpopular institution managed to portray itself as a martyr and act as the rallying flag for the forces of the right.

The church was detested by the workers and labourers for preaching acceptance of poverty while amassing vast riches. Its attitude towards the poor was that of the traditional reply to a beggar when refusing alms: 'Have patience, brother.' Most of the professional middle class disliked the repressive influence it had on many aspects of life, above all on education. In some areas the church stopped teaching children to read so as to prevent them from studying socialist tracts later. Catechisms were recited instead. The illiteracy rate ranged by area from a quarter to just over half of the population, while the church schools for children of parents able to afford high fees were usually good. And, since the ecclesiastical hierarchy sabotaged state education by persuading the caciques to divert the money intended for schools, it is not surprising that anti-clericalism was strong among teachers. Doctors, too, had a long tradition of resenting church influence. In the nineteenth century they were liable to a large fine if they did not prescribe confession on a patient's first visit. Priests often accused them of sorcery and interfered in every way out of a fear that science and learning would weaken the church's hold over its flocks. Intellectuals were scornful of the dispensations to eat meat during Lent, which were sold by the church 'like a game licence', and of the spectacle of priests picketing theatres while on the other hand the church encouraged bullfighting.

It was the fanatical mysticism of the church which provoked most people, especially the 'miracles', which in the 1930s seemed usually to consist of a 'communist' supposedly committing a sacrilegious act and dropping dead on the spot. The novelist, Ramón Sender, attributed anti-clerical vandalism, such as the desecration of mummies, to the church's obsession with the kissing of saints' bones and limbs. Anything, however ridiculous, was believed by the *beatas*, the black-clothed women who obeyed their priests' every word like the devotees of a cult leader. In Spain there were more psychological disorders arising from religious delusions than all other kinds. In reaction to traumatic superstition, workers formed gruesome ideas of torture in convents, and many natural catastrophes were attributed to the Jesuits in the same way as the church blamed freemasons, Jews and communists.

Two weeks after the publication of the primate's pastoral, serious disturbances were sparked off by an incident outside a monarchist club in Madrid, when a taxi driver was apparently beaten up for shouting *'¡Viva la República!'* After Segura's defiant support of Alfonso, between 20 and 30 churches were set on fire, although the bishops claimed four times that number. It started with the buildings of the monarchist newspaper *ABC* and the Carmelite church in the Plaza de España and stretched down into Andalucia. There was apparently no frenzy in the proceedings and onlookers watched blankly. Churchmen blamed dark forces, which meant agents paid with Moscow gold, but of that there was no evidence. Nevertheless, the bishops' greatest hatred was reserved for the government, which had refused to call out the civil guard on the grounds that citizens' lives were worth more than religious buildings. For the right, these events marked the first step towards civil war.

The government began with several minor measures to reduce the power of the church, but its main attack came in the constitution. Church and state were separated, while the civil list paid in return for previously confiscated land was to be stopped in two years. Religious orders were forced to register (at this period there were about 35,000 priests, 20,000 monks and 60,000 nuns) and were allowed only enough wealth for their own needs. Civil marriage was instituted and divorce allowed. The Jesuits were made to dissolve on the grounds that their senior members had to swear an oath of allegiance to the Pope. These measures did not persecute the church, but they certainly represented an attack on an institution which was argued to have power far in excess of its following. Conservatives were outraged; the Catholic church was the heart of Spain and Spanish civilization.

The next act of the government which greatly offended traditionalists was the granting of home rule to Catalonia. A referendum on home rule in the region received an overwhelming majority, though the poll was low because of anarchist abstentions. On 9 September 1932 the statute of autonomy became law and the historic *Generalidad* (Catalan government) was restored.

The Basques also pressed for autonomy, but without success. Basque society was very conservative in its own way. It had never passed through a feudal stage and the mountain pastures were usually still farmed on a co-operative basis. Even the mines were owned by the local municipality until after the Second Carlist War in 1876. This was the time when the Basques were deprived of their *fueros*, which the Spanish monarchs used to swear to uphold under the oak tree of Guernica. Their traditional way of life also began to be affected at this time. With their oak forests they had always been a seafaring race, but the heavy industry which developed round Bilbao was capitalist and often foreign-owned, as in Catalonia. And, as in Barcelona, the demand for labour drew workers from depressed agricultural areas outside the region.

In contrast to the majority of Spaniards, the Basques, whose priests had stayed closely identified with the people, remained devout Catholics. They also remained attached to their old social system. The monarchists, therefore, sought to win the support of fellow conservatives against the 'atheist' Republic. Alfonso even indicated that he was prepared to restore their *fueros*, but José Antonio Aguirre, the Basque nationalist leader, rejected these advances. Right-wing centralists remembered this decision with great bitterness.

For the 'Castilian' army, Basque and Catalan regionalism threatened the break-up of Spain against which the liberal generals of 1873 had moved so firmly. The new government was aware of the discontent in the top-heavy military hierarchy, but it was not alarmed. Azaña introduced legislation to thin out their numbers, but the provisions enabled several thousand officers to retire on full pay and plot against the Republic. His other measures to prevent military revolts through the promotion of loyal officers bore little fruit; but then the only regime which had ever managed to deal effectively with a hostile army in Spain was that of the arch-reactionary Ferdinand VII, who disbanded it and called up his own militias.

The forces of 'Eternal Spain' had started plotting against the Republic within weeks of Alfonso's departure. Monarchists schemed, and Cardinal Segura was said to have travelled around secretly with a project of selling church treasures to help fight the Republic. When the government's legislative programme got under way, the monarchist Major Ansaldo was sent to Italy, where Marshal Balbo offered support for a military rising. In August 1932 General Sanjurjo made a *pronunciamiento* in Seville with a cry against devolution of '¡*Viva España Indivisible!*', while monarchist officers rose in Madrid. The government crushed the revolt effortlessly in Madrid, and in Seville the immediate declaration of a general strike by the CNT made Sanjurjo decide to flee. The element of farce in this plot encouraged Azaña and his colleagues to underestimate the threat in the spring of 1936.

The army was not the only entrenched remnant with which the new regime had to deal. The civil service was still run by the appointees of the monarchical government. Largo Caballero claimed, no doubt partly in self-defence, that most of his measures on industrial relations were sabotaged by officials in the ministry of labour. The great financial institutions, particularly the Bank of Spain and the major industries, were opposed to change. In addition, there was an immense flight of capital out of the country on the fall of the monarchy: about $250 million (at 1931 value) was exported illegally. This coincided with the world depression and although the low-geared economy of Spain was probably less vulnerable than other European countries, the profligate policies of Primo de Rivera's finance minister, Calvo Sotelo, had substantially reduced the gold reserves.

The greatest problem which the government faced was agrarian reform, which exposed the dilemma of the liberal position. The new constitution guaranteed 'to every worker the necessary conditions for a dignified existence'. It also said that property would be 'the object of expropriation for social utility', but guaranteed compensation. No government could solve the appalling problem of the landless peasants by what amounted to purchasing odd strips from landowners with the limited funds available. The situation had been recognized as intolerable in the eighteenth century, but the king's will proved weaker than the vested interests. In the 1930s vast tracts of land were still kept uncultivated despite food shortages, and two million labourers received as little as 40 days' badly paid work a year. These peasants had little reason to love the liberals of the nineteenth century who had followed the advice of Jovellanos, a disciple of Adam Smith. He advocated that church estates and common land should be sold off to the highest bidder. This 'de-communalization' only benefited merchants who wanted cheap land as an investment and as a mark of social status. The peasants not only lost their common land and vital benefits like gathering firewood, but their destitution forced them to work for the new landlords at pitiful wages. It was not surprising that Proudhon's aphorism, 'property is theft', should have struck such a responsive chord among the landless peasantry of the south-west.

Agricultural conditions varied as much as the climate in Spain. Galicia resembled nineteenth-century Ireland, with tenant farmers barely managing to survive on tiny plots of land. The Basques enjoyed rich pastures and no landlords. To their south, in the mixed agriculture of Catalonia, the main dispute was between the tenant wine growers, whose vines suffered from phylloxera, and the landlords who refused to change the terms. The steppe-like plain of Castile was an endless dusty cornland of large estates and poor sparse villages. But the regions of greatest suffering were Estremadura and Andalucia.

There, most of the landless *braceros* had never tasted meat and lived in adobe huts with a hole for a window. On occasions these day-labourers would try to move into newly built pigsties because the accommodation for animals was so much better. The *bracero* earned in the region of three pesetas a day if he was lucky enough to be chosen for work. The leader of the fascist-style Falange, José Antonio Primo de Rivera, the son of the dictator, cites women working a nine-hour day for one peseta. Many were often prepared to work just for a bowl of soup and some bread. The right-wing Catholic paper, *El Debate*, admitted that around Ciudad Real the peasants were eating grass to stay alive.

It was a vicious circle. There was a surplus of labour for the under-used estates so that employers were able to depress wages without risk. As a result the workers were either so weak from malnutrition that they could do little, or they determined to share the work round among their fellow sufferers. The former granary of the Roman empire now had the lowest agricultural productivity in Europe. The *braceros* were unfed human donkeys, or *máquinas de sangre* (machines of blood), and would have been better off as outright slaves. In fact, the villagers of Paredes, whom Prieto

31

described in his speech at Cuenca, were like bond serfs. 'What was the use', he demanded, 'of our romantic Cortes abolishing black slavery in the nineteenth century if we still permit white slavery in Spain?'

For many years the *braceros* would stubbornly bear their lot; then suddenly it would become too much and there would be a violent uprising, desperate and doomed. Strikes were useless because the landowners had no difficulty in finding blacklegs who would do anything to provide a meal for their families. On many occasions the *braceros* would occupy unused land and start to cultivate it until the civil guard was called in by the owner; that usually meant a volley from their Mauser rifles.

The men of this 30,000-strong force, commanded by army officers, were never posted to their home province. Forbidden to mix with the local population, they were regarded as an occupying army of foreigners, which only protected the interests of the landowners and the clergy. (The Republican government also created a new force of 'assault guards', or *asaltos*, as they were called. This para-military riot police was intended mainly as an urban equivalent of the civil guard.) The civil guard was so hated in rural areas that extraordinary violence could be triggered off. At Castilblanco, on 1 January 1932, four civil guards, who tried to prevent a meeting by force, were hacked to pieces by the villagers. As in Lope de Vega's play, *Fuenteovejuna*, the whole community insisted on taking collective responsibility for the deed.

Under such conditions, it was inevitable that the end of the monarchy would arouse hopes which the Republic could not satisfy. Having rejected expropriation, the government could only afford to buy small tracts of land on which it resettled 12,260 families in two years (less than one per cent of the total). Largo Caballero was bitterly disillusioned by this programme, calling it 'an aspirin to cure an appendicitis'. Many others observed that it would take several centuries to solve the land problem at such a rate.

The poor were no longer, in the early twentieth century, prepared to wait patiently. Spanish working-class organizations had been greatly affected by events abroad, particularly in Russia. At first all were overjoyed by the Revolution and delegations were sent to Moscow. The CNT learned of the true situation, however, when one of their observers was released, after having been imprisoned on returning to Spain. The Bolsheviks were liquidating all opposition and the anarchist-influenced Kronstadt uprising had been crushed ruthlessly. The CNT was also horrified to learn that Trotsky's Red Army had attacked Nestor Makhno's anarchist army in the rear, once it had fought off the Whites under Denikin in the Ukraine, despite the treaty which the Soviet government had signed. Only a few syndicalists left the CNT when it condemned the 'Bolshevik dictatorship' and refused to join the Communist International (known as the Comintern or Third International), but the struggle within the socialist PSOE was intense. Their delegation to Moscow had included the Granadine professor, Fernando de los Ríos. He was spirited away from the official visit by the American anarchist, Emma Goldman, who took him to see Kropotkin who had recently issued his open letter attacking Lenin's use of hostages. De los Ríos heard the full story of the Cheka's activities and the Bolshevik consolidation of power. At his subsequent meeting with Lenin he challenged him on what he had been told, to which the Russian leader made his famous retort, 'Liberty? What for?' On his return to Spain he spoke out strongly against affiliation to the Comintern. Greatly aided by a letter from the aged Pablo Iglesias, he succeeded in reversing the earlier decision to join. The convinced *moscovitas* had little option but to leave the PSOE.

The Spanish Communist Party, the PCE, was thus formed by the socialists and syndicalists who supported the Soviet government. It adopted the militantly revolutionary line of the Bolshevik vanguard, differentiating itself entirely from the socialists. In 1931 it in turn suffered a split when Joaquín Maurín and Trotsky's former assistant, Andrés Nin, set up a 'Left Communist' party. (Once again trends in Russia influenced the development of Spanish politics.) This splinter was eventually to become the anti-Stalinist POUM (Workers' Party of Marxist Unification) in September 1935.

The socialists were still maintaining their moderate line in 1932, but many were starting to doubt how much their role in government was achieving, especially with regard to agrarian reform. Meanwhile the anarchists had made clear from the beginning that, although a Republic was obviously preferable to an autocracy, they would always be opposed to the concept of the state. Their relations with the new Republican government could hardly have started in a worse way. During a Barcelona building strike CNT workers barricaded themselves in and said they would only surrender to regular troops. The army arrived and then machine-gunned them as soon as they surrendered. In Seville, after the CNT declared a general strike, 20 anarchists were killed and another 100 wounded when the army besieged their meeting place and reduced it to rubble with artillery.

The libertarian movement was also undergoing an internal struggle at this time. The FAI (Iberian Anarchist Federation), who were the purists of anarchism within the anarcho-syndicalist CNT, had a major dispute with the more conventional trade unionists. They advocated the tactic of sudden uprisings, which the syndicalists described as believing 'in the miracles of holy revolution'. These fragmented revolts to instal their libertarian society took a fairly predictable course. The anarchists and their supporters would march into a town, take over the civic offices, run up the red and black diagonal flag and declare 'libertarian communism'. The besieged civil guard would eventually surrender and, if they had not resisted, they were left unharmed. However, on some occasions, terrible retribution was exacted.

All property deeds were then set on fire, land was declared communal and money abolished. These local declarations of independence against the state were usually suppressed with heavy casualties. The anarchists accused the socialists of being implicated in the repression because of their participation in the government. In return, the socialists accused the anarchists of undermining the Republic and playing into the hands of the right.

On 8 January 1933 there was a rash of minor uprisings and declarations of 'libertarian communism' in Catalonia and Andalucia. At Casas Viejas in the province of Cádiz the usual ceremony took place; nobody was hurt and the civil guard were called on to surrender. Instead, they shut themselves in and waited for reinforcements. A group of *asaltos* soon arrived and surrounded the major party of anarchists, who surrendered peacefully. But one old militant called *Seisdedos*, or 'Six fingers', barricaded himself and his family in his house and resisted with shotguns. The *asaltos* set fire to the house with petrol. One daughter, Libertaria, escaped; the rest of the family was burned to death. The *asaltos* then shot all those who had surrendered previously.

This incident provoked such a political storm that it was a major reason for the government's fall six months later. The right made outrageously hypocritical attacks, while even conservative republicans like Ortega y Gasset and Martínez Barrio (who was later one of Azaña's closest political friends) condemned the administration. In the meantime, tension was increasing in many regions. Local socialist councils tried to fetter the church with regulations and there was much barracking of religious processions; these in turn were increasingly used as right-wing political demonstrations with the protection of armed vigilantes.

The right started to reorganize itself on a national level as well as locally. In the important municipal elections of April 1933 the government fared badly. Only 5,000 left and centre councillors were elected, as opposed to more than 9,000 for the right and centre-right. Azaña became increasingly dejected, both by the attacks of the right and by the criticism of the left at how little had been done to improve the lot of the worker and landless peasant. He resigned in the autumn, leaving Martínez Barrio to lead a caretaker government until the general elections on 19 November 1933.

The results were a shock for Azaña, even though he admitted that the government had not realized its 'many promises'. His party, Republican Action, won only eight seats and the socialists only 60. In contrast, the centre-right Radical Party won 104, the conservative Catalan Lliga 24, the agrarians 29, the new Catholic CEDA alliance 117, and the monarchists and Carlists 35 seats. The swing of power to the right that this distribution of seats represented was more dramatic than was actually indicated by the voting figures, because the electoral system of the Republic had been designed to favour coalitions. In fact, the right obtained twice as many seats as the left for slightly fewer votes.

The socialists had refused to ally with Azaña again because of the Republic's failure to reform a tax system which continued to favour the rich, and because so little had been achieved in social reform. In contrast, the Catholic right and the landowners had reorganized themselves and their success lay in creating a sizeable authoritarian party, the CEDA (The Spanish Confederation of the Autonomous Right), out of a coalition. They had wisely left the monarchists to make the unpopular call for a restoration, but that did not stop an unofficial alliance with the monarchists after the meeting of Gil Robles, the CEDA leader, with King Alfonso at Fontainebleau in June.

The CEDA had the largest number of deputies in the Cortes, but the new government was based on Lerroux's Radical Party, because President Alcalá Zamora so hated Gil Robles that he refused to call on him to form an administration. CEDA election tactics had been well-funded and energetic. According to José Antonio Primo de Rivera, even nuns were dragged out of their convents to vote. Basically the CEDA was following a strategy of the parliamentary road to a Catholic corporate state on the model which

Dollfuss established in Austria. Gil Robles was called *Jefe* (leader), the Spanish equivalent of Führer, and the Catholic Youth organization, the JAP, was, in style at least, reminiscent of its Nazi equivalent in Germany, where their leader had been studying Nazi party methods. Although Gil Robles was initially impressed by Nazi Germany, he soon became disaffected by its anti-clerical nature.

A major reason for the defeat of the centre-left was the refusal of the anarchists to support them after the Casas Viejas incident. They had shown themselves prepared to vote for specific objectives, such as the downfall of the monarchy in 1931, but never for a political programme. In 1933 the abstention rate in major anarchist areas rose to between 40 and 45 per cent, as opposed to about one-third elsewhere. The centre and the left were furious at the way this allowed the victory of the right. The communists were the most angry. In Barcelona, the largest city in Spain and the anarchist stronghold, the communists obtained only 1,500 votes. Bitterness between anarchists and communists was intensifying at this time, partly because of their rivalry in Seville and partly because of the 'Reconstructed CNT' which the PCE had set up on Comintern orders in an attempt to poach anarcho-syndicalist unions.

Almost immediately the FAI anarchists launched their own counter to the new right-wing government with a mass of minor risings, especially in Aragon. They were put down ruthlessly and served only to increase the split with the syndicalist wing of the libertarian movement. The socialists were also divided, for Largo Caballero had been disillusioned by the negligible effect of their participation in Azaña's government. As a result he now took a far more militant line, encouraged by the Young Socialists as well as by the mass of peasants swept up in the UGT's great recruiting drives. The moderates stayed with Indalecio Prieto so the rivalry between the two men increased. Meanwhile, the left as a whole was casting anxious eyes towards Germany and the issue of Gil Robles' entry into the government was one on which the workers declared themselves ready to resort to arms. Hitler had come to power through the parliamentary system and they clearly saw Gil Robles as his equivalent. It was an impression which his propaganda methods and utterances had not attempted to dispel. CEDA posters had called on the population to save Spain from 'Marxists, Masons, Separatists and Jews'. Gil Robles proclaimed openly that he would create an authoritarian state once he was elected. 'The cowardice of the right', he declared, 'has allowed those who come from the cesspools of iniquity to take control of the destinies of the Fatherland.' The left knew that files on its union leaders were being amassed and that projects for drafting the unemployed into labour camps were being discussed.

In the months following the elections Lerroux's government concentrated on undoing almost every reform made by the previous administration. The repeal of the labour laws increased unemployment. Wages were cut or, in some cases, even halved. Those who protested were fired as subversives. There was now no protection of employment or accommodation, and many who had voted for the centre or left against their employers' instructions found themselves without work or home. In Andalucia the civil guards uprooted the crops on the land which had been purchased for landless peasants under the agrarian reform measures. Some conservatives acknowledged the terrible suffering in depressed areas, but the right's only solution was to increase the strength of the civil guard to protect property. Peasants who collected acorns to eat were arrested as criminals; hunger marches were fired upon; and the *casas del pueblo* or *ateneos libertarios* were broken up by the civil guard or attacked by thugs hired by landowners.

Only the CEDA's support maintained the Radical Party in government, for whose members being in power seemed to be an end in itself. Its programme was determined by Gil Robles, who was waiting for the right moment to take over himself. In various speeches he made it clear that the next step would be to organize a crushing electoral victory and then re-write the constitution entirely. In the first week of October 1934 the Radical Party government of Ricardo Samper, who had succeeded Lerroux five months earlier, resigned. Gil Robles demanded a CEDA majority in the new administration, but the socialists warned the president that they would take this as a declaration of war on the left. Even moderates like Prieto and De los Ríos were convinced that there was no alternative but to fight if Gil Robles took over. They feared that Gil Robles' policies would develop along the lines of Dollfuss' suppression of the socialists in Austria. A year before Gil Robles had stated openly that 'democracy is not an end for us, but a means to arrive at the conquest of the New State. When the moment comes parliament will either submit, or we will make it disappear.'

Alcalá Zamora was forced into a compromise solution. He called on Lerroux to form a government again, but with three minor posts going to the CEDA. Azaña, Martínez Barrio and even Miguel Maura rejected what they saw as the handing over of the Republic to its declared enemies. The left started to obtain arms, though not to the degree claimed by the Falangist leader, José Antonio Primo de Rivera, who wrote on 24 September to General Francisco Franco, the future leader of the military rising of 1936, that they had 'first-rate weapons'. José Antonio, as he was always known, also suggested that Trotsky was in Spain and 'all this against a background of rampant social indiscipline. The Spanish state run as it is by amateurs simply does not exist.'

An uprising of the centre-left and left, intended as a pre-emptive strike against an imminent fascist take-over, broke out on 5 October 1934. The Catalan nationalists revolted, but Luis Companys, the head of Esquerra (Catalan Left), was not allowed by his allies to call on the CNT to join them. A rising in Barcelona without libertarian support was doomed and Companys was forced to surrender in a few hours. Meanwhile, Largo Caballero's socialists started an ineffective revolt in Madrid, which collapsed rapidly. In Asturias, however, fighting developed into a small-scale civil war. An effective alliance in this mining region had been made between the UGT and the CNT. In many ways it was the forerunner of the Popular Front of 1936. The communists, who represented only a small group, joined at the last moment because Comintern policy had changed on Stalin's orders. Moscow was moving towards a Popular Front strategy as a defence against the growing strength of fascism and nazism in Europe. That meant that communist parties in Europe should make common cause with other working-class and progressive middle-class parties.

In Asturias the rebel forces amounted to some 50,000 workers, most of whom were miners. What they lacked in arms was made up in part by the skill of the blasting experts from the mines. The rebels captured Oviedo after heavy fighting which prompted the government to react quickly under pressure from the CEDA leaders. General Franco, the chief-of-staff, ordered units of the Spanish Foreign Legion and Moorish *regulares* to Asturias, because the Army of Africa was undoubtedly Spain's most effective and ruthless fighting force. Also the government was afraid that the conscripts of the home army might join the rebels.

As soon as the rising started, wild propaganda stories appeared in the right-wing press. Nuns were alleged to have been raped (the Mother Superior of the convent concerned firmly denied the reports afterwards), children's eyes to have been gouged out and priests' flesh sold for stewing meat. Not one of these accounts was supported by any evidence in subsequent investigations. The violence against civilians amounted to the killing of about 12 priests and 15 businessmen during the turmoil.

It has been alleged that these horror stories were made up to justify the conduct of the troops. Prisoners were summarily shot in batches on the orders of Colonel Yagüe. Moroccan troops engaged in their battle-practice of castrating fallen enemies and these were said to have included some wounded. The Foreign Legion's treatment of the wives and daughters of insurgents was horrific and included rape and mutilation. But it was the action of the torture squads under Major Doval of the civil guard which caused the most revulsion. They were prepared to go to any lengths to find out where arms might still be hidden. Some of their victims died of pain and others went mad. Doval himself stated that he was 'determined to exterminate the seeds of revolution even in the bellies of mothers'.

The number of political prisoners is estimated to have risen to about 30,000 after the October rising. They included Azaña and Largo Caballero (who started to read Marx and Lenin for the first time). Among those condemned to death was Luis Companys. The CEDA demanded that all capital sentences be carried out, but Alcalá Zamora, the president, resisted the demand on the grounds that Sanjurjo and the monarchists had been reprieved two years before.

In April 1935 Gil Robles entered Lerroux's cabinet along with four other CEDA ministers, despite the president's intense dislike for him; Alcalá Zamora had at least managed to prevent his becoming prime minister. In October Lerroux was brought down by the *'straperlo'* gambling scandal, which revealed how deeply his party was riddled with corruption. Gil Robles was certain that his moment had come, but Alcalá Zamora was still determined to keep him out. An independent, Joaquín Chapaprieta, was appointed, but his government fell in December, when the CEDA vetoed a proposed increase in death duties from one per cent to three-and-a-half per cent. The president then appointed Portela Valladares. This change of government meant the removal of Gil Robles from the war ministry where he had been trying to have the civil guard brought under his command. The forced departure of the CEDA leader nearly provoked a military rising in the capital, but apparently General Franco stopped such an ill-prepared move. Portela Valladares' administration enjoyed negligible backing, and could only act in a caretaker capacity until elections were called. The Cortes was dissolved within a week of the new year of 1936.

The Asturian rising was a dramatic indication of the direction of events. The cruelty of the repression embittered the workers, while the determined attempt at revolution had appalled the conservative classes. For both sides the question of the constitution and a duly elected government was shown to be little more than a legalistic concept to be employed only when it was advantageous. Even the architects of the Republic's constitution like Azaña and Alcalá Zamora demonstrated how selective their commitment was to their own creation when they felt circumstances demanded. It was now clear that the clash of attitudes throughout the country was so great that the forces of conflict could not be contained within the Cortes.

THE POPULAR FRONT

The election campaign during the first weeks of 1936 was charged with powerful emotions. The events in Asturias made most people aware that this might be the last stretch of the parliamentary road. The increasingly revolutionary workers would be totally opposed by the immovable right. Both sides had learned the necessity of coalitions to exploit the advantage given by the electoral laws and the centre ground started to empty with the forced polarization.

A mass of large posters appeared with a dictatorial-looking portrait of Gil Robles and a slogan demanding power. His efficient propaganda machine was backed with enormous funds from landowning and business interests. The CEDA dominated the newly formed alliance of the right, which now included the Alfonsist monarchists and Carlists. This electoral bloc was called the National Front and, according to the church, a vote for them was a vote for Christ.

The centre and left-wing parties, republicans, socialists, communists and the POUM, grouped themselves in the Popular Front alliance under Azaña, who had become a symbol of unity after his imprisonment following the October 1934 rising. This electoral pact, first arranged between the socialists and liberal republicans, was born of the unity forged during the Asturias revolt. It was also the Comintern's policy in Europe to create broad left alliances in the democracies to combat the threat of nazism and fascism. At the same time it provided satellite communist parties with a 'Trojan horse' method of entry 'to the very heart of the enemy camp'. Spain was to witness both the effectiveness and the limitations of this strategy.

The socialists were the largest party in the Popular Front and their leader with the greatest support, Largo Caballero, had now become, at the age of 66, a militant revolutionary (though more in rhetoric than intention). Urged on by the Socialist Youth, he was suspicious of the broad centre-left alliance advocated by Prieto and Azaña. He had to be won over by the Comintern representative, Jacques Duclos. The Comintern had decided that Largo was the most appropriate leader to unite the militant Spanish workers, and the communist press throughout Europe helped in the building of his image. He was flattered by epithets such as the 'Spanish Lenin' and his proletarian virtues were extolled. Hints were also made of some future amalgamation of the socialist and communist organizations, which was a major step in the Communist Party's strategy.

Until 1934 the communists had maintained their 'Bolshevik vanguard', 'class against class' policy. Now the Popular Front line meant that they must not alarm the parliamentary states and the middle classes. The wolf had to convince the bourgeois flock that it was now a sheepdog. This was not made easy for them when Largo Caballero, primed with revolutionary rhetoric from his prison studies, started to make rousing speeches up and down the country. Their star property was embarrassing them. A wit from the socialist camp even coined the slogan: 'Vote communist and save Spain from Marxism!'

The effectiveness of communist organization and tactics can only be appreciated when their minute size is compared with their influence. Their numbers had risen from around the thousand mark before 1934 to about 30,000 in early 1936. This is against approximately one-and-a-half million socialists, and an even larger number of libertarians in the CNT, which was still suffering from its split between the anarchist purists of the FAI and the syndicalists, who had condemned the 'revolutionary gymnastics' of the uprisings.

It was evident that the election result was going to be close. The vital factor was whether the anarchists would vote. In the south the right tried to bribe prominent anarchists to campaign for abstention, but the issue was clear to the CNT. There were political prisoners; so the paramount demand for solidarity meant voting for the Popular Front candidate.

The polling was completed with little violence and only isolated cases of interference. The Popular Front was only some 150,000 votes ahead out of nearly 10 million cast, but, with the weighting of the electoral law, they ended up with an absolute majority, and CEDA and monarchist leaders made speeches accepting their electoral defeat. Of the major parties, the socialist PSOE won 88 seats, Azaña's Republican Left Party (an amalgamation of his Republican Action, Casares Quiroga's Galician party and the Radical Socialist Party) won 79 seats, Martínez Barrio's Republican Union (a liberal breakaway from Lerroux's Radical Party) won 34, the Communist Party 14 and Companys' Catalan Esquerra 22 seats. On the right, the CEDA retained 96 seats, the monarchists 13, the Carlists 15, the Catalan Lliga 11 and the Radical Party 8. Outside the two electoral blocs the uncommited centre party of Portela Valladares won 21 seats and the Basque nationalist PNV 9 seats.

As soon as the results were known, a group of monarchists asked Gil Robles to stage a *coup d'état*, but he realized he was not suited to the role of pre-fabricated dictator. The parliamentary way to a corporate state had failed and at the moment of truth he did not have the nerve to seize power. It may have been the bitterness of defeat, but soon afterwards Gil Robles made a surprising, and hypocritical, attack on the CEDA's financial backers, the employers and landowners, 'who as soon as the Right came to power [1933] revealed a suicidal egoism by lowering wages, raising rents and trying to carry out unjust evictions'. But if Gil Robles lacked the courage to act, others, especially Generals Fanjul and Goded, were more than tempted. The chief-of-staff, General Franco, counselled caution once more, insisting that they could not be sure of the civil guard's support.

Franco was not prepared to move unless everything possible was in his favour. Even so, he tried to persuade Portela Valladares, the caretaker prime minister, not to hand power to the Popular Front. But Portela was on the edge of a nervous breakdown and resigned on 18 February. A general strike was threatened by the UGT, so the president, Alcalá Zamora, asked Azaña to form a government. This administration came from the liberal wing of the Popular Front alliance (Republican Left, Republican Union and Esquerra). The 'left socialists', as Largo Caballero's wing of the party was called, vetoed PSOE participation to stop Prieto's project of a social-democratic alliance with Azaña.

In spite of the extremely moderate composition of the new government, the politicians of the right reacted as if revolution loomed. They were horrified to see political prisoners freed by crowds who did not bother to wait for the official amnesty to be announced. But it was the failure of the National Front coalition in the election which made them decide that protecting their version of Spain meant abandoning the parliamentary process.

Azaña was depressed to find that the problems facing the new liberal government were much greater than in 1931. The frustration on the left caused by his first disappointing term of office propelled the new administration towards even more of a clash, since the economy and civil service were dominated by the right wing. The flight of capital was enormous and investment virtually came to a halt. Although it is evidently facile to create a conspiracy theory around this, there was undoubtedly economic sabotage. The most notorious practitioner was the multi-millionaire, Juan March, who backed the Falange. He had started to amass his vast fortune by smuggling tobacco with the connivance of handsomely bribed officials. When put in prision, he escaped with his warder and the prison governor, both of whom joined his payroll. On 16 February he did not wait for the election results to come through. Although he was certain of being re-elected to the Cortes from his fiefdom in the Balearics, he knew that the new government would send him back to prison. Once out of the country he started to work against the peseta on the foreign exchange, as well as act as banker to the army officers who were plotting to overthrow the government.

The Cortes was no longer regarded by the right as serving any purpose beyond providing a platform from which to insist that democracy could not work. Their leader in this task was Calvo Sotelo, the finance minister of Primo's dictatorship and a monarchist who was soon to state that he was proud to call himself a fascist. The strength of traditional Spain was now devoted to extra-parliamentary activity. Army officers were called cowards in public for not overthrowing the new government. The right-wing press ceaselessly repeated that the country was ungovernable, and ordinary crimes were reported in their pages as political so as to further this impression. Statistics were manipulated or even invented, and there is still great debate over the real level of turmoil.

Of the right-wing groups openly rejecting the parliamentary system, the most conspicuous and the fastest-growing was the para-military Falange. Up until 1936 it had been a minor embarrassment to conservatives. Now it provided an independent terrorist front which could be disowned by its

41

monarchist and industrial backers. A secret agreement had in fact been signed with the monarchists as early as August 1934, and the major donors to Falange funds were Juan March, the Bank of Vizcaya and Mussolini's government (which provided 50,000 pesetas a month).

Meanwhile, the members of the Catholic Youth organization, JAP, were no longer satisfied with rhetoric and rallies. They began to imitate the Falangist squads and large numbers of them switched to the Falange during the spring – 15,000 according to Gil Robles. From never having mustered more than a couple of thousand members up to the time of the CEDA's defeat, the Falange was now the active arm of the right, with some 30,000 members.

The Falange Española, the 'Spanish Phalanx', was started in 1933 by José Antonio Primo de Rivera, the lawyer son of the dictator. Many of its original members had belonged to his father's Patriotic Union, and support came from leading figures in society who wanted a totalitarian party. In the early stages its ideology was basically patriarchal nationalism; the 'socialist' element – here it differed from nazisn and fascism – developed later. This socialist concern, though it partly reflected José Antonio's awareness of injustice, was chiefly the result of the Falange's amalgamation with the more proletarian JONS, the Nationalist Syndicalist Offensive Juntas (Unamuno called it the Offensive of the Mentally Retarded). Its leader, Ledesma Ramos, who despised the old order, was suspicious of the urbane young marquis with his *señorito* (young gentleman) followers. Ledesma tried to break the JONS away from the Falangists soon afterwards but did not succeed.

The Falange's paradoxical ideology reveals the true strength of the centralist-authoritarian mentality of traditional Spain. Falangism (like fascism and nazism) made much of its socialist pretensions. José Antonio attacked the 'social bankruptcy of capitalism' and recognized the suffering of workers and peasants. He understood their turning towards Marxism. But Marxism was not Spanish. 'A socialist victory has the significance of a foreign invasion', he wrote in a letter to Franco. Marxism advocated class war which would weaken the nation. To avoid that, the country must be forcibly united in a system in which the employer could no longer exploit the worker, nor the worker fight the employer. This suppression of strife was the only way to make Spain great again. José Antonio expressed it thus: 'Fascism is a universal attitude of self-recovery.'

Falangism differed from nazism and fascism in its profoundly conservative nature. Mussolini used Roman symbols and imperial imagery in his speeches merely for their propaganda effect. The Falange, on the other hand, used modern and revolutionary phraseology while remaining fundamentally reactionary. The church was the essence of *Hispanidad* (Spanishness). The new state would 'draw its inspiration from the spirit of the Catholic religion which is traditional in Spain'. The ideal Falangist was to be portrayed as a political warrior Jesuit. Their symbols were those of Ferdinand and Isabella: the yoke of the authoritarian state and the arrows of annihilation to wipe out heresy. But it was not just the symbols which they borrowed. It was the mentality. 'Castile has never been resigned to being a mere province: it could not help but aspire at all times to being an empire.' 'Separatism disregards or forgets the reality of Spain, ignoring the fact that Spain is, above all, one great INDIVISIBLE DESTINY.'

The ideology was not just contradictory, but schizophrenic. One moment José Antonio was making vain approaches, first to Prieto and then to the CNT. The next, he was reminding Franco that 'as Spengler has said, in the last resort civilization has always been saved by a platoon of soldiers'. But a civilization which has to be saved by soldiers is a conservative's image of a perfect world, rather than a revolutionary national socialist's. It was inevitable that the 'nationalist' would always take complete precedence over the 'socialist', because nationalism is retrospectively inspired and therefore conservative. 'The Left is more numerous than the Right,' José Antonio wrote, 'but it is unpatriotic.' Only a rump of meaningless rhetoric could survive from the often fierce social conscience of the Falangists, so the businessmen and landowners who backed them had little difficulty foreseeing the movement's final direction. Falangism was an emotional resurrection of the old Castilian dictatorship in modern dress. One of its theorists, Federico de Urrutia, stated that the Falange's objective was 'to kill the old soul of the liberal, decadent, masonic, materialist and frenchified nineteenth century, and return to impregnate ourselves with the spirit of the imperial, heroic, sobre, Castilian, spiritual, legendary and knightly sixteenth century'.

Meanwhile, the Carlists, who also saw liberalism as the source of all modern evils, dreamt of reviving a royal Catholic autocracy in a populist form. Their main strength lay in the Pyrenees, though they did have supporters in other areas, such as Andalucia. Carlism's official title was the Traditionalist Communion, and it has been described as a form of lay Jesuitry. The Carlists no longer showed their former sympathy with regionalist aspirations. This sympathy had stemmed from their stronghold being in the former kingdom of Navarre and had also been a means of winning Basque and Catalan support for the Carlist wars in the nineteenth century. By 1936 they had come to detest Basque nationalism.

The ideal of defending traditional Spain required active preparation, now that the authoritarian right had discarded any further attempt to make use of the parliamentary system. The Carlists had started to arm and train their *requeté* militia in the Pyrenees even when the right was still in power. A number of their officers were trained in Italy with the help of Mussolini, while their leaders, Fal Conde and the Count of Rodezno, organized the purchase of weapons from Germany. Meanwhile, the Falange wanted more weapons for their street-fighting, and José Antonio's request put in motion a Bulldog Drummond-style intrigue. Luis Bolín, the London correspondent of the monarchist *ABC*, met a prominent, but anonymous, Englishman by a secret recognition signal in Claridges Hotel. They arranged for large quantities of submachine guns to be packed in champagne cases and shipped from Germany in a private yacht. In fact, they did not arrive in time, but it was not long before Bolín in London began to organize a far more important delivery.

The uncertainty of the political situation was a major factor in halting industrial development, which was already affected by the quantity of funds transferred abroad. And in the countryside landowners left much of their land uncultivated. The Institute of Agrarian Reform started work again resettling landless peasants, but as it could still only scrape at the surface of the problem, the frustrations among the labourers built up even more strongly as a result. On 25 March at dawn 60,000 of them took over unused land in Estremadura and started ploughing in an operation which was co-ordinated by the agricultural branch of the UGT. The government kept the civil guard away, because the possibility of a Casas Viejas on such a scale appalled them. Even so, there was another incident at Yeste, where the civil guard arrested peasants gathering firewood. When they resisted, the civil guard shot 20 dead and wounded many more.

In Madrid there were moves afoot to remove the conservative republican, Alcalá Zamora, from the presidency. Although he had manipulated the constitution to keep Gil Robles from the prime ministership, he was brought down by a manœuvre of the socialists and left republicans. The right did nothing to help him after the way he had prevented their seizing power through the Cortes. Azaña was confirmed as presidential candidate by Prieto and his wing of the socialists. The intention was for Prieto to succeed to the leadership of the government. But his position in the PSOE was not strong enough to counter the *Caballerista* wing's opposition to a coalition with the liberals. As a result, the Galician republican, Casares Quiroga, was asked to form a government.

On 15 April, eight days after the Cortes deposed Alcalá Zamora, a bomb was thrown at Azaña in the presidential box during the anniversary celebrations of the Republic. *Asaltos* then shot down a civil guard officer of known right-wing views. His funeral, two days later, developed into a running battle between Falangists and the young socialists. Most of the street-fighting of this spring was between these two groups, a vicious circle of attack followed by reprisal. The first main Falangist attack had come immediately after the general election results were announced, when they started to shoot at wives and friends hurrying to release the political prisoners. On 11 March they attempted to assassinate the deputy speaker of the Cortes. Four days later they tried to kill Largo Caballero. Then on 16 April they machine-gunned labourers working in the centre of Madrid, killing three and wounding 40.

The government closed down Falangist headquarters in Madrid and arrested José Antonio for not having a gun licence. His imprisonment did not cut him off completely from his *sub-jefes*, but he was uneasy at not being able to influence events. He feared that the Falange would be changed by the influx of new members and that it might lose its identity when the military rebelled. At times it is difficult to reconcile José Antonio's famous charm with the brutality of his followers. He cannot, however, escape responsibility, because his speeches were a clear incitement, even if violence remained an abstract quantity to the fastidious Andalusian.

Largo Caballero was also intoxicated by rhetoric stronger than his intentions. His declaration that 'the revolution we want can only be achieved through violence' was taken by the Socialist Youth as an unwavering commitment to Leninist strategy. The fact that many of them soon went over to the Communist Party proves that there was a strong authoritarian element within the PSOE. The May Day parade in Madrid of socialists and communists horrified the conservative classes watching from their windows. There were red banners everywhere and huge portraits of Lenin, Stalin and Largo Caballero. But it was not just these obvious political symbols which frightened them. The workers in the street had a new confidence, or, in their view, insolence. Beggars had started to ask for alms, not for the love of God, but in the name of revolutionary solidarity. Girls walked freely and started to ridicule convention. José Antonio wrote in a shocked tone: 'Have you not heard Spanish girls these days shouting "Children, yes! Husbands, no!"?' For him and those of his background Spain was on the brink of 'a barbarian invasion'.

Prieto, meanwhile, was attacking 'childish revolutionism' and warning that it was pushing a frightened middle class into the arms of fascism. This was undoubtedly true, but the assumption that the army would not stage a coup, or that Falange attacks would cease if a gradualist approach was adopted, could not be justified.

The right was not prepared to concede any ground at all, as they had demonstrated so obviously when in power, while a social-democratic line could never satisfy the aspirations of the workers, especially the *braceros*. Moderation was rejected because there was a feeling that, after centuries of exploitation, the workers could not be asked to forget that past while the upper classes still profited from it.

The actions of landowners and industrialists during the right-wing government of 1933–35 led to a backlash in 1936. The memory of evictions, sackings and drastic reductions in wages provoked a feeling of 'we are the masters now' once the Popular Front won. The national level of unemployment was at least 17 per cent of the working population and, with a particularly bad winter, conditions were desperate in the centre and south-west. Strikes broke out almost everywhere that spring, not only to obtain employment and a decent wage, but also to prove working-class muscle. There was inevitably a vindictive element, a powerful satisfaction of turning the tables. The demands frequently bore no relation to what the company or farm could afford.

The socialist philosopher, Julián Besteiro, warned his colleagues that Spain was not Russia in 1917, when conservative strength had collapsed after the Great War. However, there were in fact only two real options open to the workers: to go straight at the enemy trenches or to return to social-democratic lines for a stalemate of sniping. And the latter alternative did not guarantee them immunity from what had happened in Germany and Italy. The liberal ministers and the moderate *Prietista* wing of the PSOE were worried at the way in which Largo and the Socialist Youth were provoking the right, while they in turn were accused of being complacent about the threat of a military rising.

The CNT was relatively quiet in this turbulent spring, being preoccupied with internal union matters. Many of their unions were engaged in all-out competition with the UGT, which involved the CNT in trials of bargaining strength – the 'reformist syndicalism' to which the anarchist purists were opposed. The FAI felt that dealing with capitalist society on its own terms was inevitably corrupting. In 1907 Malatesta had remarked of trade unionism that 'the more powerful this movement becomes, the more it starts to be selfish, conservative, exclusively concerned with short-term interests, and it develops an internal bureaucracy which, as always, is only interested in growing larger and stronger'. The syndicalists, on the other hand, believed that theirs was the only effective strategy for helping the working class. Nevertheless, the threat of civil war brought the FAI anarchists and the syndicalists back together again. The CNT conference in May at Saragossa, the capital of Aragon and the 'second city of anarchism', was proof of their regained strength. With many new members in Madrid and other traditional UGT areas, the CNT was probably larger than the socialists and communists combined.

Largo Caballero addressed the Saragossa conference and urged the amalgamation of the UGT and the CNT. This was precisely the communist strategy, part of their long-term plan to unite and infiltrate, then divide and rule. This would be achieved, despite their small numbers, by superior organization and the ruthlessness which their recruits so admired as the only way of advancing the cause of the working class. The Popular Front alliance, as it stood, was insufficient for their needs. They wanted a complete integration of working-class parties and unions so that their appointees and secret supporters in key positions could organize one coup after another. Largo Caballero was totally unaware that his most trusted adviser and future foreign minister, Alvarez del Vayo, had just helped the Comintern agent, Vittorio Codovilla (who had the cover-name 'Medina'), to organize the take-over of the Socialist Youth. Together they had secretly interviewed likely candidates in the Socialist Youth, whom they persuaded to join the Party with promises of power and with the argument that only the Communist Party had the professionalism and international strength to defeat fascism. Ettore Vanni, a prominent Italian communist in Spain, explained that their discipline was 'accepted with a fanaticism which at once dehumanized us and constituted our strength'. The deterministic idea of 'scientific socialism' convinced young militants that nothing could stop the eventual triumph of Marxism. They believed that absolute power was the only means for achieving their ideals, which one recruit, Manuel Tagüeña (later an important military commander), described as the same 'as the anarchists, but by a different path, with organization and discipline'. They were strongly influenced by the myths of the Russian revolution, which blended romantic heroism and a ruthless rejection of sentimentality into a powerful appeal. They felt that they were the only efficient leaders of the masses. Any weakness of resolve was petit-bourgeois indulgence, if not treason to the international proletariat. Libertarian fears of the corrupting influence of power were scorned as the delusions of amateurs in a battle against an implacable enemy. Among those attracted to the communists was the head of the Socialist Youth, Santiago Carrillo, best known today as an important exponent of Euro-Communism. The new United Socialist Youth, the JSU, had been brought together on 1 April. Then, soon after the outbreak of the civil war, Carrillo brought the 200,000 members of the joint organization under communist control in a coup carefully staged during the confusion of the fighting.

The communists were also successful that summer in carrying out a similar manœuvre with their tiny Catalan party and the Catalan socialist groups. The united Socialist party of Catalonia, the PSUC, under Juan Comorera, was Comintern-controlled from the early days of the civil war. A similar tactic was followed with the miniature communist union, the CGTU. (The CGTU had been set up after the Party abandoned its attempts to split the anarcho-syndicalists with its 'Reconstituted CNT'. Its name was presumably an intentional blend of UGT and CNT.) Nevertheless, the communists had little success within the UGT during the summer of 1936, except in Catalonia, where the PSUC coup was successful. Their most ambitious attempt was to urge the outright amalgamation of the socialists and communist parties. Largo's Madrid branch and the militant Socialist Youth were in favour, but Prieto's social-democratic wing and the Asturian miners managed to defeat this move.

The rhythm of political violence and strikes increased in the early summer, enabling the right-wing press to sensationalize the public-order issue to the maximum. On 1 June 70,000 Madrid building workers began a joint UGT–CNT strike. Falangists machine-gunned the pickets from cars in hit-and-run raids or attacked isolated workers. As the strike progressed many hungry builders seized food from restaurants and there were clashes with the police. The UGT agreed to the settlement arranged by the ministry of labour early in July, but the CNT decided to carry on. It had now become a political strike for them. Fights broke out between CNT and UGT members, while the Falangists renewed their attacks to increase the confusion. CNT members then carried out a reprisal raid on a Falangist café and killed three of José Antonio's bodyguards. The government promptly closed the CNT headquarters in Madrid and arrested the strike leaders, David Antona and Cipriano Mera. Fighting had also broken out between anarchists and socialists in Málaga in mid-June, which was condemned by both the UGT and the CNT. Also at this time nearly 100,000 peasants of the CNT were on strike in the surrounding countryside.

The socialists and anarchists were starting to take over in central and southern rural areas. There was little outright violence, though there was much intimidation. However, in the main Andalucian towns, as in Madrid, Falangist squads drove at top speed through working-class districts shooting people indiscriminately. There were bomb attacks on newspaper offices and Falangists shot down a judge who had sentenced one of their number to 30 years' imprisonment for murder. The communists had organized the most effective of the left-wing para-military bodies in their MAOC (Anti-Fascist Workers' and Peasants' Militia), while the socialists only had their *motorizada* column in the capital. Almost everyone who could went around armed and deputies entering the Cortes were relieved of their weapons in case debates became heated.

There were undoubtedly attempts to increase the sense of chaos. Such tactics had been used on several occasions in the past, the events in Barcelona just after the First World War providing an obvious example. But there has not been any evidence to point to a concerted campaign. Apart from provocative attacks, there were violent acts apparently carried out under false colours. Black propaganda included Carlists faking anarchist pamphlets with terrifying language; and it has been said that the wild rumours of nuns giving poisoned sweets to children were started by the right in order to provoke anti-clerical riots. During all this time the right-wing press repeatedly compared Azaña to Kerensky, and José Antonio reminded the army of the fate of Tsarist officers. In the other camp Besteiro warned the left against Russian comparisons, for the Spanish army was not in a state of mutiny and collapse like the Russian army in 1917.

In 1936 the Spanish army was officially about 100,000 strong, of whom

30,000 were the tough and effective colonial troops in Morocco. The metropolitan army, on the other hand, was almost useless. There were probably fewer than 50,000 of them in uniform. (Inflated figures were given by officers and quartermasters, enabling them to collect extra pay and sell surplus rations.) The conscripts had almost no training, many had never fired a rifle and they were usually treated as cheap labour by the officers. Their equipment was notoriously shoddy, the Spanish phrase for the worst possible quality of anything being *de munición*, or army issue.

The low effectiveness of Spanish troops had not hindered the *pronunciamientos* of the past and, despite the Asturian fighting, it does not seem that the conspirators thought it would matter this time. Right-wing officers had started to plan a coup on the removal of Gil Robles from the war ministry at the end of 1935. The Popular Front government's arrest of General López de Ochoa, commander in charge of the suppression of the Asturian uprising, provided fresh impetus. Most of the original plotting was organized through the Unión Militar Española, a group of 'patriotic officers' formed in 1933.

The government took the precaution of sending suspect generals like Franco and Goded to minor commands in the Canaries and the Balearic islands, but Las Palmas was close to the Army of Africa and Majorca to Barcelona. General Mola, the chief organizer of the conspiracy, who was code-named the 'Director', was sent as military governor to Pamplona, the centre of the Carlists. They were able to offer him 7,000 fully armed *requetés*. The other force available to the plotters was the Falange, but their action squads were wild groups unlike the organized Carlists. The monarchists were also committed to the rebellion, as were most of the CEDA, although Gil Robles had started to back away from this path.

The agreed figurehead for the rising was General Sanjurjo, who glorified in the nickname, the 'Lion of the Rif'. He was most in favour with the Carlist faction, since his family had fought for Don Carlos in the nineteenth century. Sanjurjo was in exile in Lisbon as a result of his failed *pronunciamiento* during the first Republican government, thus making another stop-off point in a circuit of conspiratorial negotiations which included London, Paris, Biarritz, Berlin, Rome, the Canary Islands and Spanish Morocco. (The conspirators were aided by the Royal Navy at Gibraltar, which allowed them to use their telephone link to the international system to avoid going through Spanish exchanges. The American company, ITT, which had been awarded the telephone monopoly in Spain by Primo de Rivera, also provided special lines.)

Sanjurjo had been the commander of the risky, but successful, landings at Alhucemas in 1925 which enabled Primo to defeat Abd-el-Krim. But the young officer who commanded the landing party was to prove the most important *africanista*. Francisco Franco y Bahamonde was the son of a dissipated naval paymaster in Galicia. The family was reputedly of Jewish blood, though this was hushed up by Nationalist genealogists. He joined the army because the navy had few ships and no vacancies after the Spanish–American war. Franco appears to have been an unexciting, but conscientious, cadet. He achieved rapid promotion, and in 1920 was sent as second-in-command to the new Spanish Foreign Legion. This unit, founded by Colonel Millán Astray, was modelled on its French equivalent, except that Spaniards, not foreigners, formed the majority in its ranks.

In contrast to his rough soldiers, Franco was a small man with a squeaky voice and an incipient pot belly. At his first parade a legionnaire mimicked his high-pitched tone. Franco apparently drew his revolver, shot him dead and then continued as if nothing had happened. (As an English volunteer officer in the Legion later affirmed, 'insubordination, whether or not in the face of the enemy, was punishable by death on the spot'.) One event of this period, which is said to have influenced him, was the severe wounds which he received in a battle after he thought the tribesmen beaten. The experience apparently made him determined never to give quarter.

The young general was undoubtedly brave, but he was never reckless. In fact his caution during the spring led many senior officers to think that he might not join the rising, even though his direction of the Asturian operation made him hated by the left. He was introvert and at that time unreligious, as Nationalist historians emphasize when building up the 'crusade' aspect. Everything was played with his cards very close to his chest. The bombastic Sanjurjo, the suspicious Mola and the reserved Franco made a triumvirate of contrasts. They were then surprised to find another important general join them. Queipo de Llano was thought to be a convinced Republican, because he had taken part in the ineffective plot against the monarchy in 1930. But Queipo, a key officer on whom the prime minister counted, started to organize the rising in Andalucia, the vital link with the Army of Africa.

The left, meanwhile, was making attempts to win over members of the army and the para-military forces. (There were already a few militant left-wing officers, as opposed to those who were simply loyal to the Republic.) A certain measure of success was achieved, particularly among the *asaltos*, by the communist infiltration programme which was organized by the Moscow-trained Enrique Líster. The communists and the socialists also won over a number of non-commissioned officers around Madrid.

It was the political involvement of left-wing para-military officers which led to the most important event just before the rising. On 12 July Falangist gunmen succeeded in finding Lieutenant José Castillo of the *asaltos* alone. He had been a marked man ever since the violent clashes of mid-April, and was the second socialist officer to be killed. Several of his comrades tried to arrest those whom they thought responsible for his murder, but, not finding them, they went to Calvo Sotelo's flat. In their anger they blamed his extreme oratory in the Cortes. They took him out to their car on an official pretext and shot him dead. His body was dumped outside a cemetery.

The outrage of the right was overwhelming, but the killing was definitely not carried out on the government's orders. That claim was made to help justify the rising against the Republic. Also the notion that this was 'the final straw' is false. An aeroplane, organized in London by Luis Bolín, was already en route to take Franco to the Army of Africa. Mola, moreover, had issued detailed orders for the rising long before. The Falangists were already in touch with rebel officers to co-ordinate plans. Their secret recognition was the codeword 'Covadonga', the point in the Asturias where the *Reconquista* of Spain from the Moors had started. It was a melodramatic touch which had little to do with security.

Despite these preparations, the Republican leaders discounted all warnings. Azaña, the president, and Casares Quiroga, his replacement as prime minister, were on a par with Chamberlain facing Hitler. At times it almost seemed as if they wanted to be deceived. Azaña certainly appeared to have lost all political sense. He was suffering from bouts of depression, interspersed by occasional flashes of flippancy. 'The only Spaniard who is always right is Azaña,' he remarked to one visitor. 'If all Spaniards were *Azañistas* all would be well.' He and the government seemed to have no understanding of the military threat. They scornfully dismissed all warnings, whether from loyal senior officers, like General Nuñez de Prado, or from the communist deputy, Dolores Ibarruri, better known as 'La Pasionaria', who came with the communist organizer in Pamplona to tell Casares Quiroga of Mola's preparations. The prime minister maintained his belief that 'Mola is a general loyal to the Republic', just as the government had earlier announced that the Spanish army officers were maintaining 'themselves within the limits of the strictest discipline, disposed at any moment to fulfil their duties scrupulously and, needless to say, to obey the orders of the legally constituted government'. On 11 July, a week before the rising, Falangists seized Valencia radio and announced that 'tomorrow the same will happen in broadcasting stations throughout Spain'.

The final, fatal paradox of the liberal Republic was expressed by its government not daring to defend itself against its own army by arming the workers who elected it. It merely proclaimed that it was 'the legally constituted government'. But Spanish history showed how legitimacy tended to be an arbitrary and subjective term, little more than a euphemism for right of conquest and subsequently maintained power.

THE GENERALS' RISING

The generals had planned a *coup d'état* with a rising of garrisons in Spanish Morocco and throughout Spain. The success of such an action depended more on the psychological effect of speed and ruthlessness than on numbers. Although an outright coup was not achieved, the Republic failed to crush the rising in the first 48 hours, the most important period of the whole war, when the possession of whole regions was decided.

In a rapidly developing crisis, initial uncertainty enforces a defensive mentality, and for the Republic hesitancy was fatal. The politicians did not dare arm the UGT and CNT. They refused to depart from the legal constitution of the state, even though a state attacked by its own 'spinal column' has ceased to exist for all practical purposes. The delay in issuing weapons discouraged pre-emptive or counter-offensive moves against the rebel military.

A virtue was made of necessity. The Republic was to encourage the idea that 'to resist was to win', as a slogan later put it. Even during the rising the communist deputy, La Pasionaria, had expressed this dangerously appealing idea with her famous plagiarism of Pétain's phrase at Verdun, *'¡No Pasarán!'* ('They shall not pass!').

The military plotters seldom had complete surprise on their side, but doubt and confusion were certainly in their favour. If the workers held back on the advice of a civil governor who was afraid of provoking the local garrison into revolt, they were lost. They paid for this hesitation with their lives. But if they demonstrated from the beginning that they were prepared to assault the barracks, then most of the para-military forces would join them and the garrison surrender.

The final orders, sent out by General Mola in coded telegrams, provided for the Army of Africa to revolt at 5 am on 18 July, and the army in mainland Spain to rise 24 hours later. The difference in timing was to allow the Army of Africa to secure Spanish Morocco before being transported to the Andalucian coast by the navy.

The rebel generals could count on this force because the rank and file were not conscripts, but regulars, or, more accurately, mercenaries, whose reliability had been proved in the Asturias. There were few officers of liberal sympathies, perhaps because colonials always exaggerate what they believe are national virtues. They despised politicians and had a virulent hatred of 'reds', a term including all those opposed to a right-wing dicta-torship. It was an attitude which Mola expressed in his instructions for the rising: 'He who is not with us is against us.'

The elite force, and the most introvert, was the Foreign Legion. Com-posed in large part of fugitives and criminals, its ranks were indoctrinated with a cult of virility and slaughter. They were taught to be useful suicides with their battle cry of '¡Viva la Muerte!' ('Long live death!'). The Legion was organized in *banderas*, compact battalions with their own light artil-lery. The Moroccan troops, on the other hand, were divided into *tabores* of some 250 men each. These *regulares* were Riffian tribesmen commanded by Spanish officers. Their ferocious efficiency had been amply proved resisting colonial power during the first quarter of the century. Probably their most important skill was the ability to move across country using the folds in the ground. Such stealth had a decided advantage over the Spanish idea of conspicuous bravery.

The rebels could hardly have failed to take Spanish Morocco. There was only a handful of Republican officers, while the legionnaires obeyed the order to join the rising without question. The *regulares* were told that the Republic wanted to abolish Allah. The Spanish workers, who had virtually no arms and little contact with the indigenous population, were completely isolated.

During the afternoon of 17 July the plan for the next morning was discovered in the Moroccan town of Melilla, but General Romerales, who was a loyal Republican, could not make up his mind whether to arrest the officers concerned. Colonel Seguí moved faster and arrested the general, having decided that it would be dangerous to delay, even though the other conspirators would not be ready. The *asaltos* were persuaded to join the rising and key buildings in the town were rapidly seized. The Foreign Legion attacked the *casa del pueblo*, where trade unionists fought to the end. While the remaining pockets were being finished off, Seguí had General Romerales and the mayor shot. He then signalled the garrisons at Tetuán and Ceuta before informing General Franco in the Canaries about his premature action.

As dusk fell, the commanders of the Legion and the *regulares* moved their forces into position in the other garrison towns. The Spanish working-class areas were quickly occupied and prominent unionists shot on sight. The declaration of a general strike was no more than a brave gesture as the *regulares* were let loose. In Larache the workers fought desperately with very few weapons through the night, but in Ceuta, Yagüe's legionnaires crushed the resistance in a little over two hours. All this time the commander-in-chief in Morocco, General Morato, was gambling. Having carried out Azaña's reshuffle, he was hated by the rebel officers. He knew nothing of the rising until a telephone call for him from Madrid was put through to the casino.

The only remaining centres of Moroccan resistance at dawn on the 18th were the governor's residence and the air force base at Tetuán; both surren-dered a few hours later when threatened with artillery. All those who had resisted were executed, including Major de la Puente Bahamonde, whose fate was approved by his first cousin, General Franco. The rebels approached the Caliph and Grand Vizier to secure their support. They were warned that the Republican government could declare Morocco independent in order to undermine the rebel base. And any encouragement of Moroccan nationalism would be a serious threat after their collaboration with the colonial power.

In Madrid the government had been aware of the rising since the evening of the 17th. The next morning they issued the following communiqué: 'The government states that the movement is confined to certain areas in the Protectorate and that no one, absolutely no one, on the mainland has joined this absurd venture.' When the prime minister, Casares Quiroga, was told the news, he is alleged to have said: 'They're rising? Very well, I shall go and lie down.' At 3 pm he firmly rejected offers of aid from the CNT and UGT. He urged everyone to carry on as normal and to 'trust in the military powers of the state'. He claimed that the rising in Seville had been suppressed, still believing that General Queipo de Llano would manage to secure central Andalucia for the Republic. He had already done precisely the opposite. 'Thanks to preventative measures taken by the government,' Casares Quiroga proclaimed, 'it may be said that a vast anti-Republican movement has been wiped out.' He again refused to arm the workers.

That night the CNT and UGT declared a general strike over Unión Radio. It was the nearest they could get to ordering mobilization. The news coming in showed the administration's statements to be a mixture of contradictions, lies and complacency. The workers began to dig up weapons hidden since the Asturian events of October 1934 and, although Casares Quiroga's government began to understand what it faced, its basic attitude did not change. 'His ministry is a madhouse,' an observer remarked, 'and the maddest inmate is the prime minister. He is neither sleeping nor eating. He shouts and screams as if possessed. He will hear nothing of arming the people and threatens to shoot anybody who does it on his own initiative.'

When the rising was successful in a town, the pattern of events usually started with the seizing of strategic buildings like the town hall. If there was no military garrison, the rebel forces would consist of civil guards, Falangists, and right-wing supporters armed with hunting rifles or shotguns. They would proclaim a state of war in official terms, and in several places confused townsfolk thought that they were carrying out the orders of the Madrid government.

The response of the working-class organizations like the CNT and UGT was to order a general strike and demand weapons from the civil governor. Arms were either refused them or were unobtainable. Barricades were thrown up, but workers who resisted the rebels were massacred, and potential opponents who survived, from the civil governor down to the lowest union official, were executed. On the other hand, if the troops wavered or delayed in coming out of their barracks, and the workers were ready, the outcome was usually very different. An immediate attack, or an encirclement of the barracks, was enough to ensure the rebels' surrender.

A very important factor was the decision of the para-military forces, who were much better trained and armed than the conscript infantry. But it was wrong to say that their loyalty or disloyalty to the government was the crucial element. Like the general population, they were often unsure in their minds, and only the most dedicated would fight when the battle was obviously lost from the beginning. They often hung back to see which way things were going before committing themselves. If the workers' organizations took immediate and firm action, then they usually remained loyal, although the civil guard often revealed their true colours later on. Of the two corps, the *asaltos* showed more loyalty to the government than the civil guard, but then they tended to be an urban force, and the big cities had a better prepared working class.

The events in Seville demonstrated in a spectacular manner what could be achieved by sheer nerve in the face of indecision. The capital of Andalucia was of great strategic importance to the rebels' plans, yet the weak garrison there had virtually no officers committed to the rising. It was only four years since Sanjurjo's attempted rising collapsed in fiasco. General Queipo de Llano, the commander of the *carabinero* frontier guards, only arrived on 17 July. He was irreverent, cynical, unpredictable, and possessed a black sense of humour. Early on the morning of the 18th, accompanied by his ADC and three other reliable officers, he marched into the office of the commander of the military region, General Villa-Abrille, who was given no time to recover from the surprise intrusion. When told to decide immediately whether he was with the rising or against it, Villa-Abrille dithered. Queipo arrested him and had a corporal guard the door with orders to shoot anyone who attempted to leave the room.

Queipo next went to the infantry barracks where he found the 6th Regiment drawn up on parade, fully armed, but well below strength. He went straight to the colonel to congratulate him on joining the rising. The colonel replied that he was for the government. Queipo suggested that they should discuss the matter in his office. Once inside, he arrested him too. He then tried other officers to see if they would lead the regiment, but Sanjurjo's failure was evidently strong in their thoughts. Eventually a young captain volunteered and all the other officers were locked up.

With the infantry on his side, Queipo managed to persuade the artillery regiment to join him as well. Falangists, who arrived to help, were given weapons from the armouries. Yet Queipo's force was still only about 300 strong when it moved on the centre of the city. An artillery salvo ensured the surrender of the civil governor and the *asaltos*. Then, despite Queipo's promise to save the lives of all those inside if they gave in, they were all shot. Just before the chief-of-police was due to be executed, he was told that his wife would be given his full salary if he handed over the secret files on the workers' organizations. He explained where they were hidden, but his widow probably received nothing after he was shot.

The civil guard joined the rebels as soon as they saw the surrender of the *asaltos*. It was only then that the workers started to react. A general strike was ordered over Radio Seville and peasants were called in from the surrounding countryside to help. Barricades were constructed in desperate haste, but the feud between anarchists and communists undermined the organization of an effective counter-attack. They withdrew into their own districts around the perimeter of the town where they prepared their defence. The rebels captured the radio station, which was used by Queipo to broadcast threats of violence against those who resisted him and, more importantly, to deny government claims that the revolt had been crushed on the mainland. The rising of 18 July 1936 was the first modern coup in which radio stations, telephone exchanges and aerodromes were of major importance.

In Málaga the workers were strong, but they had no weapons. Their leaders maintained contact with the *asaltos*, the only government force they felt they could trust. On the afternoon of the 17th, when the news of the rising in Melilla arrived, a rash young army officer led his company out towards the centre of the town. On its way it ran into a strong force of *asaltos*, who attacked at once. The soldiers came off worse. The senior officer in Málaga, General Paxtot, felt that he had no option but to move immediately. The rest of the garrison was marched out, but their commander was to show himself a worthy successor to the grand old Duke of York, for he changed his mind and marched them back to barracks. The colonel in charge of the civil guard was, most unusually for that corps, arrested by his own men when he also declared for the rising. The workers then surrounded the barracks and set fire to the buildings on its perimeter. The garrison surrendered immediately.

In Almería the civil governor refused to arm the workers, using the argument that he did not wish to provoke the military into open revolt. He later claimed that he had had no weapons to issue anyway. 'Arm the people, but with what? ... Where do Governors get arms to distribute to the people? The arms of the state are always placed in the power of the army.' Only the arrival on 21 July of the destroyer *Lepanto* with a loyal captain secured the port for the Republicans. Its guns were trained on the headquarters of the civil guard, which surrendered immediately. The threat of shelling proved a strong factor in many towns.

The civil governor in Jaén took a more positive approach. He called in the civil guard and persuaded them to lay down their weapons, even though they protested that they were loyal to the Republic. He then gave the weapons to the UGT and CNT for distribution and the town was secured. Obviously many more towns would have been saved if such a course had been followed, but there were few governors prepared to admit the total ineffectiveness of normal channels.

In the naval port of Cádiz, Colonel Varela was freed from prison by the local garrison and took command of the rising there. His troops attacked the *comandancia*, which was defended by the civil governor, Mariano Zapico, and improvised workers' militia. The town hall was another centre of resistance, but artillery was brought up. Then at first light on the next day, 19 July, the destroyer *Churruca* arrived with the first reinforcements from the Army in Africa. The insurgents had captured a major naval port on the Andalucian coast.

They were also to secure all the coast westwards to the Portuguese frontier, including Algeciras, La Línea (where the Carlists shot 200 freemasons) and Jeréz. In Huelva, however, the left retained control for the first few days. The civil guard commander in Madrid ordered the local detachment to attack Seville but it joined Queipo's forces immediately on arrival.

In the capital Casares Quiroga resigned as prime minister at four o'clock in the morning of 19 July. The atmosphere in Madrid had been very tense throughout the night. Even the backfiring of a car would lead people to think that the rising had started there too. During the hot night the cafés stayed open and the streets were noisy. Popular frustration and anger at the government was increased by contradictory news items broadcast on the wireless. The UGT and CNT were beginning to suspect treachery.

On receiving Casares Quiroga's resignation, Azaña then asked another personal friend, Martínez Barrio, the president of the Cortes, to form a government. His cabinet was composed of republican parties only and purposely ignored the left-wing elements of the Popular Front alliance, since it was the new prime minister's intention to achieve a reconciliation with the right.

Nevertheless, Martínez Barrio's peace overture to Mola by telephone was firmly rejected. 'If you and I should reach agreement,' Mola told him, 'both of us will have betrayed our ideals and our men.' It was perhaps ironic that a rebel general should remind the prime minister that he was the representative of those voters to whom he owed his appointment. The workers were furious with what they regarded as an utterly *fainéant*, if not treacherous, government. 'Large demonstrations are formed simultaneously,' an eye-witness wrote. 'They move towards the war ministry like an avalanche. The people shout, "Traitors! Cowards!".' Martínez Barrio's government collapsed instantly. He described the event himself: 'Within a few minutes the political demonstration had brought about the ruin of my government. It was senseless to ask me to combat the military rebellion with mere shadows, stripped of authority and ludicrously retaining the name of ministers.' His ministry had lasted less than 12 hours.

Azaña asked yet another personal friend of his to form a government. José Giral, a university professor, was the only liberal politician who realized that the politicians of the Republic could not refuse to face reality any longer. During the morning of the 19th, he dissolved the army by decree and ordered that arms should be given to the workers' organizations. Even so, there were governors who refused to carry out this instruction. In Madrid the government had to order General Miaja point-blank to comply with the order. More than 60,000 rifles were then delivered in lorries to UGT and CNT headquarters, where the heavy grease was cleaned off with party newspapers. Only 5,000 of them had bolts, the remainder being in the Montaña barracks where Colonel Serra, who was one of the conspirators, refused to hand them over.

David Antona described the scene inside CNT headquarters, which the government had closed by order only a few weeks before. 'A narrow dark room. We could hardly move. A jabber of voices, shouts, rifles – many rifles. The telephone never stopped ringing. It was impossible to hear yourself speak. There was only the noise of rifle bolts from comrades who wanted to learn quickly how to handle them.'

The loyalists were lucky that there was also confusion among the conspirators in Madrid. Nobody seemed certain who was to take command, until eventually General Fanjul assumed this ill-fated responsibility. The rebel generals had always realized the improbability of their capturing Madrid at once. But considering that their strategy was based on a holding action until reinforcements arrived from Pamplona, Saragossa and Barcelona, astonishingly little preparation was made for a siege.

Late in the afternoon of the 19th, Fanjul went to the Montaña barracks, where he addressed the officers and those Falangists who had come to help. But when they attempted to march out, they found that they were hemmed in by crowds of *madrileños* who had been directed there by the UGT and CNT. Fire was exchanged and the troops withdrew into the barracks. The rebels' action had more the air of a ritual than a military operation. Outside, La Pasionaria's speech on the radio calling for resistance was relayed over loudspeakers, then the besiegers settled down to wait for the morning.

While the fighting on the mainland intensified, the Dragon Rapide aeroplane, organized by Luis Bolín in London, had collected General Franco, in civilian clothes, from Las Palmas during the afternoon of the 18th. The English pilot was supposed to match half a torn playing card with its counterpart in his passenger's possession. Franco dispensed with such a trivial touch of amateur conspiracy; perhaps he felt it was beneath the dignity of a man of destiny. Sanjurjo may have been accepted as the figurehead, but Franco had an unshakeable belief that his own abilities were indispensable to the success of the rebels' great undertaking.

Franco flew to Casablanca, in French Morocco, so that he could first make sure that the Army of Africa was in control. At dawn on 19 July he left for Tetuán, changing into uniform in mid-flight. There were senior officers waiting for him at the airport. Immediately after landing a conference was held around the aircraft, when Franco learnt that the rising had not been entirely successful. It was decided that Bolín should leave at once with an authorization to 'purchase aircraft and supplies for the Spanish non-Marxist army' – a somewhat bland description for the forces of what was later to be called *La Cruzada*. Reinforcements were urgently needed on the mainland and, since the rising in the fleet had failed, aeroplanes were essential to carry the Army of Africa to Spain.

On the northern coast Santander was secured for the Republic without bloodshed on the morning of the 19th, when the 23rd Infantry Regiment refused to rise. But in Oviedo, where the military commander, Colonel Aranda, had managed over the previous months to convince the civil governor and most of the workers' leaders that he was loyal to the government, the left was too confident after the strength it had demonstrated in the Asturian rebellion of 1934. Aranda, insisting that he acted on Madrid's orders, refused to hand over any weapons. The civil governor, reassured by his promises of loyalty, described him to the workers' leaders as a man of honour. Aranda suggested that he hold Oviedo while the miners form a column to go and help in Madrid. As soon as they had left, he declared for the rising. The governor was one of the first to be executed once Aranda's troops and civil guards secured the town. It was to withstand a long and furious seige once the workers realized that they had been tricked.

Events were much less dramatic in the Carlist city of Pamplona. On the morning of the 19th the 'Director' scrupulously followed his own timetable and declared a state of war in Navarre. There was no resistance in this stronghold of traditionalism, often described as the Spanish Vendée. All that day a continual stream of Carlist farmers arrived in the main square to volunteer. Wearing their large scarlet berets, they shouted the old battle cry, '¡*Viva Cristo Rey!*' A French observer of the scene said that he would not have been surprised to see an *auto-da-fé* of heretics organized at the same time. A total of 8,000 *requetés* assembled, singing,

> Give me my beret,
> Give me my rifle,
> I'm going to kill more reds
> Than there are flowers in April and May.

Navarre had voted to reject the statute of Basque autonomy offered by the Republic, so the Basques were well aware of the threat posed by the Carlists joining the military rebellion. On 19 July the Nationalists captured the city of Vitoria, heart of the southern Basque province of Alava, but in Bilbao the army commander refused to revolt. A council of defence for the province of Vizcaya was set up, the fortress of Basurto was surrounded, and the soldiers were disarmed. In Basque territory to the east, the initiative came almost entirely from working-class organizations, such as the UGT in Eibar and the CNT in San Sebastián. In San Sebastián events resembled those which had taken place in Oviedo. Colonel Carrasco declared that he was loyal to the government, so a column was sent off to help at Mondragón. When the colonel eventually showed his hand, his men were besieged in the María Cristina Hotel and the Gran Casino Club. San Sebastián, the summer capital and the most fashionable seaside resort in Spain, contained a considerable number of right-wing supporters, but they were unable to withstand the workers' unexpectedly ferocious attack. In their unsuccessful defence of the María Cristina, the rebels were alleged to have used live hostages as sandbags in the windows, but this was probably an example of the exaggerated rumours of the time being used as propaganda. The anarchists seized the weapons in the Loyola barracks, since they were not certain that the Basque nationalist party would oppose the rising. This, and their subsequent shooting of some right-wing prisoners, worsened their relations with the PNV.

In Old Castile, Burgos, the city of soldiers and priests, was secured for the rising without opposition, but that did nothing to lessen the mass executions once names and addresses had been obtained from police headquarters. Generals Batet and Mena, who stayed loyal to the government, were among the first to be shot. The most prominent right-wing civilians in the conspiracy had already gathered at Burgos to welcome General Sanjurjo as the new head of state, but they waited in vain. His aeroplane from Portugal crashed on take-off and the 'Lion of the Rif' was killed instantly.

At Valladolid, the heart of that austere Castile romanticized by José Antonio, the civil war began with a pistol battle between army officers. General Molero's loyalist faction was overpowered and the garrison was marched out for the rising. The railwaymen of the UGT fought with great bravery, but were soon annihilated.

The failure of the left to secure Saragossa, the capital of Aragon, was a major disaster, especially for the anarchists. The government, suspicious of General Cabanellas' intentions, sent a friend of his, General Nuñez de Prado, to confirm his loyalty to the Republic. Cabanellas declared for the rising and had Nuñez de Prado and his ADC shot. There were about 30,000 CNT members in Saragossa, but their leaders insisted on working through the civil governor, even though he gave them no arms. Troops led by

Colonel Monasterio marched into the streets at dawn on the 19th and the scarcely armed workers suffered a fearful massacre.

Barcelona presented a very different story, even though it had been regarded by the military conspirators as the most certain conquest of all. The Nationalists had 12,000 troops to bring in from their barracks to dominate the central area. Then General Goded was to fly in from Majorca, once the island was secured, and take command.

On the evening of 18 July, Companys, the president of the Catalan *Generalidad*, refused to issue arms to the CNT, even though news of events in Morocco and Seville had reached him and he had been given documentary proof of plans for the rising in Barcelona. Catalan police arrested anarchists carrying arms, but they were released after vigorous protests by the CNT regional committee.

The anarchists, who knew very well what awaited them if the army seized the city, decided not to leave their fate in the hands of politicians. During that night the CNT local defence committees went ahead with full preparations for war. Isolated armouries were seized (a couple with the active assistance of sympathetic NCOs) and weapons were taken from four ships in the harbour. Even the rusting hulk of the prison ship *Uruguay* was stormed, so as to take the warders' weapons. The UGT dockers' union knew of a shipment of dynamite in the port, and once that was seized, home-made grenades were manufactured all through the night. Every gun shop in the city was stripped bare. Cars and lorries were requisitioned and metal workers fixed crude armour plating while sandbags were piled behind truck cabs. All vehicles were given clear identification with large white letters daubed on the roof and sides. The vast majority were the anarchist initials, CNT-FAI, but POUM and PSUC were also in evidence. Some bore the letters UHP (United Proletarian Brothers), the joint cry of the workers' alliance in the Asturian revolt.

The atmosphere of that hot night was highly charged. The Popular Olympiad (organized as a boycott of the Olympics in Nazi Germany) was due to open the next morning. The event was forgotten in the threatening crisis, and the foreign athletes waited uneasily in their hotels and dormitories. (Many of them joined the fighting the next day alongside the workers, and around 200 later joined militia columns.) Companys, realizing he was superfluous for the moment, went for a walk on the Ramblas with a felt hat pulled down over his eyes to avoid being recognized. The streets were crowded and noisy, with loudspeakers attached to the trees playing music interrupted by announcements. In the favourite anarchist meeting place, the café '*A la Tranquilidad*', CNT members were dashing in and out to hear the latest news and report on the arming of the workers. The members of the regional committee, such as Buenaventura Durruti, Juan García Oliver and Diego Abad de Santillán, maintained a close liaison with the *Generalidad* despite Companys' decision. In fact a few *asaltos* ignored the *Generalidad's* instructions and handed out rifles to the CNT from their own armoury.

Just before dawn on the 19th, the soldiers in the Pedralbes barracks were given rum rations by their officers, then told that orders had been received from Madrid to crush an anarchist rising. Falangists and other supporters wearing odd bits of uniform joined the column as it set off up the *Diagonal*, one of the major thoroughfares of Barcelona. Almost immediately factory sirens all over the city were sounded to give the alarm.

The move out of the barracks was badly co-ordinated. The infantry regiment from the Parque barracks was vigorously attacked and forced to make a fighting retreat back behind its own walls, while the Santiago cavalry regiment was scattered at the Cinc d'Oros. Some units never even broke out into the streets. Those that did manage to, made their way to seize strategic buildings near the Plaza de España and the Plaza de Cataluña. They barricaded themselves in the Hotel Colón, the Ritz and the central telephone exchange. Detachments attacked en route made barricades to defend themselves, but these were charged by heavy lorries driven in suicidal assaults. The soldiers were also attacked with home-made bombs lobbed from rooftops and by snipers. Barricades to bar their way to the centre were constructed by almost everyone who could not take part in the fighting. Those made with paving stones could withstand light artillery if properly laid.

At about 11 am General Goded arrived from Majorca by seaplane. The island had been easily secured for the rising, although Minorca, with its submarine base at Port Mahon, was won for the left by soldiers and NCOs who resisted their officers. Goded went immediately to the *capitanía* (the captain-general's headquarters), where he arrested the loyal divisional commander, Llano de la Encomienda. It was not long, however, before all the rebel-held buildings in the centre of the city were besieged. The black-and-red diagonal flag of the CNT-FAI appeared everywhere on barricades, lorries and public buildings. Loudspeakers in the streets continued to relay news, instructions and exhortations throughout the long hot Sunday. Churches were set on fire after reports of sniping from church towers (not by priests, as rumour said, but by soldiers who had occupied the belfries of La Carmelita and Santa Madróna). Attacks across open ground surrounding the besieged buildings caused heavy casualties. Then, at about two o'clock, when it was evident that the army would not be able to defeat such determined numbers, Colonel Escobar brought in his 4,000 civil guards on the side of the workers. A mounted squadron trotted down the Ramblas, giving the clenched fist salute to roars of approval from the crowds. It was the first time that this para-military force had been cheered by the workers of Barcelona, though their instinctive suspicion of the civil guard did not disappear.

With their excellent marksmanship, the civil guards were to prove a great help in the attack on the Hotel Colón and the Ritz, although the anarchists recaptured the telephone building on their own. The real turning-point came in the Avenida Icaria, where barricades were improvised with huge rolls of newsprint to stop cavalry and the 1st Mountain Artillery Regiment from the San Andrés barracks who were on their way to help the besieged rebels in the centre. At one moment during the fighting, a small group of workers and an *asalto* rushed across to an insurgent artillery detachment with two 75 mm guns. They held their rifles above their heads to show that they were not attacking as they rushed up to the astonished soldiers. Out of breath, they poured forth passionate arguments why the soldiers should not fire on their brothers, telling them that they had been tricked by their officers. The guns were turned round and brought to bear on the rebel forces. From then on more and more soldiers joined the workers and *asaltos*.

It was a salvo from captured artillery under the command of a docker which brought the surrender of General Goded in the *capitanía*. Many Republicans wanted to shoot this leading conspirator on the spot, but he was saved by a communist, Caridad Mercader, the mother of Trotsky's assassin. Goded was taken to Companys, who persuaded him to broadcast a statement over the radio to save further bloodshed. 'This is General Goded,' he said. 'I make this declaration to the Spanish people, that fate has been against me and I am a prisoner. I am saying this so that all those who are still fighting need feel no further obligation towards me.' His words were of great help to the left-wing forces in other parts of Spain, but agreeing to make the statement did not save him. A court martial of Republican officers in August condemned him to death for rebellion.

By nightfall only the Atarazanas barracks, near the port, and the San Andrés barracks still held out. The machine-gun emplacements round the Columbus monument had been silenced in the early evening. The airport at Prat was commanded by a sympathetic officer, Colonel Díaz Sandino, and his planes had attacked this position, enabling a wave of workers and *asaltos* to overrun it. In the castle of Montjuich the garrison had shot the rebel officers and then handed over the weapons in the armoury to the CNT.

The next morning the anarchists, insisting that the storming of the Atarazanas barracks was their prerogative, told the para-military forces to stay clear. Buenaventura Durruti gave the order for the mass attack: '¡*Adelante los hombres de la CNT!*' He led the charge with his companion in arms, Francisco Ascaso, who was killed immediately. That final action brought total casualty figures to about 600 killed and 4,000 wounded. As in all the fighting, a desperate, selfless bravery was shown by the attackers. Many of the casualties were unnecessary, especially those suffered in the final assault when the anarchists had artillery and air support available. Nevertheless, the courage of that attack passed into anarchist folklore, obscuring the fact that dash and guts are dangerous substitutes for military science.

THE STRUGGLE FOR CONTROL

The rebels' plan for the military rising had assigned to the navy the key role of bringing the Army of Africa to the mainland. This had been worked out in advance between senior naval officers, on fleet exercises near the Canaries, and General Franco. Warships were to make all speed for Spanish Morocco on the outbreak of the rising. The conspirators were convinced that few officers would remain loyal to the Popular Front government. In common with the naval officers of most Latin countries, those in Spain were more aristocratic than their counterparts in the army, which had become a ladder for the social-climbing middle class in the nineteenth century. They tended to be strongly monarchist; there was little trace of that liberal tradition which still existed in parts of the army. And the average naval officer's attitude towards the lower deck was scarcely progressive.

On the morning of 18 July the ministry of marine in Madrid instructed three destroyers to sail for Melilla from Cartagena. They were radioed orders to bombard the insurgent town; the officers knew that the rising had begun. In two of the destroyers all hands were called on deck, where their captains explained the objectives of the rebellion. But if the officers had been expecting shouts of enthusiasm, they were disappointed.

The junior ranks in the navy were far better organized than their counterparts in the army. They had held a secret conference in El Ferrol on 13 July to discuss what they should do if the officers rebelled against the government. In Madrid a telegraphist promptly arrested the officer commanding the signals section when he realized that he was in the conspiracy. Immediately afterwards, this junior NCO issued instructions to fleet radio operators that all messages must be sent in clear, since only officers had code books on board ship. As a result of his actions, the majority of ships' crews were informed of events and could not be tricked by false stories. Following this up, Giral, still at this point minister of marine, sent a signal dismissing all officers who refused government orders.

Of the three destroyers off Melilla only the officers on the *Churruca* stayed in command because the radio was out of order. On the *Almirante Valdés* and *Sánchez Barcaíztegui*, however, the crews rushed their officers and overpowered them. They then elected a ship's committee, bombarded

Melilla and Ceuta and returned to the loyal naval base of Cartagena. The rebels had only one destroyer and one gunboat, the *Dato*, to start ferrying the badly needed reinforcements across to Spain.

By the morning of the 19th the government had ordered all available warships to steam to the Straits of Gibraltar to prevent the Army of Africa from crossing. The officers who wished to join the rising could not prevent the news from reaching the lower deck. On the cruiser *Miguel de Cervantes* the officers resisted to the end; but on most ships they surrendered once ratings had seized the ship's armoury. The only seaworthy battleship, the *Jaime I*, was won back by the sailors, as were the cruiser *Libertad* and even the destroyer *Churruca*, after it had landed half a *tabor* of *regulares* at Cádiz. The Nationalists later claimed that 'mutinous' sailors had assassinated their officers and accused Giral of being responsible.

After the ministry of marine had sent instructions relieving rebel officers of their command, the following famous exchange of signals occurred: 'Crew of *Jaime Primero* to ministry of marine. We have had serious resistance from the commanders and officers on board and have subdued them by force ... Urgently request instructions as to bodies.' 'Ministry of marine to crew *Jaime Primero*. Lower bodies overboard with respectful solemnity. What is your present position?'

The officers of the Royal Navy at Gibraltar were watching events carefully. The very idea of such action by the lower deck sent shudders down their spines. The Invergordon mutiny was fresh in their memories, and only 17 years had passed since the revolt of the French fleet in the Black Sea. There was no doubt as to where their sympathies lay, and this was to have an appreciable influence in several areas. The most important was passing intelligence on Republican shipping to the Nationalists; the most immediate was allowing Franco to set up a signals centre in Gibraltar itself (it is not clear whether London was informed of this).

With the rising crushed on most ships, many of the rebels were sure that they were doomed, since it seemed the Army of Africa could not cross to the mainland. Mola, convinced that their project had failed, continued only because there was no choice. The German *chargé d'affaires* reported to the Wilhelmstrasse that 'the defection of the fleet may frustrate completely the project of Franco. This quite serious organizational setback threatens the plans from the beginning. The resultant weakness can sacrifice the garrisons of the major cities. Above all precious time is being lost.'

This setback did not turn out to be a disaster for the Nationalists because they managed to start the first major airlift of troops in history. Although the airlift began almost immediately with a few Spanish air force Breguets and Italian Savoias, it was chiefly effected by Junkers 52s sent by Hitler, who remarked later that Franco should erect a momument to the plane because it was so vital to his victory. But the Nationalists also benefited from the fact that the new ships' committees were badly co-ordinated, thus severely reducing the effectiveness of the Republican navy. The Republican navy was also deterred from attacking ships transporting units of the Army of Africa because they were screened by the German pocket battleships *Deutschland* and *Admiral Scheer*.

The most furious fighting within the navy did not take place at sea, but in the port of El Ferrol at the north-west tip of Spain. On the 19th the

CNT and UGT demanded that the civil governor comply with the orders to issue arms, but the head of the naval arsenal refused to hand any over and a state of war was declared by the conspirators. The 29th Marine Infantry and detachments from the 3rd Regiment of Coastal Artillery managed to clear the town for the rebels, but many workers joined with sailors to seize the arsenal.

Loyalists also manned the cruiser *Almirante Cervera*, which was in dry dock, as well as the immobilized battleship *España*. These two ships managed to knock out the destroyer *Velasco*, which had been secured by its officers for the rising, but they could not traverse their heavy guns landwards at the coastal batteries because of installations alongside the dock. The destruction caused by a major naval battle in such a restricted area was enormous. Eventually, on 21 July, Nationalist officers faked a signal from the ministry of marine ordering the ships to give in and avoid useless bloodshed. The loyalist commander of the *Almirante Cervera* accordingly offered to surrender on the condition that there were no executions. This was promised, but later ignored.

The military rising elsewhere in Galicia had begun, after a delay, early on 20 July. In Corunna the civil governor refused arms to the UGT and CNT. He assured them that the military governor had received a solemn promise from his officers that they would not rebel. But General Pita was then arrested and shot, along with the divisional commander, General Salcedo, the civil governor and his pregnant wife. Groups of workers with very few weapons held out bravely against the troops and a large detachment of the Falange under Manuel Hedilla. They were finally crushed in a last stand near Sir John Moore's grave, just as reinforcements were arriving in the form of *dinamiteros* and miners armed with rifles. Finding they were too late and coming up against strong counter-attacks, the relief column fell back into the hills and broke up into guerilla forces.

In Vigo, which also fell to the Nationalists, the soldiers were given a great deal of alcohol, so the column marched to the centre of the town half-drunk. The officer in command proclaimed a state of war and, when unarmed civilians shouted protests, gave the order to fire. The soldiers started shooting in every direction.

Early in the morning of 20 July the sparsely armed citizens of Madrid around the Montaña barracks were joined by many others, including women. A lawyer who was with them described the scene: 'Rifle shots were cracking from the direction of the barracks. At the corner of the Plaza de España and the Calle de Ferraz a group of *asaltos* were loading their rifles in the shelter of a wall. A multitude of people were crouching and lying between the trees and benches of the gardens.' A loyalist plane arrived from the nearby airfield of Cuatro Vientos where the rising had been suppressed the day before. As it dropped its bombs on the barracks the thousands of civilians cheered and jumped for joy, but the machine-guns in the barracks opened up again, killing some of them. A lorry arrived towing a 75 mm gun. The crowds rushed upon it and manhandled it into position. An *asalto* officer explained that they needed to give the impression of being a whole battery; the moment after he fired, the gun was lifted bodily and rushed across to a new position.

Not surprisingly, emotions were often stronger than common sense. Old

1 Don Carlos and his staff during the Second Carlist War (1873–6).

2 Civil guards in Barcelona during the Tragic Week of July 1909.

3 Tram overturned in Valencia during a general strike.

4 Alfonso XIII and Queen Victoria Eugenia (of Battenberg).

5 Population of Castilblanco on trial for killing civil guards, January 1932.

6 Anarchists killed in the Casas Viejas massacre, January 1933.

7 From left to right, Lerroux, President Alcalá Zamora and Gil Robles in 1934.

8 Civil guards arrest socialist in Madrid, October 1934.

9 Asturian peasants rounded up after fleeing to the woods, October 1934.

10 Crowd in Madrid celebrates the Popular Front victory on 16 February 1936.

11 Shooting breaks out during the funeral of a civil guard officer, who was suspected of having attempted to assassinate President Azaña, April 1936.

12 Martínez Barrio, leader of the Cortes, and President Azaña (right), March 1936.

13 The May Day procession of 1936 descends the Paseo del Prado in Madrid.

14 José Antonio (seated centre) and fellow Falangists.

15 Asaltos, CNT workers and captured field gun in Barcelona, July 1936.

16 Rebels defend the telephone exchange in Barcelona, July 1936.

17 Civil guards join the fight against the rising in Barcelona, July 1936.

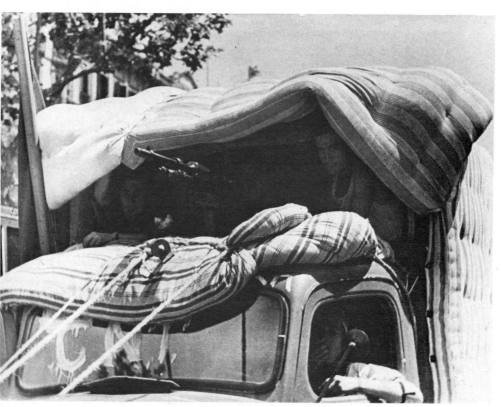

18 Commandeered lorry with machine-gun in Barcelona, July 1936.

19 Soldiers from the Montaña barracks in Madrid proclaim their loyalty to the Republic.

20 Rebel bodies lying in the courtyard of the Montaña barracks, July 1936.
22 Right Rebel officer led off for execution, July 1936.

21 The cruiser *Miguel de Cervantes* is secured for the Republic, August 1936.

23 Republican militiamen shoot at statue of Christ at Cerro de los Angeles, near Madrid.

24 Improvised armoured vehicles in Barcelona, July 1936. Note CNT salute.

25 Republican prisoners led off by Nationalist soldiers.

26 A suspected rebel sympathizer shot in Madrid, July 1936.

27 General Sanjurjo near Lisbon just before his fatal aircrash on 20 July 1936.

28 Millán Astray, the founder of the Foreign Legion, raises his remaining arm.

29 Queipo de Llano's daughter (in black *mantilla* and flowered dress) at a bullfight.

30 Franco surrounded by church hierarchy.

31 Falangist poster.

revolvers were fired at the thick stone walls by those privileged few who had weapons. The assault on the Montaña barracks was to prove what horrors can result from confusion. Many of the soldiers wanted to surrender and waved white flags from their windows. The crowds ran joyfully forward but the machine-guns commanded by officers opened up again, killing many in the open. This happened several times so the mass of people were utterly enraged by the time the barracks were stormed. This was only achieved because a Republican sapper sergeant within managed to throw open the gate before being shot down by an officer. The slaughter which followed was terrible. One cannot help remembering Borrow's words about the 1808 revolt against Napoleon, 'genuine sons of the capital, rabble of Madrid, ye twenty thousand manolos, whose terrible knives on the second morning of May worked such grim havoc against the Legions of Murat'.

In Granada General Campins held back for two days. He was finally arrested on 20 July by a Falangist army officer, to be shot later. The workers, who had believed that the garrison was loyal, realized too late what was happening. They withdrew to the district known as the Albaicín, which they barricaded, but artillery was brought up, and scores of families were buried in the rubble of their houses.

Of all the major towns, Valencia experienced the longest delay before the situation was clear because the military commander refused to declare himself for either side. General Goded's broadcast from Barcelona was a great blow to the conspirators there, who found it very difficult to persuade fellow officers to join. The CNT had already declared a general strike in the Valencian region and joined the executive committee set up by the Popular Front parties in the office of the civil governor. This dignitary had been deposed by the committee because he refused to do anything.

The CNT, with its large docker membership, was the most numerous of the worker organizations. In co-operating with the Popular Front it insisted on various conditions. One of these was that the para-military forces should be divided up among much larger groups of workers in order to ensure their loyalty. The condition was accepted and the mixed 'intervention groups' occupied the radio station, telephone exchange and other strategic buildings. Even so, when a detachment of the civil guard was sent together with some workers to help in another area, they shot their companions and went off to join the Nationalists.

The general commanding the Valencian garrison continued to insist on his loyalty although he refused to hand over any weapons as ordered by the government. Few were convinced by his protestations, since he was evidently waiting to see how events developed in other towns. The argument over whether to storm was further confused when a delegation under Martínez Barrio arrived from Madrid. Eventually even those who were afraid of forcing neutrals into the enemy camp agreed that the situation was intolerable. The barracks were finally taken two weeks after the rising had begun.

In Andalucia, Queipo's small force had not managed to secure much more than the centre of Seville and the aerodrome. The private planes housed at the aeroclub were to prove very useful for reconnaissance work and amateur bombing raids, but the vital function of the airstrip was to provide a landing-ground for the airlift from Morocco. It was not long before the rebels had sufficient reinforcements from Africa, both legionnaires and *regulares*, to crush all remaining resistance in the working-class districts.

Queipo de Llano's assistant, Antonio Bahamonde, who later changed sides, described the action against these areas, which were defended by their inhabitants with hardly any weapons (the Triana area was the *barrio* of the *gitanos* [gypsies] and the home of flamenco): 'The lower part of Triana was shot to pieces by cannons on the opposite bank of the river. The Moors, with savage ferocity and in obedience to terrible orders which it seems incredible could have been given by Spanish soldiers against their own brothers, entered the houses from which they supposed that shots had come, and killed with knives all the inhabitants, excepting not even the women and children.' A French journalist described the scene afterwards: 'It was implacable, inexorable slaughter ... one found the corpses of men intertwined and seemingly prepared to be strung like beads by the gaping wounds of bayonets and knives, which had been thrust into their bodies to the hilt.'

News of these actions triggered off reprisal killings in the Andalucian countryside, where the peasants had risen in their traditional fashion against their landlords and the civil guards. Then, once Queipo's forces had secured Seville, the rebels started to dominate the countryside around. Falangist sons of landowners organized peasant hunts on horseback. This sort of activity was jokingly referred to as the *'reforma agraria'* whereby the landless *bracero* was finally to get a piece of ground for himself.

In many outlying areas of Spain a shocked stillness followed the sudden violence, but there was little pause for breath after control of the major towns had been decided. Columns were rapidly organized to help in other areas, or recapture nearby towns. In Madrid the UGT had organized an effective intelligence system through the railway telephone network to find out where the rising had succeeded and where it had failed. Lorry loads of workers' militias rushed out from the capital. Guadalajara was retaken after a bitter struggle, Alcalá de Henares was recaptured from the civil guards who had declared for the rising and Cuenca was recaptured by 200 men led by Cipriano Mera. Other hastily formed militia detachments moved quickly north to block General Mola's troops along the line of the Guadarrama mountains.

A large column of militiamen drove south in a convoy of lorries, across the Castilian plain towards Toledo, where Colonel Moscardó was organizing the Nationalists' defence of the military academy in the Alcázar fortress. Only a handful of the cadets assembled, as it was the summer vacation, but a strong force of civil guards had been brought in from the surrounding countryside. A mixed bag of officers and a large number of Falangists brought the total of active defenders to around 1,100. Inside the fortress were also more than 500 women and children and 100 left-wing hostages. Moscardó, who had not been involved in the conspiracy, was acting on his own initiative. He had managed to stall the war ministry's orders to despatch the contents of the Toledo arms factory to Madrid, and his men had withdrawn into their fortress with most of its contents just as the militia column reached the edge of the town. The siege of the Alcázar had begun. It was to be exceptionally rich in emotive symbolism for the Nationalists.

In Barcelona the greatest concern of the anarchists was the fall of Saragossa to the army and the resulting slaughter of their comrades. Flying columns of armed workers assembled in great haste and rushed forth into the Aragon countryside. Villages and small towns which had been secured for the rising by the local civil guard detachment and right-wing sympathizers were seized on the way. The militia usually shot all those who they felt represented a threat before moving on. However, the columns were primarily made up of urban workers. Their fighting effectiveness was in the streets, not in the countryside where they had no sense of terrain.

Of the advancing columns only Durruti's did not fall to the temptation of securing rural areas, which was shown to be a dangerous distraction when the principal town was in enemy hands. The regular commander of the Republican forces, Colonel Villalba, even ordered Durruti not to rush on so tempestuously towards Saragossa. A strong detachment of Carlists, sent by General Mola in Pamplona, arrived to reinforce the Saragossa garrison and Durruti's force was unsupported. The militia columns from Barcelona, amounting to about 20,000 men, would have been far more effective if they had been concentrated on fewer objectives. But such a spontaneously mobilized body could not act like troops controlled by a general staff.

The early days of fighting were chaotic. Improvisations on both sides ranged from the inspired to the impractical. Field guns were fixed on to the rear of lorries, forming an early version of self-propelled artillery; armoured cars were built round trucks, sometimes effectively, though often the weight of steel plate was too much for the engine; every form of grenade, or *petardo*, was tried out (the so-called Molotov cocktail was in fact invented by the Foreign Legion when it was attacked by Russian tanks outside Madrid that autumn). But with the originality came a contempt for more prosaic military customs, such as digging trenches. To fight from the ground was utterly contrary to the Spanish concept of war. There was a subconscious moral certainty that bravery must lead to victory.

It was not until the early days of August that the respective zones became clear and fronts recognizable. The insurgents had a broad horizontal strip of territory from Galicia and León in the west to Navarre and north Aragon in the east. This surrounded the Biscay coast regions of Asturias, Santander and the Basque country, which had defeated the rising. In the south and west the rebels had seized no more than a small part of Andalucia.

Only at this stage did the realization that Spain faced civil war, rather than a violently contested coup, penetrate people's minds. The Republican failure to win outright in the early days, when dash and instinct outweighed weaponry and military science, meant that they were to become involved in a totally different type of fighting, one in which very different qualities were needed to win.

The Nationalists' greatest military asset was the 30,000 men of the Army of Africa, with its combat experience. They had also secured just over half of the badly trained and poorly equipped 70,000-strong metropolitan army. In addition, the great majority of the officers had joined the rising. They had about two-thirds of Queipo's *carabineros*, 40 per cent of the *asaltos* and 60 per cent of the civil guard. In all, this represented about 35,000 men out of the combined strength of the three para-military forces, which totalled just under 65,000 men.

For a long war it looked as if the Republic had the advantage: the large cities with their industry and manpower, most of the navy and merchant marine, two-thirds of the mainland territory, the gold reserves, and the citrus fruit export trade from Valencia, which was the country's largest foreign currency earner. However, the Nationalists were more than compensated by help from outside Spain. Their primary supply of recruits for some time was to be the Riffian tribes. Hitler and Mussolini were to provide military, naval, air, logistical and technical support, while American and British business interests supplied vital credits and oil.

The Nationalists at this point were starting to organize a military state, while in the Republican zone revolutionary processes were set on foot. The army's attempt at what they claimed was a pre-emptive counter-revolution had undermined the structure of the state. Andrés Nin of the POUM described it thus: 'The government do not exist. We collaborate with them, but they can do no more than sanction whatever is done by the masses.' The rising of the right had pushed an unplanned revolution into the willing arms of the left.

STAGES OF THE WAR,
July 1936-July 1938

Nationalist controlled territory July 1936
Nationalist gains by October 1937
Nationalist gains by July 1938

THE ATROCITIES

The most emotive issue in warfare is that of atrocities and it is nearly always the most visually horrific of them which become fixed in the imagination. The Spanish war had many, but it was those of religious significance which tended to prevail in people's minds: workers killing priests and disinterring the mummies in convent vaults, or Carlist *requetés* making a Republican lie in the form of a cross before hacking off his limbs while shouting 'Long live Christ the King!' The French Catholic writer, Bernanos, reported a Jesuit priest's statement that Christianity could only be re-established in Spain after two million 'incorrigibles' had been killed.

If people in other countries were reminded of the Thirty Years' War, or the religious persecutions of the Dark Ages, if they shuddered at this 'new barbarism', it was not surprising. But it must be remembered that the techniques of propaganda had recently been developed with improved communications to accompany mass mobilization. The purpose was to stiffen the resolve of both civilians and troops just as much as to win over the outside world. And, as in elections, it is obviously more effective to denigrate the enemy than indulge in self-praise. The lurid stories, such as of 'Huns' impaling babies on bayonets during the First World War, had quickly become weapons in the new total warfare.

The Spanish civil war was a war of foreign correspondents as well as of foreign intervention and the enemy atrocities related by press officers provided sensational copy. The initial, hasty impressions passed on by journalists with little first-hand evidence seriously affected the Republic's foreign relations when it needed to buy arms in the crucial months of the war. The violent excesses recounted in many papers justified that distaste for the Republic's politics which ran strongly in British conservative and diplomatic circles. The left-wing administration in France under Léon Blum suppressed its own natural sympathies and, alarmed by Hitler's occupation of the Rhineland that spring, felt obliged to follow British policy. Not until the bombing of Guernica in April of 1937 did the battle for world opinion really change in the Republic's favour, but by then the Republicans were already losing the war.

In the early days little was done, or could be done, by correspondents to examine the truth and background of most incidents. Refugees often justified their panic with exaggerated or imagined tales of horror. The gang of Barcelona workers said to be covered in blood from a massacre on 19 July were, in fact, from the abattoirs and had rushed straight out to resist the military rising. Wild estimates of the killing were reported: the Nationalists stated at the time that half a million people had been slaughtered in Republican territory, and claimed the still excessive figure of 55,000 after the war. Perhaps the confusion and speed of events made journalists fall back on clichés, rather than investigate what lay behind the ferocity of the war. Having tended to ignore Spain, Europe did not understand the turbulent cycles of repression and revolt which had now built up to an explosion affecting every corner of the country.

The slaughter did not follow the same pattern on each side. In Nationalist territory the relentless purging of 'reds and atheists' was to continue for years, while in Republican territory the worst of the violence was mainly a sudden and quickly spent reaction of suppressed fear, exacerbated by desires of revenge for the past.

The attacks on the clergy were bound to cause the greatest stir abroad, where there was little understanding of the church's powerful political role. The Catholic church was the bulwark of the country's conservative forces, the foundation of what the right defined as Spanish civilization. Not surprisingly, the outside world had a fixed impression of Spain as a deeply religious country. The jest of the Basque philosopher Unamuno, that in Spain even atheists were Catholic, was taken seriously. Centuries of fanatical superstition enforced by the Inquisition had engraved this image on European minds. Even so, it was surprising how few foreign newspapers made the connection between the religious repression dating back to the Middle Ages and the violent anti-clericalism which developed in the nineteenth century. For the anarchists, at least, the church represented nothing less than the psychological operations branch of the state. As such it was a target which ranked in importance with the civil guard.

The rage which led to such excesses in some areas was fired by one great conviction: the promise of heaven for the meek was the age-old trick by the rich and powerful to make the poor accept their lot on earth.

During the war the Nationalists claimed that 20,000 priests had been slaughtered; afterwards they said that 7,937 religious persons were killed out of a total community of around 115,000. This figure would still appear to be high, but undoubtedly there was a terrible slaughter. Even so, liberal Catholics abroad were later to state that the killing of priests was no worse than the right's killing of left-wingers in the name of God. The Spanish church was furious at this attitude, yet it said nothing when the Nationalists shot 16 of the Basque clergy including the arch-priest of Mondragón. The most sensational item of propaganda in the world press involved the raping of nuns, yet the detailed Nationalist indictment of Republican crimes published in 1946 offers no evidence for any such incident, while hinting at only one.

On the other hand, there were certainly occasions when wanton cruelty was inflicted on priests before they died. A few were burned to death in their churches and there are reports that some were buried alive after being made to dig their own graves. In the overwhelming majority of cases, however, it would appear that the killing was carried out instantly even if some corpses were mutilated afterwards. It is worth noting that the few Protestant churches were untouched. On the other hand, Protestants in Nationalist Spain, especially in Old Castile, such as the communities of Piedralaves and El Barraco near Avila, were killed on the urging of priests, who described them as 'these sons of Satan'.

Copes were used for mock bullfights in the street. A Republican who dressed himself in the archbishop of Toledo's ceremonial garments as a joke was nearly shot by a drunken *miliciano* who mistook him for the primate. Communion wine was drunk out of chalices, stained glass windows were broken, and militiamen shaved in the fonts. Despite what was said at the time, however, the loss of major works of art was remarkably small considering the destruction and damage to buildings.

The killing of the clergy was far from universal and with the exception of the Basque country, where the church was untouched, there was no marked regional pattern. In depressed rural areas the priests were often as poverty-stricken and ill-educated as their parishioners. Those who had taken as much trouble over burying the poor as the rich were almost certain not to be harmed.

The same was usually true of the killing of shopkeepers and members of the professional class. A lawyer or shopkeeper who had not taken advantage of the poor was rarely molested. Factory-owners and managers with a reputation for dealing fairly with their workforce were nearly always spared, and in many cases kept on in the new co-operative. On the other hand, any 'known exploiter' had little chance of survival if caught in the early days. Obviously there were exceptions to this pattern, but the rumours of people being shot merely for wearing hats and ties were the product of an inevitable middle-class persecution complex.

The relationship between the anarchists and the middle classes was extremely confused. Middle-class fears of what anarchist social revolution might mean were revealed in the slightly surprised account of a prominent christian democrat lawyer in Barcelona. 'In all my walks through the many different types of neighbourhood, I didn't see a single drunk. And that was a time which lent itself to excesses. Nor were there any sexual crimes ... While there was total social disorder you might say, there was no moral disorder. People were being assassinated – though in far fewer numbers than, propagandistically, has been claimed ... but at the same time the total decomposition that one could have expected did not occur.'

In Madrid the left-wing parties set up their own *checas*. Supporters of the rising were dragged in front of these revolutionary tribunals when they were not shot out of hand. The names and addresses of those belonging to groups involved in the rising were taken from official departments or the respective party headquarters, if their records had not been destroyed in time. Evidently some victims were denounced by servants, debtors and enemies. With the intense atmosphere of suspicion and the speed of events, many mistakes were undoubtedly made.

This superficial institutionalizing of justice happened mainly in places where the socialists and communists were dominant. Fake Falange membership cards, said to belong to the defendant, were often produced so as to ensure that the proceedings were rapid. When declared guilty, prisoners were taken away to be shot. Their bodies were then often left in prominent positions with placards stating that the victims were fascists. Anarchists tended to despise this farce of legality and simply got on with the shooting. Believing in the individual's responsibility for his actions, they rejected any form of corporate 'statism' for officials to hide behind. The other reason for immediate execution was their genuine horror of putting anyone in a prison, the most symbolic of all state institutions.

The wives and daughters of Nationalist supporters were hardly ever brought before the *checas*. They were only liable to be harmed if they put up resistance when the militia arrived at their homes. There were also notably few cases of rape in Republican territory, and this does not seem to have been due to the death-sentence which the militias imposed for the crime.

The establishment of the *checas* was inevitable, considering the spy mania and the frustration caused by the government's lack of resistance to the military rising. It is hardly surprising that some of them became gangs ruled by opportunist leaders. One of them was run by García Atadell, a former secretary-general of the Communist Youth, who set off for Argentina with his loot, but was captured by the Nationalists en route and later garrotted. Exploiting the fear and turmoil, a great number of criminals found it easy to act under political flags of convenience. Many of those who took real and imagined fascists for rides (in the movie jargon used at the time) were often teenage workers or shop assistants who were not political fanatics. The actress, Maria Casares (daughter of the ex-prime minister), who worked at a Madrid hospital with her mother, described what happened when they found blood in their car one morning. Their young driver, Paco, gave 'an imperceptible shrug. Then he said: "We took a guy for a ride at dawn, and I'm sorry I haven't had time to clean up the car." And in the rear-view mirror I saw his indefinable little smile; a smile of bragging and shame at the same time, and also a sort of atrocious innocence. The expression of a child caught red-handed.'

In spite of the wave of political killings in Madrid during the first few weeks, there remained a very large population of Nationalists, judging by the 'fifth column' which emerged two-and-a-half years later when Franco's troops approached. Those of the upper and middle classes who knew they were in danger usually tried to go into hiding, disguise themselves as workers to flee Madrid, or seek refuge in overcrowded embassies. Foreign legations were estimated to have held a total of 20,000 people. Hatred was aroused against them because some embassies, representing governments sympathetic to the Nationalists, acted as espionage centres, using both radio and diplomatic bag to pass information to the other side. One *checa* opened a fake embassy some months later and killed all those who came there for shelter. The indiscriminate killing was to decline, once control was exercised over the criminals released from prison and military action began in the Madrid area.

The worst mass killing in Madrid occurred on 23 August, just after an air raid and the arrival of reports of the massacre of 1,500 Republicans in the bullring at Badajoz. Enraged militiamen and civilians marched on the Model Prison when rumours spread of a riot among the Nationalist prisoners. Seventy of them, including many prominent right-wingers, were dragged out of the prison and shot.

There was relatively little violence in Málaga before 27 July. On that day Nationalist aircraft bombed the market, killing women and children. Coming just after Queipo de Llano's boasts over Seville radio that he knew from spies everything that happened in the town, the air raid had a traumatic effect. Suspects were hauled out of prison and shot against the nearest wall, and there was a further round-up in the wealthy areas of the town. Later on, in October, there was a similar incident in Bilbao after a bombing raid, but these incidents were not confined entirely to the Republican zone. A wholesale lynching of prisoners happened in Navarre when a Carlist mob took 50 men and women from their cells and drove them off to be shot after the emotional burial of a *requeté* killed in action. The Falange often used the local prison as a reservoir of victims when their patrols were unsuccessful. In Granada alone, 2,000 were thought to have been killed in this way.

In Barcelona the top priorities for revenge (after certain police officials like Miguel Badia) were the industrialists who had employed *pistoleros* against union leaders and, of course, the gunmen themselves. There was inevitably a wide-ranging settlement of accounts against blacklegs. One or two killings even went back to old inter-union disputes. Desiderio Trillas, the head of the UGT dockers, was shot down by a group of anarchists because he had prevented CNT members from receiving work. This murder was immediately condemned by the CNT-FAI leadership and they promised immediate execution of any of their members who killed out of personal motives. It was a threat which they carried out. Several prominent anarchists, such as their building union leader and the head of the catering syndicate who had taken vengeance on people who had denounced him to the police during Primo's dictatorship, were shot.

It appears that a considerable part of the violence, and most of the looting, was done by freed convicts. The real anarchists burned banknotes because they symbolized the greed of society, but those they had released from prison did not immediately change their habits with the arrival of the social revolution. The Iron Column of anarchist militia incorporated 300 convicts from Valencia in their ranks. 'We, who have always held society responsible for its own defects,' they explained, 'regarded them as our brothers. Imprisonment had earned them the contempt of society, but we gave them their freedom and the chance to rehabilitate themselves.' The excesses of unreformed criminals caused the CNT-FAI to complain bitterly that the 'underworld is disgracing the revolution', but they were reluctant to admit that they had allowed almost anybody to join their organization. Falangists sought refuge in their ranks, as well as others who had no interest in libertarianism. Many on the left also alleged that civil guards were often the most flagrant killers, as they sought to protect themselves from suspicions of sympathizing with the right.

The random killing started to be contained once the individuals exploiting the situation were suppressed by the 'control patrols', organized within a few days of the rising by the Central Committee of Anti-Fascist Militias, the new power in Catalonia.

The worst of the violence occurred in the first few days throughout Republican Spain, though it varied greatly from region to region. On the whole the depressed areas saw more ferocity, especially the province of

Ciudad Real, and parts of Andalucia like Ronda where the victims were thrown over the cliffs. (Hemingway used this incident in *For Whom the Bell Tolls*.) But in Ronda, as in many towns and villages, the executions were carried out by groups from other parts. It was a phenomenon which bore a remarkable resemblance to the way in which villagers had burned each other's churches, almost by mutual agreement, during the uprisings of the previous century.

On the Republican side there was a strong mixture of feelings when the worst of the rearguard slaughter was over. The majority of Republicans were sicked by what had happened. The anarchist intellectual, Federica Montseny, referred to 'a lust for blood inconceivable in honest men before'. La Pasionaria intervened on several occasions to save people, but other communists took a fatalistic attitude to the violence. Stalin's ambassador is said to have commented, with a shrug, that the scum was bound to come to the top at such a time. However, the dubious rationale that the atrocities had been far worse on the other side was not used until the propaganda campaign became effective during the next year.

The pattern of killing in 'white' Spain was different. It started as soon as an area had been secured by the Nationalist forces. Even Republicans who were promised their lives before surrendering were killed. Officers who had stayed loyal to the government in word only were also shot or imprisoned. Once the troops had moved on, a second and more intense wave of slaughter would begin, as the Falange, or in some areas the Carlists, carried out a ruthless purge of the civilian population. Their targets included union leaders, government officials, left-of-centre politicians (34 members of the Cortes were shot), intellectuals, teachers, doctors, even the typists working for revolutionary committees; in all, anyone who was even suspected of having voted for the Popular Front was in danger. It was a political slaughter which dwarfed its counterpart in Republican territory. Estimates of Nationalist victims vary enormously: from 50,000 to more than half a million. Queipo de Llano boasted of a ratio of 10 leftists to every Nationalist supporter killed. The boast was also a threat, but, if the executions which continued long after the end of the war, amounting to nearly 200,000 more, are included, the final figure may not be so far from the truth.

Estimates of non-combatants and surrendered troops killed by the Nationalists during the war vary for a host of reasons – propaganda motives, confusion, exaggeration through fear and the different definitions of rearguard slaughter. Nevertheless, if one takes some of the provinces where relatively reliable figures have been quoted, the figure for the war must exceed 100,000 and may be closer to 200,000. These provinces, which cannot be typical, include Seville where around 9,000 were killed, Granada 8,000, Majorca over 3,000 and Navarre over 7,000. Using official Nationalist statistics, the British consul in Málaga reported in 1944 that while 'the "Reds" were in control of Málaga from July 18th 1936 until February 7th 1937 ... they executed or murdered 1,005 persons'. But that 'during the first week of "liberation", that is from February 8th to 14th ... 3,500 persons were executed by the Nationalists.' And that 'from February 15th 1937 to August 25th 1944, a further 16,952 persons have been "legally" sentenced to death and shot in Málaga.' Historians had been doubtful about the numbers which the left claimed were killed in Saragossa, but in 1979 a mass grave 500 metres long with around 7,000 corpses was discovered near the city. The truth about the numbers killed by each side will never be known. Only a general measure or comparison can be given.

The Nationalist counterparts to the Republican *checas* were the local purge committees, usually composed of prominent right-wing citizens like the most prominent local landowner, the senior civil guard officer, a Falangist and, often, the priest. (In some places, however, clergymen risked their lives trying to stop the slaughter.) The committees inevitably inspired in neutrals a great fear of denunciation. All known or suspected liberals, freemasons and left-wingers were hauled in front of them. The voting register was referred to in many areas. A few prisoners might accuse others in a panic-stricken attempt to save themselves, but otherwise they had either a dazed or a defiant manner. Their wrists were tied behind their backs with cord or wire before they were taken off for execution. In Navarre a priest gave last rites to Basque nationalists *en masse* in front of an open trench before the volley, but in most places the condemned were taken in batches to the cemetery wall. Those who 'knew how to die well' shouted *'¡Viva la República!'* or *'¡Viva la Libertad!'* in the same way as condemned Nationalists called out *'¡Viva España!'*.

Nobody can tell what proportion of the victims were seized and shot at night lined up in front of car headlights. People lying awake in bed would cross themselves instinctively on hearing shots in the distance. The corpses of these 'clients', as they were sometimes called, were left in the open. If they were union members they often had their membership cards pinned to their chest as proof of guilt. In some areas the Nationalist authorities had to insist on burial for public health reasons.

It seemed to make little difference to the Nationalists whether or not there had been open opposition to their forces. In the military centre of Burgos and the Carlist capital of Pamplona they had not been resisted, yet the purge began immediately. The bishop of Vitoria later said that 'with astonishment and terror we learned from the lips of a chief of *requetés* of Navarre that in the month of September 1936 the Franco adherents had killed some 7,000 people of the left in Navarre alone. And this in an area which the Nationalists had taken without a fight.' In Seville, where Quiepo de Llano's bluff had won over the confused soldiers, the initial killing was said to be part of a military operation. But when reinforcements from the Army of Africa arrived under Major Castejón, the mopping-up was nothing more than a fearful massacre, with survivors finished off by knife or bayonet.

The subsequent actions of Franco's main force, composed of legionnaires and Moroccan *regulares*, showed that events in Seville were not exceptional. Their operations in Andalucia and the massacre after the fall of Badajoz left horrifying evidence of their obsession with knives and bayonets. A pro-Nationalist reporter, Mario Pires, suffered a nervous breakdown because of the scenes he witnessed. The continuing advance towards Madrid followed the same pattern. War correspondents were held back from Toledo so that they should not witness the events which followed the relief of the Alcázar. There 200 wounded militiamen in hospital were finished off with grenades and bayonets. The conduct of the campaign was compared to the *furia española* of Philip II's infantry in the sixteenth century, which terrorized Protestant Holland in its all-destructive advance. Villages which the Nationalists subdued along the way were laid waste, and graffiti such as 'your women will give birth to Fascists' were daubed on their walls. Meanwhile, General Queipo de Llano menaced Republicans who listened to Radio Seville with stories about the sexual powers of the African troops, to whom he promised the women of Madrid as an inducement. Near Gibraltar a Falangist reported that the wife of a left-winger was raped by a whole firing squad of Moors before being shot. An American journalist, John T. Whitaker, was present when two young girls were handed over to Moroccan troops near Navalcarnero by their commanding officer who told him calmly that they would not survive more than four hours. These *regulares* were later made 'honorary Christians'. The horror they inspired in Republican territory led to two of them being torn to pieces by a crowd when the truck in which they were being sent back as prisoners stopped for petrol.

The violence of their forces was justified by the Nationalists as reprisals for 'red terrorism' but, as with the fall of Málaga some six months later, it far surpassed Republican killings. In fact the retribution exacted in Málaga after the militias had retreated made the earlier slaughter look almost mild in comparison. Mussolini's ambassador, Cantalupo, protested vehemently to Franco that the Italian forces who were there under the overall command of the Duke of Seville had been brought into disrepute. The Italians were shocked by the behaviour of Nationalist women, particularly the *beatas* who mutilated bodies and desecrated graves. People who supported the rising were deeply disturbed at the scenes surrounding the executions. Such large crowds came to watch that coffee and *churro* stalls were set up. The civil governor of Valladolid called on 'people whose religious convictions are in many cases openly displayed, not to attend, even less take their wives and children'. It was widely known for women of high social standing to take their young children to watch as if it were some medieval morality play.

Military custom required that loyalist or neutral regular officers be accorded court martials where possible. On the whole, waverers were imprisoned, while most of those who had continued to serve the government, including seven generals and an admiral, were shot on the grounds of 'rebellion'. This remarkable reversal of definitions had also occurred in the navy, where Nationalists described sailors who followed ministry of marine instructions as 'mutinous'.

In the rear areas the Falange rapidly developed into the Nationalists' para-military force, assuming the task of 'cleaning up' – a legitimized version of their tactics earlier in the year. The young *señoritos*, often aided by their sisters and girl friends, organized themselves into mobile squads, using their parents' touring cars. Their leader, José Antonio, had declaimed that 'the Spanish Falange, aflame with love, secure in its faith, will conquer Spain for Spain to the sound of military music'. The real militants were obsessed with their task of cutting out 'the gangrenous parts of the nation' and destroying the foreign, 'red' contagion. The rest simply seemed to find sanctified gangsterism appealing. The Carlists, on the other hand, were fired by religious fanaticism to avenge the church by wiping out such modern evils as freemasonry, atheism and socialism. They also had a far higher proportion of their able-bodied men at the front than the Falange and, despite their violent excesses on many occasions, were reputed to have treated their prisoners of war the most correctly.

The fascist and military attitude to intellectuals showed itself to be one of deep distrust at the least, and usually consisted of an inarticulate reaction mixing hate, fear and contempt. The most famous victim of 1936 was undoubtedly the poet, Federico García Lorca. Lorca had returned to his home town of Granada just before the rising. (With the start of the summer holidays many on both sides were saved or killed simply by their travel plans.) He realized immediately that he was in danger because of his liberal sympathies even though he belonged to no party. His brother-in-law, the socialist mayor, and five of the university's professors had been shot in the first days. Yet even taking refuge with an old friend in the Falange did not save him. On 16 August he was arrested by a former CEDA deputy, Ruiz Alonso, who later asserted that Lorca 'did more damage with his pen than others with their guns'. He was condemned on the orders of the new governor, Colonel Valdés Guzmán, the commander of the Falangist militia. The precise details of his execution on 19 August remain unclear, but members of the CEDA group, Popular Action, claimed responsibility. H. G. Wells, the president of PEN, demanded details on the fate of Lorca as soon as the news reached the outside world, but the Nationalist authorities denied knowing what had happened to him. Lorca's death remained a forbidden subject in Spain until the death of Franco in 1975.

The Nationalists soon set up 'emergency military tribunals' as a legal cosmetic to the shootings. In Valladolid 448 people were tried in under six hours, while, in its account of one mass trial, *ABC* of Seville reported on 29 August that 'various terms of life imprisonment were demanded, but the impression is that they will all be shot'. The description of this type of proceedings by Luis Bolín, Franco's press officer, was revealing: 'Culprits usually confessed. When confronted with their guilt, their defence was the same: they had been deceived by red agitators, made to believe that by eliminating those who disagreed with them, burning crops and devoting themselves to wholesale plunder, a new order would be established and all need to work done away with for ever.'

Nationalist killings reached their peak in September, and continued for a long time after the war. Not surprisingly, people wondered if Franco wanted to repeat the deathbed answer of the nineteenth-century General Narváez when asked if he forgave his enemies: 'I have none. I have had them all shot.' A prominent monarchist, Eugenio Vegas Latapié, protested at the scale of killings to Franco, who 'displayed the simple cold cruelty for which he was well known in the Foreign Legion'.

The fanaticism of these self-appointed surgeons of the body politic provides only a partial explanation for the violence of Nationalist Spain. Behind it lay also, as General Mola explained, a deliberate political purpose: 'It is necessary to spread an atmosphere of terror. We have to create an impression of mastery.' At the beginning the corpses were left by the roadside with the express purpose of intimidating potential opponents into submission. Queipo de Llano was furious that exemplary killings had not been carried out in Córdoba, though he was soon satisfied when Major Bruno Ibañez of the civil guard arrived. The former public prosecutor of the city recounted to Ronald Fraser the story of a certain count, known to be a friend of Ibañez, who discovered that a friend of his was to be executed. He managed to stop the lorry load of victims en route to their death, but the squad leader insisted that he was under orders to deliver 18 corpses. The count grabbed the first passer-by, who was then shot as a substitute for his friend.

Several historians have pointed out that Nationalist policy was one of a foreign army conquering a large and hostile population. The war was substantially affected by the knowledge that the killings would go on. There was little incentive for the Republicans to negotiate terms when they knew that the execution squads were waiting. Antoine de Saint-Exupéry saw this in the faces of militiamen when leaving for the front: 'These men stand round and stare at me, and I read in their eyes a mournful sobriety. They know the fate that awaits them if they are captured. I begin to shiver with cold and observe of a sudden that no woman has been allowed to see them off.'

THE NATIONALIST ZONE

A *coup d'état* does not need a positive creed. A civil war, on the other hand, demands a cause, a banner and some form of manifesto. During the preparation for the coup, the military plotters had not concerned themselves greatly over the exact form of government which their *pronunciamiento* would herald. The urgency of the conspiracy did not allow them to waste time discussing hypothetical constitutions. They would discuss the finer points and formulate a detailed justification for their action after the country was secured. The substance was clear to all: centralized authoritarian rule. The form, however, was not clear, although the possibilities included Falangism, Carlism, a restoration of the Alfonsine monarchy and a republican dictatorship.

Until this problem was resolved the nominal command of Nationalist Spain was constituted in the Burgos junta presided over by General Cabanellas, the divisional commander at Saragossa. This figurehead establishment was organized by Mola, who commanded the Army of the North. It appears to have been an attempt to reduce the power of Franco, who commanded the most important military formation. Before the rising, General Hidalgo de Cisneros, the loyal commander of the Republican air force, had said that 'General Goded was more intelligent, General Mola a better soldier; but Franco was the most ambitious.' (His verdict on Mola was to prove highly inaccurate.)

Mola had talked of a republican dictatorship which would maintain the separation of church and state. He had even ordered that the monarchist flag be taken down in Pamplona. The Carlists were so horrified by his attitude that in the last few days before the rising there had even been doubts whether they would commit their *requetés*, who were needed to assure the obedience of the regular troops to the Nationalist cause. Queipo de Llano's sudden rise to prominence in the rebellion with his seizure of Seville must have worried them almost as much. He not only finished his radio broadcasts with '¡Viva la República!' and the liberal anthem, the *Himno de Riego*, but, worst of all, he was a freemason. The idea of fighting under the Republican tricolour was anathema to all traditionalists. Only the military plotters had sworn loyalty to it.

The Carlists' main hope for safeguarding their interests was destroyed on 20 July with General Sanjurjo's death. Major Ansaldo, the monarchist airman, had arrived in Portugal to fly him to Burgos with the announcement that he was now 'at the orders of the head of the Spanish state', which caused very emotional scenes among the general's entourage. Their light aircraft crashed on take-off and Sanjurjo died in the flames. This accident has been attributed either to sabotage by a Franco supporter or to Sanjurjo's vanity in taking so many cases of uniforms. The latter explanation seems the more probable, although Ansaldo claims it was sabotage.

During this time of uncertainty over the form of the new state, the Catholic church provided the Nationalist alliance with both a common symbol of tradition and, more important, a cause to transcend ideological confusion within their ranks. Its authoritarian, centralist nature and its attitude to property were acceptable to all factions, except the left wing of the Falange. Its hierarchy rallied to the cause of the right and prominent churchmen were seen giving the fascist salute. Cardinal Goma stated that 'Jews and masons poisoned the national soul with absurd doctrines'. The medieval idea of possession by the devil was used to justify the violent exorcism practised on 'traitors and bad Spaniards'.

A few brave priests put their lives at risk by criticizing Nationalist atrocities, but the majority of the clergy revelled in their new-found power and the increased size of their congregations. Anyone who did not attend mass faithfully was likely to be suspected of 'red' tendencies. Entrepreneurs made a great deal of money selling religious symbols, which were worn ostentatiously to ward off suspicion rather than evil spirits. It was reminiscent of the way the Inquisition's persecution of Jews and Moors helped make pork such an important part of the Spanish diet.

The disparate groups which made up the Nationalist movement were well aware of the danger in their undertaking, for they controlled only a third of Spanish territory and just under a quarter of the population. It was this uncertainty and the desire for strong leadership which Franco was able to exploit in the following months. He was a great admirer and worthy successor of that most cynical of statesmen, Ferdinand of Aragon, whom Spanish historians cite as the original of Macchiavelli's Prince. During August it became almost certain that Franco was to be the Nationalists' *Caudillo*, or leader, but nobody really knew what beliefs were hidden behind his bland, complacent expression, nor to what extent he would be able to reconcile the markedly different opinions about the future form of the Nationalist state. The Falange was worried that it would be little more than an auxiliary force under army command. The monarchists wanted Alfonso returned. The Carlists wanted a royal Catholic dictatorship with a populist flavour, although they realized that their pretender to the throne would not be accepted by their allies.

Franco's constitutional formula for unifying the Nationalists was as brilliant in what it included as in what it left unresolved. The basis of his approach was to have a monarchy without a king. Alfonso was not acceptable to the majority of Nationalists and he had little popular appeal; yet the arrangement satisfied the traditionalists without provoking the Falange or republicans like Queipo or Mola. It also avoided the kind of frustration Mussolini felt over King Vittorio Emmanuelle, which had resulted in serious tensions between royalists and fascists in the Italian armed services.

On 15 August, the Feast of the Assumption, a great ceremony was organized in Seville. The purpose was to pay homage to the old monarchist flag and adopt it as the banner of the 'new *Reconquista*'. The ceremony was also a part of Franco's plan to assert his ascendency over potential rivals for the Nationalist leadership. Queipo said that he would not attend, remarking that 'if Franco wants to see me, he knows where I am'. The Republican tricolour was lowered, then the monarchist flag of red-gold-red hoisted to the strains of the Royal March. Franco made a fervent speech, in which he hailed 'our flag, the authentic one, one to which we have all sworn loyalty, and for which our forefathers died, a hundred times covered with glory'. He then embraced the flag, followed by Cardinal Ilundaín. Queipo, who had decided to turn up at the last moment, made a long rambling speech worthy of General Primo de Rivera (he may have been either slightly drunk or else mocking the whole performance).

Seville had rapidly become the personal fief of Queipo and Franco was galled by his cavalier behaviour. Queipo's portrait was everywhere. His face dominated the town and was reproduced even on vases, ashtrays and mirrors. Households where 'reds' had been killed were the first to be forced to display his photograph in their windows. Against this barrage of publicity Franco's staff desperately sought to obtain exposure for their chief. Eventually they managed to arrange for his photograph to be projected on cinema screens to the tune of the Royal March. The audience gave the fascist salute during the five minutes that this lasted. Later on, public establishments in the Nationalist zone were obliged to display his portrait. And whenever the Royal March was played on the radio all who did not want their loyalty to be suspect saluted it.

The publicity of other Nationalist groups was just as strident. Posters appeared everywhere. The Carlist message proclaimed: 'If you are a good Spaniard, love your country and her glorious traditions, enlist with the *Requetés*.' The Falange's slogan was briefer and more threatening: 'The Falange calls you. Now or never.' More than 2,000 new Falange members were said to have enlisted in a 24-hour period in Seville alone. Queipo de Llano was both cynical and accurate when he referred to the blue shirt as a 'life-jacket'. Many a left-winger or neutral who wanted to avoid the *máquina de matar*, the killing machine, rushed to enlist and often tried to prove himself more fascist than the fascists. This phenomenon also occurred in Republican territory.

José Antonio's pre-war fears were confirmed, when this influx swamped the surviving *camisas viejas*, the 'old shirts'; nearly half of the pre-1936 veterans had died in the rising. Meanwhile, José Antonio was in Alicante jail guarded by militiamen, Onésimo Redondo had been killed and Ledesma was also in enemy hands. The Falange was thus in an uncomfortable position. Its membership was greatly swollen just at the time that its leaders were out of action. As a result the Falange operated in an unpredictable fashion. Some militia units went to the front, but the majority stayed in the rear areas to provide an improvised bureacracy and an amateur political police. The Falangist patrols supposedly checking suspicious characters, were blue-shirted and flamboyantly conspicuous as they forced passers-by to give the fascist salute and shout '*¡Arriba España!*'. Girl Falangists went into cafés to ask men why they were not in uniform. They then presented them with sets of doll's clothing in a contemptuous manner while a back-up squad of male comrades watched from the door.

The Nationalist obsession with *macho* qualities and the traditional male values of 'Old Spain' was emphasized in the slogan 'Young men of Spain – either military or castrated' (*o castrenses o castrados*). A man in civilian clothes was derided as being effeminate or homosexual. Trescastro, the self-proclaimed executioner of García Lorca, said that 'we were sick and tired of queers in Granada ... I fired two bullets into his arse for being a queer'. The mentality was not new, even the mild military regime of Primo de Rivera had claimed: 'This is a movement of men, and let him who does not have a complete sense of manhood wait in a corner without disturbing the good days that we are preparing for the nation.'

José Antonio had been transferred to Alicante jail by the Republican authorities early in July. A dramatic attempt to rescue him failed soon after the rising. It had been prepared by the leaders of the Falangist militia and the German consul, and involved the use of the pocket battleship *Admiral Graf Spee*. The trial of José Antonio was inevitable considering the role of the Falange and his own part in encouraging the rising. He was allowed to defend himself and his legal training helped him put up an impressive performance. Knowing he was doomed, he did not stoop to ask for clemency. He was, however, successful in having his brother's and sister-in-law's sentences commuted, remarking that 'life is not a firework to be let off at the end of a party'. José Antonio was eventually executed on 20 November, despite attempts by the central government to reduce the sentence to life imprisonment. The Falange had a great martyr as a result, but was left without any leader of stature – a situation which could hardly have displeased Franco. He was happy to allow the cult of José Antonio to develop later, being far too pragmatic to be jealous of a dead rival.

Behind the military edifice of Nationalist Spain trade developed rapidly. In Andalucia Queipo de Llano proved himself to be a surprisingly competent commercial administrator. He quickly ensured that the production of foreign exchange earners, such as the region's sherry, olives and citrus fruit, was increased. He organized trade agreements with the Salazar regime in Lisbon. However, the granting of import licences, monopolies and commercial rights led to the corruption and profiteering which was to permeate Nationalist Spain. Contributions to the movement were a good investment for those who were quick. At the same time charities mushroomed, occupying the time of clergy, *beatas*, war widows and other civilians with an ambitious eye to the future.

Meanwhile, the loudspeakers in the streets played music such as the violent Legion marching song, *El Novio de la Muerte* (the fiancé of death). And at the radio station every evening a bugler stood in front of the microphone to herald the daily bulletin from the Generalissimo's headquarters. It was against this atmosphere that a remarkable act of moral courage was to take place, an incident highlighted by the emphasis on physical bravery in that war. On the anniversary of Columbus' discovery of America, a Festival of the Spanish Race was organized at the University of Salamanca. The audience consisted of prominent supporters of the

Nationalist movement, including a large detachment of the local Falange. Among the dignitaries on the stage sat Franco's wife, the bishop of Salamanca, General Millán Astray, the founder of the Foreign Legion, and Miguel de Unamuno, the Basque philosopher who was the rector of the university. Unamuno had been disappointed by the Republic, so in the beginning he had supported the Nationalist rising. But he could not ignore the slaughter in this city where the infamous Major Doval from the Asturian repression was in charge.

Soon after the ceremony began, General Millán Astray, who looked the very spectre of war with only one arm and one eye, stood up to speak. He violently attacked the Basques and Catalans: 'On this day of the Spanish race one half of all Spaniards are criminals guilty of revolution and high treason.' Describing them as 'cancers in the body of the nation', he went on: 'Fascism, which is Spain's health-giver, will know how to exterminate both, cutting into the live healthy flesh like a resolute surgeon free from false sentimentality.' This metaphor was a constant refrain; Sanjurjo had said that 'only an operation can save Spain'. However, despite this unoriginality, the acclaim from the audience was set off by a Falangist yelling the battle cry which Millán Astray had given to his Foreign Legion, '¡Viva la Muerte!' ('Long live death'). This was followed by the chanting of Falangist slogans in reply to the prompting of cheer leaders. The audience screamed themselves hoarse, standing in their blue shirts with right arms thrust up in fascist salutes towards the portrait of General Franco hanging above where his wife sat.

The noise died as Unamuno stood up slowly. His quiet voice was an impressive contrast.

> All of you are hanging on my words. You all know me and are aware that I am unable to remain silent. At times to be silent is to lie. For silence can be interpreted as acquiescence. I want to comment on the speech, to give it that name, of General Millán Astray, who is here among us. Let us waive the personal affront implied in the sudden outburst of vituperation against the Basques and Catalans. I was myself, of course, born in Bilbao. The bishop, whether he likes it or not, is a Catalan from Barcelona.

The bishop of Salamanca seemed discomforted at the public reminder of his birth, which was almost in itself an implication of disloyalty to the Nationalist crusade. Everyone stood in numbed silence as Unamuno went on:

> Just now I heard a necrophilous and senseless cry: 'Long live death'. And I, who have spent my life shaping paradoxes must tell you as an expert authority, that this outlandish paradox is repellent to me. General Millán Astray is a cripple. Let it be said without any slighting undertone. He is a war invalid. So was Cervantes.* Unfortunately there are all too many cripples in Spain now. And soon there will be even more of them if God does not come to our aid. It pains me to think that General Millán Astray should dictate the pattern of mass psychology. A cripple who lacks the greatness of Cervantes is wont to

* Cervantes' satire on chivalry in *Don Quixote* was said to have been partially inspired from his wounds received at Lepanto in 1571.

83

seek ominous relief in causing mutilation around him. General Millán Astray would like to create Spain anew, a negative creation in his own image and likeness; for that reason he wishes to see Spain crippled as he unwittingly made clear.

The general was unable to contain his almost inarticulate fury any longer. He could only scream, *'¡Muera la inteligencia. Viva la Muerte!'* ('Death to intellectuals! Long live death!'). The Falangists took up his cry and army officers took out their pistols. Apparently, the general's bodyguard even levelled his submachine-gun at Unamuno's head, but this did not deter Unamuno from crying defiance.

> This is the temple of the intellect, and I am its high priest. It is you who profane its sacred precincts. You will win, because you have more than enough brute force. But you will not convince. For to persuade you would need what you lack: reason and right in your struggle. I consider it futile to exhort you to think of Spain.

He paused and his arms fell to his sides. He finished in a quiet resigned tone. 'I have done.' It would seem that Franco's wife saved him from being lynched on the spot, though when her husband was informed of what had happened he apparently wanted Unamuno to be shot. This course was not followed because of the philosopher's international reputation and the reaction caused abroad by Lorca's murder. Unamuno died six weeks later, broken-hearted and cursed as a 'red' and a traitor by those he had thought were his friends.

THE REPUBLICAN ZONE

The rising fragmented the country into a mass of localized civil wars, but it was not the main reason for the collapse of the Republican state. This was caused partly by the central government's disastrous response to the crisis and partly by the sympathy which a majority of its functionaries, from the diplomatic corps to the police force, felt for the rebellion. As a result the CNT and UGT, which had borne the brunt of the fighting, also acted as the basis for a revolutionary reorganization of all Republican territory except the Basque country. The membership of the two unions increased enormously, partly out of admiration for what they had done, but mostly for opportunistic reasons as they were now the power in the land. They soon had around two million members each, a striking total when the lost territories are taken into account. The POUM and the Communist Party were also to increase rapidly. The communists' vast gains came from middle-class Republicans attracted by the Party's disciplined anti-revolutionary approach, ambitious men who were sure that they would come out on top, and people frightened of being arrested as Nationalist supporters.

In the early days of the rising, Madrid had the air of a revolutionary city, in contrast to its later appearance of a city merely at war. Militiamen of the UGT and CNT could be seen in almost every street checking identities. Their usual dress consisted of dark blue *monos* (which were like boiler suits) and badges or coloured scarves to denote their political affiliation: black and red for the anarcho-syndicalists, red for the socialists and communists. The lack of opportunity, or the unwillingness, to shave made most of them look especially villainous to foreign observers. None of them went anywhere without a rifle. The government's original refusal to issue arms, which produced a feeling of impotence against the military rising, had left a deep mark. This lingering distrust meant that a vast number of weapons was kept in rear areas during the early months. Also, ruses like those at Oviedo and San Sebastián meant that there was a reluctance to commit too many men in case there were more unpleasant surprises.

The socialist UGT was still the most powerful organization in Madrid, even though the CNT continued to gain rapidly at its expense. Girls wearing the red and blue of the Socialist Youth were everywhere collecting money for left-wing charities, encouraged by their new freedom to talk to whomever they wanted without being thought loose. Also, schoolchildren dressed as Young Pioneers (a Spanish attempt at the Komsomol) might be seen walking along in crocodile chanting slogans in shrill voices like a monotonous multiplication table. Much was made later of the fact that 'middle-class' jackets and ties were hardly to be seen in the streets any more. However, this probably owed more to the exceptionally hot weather and the new informality than to persecution of those who were respectably dressed. Obviously Nationalist supporters trying not to be recognized would do everything possible to look proletarian if they did venture outside, and neutrals preferred to be on the safe side in the atmosphere of suspicion.

Once most of the militia left for the various fronts, the revolutionary aspect of Madrid began to disappear. There were still beggars on street corners and the expensive shops and restaurants soon reopened. The war could almost have been overseas. Only the foreign journalists who crowded the cafés and hotel bars of the Gran Vía seemed to think that the capital was at the centre of events.

The shock of civil war made Spanish workers both outward looking in the way they hoped for 'international support against fascism', and inward looking in the way they trusted only the local community. Every town and village had its revolutionary committee, which represented the political balance in the community. It was responsible for organizing everything which the government and local authorities had done before. On the Pyrenean border, anarchist militiamen in their blue *monos* stood alongside smartly uniformed *carabineros*, checking passports. It was the committee of the border town, not a government official, who decided whether a foreigner could enter the country.

The local committees organized all the basic services. They commandeered hotels, private houses and commercial premises for use as hospitals, schools, orphanages, militia billets, and party headquarters. They established their own security forces to stop random and personally motivated killings perpetrated as 'anti-fascist operations'. Justice became the responsibility of revolutionary tribunals, whose proceedings were an improvement on the sham trials of the early days. The accused were allowed to have legal assistance and to call witnesses, although standards varied widely and in some places justice remained a grotesque piece of play-acting. Once the initial fears of the first weeks had started to abate, the death penalty became much rarer.

In Asturias the CNT set up the Gijón War Committee. The CNT's strength came from dockers, seamen and, above all, fishermen, who set up a co-operative covering every aspect of their trade. The UGT were stronger inland, among the miners. Eventually its committee merged with the anarchists, and a socialist became president of the joint council. On the other hand, in Santander socialists took over the war committee, prompting anarchists to attack their 'authoritarian manner'.

The Basque juntas of defence were replaced by the independent Republic of Euzkadi, with José Antonio Aguirre as president. (Its red, green and white flag had already replaced the Republican tricolour.) The formal establishment of the Basque republic was confirmed by a meeting of municipal delegates in the traditional fashion, with oaths sworn under the sacred oak tree of Guernica. The conservative Basque nationalist party held the most important portfolios, while republicans and socialists were allowed the lesser ones. The anarchists, who were strong in San Sebastián and the fishing communities, neither demanded nor were offered any role in the administration. The Basque nationalists established a very rigid control with their para-military militia which excluded left-wingers and non-Basques. However, both the UGT and the CNT later formed their own battalions to fight in the army corps of Euzkadi.

Of all these regional moves to self-government, the most extraordinary and the most important took place in Catalonia. The journalist, John Langdon-Davies, described the contradictions in Barcelona, calling it 'the strangest city in the world today, the city of anarcho-syndicalism supporting democracy, of anarchists keeping order, and anti-political philosophers wielding power'. On the evening of 20 July, Juan García Oliver, Buenaventura Durruti and Diego Abad de Santillán met with President Companys in the palace of the *Generalidad*. They still carried the weapons with which they had stormed the Atarazanas barracks that morning. In the afternoon they had attended a hastily called meeting of more than 2,000 representatives of local CNT federations. A fundamental disagreement arose between those who wanted to establish a libertarian society immediately and those who believed that it had to wait until after the generals were crushed.

Luis Companys had defended anarchists for nominal fees when a young lawyer. His sympathy for them was unusual among Catalan nationalists, who often referred to them in almost racial terms as 'Murcians', because the major source of anarchist strength had been among non-Catalan immigrant workers. At the meeting on 20 July Companys greeted anarchist delegates warmly:

> Firstly, I must say that the CNT and the FAI have never been treated as their true importance merited. You have always been harshly persecuted and I, with much regret, was forced by political necessity to oppose you, even though I was once with you. Today you are the masters of the city and of Catalonia because you alone have conquered the fascist military . . . and I hope that you will not forget that you did not lack the help of loyal members of my party . . . But you have won and all is in your power. If you do not need me as president of Catalonia, tell me now, and I will become just another soldier in the fight against fascism. If, on the other hand . . . you believe that I, my party, my name, my prestige, can be of use, then you can depend on me and my loyalty as a man who is convinced that a whole past of shame is dead.

Azaña was later to call this 'a plot to abolish the Spanish state', but the Catalan president was a realist. The official Republican force in Barcelona amounted to about 5,000 men of the para-military corps, and events elsewhere had shown that it was very dangerous to rely on them entirely. The regular army no longer existed in Barcelona, for most of the rebel officers had been shot and the soldiers had either gone home or joined the workers' militias. Meanwhile, with rifles from the San Andrés barracks and from elsewhere, the anarchists were estimated to have some 40,000 weapons distributed among their 400,000 members in Barcelona and its suburbs. It would have been folly for Companys to have considered attacking them at their moment of greatest strength and popularity. The anarchists were, also, his best allies against the re-imposition of Madrid government. Companys expressed the situation drily: 'Betrayed by the normal guardians of law and order, we have turned to the proletariat for protection.'

The Catalan president had presented the anarchists with a fundamental dilemma. García Oliver described the alternatives as 'anarchist dictatorship, or democracy which signifies collaboration'. Imposing their social and economic self-management on the rest of the population appeared to violate libertarian ideals more than collaborating with political parties. Abad de Santillán said that 'we did not believe in dictatorship when it was being exercised against us and we did not want it when we could exercise it only at the expense of others'. At their Saragossa conference only seven weeks before, the anarchists had affirmed that each political philosophy should be allowed to develop 'the form of social co-existence which best suited it'. This meant working alongside other political bodies with mutual respect for each other's differences. Though genuine, this was a simplistic view, since the very idea of worker-control and self-management was anathema both to businessmen and the communists.

Even if the anarchist leaders sitting in Companys' ornate office, having just been offered the keys of the kingdom, could have foreseen the future, it is doubtful whether their choice would have been made any easier. They had the strength to turn Catalonia and Aragon into an independent non-state almost overnight. But Madrid had the gold, and unofficial sanctions by foreign companies and governments could have brought them down in a relatively short space of time. However, what influenced their decision the most was concern for their comrades in other parts of Spain. The demands of solidarity overrode other considerations. They could not abandon them in a minority which might be crushed by the Marxists.

They therefore proposed a joint control of Catalonia with other parties and on their recommendation the Central Committee of the Anti-Fascist Militias was set up. 'Being in the majority, the least we can do is to recognize the right of minorities to organize their own lives as they want and to offer them our cordial solidarity. In the case where we are in a minority [the central and northern parts of the Republican zone], we as anarchists would require a similar treatment.' In Barcelona the CNT-FAI took only five of the 15 seats.

The Central Committee of Anti-Fascist Militias literally ran everything from security and essential services to welfare; the *Generalidad* was nothing more than a shadow government, or rather a government-in-waiting. Its councillors might make plans and charts, but they had little to do with what was already being put into practice on the ground. The all-important conversion to war industry had been started by Juan García Oliver and Eugenio Vallejo during the initial fighting. The *Generalidad* did not set up its war industries commission until August and for a long time it had little influence.

The contradictions of political power were to confront the anarchists in many forms. Their manifesto of 1917, for example, had condemned 'all festivals, such as bullfights and indecent cabarets which can brutalize the people'. But to act as dictatorial censors was an even worse affront to their beliefs. Meanwhile the *Mujeres Libres*, the anarchist feminists, were sticking posters over the walls of the red light district, trying to persuade prostitutes to give up their way of life. They offered and ran training courses for the ex-prostitutes to acquire skills for productive work. But other anarchists were less patient. According to the sympathetic French observer, Kaminski, they shot pimps and drug dealers on the spot.

A notable phenomenon of the war was the spontaneous growth of a women's movement after the 1936 elections. It was born, not of literature or theory from abroad (except a few translations of Emma Goldman), but of women's instinctive sense that the overthrow of the class system should mean the end of the patriarchal system as well. The anarchists had always declared the equality of all human beings, but, as the anarchist feminist organization, *Mujeres Libres*, emphasized, relationships still remained 'feudal'. The most blatant way in which the anarchists had failed to live up to their professed ideals was the different levels of pay for men and women in most CNT enterprises. The Socialist Youth was another major focal point for feminism. Little headway was made outside the cities, though the greatest demonstration of the new equality was the number of militia-women fighting in the front line. (The German ambassador was shocked when, one day, Franco ordered the execution of some captured militia-women and then calmly continued to eat his lunch.) No figures are available, but there were probably fewer than 1,000 women at the front. There were, however, several thousand under arms in the rear areas and a woman's battalion took part in the defence of Madrid. This move towards equal participation was severely curtailed under the increasingly authoritarian direction of the war effort as the military situation deteriorated. By 1938 women had returned to a strictly auxiliary role.

The people's attitude towards buildings was accurately described by Kaminski: 'They are inclined to destroy symbols, but they respect in an ingenuous and sometimes exaggerated way everything which seems useful.' Religious buildings, patriotic monuments and the women's prison were torn or burnt down, while hospitals and schools were respected almost with a reverence which the Nationalists accorded to churches.

The most important achievement of the liberal Republican government of 1931–33 had been in education and reducing illiteracy. The measures limiting church involvement in education created a great void in the system to begin with, but the school-building and teacher-training programmes were correspondingly ambitious. The Republic claimed to have built 7,000 schools as opposed to only 1,000 built during the previous 22 years. An illiteracy rate of nearly 50 per cent in most areas under the monarchy was drastically reduced. Many imaginative projects, such as Lorca's travelling theatres, were part of an energetic attempt to help the rural mass free itself from the vulnerability of ignorance. All the time, independently of government sponsored efforts, the *casas del pueblo* of the UGT and the *ateneos libertarios* of the anarchists continued their efforts in this direction. During the war it was above all the earnest study of uneducated militiamen in the trenches which so impressed foreign visitors like Saint-Exupéry.

The outward signs of working-class power were everywhere in Barcelona, unlike Madrid. Party banners hung from public buildings, especially the black and red diagonal flag of the CNT. The anarchists had installed their headquarters in the former premises of the Employers' Federation, while the communist-controlled PSUC led by Juan Comorera had taken over the Hotel Colón. The POUM had seized the Hotel Falcón, though their main power base was in Lérida. The POUM was growing because it seemed to offer a middle course between the anarchists and the communists. But, as Andrés Nin, their leader, had once been closely associated with Trotsky, the Stalinists hated the POUM even more than the anarchists. They ignored the fact that Trotsky and his Fourth International never ceased to attack the POUM.

Barcelona had always been a lively city and the July revolution hardly calmed it. Expropriated cars roared around at high speed, often causing accidents but such antics were soon stopped when petrol was issued only for essential journeys. Loudspeakers attached to trees on the avenues relayed music and broadcast ludicrously optimistic news bulletins from time to time. These were seized on by groups discussing events such as the 'imminent' fall of Saragossa. It was a world of instant friendship, with the formal expression of address no longer used. Foreigners were welcomed and the anti-fascist cause was explained repeatedly. There was a naive faith that, if everything was made clear, the democracies could not fail to help them against Franco, Hitler and Mussolini.

All around a heady atmosphere of excitement and optimism prevailed. Gerald Brenan said that 'visitors to Barcelona in the autumn of 1936 will never forget the moving and uplifting experience'. Foreigners who gave a tip had it returned politely with an explanation of why the practice corrupted both the giver and the receiver. Probably the greatest contrast between Madrid and Barcelona was in the use of hotels. In the capital Gaylord's was later taken over by the Communist Party as a luxurious billet for its senior functionaries and Russian advisers. In Barcelona the Ritz was used by the CNT and the UGT as 'Gastronomic Unit Number One' – a public canteen for all those in need. That may have been partly a symbolic gesture, but the hotel's enormous kitchens were ideal. Everyone who went was supposed to have a pass from his local committee, but the guards 'refused to be bureaucratic'. Not only did few people attempt to eat twice but, according to Langdon-Davies, little of the Ritz cutlery disappeared. The anarchists ascribed this to the fact that it now belonged neither to a private concern, nor to the state; the people did not steal from themselves. Their basic principle was that the community should take on all responsibility for welfare. To leave it to the state was to give authoritarianism a human face. Certainly such enterprises accounted for the lack of begging in Barcelona compared to Madrid. Meanwhile, refugees from areas conquered by the Nationalists were installed in the apartments of the rich.

The most outspoken champions of property were not the liberal republicans, as might have been expected, but the Communist Party and its Catalan subsidiary, the PSUC. La Pasionaria and other members of their central committee emphatically denied that any form of revolution was happening in Spain, and vigorously defended businessmen and small land-owners (at a time when *kulaks* were dying in Gulag camps). This anti-revolutionary stance, prescribed by Moscow, brought the middle classes into the communist ranks in great numbers. Even the traditional news-papers of the Catalan business community *Vanguardia* and *Noticiero*, praised 'the Soviet model of discipline'. Meanwhile, the model of 'unor-ganized discipline' had already made itself felt throughout the Republican zone, but above all down the Mediterranean coastal belt.

This extraordinary mass-movement of worker self-management still provokes powerful controversy. The liberal government and the Commun-ist Party regarded it as a major obstacle to their attempts to organize the war effort. They were convinced that central control was vital in a country such as Spain with its strong parochialism and reluctance to react to a threat unless it was close. For example, the anarchists of Catalonia felt that to recapture Saragossa would be tantamount to winning the war. The advance of the Army of Africa in the south-west could almost have been in a foreign country, as far as they were concerned. The exponents of self-management, on the other hand, argued that there would be no motive for fighting if the social revolution were not allowed to continue. Having done the fighting in July when the government refused to arm them, the anarch-ists bitterly resented the way the government expected them to surrender all their gains. This fundamental clash of attitudes undermined the unity of the Republican alliance. The advocates of a centralized state were to win the struggle in 1937, but the morale of the population was mortally stricken by the Communist Party's bid for power in the process.

The collectives in Republican Spain were not the state collectives of Russia. They were based on the joint ownership and management of the land or factory. Alongside them were 'socialized' industries, restructured and run by the CNT and UGT as well as private companies under the joint worker–owner control. Co-operatives marketing the produce of individual smallholders and artisans also existed, although these were not new. They had a long tradition in many parts of the country, especially in fishing communities. There were estimated to have been around 100,000 people involved in co-operative enterprises in Catalonia alone before the civil war. The CNT was, of course, the prime mover in this development, but UGT members also contributed to it. The UGT or UGT–CNT organized about 15 per cent of the collectives in New Castile and La Mancha, the majority in Estremadura, very few in Andalucia, about 20 per cent in Aragon, and about 12 per cent in Catalonia.

The regions most affected were Catalonia and Aragon, where about 70 per cent of the workforce was involved. The total for the whole of Re-publican territory was nearly 800,000 on the land and a little over a million in industry. In Barcelona workers' committees took over all the services, the oil monopoly, the shipping companies, heavy engineering firms such as Vulcano, the Ford motor company, chemical companies, the textile industry and a host of smaller enterprises.

Any assumption by foreigners that the phenomenon simply represen-ted a romantic return to the village communes of the Middle Ages was inaccurate. Modernization was no longer feared because the workers controlled its effects. Both on the land and in the factories technical improvements and rationalization could be carried out in ways that would previously have led to bitter strikes. The CNT wood-workers' union shut down hundreds of inefficient workshops so as to concentrate production in large plants. The whole industry was reorganized on a vertical basis from 'felling timber to the finished product'. Similar structural changes were carried out in other industries as diverse as leather goods, light engineering, textiles and baking. There were, however, serious problems in obtaining new machinery to convert companies which were irrelevant, like luxury goods, or under-used because of raw-material shortages, like the textile industry. They were caused principally by the Madrid government's attempt to reassert its control by refusing foreign exchange to collectivized enterprises.

There were wide disparities between rich and poor collectives, and the objective of avoiding the waste of the capitalist system or the inefficiency of state socialism was achieved only in part. The strong syndicalist presence within the CNT meant that the anarchist aim of a consumer–producer balance was upset, because the workers' committees were often out of touch with their customers' needs. In addition, the mentality induced by years of industrial strife was deeply engrained. For some it took time to realize that more pay for less work was now against their interests.

There were sometimes long discussions and wrangles within the workers' committees, but when the issues were clear, little time was wasted. Services, such as water, gas and electricity were working under their new management within hours of the storming of the Atarazanas barracks. Using the framework agreed at the Saragossa conference, a conversion of appropriate factories to war production meant that metallurgical concerns had started to produce armoured cars by 22 July. Although not sophisticated, they were not all crudely improvised contraptions. The industrial workers of Catalonia were the most skilled in Spain. The Austrian sociologist, Franz Borkenau, also pointed out the great difference it made not to have technicians obstructed as occurred in Russia.

One of the most impressive feats of those early days was the resurrection of the public transport system at a time when the streets were still littered and barricaded. One observer described employees being summoned back to work by CNT appeals over the radio. 'Five days after the fighting had stopped, 700 tramcars, instead of the usual 600, all painted in the colours of the CNT–FAI in red and black diagonally aross the sides, were operating in Barcelona.' Nevertheless, the continued success of Barcelona's collectivized transport was helped by elements which other industries lacked – a regular cash flow and little need of raw materials.

The social revolution in Catalonian industry was soon threatened in several ways. A sizeable part of the home market had been lost in the rising. The peseta had fallen sharply in value on the outbreak of the war, so imported raw materials cost nearly 50 per cent more in under five months. This was accompanied by an unofficial trade embargo which the pro-Nationalist governors of the Bank of Spain had requested among the international business community. Meanwhile, the central government tried to exert control through withholding credits and foreign exchange. Largo Caballero, the arch-rival of the anarchists, was even to offer the government contract for uniforms to foreign companies, rather than give it to CNT textile factories. (The loss of markets and shortage of raw materials led to a 40 per cent decline in textile output, but engineering production increased by 60 per cent over the next nine months.)

The communists' Popular Front strategy of defending commercial interests so as to win over the middle class was perfectly compatible with their fundamental opposition to self-management. As a result their Catalonian affiliate, the PSUC, started to persuade UGT bank employees to use all possible means to interfere with the collectives' financial transactions.

To many people's surprise the anarchists made attempts to win the trust of the middle classes. If a shopkeeper complained to the CNT that his goods were being taken by workers' patrols, a sign would be put up stating that the premises belonged to the supply committee. Small firms employing fewer than 50 people were left untouched if the management had a good record. Meanwhile, the anarchists tried to persuade the middle classes that they were in fact oppressed by an obsession with property and respectability. 'A grovelling existence,' they called it. 'Free yourselves socially and morally from the prejudices that have dominated you until today.'

There is no doubt that finance was the anarchists' greatest weakness. For most of them handling money was 'the moral equivalent of a priest running a brothel'. They confused the 'vehicle of greed with greed itself'. Many factories and enterprises were run with perfectly good economic control by their committees, but in others there was financial chaos. Income from sales was treated as profit, and no provision was made even for raw materials. But the money was not wasted on riotous living. The surplus to the wage bill was usually given away, either to left-wing charities or to agricultural collectives for investment in new machinery. In some cases, however, it was found that the owner had managed to leave just before the rising with everything in the firm's accounts.

After defeating the attempted coup in Barcelona and reorganizing production so quickly, the anarchists were angry at the Madrid government's attempt to regain control through the denial of credits. A plan for seizing part of the Spanish gold reserves so as to by-pass the central government's denial of foreign exchange was considered, but rejected, by the CNT regional committee. Apart from finance, the other main weakness was the lack of co-ordination between co-operatives within a particular industry. However, government performance on industrial matters was such that it is doubtful whether ministers in Madrid would have done much better.

At the same time as the management of industry was being transformed, there was a mushroom growth of agricultural collectives in the southern part of Republican territory. They were organized by CNT members, either on their own or in conjunction with the UGT. The UGT became involved because it recognized that collectivization was the most practical method of farming the less fertile *latifundia*. It would perhaps also be true to say that in many places the socialists followed this course to avoid being usurped by the anarchists in what they regarded as their fiefs.

In Aragon some collectives were installed forcibly by anarchist militia columns, especially Durruti's. Their impatience to get the harvest in to feed the cities, as well as the fervour of their beliefs, sometimes led to violence. Aragonese peasants resented being told what to do by over-enthusiastic Catalan industrial workers, and many of them had fears of Russian-style collectives. Borkenau showed in an example how much more effective other means could be: 'The anarchist nucleus achieved a considerable improvement for the peasants and yet was wise enough not to try to force the conversion of the reluctant part of the village, but to wait till the example of the others should take effect.' Not surprisingly, a collective begun in that way worked best.

There were few villages which were completely collectivized. The 'individualists', consisting chiefly of smallholders who were afraid of losing what little they had, were allowed to keep as much land as a family could farm without hired labour. In regions where there had always been a tradition of smallholding, little tended to change. The desire to work the land collectively was much stronger among the landless peasants, especially in less fertile areas where the small plots were hardly viable.

The anarchists continually tried to persuade the peasants that the ownership of land gave a false sense of security. The only real security lay within a community which cared for its own members by providing medical facilities and welfare for the sick and retired. In some villages great resentment was caused when individualists foisted their grandparents and sick relations on to the collective while the healthy members of the family retained all their own produce. This reinforced the collectivists' view that greed and hoarding were the inevitable result of competition.

In most anarchist collectives money was abolished. 'Here in Fraga', the local paper proclaimed in blazing pride, 'you can throw banknotes into the street and no-one will take any notice. Rockefeller, if you were to come to Fraga with your entire bank account you would not be able to buy a cup of coffee. Money, your God and your servant, has been abolished and the people are happy.' In the early months barter was not found to be easy in outside dealings; however, as currency problems and food shortages mounted, town suppliers were found to be much more ready to accept produce in lieu of cash.

There was usually a family wage, which was closer to a form of rationing than payment, since everyone had equal rights to everything whether they worked or were sick. The only sanction against the lazy was public opinion. People were to live without either the threat of starvation or the encouragement of material incentive. In some CNT collectives the committee automatically took less than everyone else so that they would never be accused of profiting from their position. Most UGT collectives replaced currency with coupons for exchange at the village shops, which now tended to be distribution centres. Doctors, barbers, carpenters and cobblers usually gave their services free and, in return, were maintained by the community. In many places small manufacturing enterprises were set up so as to take advantage of local resources, and offer a wider variety of work. It was not just the industrial worker who was no longer fearful of new technology; the supposedly reactionary peasants, too, soon came to welcome such developments. Even smallholders were often encouraged to join the collectives when they saw the advantages offered by communal working of the land. The communists attacked the self-managed collectives for inefficiency; yet production rose by about one-fifth in Aragon and declined in Catalonia, where smallholding still predominated.

The only alternative systems to the free collectives for supplying the Republican zone with food were either state collectives or dividing up the land into smallholdings. The nearest equivalents to state collectives were the municipally organized farms. In the province of Jaén, for example, where the CNT was almost non-existent and the UGT weak, the municipality took over the land and organized it. Borkenau recorded that it 'employed the same *braceros* that the former landowners employed upon the same estates for the same endless working hours for the same starvation wages . . . As nothing had changed in their living conditions so nothing had changed in their attitude. As they are ordered about as before and for the same wages, they start fighting the new administration of the estates as they did the old one.' Borkenau also described how self-managed collectives were much happier when no better off than before. What mattered was that the labourers ran their own collectives – a distinct contrast to the disasters of state collectivization in the Soviet Union, which the peasants had resisted by slaughtering livestock and sabotaging the harvest.

The *reparto*, the dividing out of confiscated land among peasant families, was obviously popular to rich peasants who thereby increased the size of their existing holdings. It also appealed to some landless labourers who believed that the only security against starvation was to possess their own little plot. However, in many cases it resulted in the distribution of totally uneconomic units. Smallholdings were not viable in Spain except in the Pyrenees, Galicia, and the rich valleys of the Mediterranean coastal belt.

The anarchists attacked the *reparto* because they thought that 'privately controlled land always creates a bourgeois mentality, calculating and egotisticial, which we wish to uproot for ever'. But whatever the ideology, the self-managed co-operative was almost certainly the best solution to the food-supply problem. Not only was non-collectivized production lower, but the 'individualists' were to show the worst possible traits of the introverted and suspicious smallholder. When food was in short supply they hoarded it and created a thriving black market, which, apart from disrupting supplies, did much to undermine morale in the Republican zone. The communist civil governor of Cuenca admitted later that the smallholders who predominated in his province held onto their grain when the cities were starving.

The other criticism levelled against the collectives was their failure to deliver food to the front line in regular quantities at regular intervals. Obviously there were cases of inefficiency, but overall the charge was unfair considering that all their lorries had already been commandeered. Whenever transport did arrive, the peasants would pile on everything possible, not knowing when it would next be available. The fault lay far more with the militia, who should have organized things the other way round and warned particular collectives of their needs in advance. The army and the International Brigades were also to suffer from bad distribution, often on an even worse scale.

In terms of production and improved standards for the peasants, the self-managed collectives appear to have been successful. They also seem to have encouraged harmonious community relations. There were, however, breakdowns of communication and disputes between collectives. The anarchists were dismayed that collective selfishness should seem to have taken the place of individual selfishness, and inveighed against this 'neo-capitalism'.

The central government was alarmed by the developments in Aragon, where the anarchist militia columns exercised the only power in the whole of an area predominantly libertarian in sympathy. In late September delegates from the Aragonese collectives attended a conference at Bujaraloz, near where Durruti's column was based. They decided to establish a Defence Council of Aragon, and elected as president Joaquín Ascaso, a first cousin of Francisco Ascaso who fell in the Atarazanas assault.

Earlier that summer the government had tried without success to re-establish its control in Valencia by sending a delegation under Martínez Barrio. It was brushed aside by the Popular Executive Committee, which consisted mainly of UGT and CNT members. Communist pleas for discipline and obedience to government orders went unheeded. Even so, the communists, who opposed free collectives, profited from local conditions in their recruiting drives. The rich countryside was held in smallholdings by extremely conservative peasants, who were joined in their resistance to collectivization by many citrus farmers.

Giral's government in Madrid did not share the anarchists' enthusiasm for self-managed collectives. Nor did it welcome the fragmentation of central power with the establishment of local committees. Its liberal ministers believed in centralized government and a conventional property-owning democracy. They also felt, along with Prieto's wing of the socialists and the Communist Party, that only discipline and organization could prevail against the enemy. Above all, they were appalled at having no control over the industrial base of Catalonia. But, after Martínez Barrio's failure in Valencia, Giral's administration could do little for the moment except try to keep up appearances. For the future, its continued control of supply and credit held out the prospect that concessions might gradually be wrung from the revolutionary organizations as a first step towards incorporating them into the state.

X
THE ARMY OF AFRICA
AND THE MILITIA

By the beginning of August the extent of the rising was clear. Both Republican and Nationalist territory quickly developed their specific characters in the wake of the upheaval. It was as if two separate nations were at war. The rebel generals urgently needed to show rapid gains of territory at the beginning so as to convince a foreign as well as domestic audience of their future success. Having failed to achieve a coup, they required the international recognition, credits and material which a war demanded. General Franco's Army of Africa was to make the most conspicuous contribution to this necessary impression of victory. The forces under General Mola played a less flamboyant role.

'The Director' sent out three columns from Pamplona mainly made up of Carlist *requetés*. The first left immediately for Madrid, a second force of about 1,400 men moved south to Saragossa to reinforce the Nationalist garrison in the first week of the war, and a third, much larger force was then sent north towards the Basque coastline. The first column of 1,000 men under Colonel García Escámez, who had set out for the capital on 19 July, found that Guadalajara had already been captured by armed workers from Madrid. García Escámez then tried another line of advance on the capital, swinging round to the north to cross the Sierra de Guadarrama by the main Burgos road over the Somosierra pass. His force came up against Madrid militias at the summit where, a century-and-a-quarter before, Napoleon's Polish lancers had opened the route to the capital with a suicidal uphill charge against artillery. García Escámez's men captured the pass after several days' fighting, but could do little except consolidate their position since they were virtually out of ammunition. A Nationalist force from Valladolid managed to secure the other pass at the Alto de los Leones to the south-west, but they also suffered from a shortage of ammunition. It was surprising that the chief architect of the conspiracy had not built up reserves in Burgos or Pamplona during the previous months. Mola's difficulties were only solved when Franco sent him large supplies from Germany via Portugal with the assistance of the Salazar regime (the Nationalists referred to Lisbon as 'the port of Castile'). But, by the time they were resupplied, the militia forces in the mountains had become less haphazard in their organization and had established a front.

97

Mola's largest force of 3,500 men attacked northwards from Pamplona. The plan was to thrust up the high hills of northern Navarre towards the coast to cut the Basques off from the French frontier, then to capture the summer capital of San Sebastián. On 11 August the column under Major Beorleguí drove a wedge between San Sebastián and the border-town of Irún. Six days later the Nationalist battleship *España*, the cruiser *Almirante Cervera* and the destroyer *Velasco* arrived to shell the seaside resort. The Republican military governor threatened to shoot right-wing hostages if heavy civilian casualties were inflicted. The Nationalists called his bluff. Their bombardment was followed by aerial attacks from Junkers 52s on both San Sebastián and Irún.

The defence of Irún demonstrated that untrained workers, providing their defensive position was well sited and prepared, could fight bravely and effectively against head-on attacks backed by modern weaponry. The CNT had been the main contributor to the defeat of the rising in the province of Guipúzcoa, and its members joined with Asturians, Basque nationalists and French communist volunteers organized by André Marty (later the chief organizer of the International Brigades) to make a total force of 3,000 men. Beorleguí's force was numerically weaker, but it had all Mola's artillery, light German tanks, and the Junkers 52s in support. In addition, Franco sent a *bandera* of the Foreign Legion and a battery of 155 mm guns.

There was ferocious hand-to-hand fighting on the Puntza ridge to the south of Irún where positions were captured and retaken several times in the course of a week. The militia fought with remarkable skill and courage. The convent of San Marcial was held to the end by a handful of Asturian *dinamiteros* and militiamen. During the final attack, when out of ammunition, they hurled rocks at the Carlists who were storming their position. Irún itself was left a burning ruin when the last of the workers withdrew, some of them having to swim to safety before reaching French territory. A parting burst of machine-gun fire hit Beorleguí in the calf. The tough old soldier refused treatment and later died of gangrene.

The anarchists in San Sebastián were angry at the lack of support from the Basque nationalists, especially when they heard that the governor was negotiating the surrender of the city with the enemy. They were extremely suspicious after the betrayals which had occurred in the first few weeks of the war, but, despite its conservatism, the Basque nationalist PNV had not the slightest intention of changing sides. Nevertheless, it was totally opposed to the anarchists' scorched-earth policy, which had led to the burning of Irún during the withdrawal, and now meant defending San Sebastián to the last. The PNV prevailed, once their militia shot several anarchists. The city was abandoned to the Nationalists on 14 September, which meant that the northern Republican zone was now firmly surrounded.

The most striking military development of the summer was the ruthlessly efficient campaign of the Army of Africa. Its early arrival on the mainland was mainly due to the help of German and Italian aircraft. Not surprisingly Republican propaganda made much of this foreign intervention at such a vital stage of the war, but the vehement protests tended to obscure two uncomfortable truths. Firstly, Republican warships run by sailors' committees seemed to lack the ability or desire for offensive action. (There is little doubt that the German battleships *Deutschland* and *Admiral Scheer* screening the Nationalist convoys across the straits had orders to avoid open conflict.) Secondly, the Republican medley of regular officers, urban workers' militias and peasants intent on staying close to their *pueblo* proved incapable of launching any effective counter-attack in the vital south-western sector before the colonial troops arrived in strength. The military importance of the airlift by the Savoias and the Junkers 52s must, therefore, not be exaggerated, even though the arrival of 1,500 men between 28 July and 5 August had an enormous influence both on the Nationalists' morale and on the international assessment of their chances of victory. Altogether, some 12,000 troops were transported in this way during the first two months of the war, before the Nationalists had won absolute control of the straits.

The airlift of legionnaires and Moroccan *regulares* from the Army of Africa was well under way during the first week of August. On the 6th Franco himself crossed to the mainland, leaving General Orgaz in command of the Protectorate. He established his headquarters in Seville, where he decided to split his forces so as to be able to secure Andalucia as well as advance rapidly on the capital.

The main force under Colonel Yagüe was to drive north, parallel to the Portuguese frontier, then swing north-eastwards on Madrid. Yagüe was to prove the most aggressive of all the Nationalist field commanders. In many ways these qualities underlined the contrast between the Army of Africa and the apathetic metropolitan army. Colonial officers have always tended to be less fashionable and more professional, but in Spain this difference was even more pronounced than in either the British or French services. Nevertheless, Franco, the supposedly archetypal *africanista*, was extremely conventional in contrast to his impetuous subordinate.

A much smaller force of only 400 *regulares* was to secure southern Andalucia under Colonel Varela, a secret instructor of Carlist *requetés* before the rising and the officer released from prison in Cádiz by the insurgents on 19 July. The first colonial troops from Seville captured Huelva before retiring to crush any remaining resistance southwards to Cádiz and Algeciras. Then, in the second week of August, Varela's force moved eastwards to help the beleaguered Nationalists in Granada. Once a promontory to the city had been established, they prepared to attack Málaga and the coastal strip beyond the mountains. But Córdoba was threatened by a Republican force of 3,000 men under General Miaja, so Varela moved rapidly on 20 August to reinforce Colonel Cascajo's small force there. Once the Córdoba front was stabilized in the first week of September (it was hardly to change for the rest of the war), Varela marched southwards to capture Ronda.

General José Miaja, the Republican commander of the southern front and later of Madrid during the siege, was one of those senior officers who probably stayed loyal from force of circumstance rather than from conviction. His force was composed of loyal regular troops, Madrid militiamen and local volunteers. The ineffectiveness of totally untrained men in conventional manœuvres was to be expected, but the uselessness and sloth of the regular officers was extraordinary. Franz Borkenau visited the headquarters on 5 September, during heavy fighting which was going

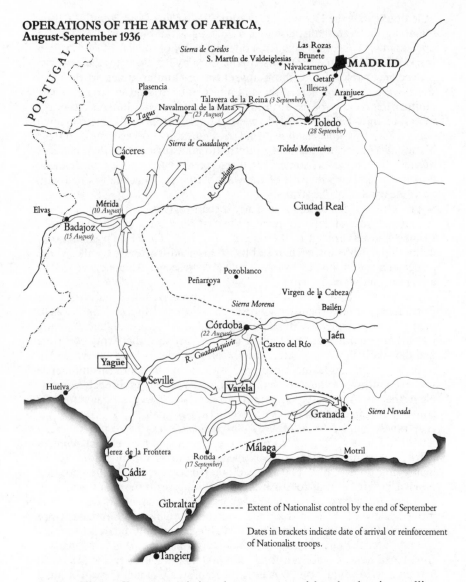

OPERATIONS OF THE ARMY OF AFRICA,
August–September 1936

Sierra de Gredos
S. Martín de Valdeiglesias
Las Rozas
Brunete
Navalcarnero
MADRID
Getafe
Illescas
Plasencia
Aranjuez
Talavera de la Reina *(3 September)*
R. Tagus
Navalmoral de la Mata *(23 August)*
Toledo *(28 September)*
Cáceres
Sierra de Guadalupe
Toledo Mountains
R. Guadiana
Elvas
Mérida *(10 August)*
Ciudad Real
Badajoz *(15 August)*
Pozoblanco
Peñarroya
Virgen de la Cabeza
Sierra Morena
Bailén
Córdoba *(22 August)*
Jaén
Castro del Río
R. Guadalquivir
Yagüe
Seville
Huelva
Varela
Granada
Sierra Nevada
Jerez de la Frontera
Ronda *(17 September)*
Málaga
Motril
Cádiz
Gibraltar
Tangier
PORTUGAL

- - - - - Extent of Nationalist control by the end of September

Dates in brackets indicate date of arrival or reinforcement
of Nationalist troops.

badly. 'The staff ... were sitting down to a good lunch, chatting, telling dirty stories, and not caring a bit about their duty, not even trying to establish any contact with the fighting lines for many hours.' Even the wounded were ignored.

Meanwhile, on the northern axis of advance Colonel Yagüe's force was organized in five self-contained columns of some 1,500 men each, with legionnaires and *regulares* mounted in requisitioned lorries and accompanied by 75 mm artillery. They were supported by Savoia-Marchetti 81s, piloted by Italians in Legion uniform, and Junkers 52s flown by Luftwaffe personnel. Yagüe struck due north into Estremadura, maintaining a momentum of advance exceeded only by the armoured punches of 1940. His tactics were simple and effective. The lorry-borne force rushed up the main road at full speed until resistance was encountered at a town or village. (No ambushes were made in the open country because the inhabitants wanted to defend their homes and needed the feeling of security which walls gave.) The Nationalists would order surrender over loudhailers provided by the Germans. All doors and windows were to be left open and white flags hung on every house. If there was no reply, or firing, then the troops would dismount and launch a rapid pincer attack.

Concentrations of defenders provided ideal targets for professional troops with artillery backed by bombers. Mobile groups would have inflicted higher casualties and delayed the Nationalists' advance more effectively. Once a village was captured, the ensuing massacre was supposed to be a reprisal for 'red' killings, but it was utterly indiscriminate. Queipo de Llano claimed that '80 per cent of Andalucian families are in mourning, and we shall not hesitate to have recourse to sterner measures'.

The Nationalist attack demonstrated the psychological vulnerability of the worker militias. In street-fighting, caught up in collective bravery, they were courageous to a foolhardy degree. But in the open the shelling and bombing were usually too much for them, since they refused to dig trenches (Irún was an outstanding exception). Most of the bombs dropped were, in fact, almost useless, but the enemy aircraft were skilfully handled, causing maximum terror to peasants who had little experience of modern technology. Also, having no idea of how to prepare a defensive position, the militiamen had a desperate fear of finding themselves facing the Moors' knives alone. Outflanking movements which surprised them usually led to a panic-stricken stampede. Chaos was increased when the population of a village clogged the roads with their carts and donkeys as they too fled from the colonial troops. Sometimes they even seized the militias' lorries for themselves. On the other hand, the Nationalist tactic of terror provoked heroism as well as flight. Peasants, having seen their families on their way, would take up shotguns or abandoned rifles and return to die in their *pueblo*.

By 10 August Yagüe's force had advanced more than 300 kilometres (185 miles) to Mérida. There, just south of the town at the bridge over the River Guadiana, his forces met fierce opposition. The defence committee of the town was organized by Anita López, who greatly encouraged the ferocious resistance. She was among those killed when Yagüe's troops finally entered the town that night. The next day the bulk of the Mérida militia counterattacked with the aid of a strong detachment of *asaltos* and civil guards sent from Madrid. Yagüe left part of his force to hold them off while he advanced due west on Badajoz, on the Portuguese border. Franco insisted on this diversion from the main axis. Apart from not wanting to leave an enemy strongpoint behind his line of advance, he wished to demonstrate that the northern and southern parts of the Nationalist zone were now linked.

Badajoz was defended by more than 7,000 militia, but they were poorly armed. They also had to suppress the civil guards, who declared for the rising just before Yagüe's arrival. His troops took up position outside the town walls on 14 August. A pincer attack was then launched, with the Foreign Legion assaulting two of the gates under the cover of artillery fire.

After suffering heavy casualties, they broke into the town and the slaughter began. House-clearing with grenade and knife, the legionnaires made no distinction between combatant or civilian. Militiamen were even shot down on the altar steps of the cathedral. Any survivors were then herded into the bullring. The smell of blood in the heat was sickening after more than 1,500 of them were machine-gunned in batches.

The search for Republicans went on during the following days. Shirts were ripped away and any man found with marks on his shoulder from rifle recoil was killed immediately. The Portuguese authorities sent back for execution refugees who had fled over the border. The report of these events by Jay Allen of the *Chicago Tribune*, together with the objective accounts of Portuguese journalists (which the Nationalists never expected), started to change the one-sided impression of rearguard killing which existed abroad.

Meanwhile, the looting of even Nationalists' property was explained by one officer as the 'war tax they pay for salvation'. Officers organized the despatch of the *regulares*' booty back to their families in Morocco because it helped recruiting. The legionnaires did not burden themselves with the often useless impedimenta which the Moors collected. They simply examined the mouths of the dead and smashed out any gold-capped teeth with their rifle butts.

On 2 August Yagüe reached the Tagus valley, where he swung eastwards towards Madrid. He had already ordered Asensio and Castejón's forces to advance on Navalmoral de la Mata via the high hills to the south of the river. They were attacked by an international air squadron organized by the French writer, André Malraux, before coming up against a militia force of about 8,000 men under General Riquelme. The colonial troops' rapid deployment, however, outflanked the Republican forces, making them fall back in disorder. The Moors' tactical movements, using every piece of dead ground available, achieved a surprise which struck panic into the inexperienced city militiamen. Yet there were independent groups, who attacked and harassed the colonial troops in guerrilla fashion. Such tactics probably offered a better chance of delaying the enemy than Riquelme's static defence in a concentrated target.

Yagüe was determined to keep up his momentum. He pushed on to Talavera de la Reina, the last town of any size before Madrid. The rapidity and success of his advance had seriously demoralized the force of 10,000 militiamen awaiting him there. It seemed as if the Army of Africa was unbeatable. Once again a flanking motion supported by air and artillery bombardment was enough to start a Republican retreat. Only the very bravest risked staying to be captured. On the evening of 3 September the road to Madrid was littered with abandoned weapons. The capital was only 100 kilometres (60 miles) away.

Yagüe had advanced nearly 500 kilometres (310 miles) in four weeks. It was a feat which, even allowing for the experience and training of his troops, took all attention away from Mola's Basque operation. The next move of the Army of Africa still provokes discussion. Franco did not force on north-eastwards to Madrid and so maintain the momentum of attack before a proper defence of the capital could be organized. Instead, he switched the axis of advance south-eastwards to Toledo, where Nationalists were still defending the Alcázar. Yagüe argued bitterly against this decision, so Franco replaced him with Varela after the capture of Ronda on 18 September.

As many observers had remarked, Franco was both ambitious and politically clear-sighted. The defence of the Alcázar had become, and still offered, the most potent source of Nationalist propaganda. Its resistance was raised to an almost mystical level. Franco was still, at this stage, little more than *primus inter pares*. To be the 'saviour of the Alcázar' would make his leadership of the Nationalist movement unchallengeable. It has, of course, been argued that Franco would have achieved the same pre-eminence by capturing Madrid. But that was a far more difficult undertaking. It was one thing to outflank and bomb untrained militiamen in the countryside. Clearing a major city was a totally different operation. Franco was too wily to take an unnecessary risk before his leadership was officially confirmed. Then, too, while foreign backers and financiers might grumble if the war took a long time, only a very serious reverse would induce them to cut their losses. Franco did not believe that the fighting qualities of the Madrid militia, or their weaponry, would improve in the immediate future. He therefore felt that he could afford to wait a couple of weeks for reinforcements to arrive. It was Mola who was to make a fatuous boast about drinking coffee on the Gran Vía in a matter of days, not Franco. But even Franco never expected Madrid to resist as it did.

During August the militia troops besieging the Alcázar misjudged both the speed of Yagüe's advance and the resilience of the fortress' defenders. There was a relaxed atmosphere on the barricades surrounding the military academy, and enormous quantities of ammunition were wasted against its thick walls. It was some time before artillery was brought up, and even the 175 mm piece which eventually arrived brought down only the superstructure. The Alcázar was like an iceberg. Its strength lay within the submerged rock. There was something Buñuelesque about the scene; militiamen, wearing straw hats against the sun, lay on mattresses behind their barricades and exchanged insults with the civil guard defenders. Twice a day there was a tacitly agreed ceasefire as a blind beggar tapped his way along the Calle de Carmen between the firing lines.

The most serious psychological mistake made by the Republican besiegers was the attempt to use Colonel Moscardó's son, Luis, as a hostage. On 23 July they rang the Alcázar, saying that they would shoot him unless the defenders surrendered. Moscardó refused and told his son, who was put on the telephone, to die bravely. In fact, Luis was not shot until a month later, in reprisal for an air raid. The dramatic appeal of the story also camouflaged the fact that the 100 left-wing hostages, whom the defenders had taken into the Alcázar at the beginning of the siege, were never heard of again.

None of this stopped the creation of the most emotive symbolism for the Nationalist movement. The defenders, believing that Luis had been shot immediately, could not consider surrendering after such a sacrifice. The story was used as a moral lesson for everyone in Nationalist territory. In addition, since the old city of Toledo was the centre of Spanish Catholicism, and 107 priests were reputed to have been killed there by the left, the incident was projected with all the fervour of the 'anti-atheist crusade'.

It was enrobed with mystical implications of Abraham and Isaac, even of God and Christ, by those carried away with the parallel. Dramatic resemblances were also drawn with the episodes in which Philip II had handed over his son to be executed by the Inquisition and Alonzo Guzmán had allowed the Moors to crucify his son outside the besieged walls of Tarifa in the thirteenth century. The young cadets of the Alcázar were extolled by the Nationalist press and their supporters abroad. In reality, there was only a handful of cadets there, since the rising took place during the Academy's summer holiday. The heroic defence which tied down so many Republicans was conducted by the less glamorous civil guard.

The rapid approach of the Army of Africa during September made the besiegers appreciate the gravity of their situation. Mines were dug into the rock under the fortress, and in a great show, witnessed by the world's press, one corner of the Alcázar was blown up. The presence of women and children inside, however, made the exercise counter-productive, while the rubble left a formidable barrier enabling the defenders to beat off the assault. Towards the end of September Varela's relief force arrived within striking distance. Some of the militia stayed on and faced the colonial troops with great courage, but the majority fled back towards Aranjuez. Varela ignored Moscardó's promise that militiamen who surrendered would be spared. Blood ran down the steep and narrow streets of the city in reprisal. Many militiamen killed themselves rather than surrender. Pockets of resistance were burned out and in the hospital 200 wounded militiamen left behind were killed in their beds with grenades and knives.

The gaunt and erect figure of Moscardó waited in his dust-impregnated uniform. He greeted Varela with the words, '*Sin novedad en el Alcázar*' ('Nothing to report at the Alcázar'). *Sin novedad* was also the codeword for the rising which nobody had bothered to ask the passed-over colonel to join. He repeated the same performance for General Franco and the newspapermen the next day, 29 September.

The Nationalists, especially the Army of Africa, had demonstrated their offensive abilities in these first two months of the war, while the Republican forces, based on the workers' militias, had neither the training nor the cohesion to mount effective operations against organized troops. At Oviedo, which had been won for the Nationalists by Colonel Aranda's trick, the siege still continued despite ingenious and brave attacks by Asturian *dinamiteros*. Armoured lorries manned by workers with improvised flame-throwers succeeded in making a breach only to be forced back. Relief for the besieged was on its way from Galicia.

In the south, near Córdoba, a strong detachment of civil guards and Falangists was holding out in the mountain monastery of Santa María de la Cabeza under Captain Cortés. Nationalist pilots devised an original method of dropping fragile supplies. They attached them to live turkeys which descended flapping their wings, thus serving as parachutes which could also be eaten by the defenders. The besieged were eventually overcome in April of the next year by a mass assault. It was a defence at least as brave as that of Toledo, but it was given remarkably little recognition by the Nationalists, perhaps because it risked stealing glory from Franco.

Although the workers' militias were the only possible response to the generals' rising, since few regular army units remained in formation, the anarchists, the POUM and the left socialists, including Largo Caballero, regarded the militias as a virtue rather than a necessity. There was a powerful belief that morale and motivation must overcome an enemy which depended on the mercenaries of the Army of Africa or brother workers who would desert at the first opportunity. The Republican left-wing seriously underestimated the Catholic zeal of the conservative small-holders of Galicia, Old Castile and Navarre, who were to become the Nationalists' best troops after the colonial professionals. Meanwhile the Madrid government, the regular officers, centrist politicians and the communists were advocating a conventional army as the sole means of resisting the Nationalists. The communists' attitude derived from the knowledge that a centralized command could be infiltrated and seized. Hence their call for 'Discipline, Hierarchy, Organization'.

Such plans for 'militarization' were greeted with great suspicion by the left socialists, who described them as 'counter-revolutionary' and looked upon them as a tactic in the government's effort to recover control of the workers' movement. The anarchists were even more strongly opposed. For them a regular army represented the worst aspects of the state. They called it 'the organization of collective crime'.

The two unions, the CNT and the UGT, provided the majority of the militia forces, though all the parties had their own. There were units from the Republican Left, the Catalan Esquerra, the POUM and the communists. A militiaman was paid 10 pesetas a day at first by his local organization, and later by the government. (This was the equivalent of a skilled workers' wage, and it became a heavy burden on the ailing economy.) His uniform consisted of blue overalls and either a beret, or more often, a fore and aft cap in the colours of his party. The standard of equipment and weapons varied greatly. Some militiamen were still carrying only shotguns after six months of war. The maintenance of weapons was universally bad. A rifle without rust was almost unknown; hardly any were cleaned and oil was seldom issued. The few machine-guns were old and lacked spare parts. There was also such a wide variety of calibres that as many as 16 different types of ammunition were needed within some units. Mortars and grenades, when available, were usually more dangerous to the operator than the enemy, so that the home-made variety, dynamite packed into tomato cans, was preferred.

The greatest shortcoming of the militia system remained the lack of self-discipline. At the beginning stories abounded of detachments leaving the front line without warning for weekends in Barcelona or Madrid. Anyone who stayed awake on sentry duty was thought a fool. Ammunition was wasted by firing at planes at impossible distances and positions were lost because nobody wanted to dig trenches. It is interesting that indiscipline was most marked among groups like factory workers, who had previously been subject to external constraints and controls. Those used to leading an independent existence like farmers and artisans had not had their self-discipline undermined.

Much has been made of the fact that leaders were elected and political groupings maintained in the militias. But this was not so much a difficulty as a source of strength. It inspired mutual confidence among men suspicious of outsiders. The real problem came in the first few chaotic weeks, when the revolutionary atmosphere made militiamen react immediately against anything that could be remotely construed as authoritarianism. Even Bakunin had written that 'in the moment of action, the roles divide up naturally according to the abilities of each, appreciated and judged by general opinion: some command and direct, others carry out the orders.' It was several months before the anarchist militias accepted this.

The election of officers and the trial of disciplinary offenders by rank-and-file courts were regarded by anarchists as fundamental principles. Each section, comprising 10 men, elected its own corporal. Each *centuria*, comprising 100 men, elected its own delegate. A militia column varied greatly in its number of *centuria*. Durruti's column had 6,000 men at its peak, while others consisted of only a few hundred. Most columns had a regular officer who acted as 'adviser' to the column leader, but unless he was known as a genuine sympathizer, he was usually distrusted. There were a certain number of very radical officers in the army, such as Colonel Romero Bassart, the colonial officer who resisted the rising at Larache and later became military adviser to the CNT. There was also the unconventional Colonel Mangada, who was treated as a hero in the first days of the war after his column advanced towards Avila and repulsed a column from Salamanca led by Major Doval in a very confused and inconclusive skirmish. Generally, however, Republican militia suspected the loyalty of army officers, because many had at first declared for the government only to betray it later. Some genuine supporters of the Republic were probably shot in error, and certainly in several cases loyal regular officers were made scapegoats for militia reverses.

In Catalonia, where the militia system was the most entrenched, the air force officer, Díaz Sandino, became the Catalan councillor of war while the secretary-general, the anarchist Juan García Oliver, took over militia organization. His main work was to arrange training programmes in the rear. Even though about a tenth of the militia force in Aragon were ex-soldiers who had joined the workers, the standard of training in the metropolitan army had been so abysmal that they provided little help.

The militia volunteers were kitted out at the former Pedralbes barracks, now the Miguel Bakunin barracks where García Oliver had based the Popular School of War. The same building was used for foreign anarchists who arrived to fight in the International Column. They came from all over Europe and Latin America. There were many Italians including Camillo Berneri, a philosophy professor, and Carlo Roselli, who organized the Giustizia e Libertà column of liberals and anarchists, but who was murdered in France the following June by Mussolini's agents. A group of Americans formed the Sacco and Vanzetti *centuria* and a detachment of Germans made up the Erich Muhsam *centuria*, named after the anarchist poet murdered two years before by the Gestapo. The POUM also used these barracks for their militia columns, which included foreign volunteers of whom the most famous was George Orwell. The communist PSUC, under Juan Comorera, found itself in a difficult position. Communist policy demanded a regular army, not militias, yet at the same time they needed to co-operate with the Catalan government.

The largest operation in the east at this time was the invasion by Catalonian militia of the Balearic Islands. Ibiza was taken easily, and on

16 August 8,000 men invaded Majorca under the command of an air force officer, Alberto Bayo, later to be Fidel Castro's guerrilla trainer. The invaders established a bridgehead unopposed, then paused as if in surprise. For once the militia had artillery, air and even naval support, yet they gave the Nationalists time to organize a counter-attack. Modern Italian aircraft arrived and strafed and bombed the invading force virtually unopposed. The withdrawal and re-embarkation became a rout.

The Aragon front had become a stalemate after the Carlist reinforcements arrived at Saragossa. The only exception was an unsuccessful attack on Huesca. Militia detachments held each hill in a rough line, while Nationalist troops were installed on the far side of the valley. (The day-to-day existence is best described in Orwell's *Homage to Catalonia*.)

In Madrid the Communist Party already had a military base on which to build. Their Worker and Peasant Anti-Fascist Militia (MAOC) provided the initial cadres for their 5th Regiment. The first communist objective was to make them look and act like disciplined soldiers. Practical military training was secondary to drilling. 'Steel' companies were formed (later to be imitated by other parties) and they paraded ostentatiously through Madrid causing an appreciable effect. Marching in step presented a great contrast to the militias. The mentality of the 5th Regiment was best described by a party official: 'We established special slogans designed to create an iron unity . . . "If my comrade advances or retreats without orders I have the right to shoot him." ' The training of the International Brigades was to follow a similar pattern with drill, discipline and political indoctrination taking up most of the precious time before they were sent up to the front. The Party manual said that a soldier would only fight well if carefully instructed on why he was fighting. This ideological drilling was the work of political commissars and the 5th Regiment was responsible for their introduction. Officially they were there to watch over the 'reliability' of the regular commander. In fact, they were agents in the Communist Party's plan to take over the Republican army, which would have to be formed if a conventional war was fought. These 'secular chaplains' were later the cause of a great power struggle between the communists and the government.

The first commander of the 5th Regiment was Castro Delgado, who was assisted by foreign communist advisers. The Party's 'common front' recruiting campaign, led by La Pasionaria, attracted many who admired the 5th Regiment's professional appearance. Some 25 per cent of the new recruits were socialists; about 15 per cent left republicans. Later they discovered that promotion was virtually impossible without Party membership, since the 5th Regiment served chiefly as a training base for future communist officers in a conventional army. The Communist Party claimed that some 60,000 men served in its ranks, but a maximum of 30,000 is probably more accurate. They included Juan Modesto, a former Foreign Legion corporal, and the Moscow-trained Enrique Líster, both of whom were to become important commanders.

Most regular officers preferred to co-operate with the communists because they were horrified by the militia system. On the whole these loyalist officers tended to be the older and more bureaucratic members of the metropolitan army, since the younger, more aggressive elements had sided with the rising. But only colonial soldiers had received any practical experience. The pre-war home army had seldom even carried out manœuvres.

The Republican commanders had therefore little to offer but second-hand theories left over from the First World War. Along with the communists and the government, who wanted all forces controlled through a central structure, they insisted that the militias adapt to an orthodox model. Eventually the militias would have to agree. They could not resist the enemy for long without major changes, and their theorists had failed to put forward any alternative strategy. The government and its allies had an additional motive for wanting to create a regular military organization. They believed that the Republic must impress foreign governments as a conventional state possessing a conventional army.

ARMS AND THE DIPLOMATS

Spain had attracted foreign interest and intervention throughout her history. After the extinction of the House of Trastamara's male line the country had had two foreign dynasties, the Habsburgs and the Bourbons, as well as Joseph Bonaparte and Amadeo of Savoy. Volunteers and mercenaries from abroad had been involved in her wars since the *Reconquista*. An English contingent helped against the Moors in the major battle of Las Navas de Tolosa in 1212, and at the end of the fifteenth century Lord Rivers' archers played an important part in one of the key actions leading to the fall of Granada. Swiss mercenaries, described by Isabella the Catholic as 'devout and loyal', also fought in this holy crusade.

In modern times the Napoleonic wars made Spain a European battleground. The British officers' peninsula experiences encouraged both an admiration for the ordinary Spaniard and a profound contempt for the Spanish aristocracy and priesthood. Further sympathy was provoked by the invasion in 1823 of 'The Hundred Thousand Sons of St Louis', sent to Spain by the Holy Alliance to re-establish that hated reactionary, Ferdinand VII. Undoubtedly, this helped in the recruiting of the 10,000 strong British Legion, led by regular officers, which fought for the liberals against the Carlists in the civil war of 1833–40. Sympathy for such causes changed, however, particularly in British governing circles where admiration for the Byronic tradition disappeared with the rise of socialism.

Of the three most important neutral governments the British played the most crucial role. The United States was wary of international commitments. France was alarmed by Hitler's rearmament and, despite having signed a pact with Russia, relied primarily on Great Britain for mutual defence. So, when on 19 July the Spanish Republic turned to France for arms, the sympathetic left-of-centre administration of Léon Blum looked to the British government for guidance.

Blum's Popular Front coalition had been in office only six weeks. His immediate reaction was to agree to help the Republic. There was, however, street-fighting in France between left-wingers and fascist groups. That violence, although not comparable to Spain's in the spring, still made army officers restless. The slightest suggestion of involving the country in the Spanish conflict risked provoking a major storm. As a result, a despatch of aircraft was organized in secret, but Nationalist sympathizers in the Spanish embassy informed the press. Blum survived the attacks of right-wing newspapers by restricting the agreement to private sales of unarmed military aircraft. The Republic was now being treated on a level similar to the insurgents. Giral's government sent a commission for arms purchases to Paris under Fernando de los Ríos, but, being inexperienced, they were sold obsolete weapons at inflated prices.

The alternative method of helping the Republic was to prevent foreign support reaching Franco. The British Foreign Office feared that the conflict might escalate and warned the French government that helping the Republic would only encourage Hitler and Mussolini to aid the Nationalists. Blum and Daladier, his war minister, were aware that French armaments were inferior to those that Franco could obtain from the dictators. Anthony Eden, the British foreign secretary, agreed with the view of Salvador de Madariaga, the former Republican representative at the League of Nations, that 'apart from foreign intervention, the sides were so evenly balanced that neither could win'. This sort of reasoning encouraged the French government to believe that it was better for the Republic if no arms were allowed to reach either zone.

A policy of 'non-intervention' was therefore proposed by the French on 2 August. There is little doubt that the British government's attitude was crucial. As Eden said, 'The French government acted most loyally by us.' On 8 August the French cabinet suspended all further arms sales, and four days later the French *chargé d'affaires* in London recommended an international committee of control 'to supervise the agreement and consider further action'. Eden, however, 'decided to announce that Britain would apply an arms embargo without waiting for other powers'. This in effect meant denying arms to the recognized government and ignoring those going to the rebels, for the British government refused to acknowledge the proof of German and Italian intervention. The government also told the Labour opposition that 'any active expression of sympathy with the Republican Government of Spain would at that time be against the interests of Great Britain and therefore unpatriotic'.

The policy of appeasement was not Neville Chamberlain's invention. Its roots lay in a fear of Bolshevism. The general strike of 1926 and the depression made the possibility of revolution a very real concern to conservative politicians. As a result, they had mixed feelings towards the German and Italian regimes which had crushed the communists and the socialists in their own countries. Much of the electorate also held anti-militarist sentiments after the First World War and feelings of guilt about the Allies' humiliation of Germany at the Treaty of Versailles. The British population, moreover, knew little of events abroad. As the British minister in Berlin, Sir Ivone Kirkpatrick, wrote later, the country 'could not be expected to take an enlightened view of the situation when the government had done nothing to inform it'.

When the Spanish civil war broke out, Eden was to handle the situation virtually on his own. Stanley Baldwin, the prime minister, was ill when the war began, then became preoccupied by the Abdication crisis. 'I hope', he told Eden, 'that you will try not to trouble me too much with foreign affairs just now.' Eden was hardly an impartial observer of the conflict. He is supposed to have told the French foreign minister, Delbos, that 'England preferred a Rebel victory to a Republican victory'. He professed an admiration for the self-proclaimed fascist, Calvo Sotelo, who had been murdered. He abhorred the killings in Republican territory, while failing to comment on Nationalist atrocities. From his diplomatic staff on the spot he received emotive descriptions of the killings in the capital and Barcelona. The ambassador, Sir Henry Chilton, was a blatant admirer of the Nationalists and preferred to stay in Hendaye rather than return to Madrid. 'I am but awaiting the time', he later said, 'when they finally send enough Germans to finish the war.' The government also listened to Royal Navy officers who supported the rebels. The naval base of Gibraltar had been flooded with pro-Nationalist refugees, among whom journalists of the British press searched diligently for 'first-hand' accounts of atrocities. Yet even after these accounts began to be offset by news of events in Nationalist Spain, Winston Churchill's condemnation of the Republic in October was distinctly one-sided: 'The hideous series of nightly butcheries have robbed the Madrid government of the lineaments of a civilized power.' Franco's admission at the end of July that he was prepared 'to shoot half of Spain' was virtually ignored.

Franco's new press officer, Luis Bolín, had, before the rising, organized a discreet but effective anti-Republican campaign in London as correspondent of the monarchist newspaper *ABC*. He claimed, with justification, that he had 'developed a not inconsiderable degree of influence in appropriate circles'. His most important ally was the Duke of Alba, who also had the English dukedom of Berwick and was addressed as 'cousin' by Churchill. In these circles Alba, with his affection for English institutions, typified the civilized Spaniard. His quiet conversations in White's club were infinitely more influential on government policy than mass rallies or demonstrations. But then anyone speaking up for the Spanish Republican government in such surroundings would have provoked the kind of horrified reaction caricatured in a Bateman cartoon.

It must be remembered that Eden did not fully recognize the dangers of Hitler and Mussolini until 1937, and that he did not speak out openly against appeasement until early in 1938. During the first part of the civil war he preferred, on balance, a 'fascist' victory to a 'communist' victory. He held a deep-rooted assumption that social upheaval automatically led to communism. But the refusal to sell arms to the Republic in fact strengthened the communists and weakened the forces of the non-communist centre and left. In the summer of 1936 the Spanish Communist Party represented a very small proportion of the Republican coalition. Its organization and unscrupulous methods quickly made up for this numerical weakness, but it was only the leverage and prestige of Russian military aid which was to give it a commanding position.

Many Spanish Republicans maintained a naive belief that Great Britain would act as the champion of the underdog in its nineteenth-century tradition. Indeed, the belief that the democracies would eventually deliver them from dictatorship persisted until 1946, seven years after the end of the civil war. Certainly, in 1938, there was a conviction in Spain that even British conservatives would be forced to recognize the necessity of 'joining the fight against fascism'. But they underestimated the deep prejudice of

111

certain governing circles: for example, at the height of the Second World War Sir Orme Sargent of the Foreign Office criticized the principle of aiding left-wing partisans such as Tito against the Nazis as 'a dangerous doctrine'.

The only circumstance likely to influence British foreign policy was a direct threat to traditional British interests, the most sensitive of which was still the route to India. It was the threat of a permanent Italian occupation of Majorca and Mussolini's immediate breaking of their 'Gentleman's Agreement' which brought Eden to reconsider his position on 7 January 1937. 'The character of the future government of Spain has now become less important to the peace of Europe than that the dictators should not be victorious in that country. The extent and character of the intervention now practised by Germany and Italy have made it clear to the world that the object of these powers is to secure General Franco's victory whether or not it represents the will of the Spanish people.' But despite this new analysis of the situation, there was to be no alteration in the non-interventionist policy.

Meanwhile, the actions of the Royal Navy were astonishing for a non-interventionist power. Not only were communications facilities provided for Franco in Gibraltar, but the battleship HMS *Queen Elizabeth* was moved in front of Algeciras bay to prevent Republican warships shelling the port. The German *chargé d'affaires*, Hans Voelckers, later reported: 'As for England we have made the interesting observation that she is supplying the Whites with ammunition via Gibraltar, and that the British cruiser commander here has recently been supplying us with information on Russian arms deliveries to the Red Government, which he certainly would not do without instructions.'

At the same time as the Republican government was appealing to France for military aid, the Nationalists were turning to their natural allies, Germany and Italy. After delivering Franco to Tetuán on 19 July, Luis Bolín flew to Lisbon. There, just before his fatal crash, Sanjurjo countersigned the authorization to purchase aircraft and supplies for the 'Spanish non-Marxist army'. Bolín flew on to Rome having been joined by an aide sent by ex-King Alfonso. Together they saw Count Ciano, the Italian foreign minister. According to Bolín, 'his reaction was enthusiastic and spontaneous. Without hesitating an instant he promised us the necessary aid. "We must put an end to the communist threat in the Mediterranean," he cried.' Time was wasted because of confusion with other monarchist envoys wanting military assistance, but a telephone call from ex-King Alfonso to Mussolini resolved the matter. On 30 July Bolín left Sardinia in one of the 12 Savoia 81 bombers bound for Morocco. Three crashed on the way and one came down in Algeria, providing documentary proof of Italian military aid. The rest were used as aerial cover for the first Nationalist convoy across the straits on 5 August.

Mussolini looked forward to the establishment of a fascist state in the Mediterranean, particularly one which would be indebted to him. His great concern was British naval power. A Spanish ally could control the straits by seizing Gibraltar and offered the possibility of bases in the Balearics, yet her fleet was not likely to be a rival. Mussolini's conquest of Abyssinia had greatly increased his delusions of Italian power and Ciano's main task was to obtain recognition of the 'Italian Empire'. The Savoias were soon followed by consignments of Fiat fighters, Fiat-Ansaldo light tanks, and artillery, all with trained personnel.

Republican propaganda later tried to prove – with forged Nazi documents – that fascist intervention was pre-arranged and that the generals would not have launched the rebellion without this guarantee. (The Nationalists, for their part, pretended to have found papers in Seville which revealed advance planning for a communist *coup d'état*.) In fact the military plotters had not received any such guarantee. Relations between Italy and Germany had been strained in the early summer of 1936 primarily because of their rivalry in Austria. Nevertheless, their aid to Nationalist Spain was to prove the forging of 'the Rome–Berlin axis', a phrase first used by Mussolini on 1 November 1936.

The Nazi government was the better informed of the situation in Spain, both through unofficial contacts and through their own sources within the German business community. At the beginning of the war their diplomats, led by the foreign minister, Neurath, were opposed to aiding Franco from fear of provoking a British reaction. Hitler despised this traditional branch of the German government, and he kept his diplomatic staff almost totally uninformed of his actions. He worked instead with the German Military Intelligence, headed by Admiral Canaris, who had met Franco in Spain on several occasions and was keen to support his forces in particular.

On 22 July Franco asked the German government for transport aircraft. The request was initially relayed by Colonel Beigbeder, a former Spanish military attaché in Berlin. Then, Franco's emissaries, two Nazi businessmen living in Morocco, arrived in Berlin on 25 July. Hitler saw them later that night in Bayreuth after the opera and within 24 hours the despatch of the first Junkers 52s was being organized. The main condition imposed by the Germans was that military aid would be sent only to General Franco's troops. Canaris (presumably prompted by the Franquist faction) argued that this would preclude dissension among the Nationalist generals. A special department was set up in the air ministry to organize 'volunteer' pilots. Goering, who had been at the Bayreuth meeting, was thrilled at the idea of testing his 'young Luftwaffe in this or that technical respect'. The Germans were far more hard-headed about the whole enterprise than the Italians. They were offering the best machines and experts available and, although Franco was an ideological ally, they wanted payment in copper and iron ore.

The first German aid sent to Spain included 20 Junkers 52s and six Heinkel 51 fighter-bombers, together with spares and personnel, all of which arrived by 1 August. The Luftwaffe pilots were followed by military advisers, led by Colonel von Thoma. Not long afterwards the variety and quantity of material increased rapidly, to include the Panzer Mark I, 20 mm anti-aircraft batteries, and later the famous 88 mm gun. The material was either sent straight to Cádiz, or via Lisbon. However, it was not until mid-November, after Franco's failure to capture Madrid, that German intervention was formalized by the establishment of the Condor Legion.

Hitler's real reasons for helping Franco were strategic. A fascist Spain would present a threat to France's rear as well as the British route to the

Suez canal. There was even the tempting possibility of U-boat bases on the Atlantic coast. (Spanish ports were used on an occasional basis during the Second World War.) The civil war also served to divert attention away from his central European strategy, while offering an opportunity to train men and to test equipment and tactics.

Within a fortnight of the rebellion it had become evident that the Nationalists would receive military aid from Germany and Italy, while the democracies refused arms to the Republic. This imbalance was increased by financial support to the Nationalists, as vital in a drawn-out war as military aid. In the early days the Republican government controlled the country's 700 tons of gold as backing for its peseta, while the Nationalists could only offer the probability of victory as collateral for their currency. Nevertheless, Prieto was wrong to claim on 8 August that the gold gave 'the Spanish government an unlimited resistance, while the financial capacity of the enemy is negligible'. The Nationalists immediately looked to foreign financial institutions for help as well as to Spanish supporters. The principal backing for the conspiracy came originally from the huge resources of the former tobacco smuggler, Juan March, who apparently contributed £15 million. Ex-King Alfonso's immense generosity to the Nationalist movement was only possible as a result of the $85 million he had reputedly managed to transfer abroad. Much of the capital which had been smuggled out of Spain during the Republic, especially in the first half of the year, was soon transferred back to Nationalist territory. The Nationalist movement demanded the gold of private citizens, in particular wedding rings, to help pay for the war. The *Voz de Galicia* newspaper proclaimed: 'Anyone who keeps his gold at this moment when the Fatherland needs it, IS A JEW.'

American and British business interests were to make a great contribution to the final Nationalist victory, either through active assistance, such as that given by the oil magnate, Deterding, or through boycotting the Republic, disrupting its trade with legal action and delaying credits in the banking system. (The Midland Bank was alleged to have been the most active in this way.)

Spanish industry had been dominated by foreign capital since its retarded start in the mid-nineteenth century. The railways and basic services such as electricity, engineering and mining all depended on heavy foreign investment. American ITT owned the Spanish telephone system and Ford and General Motors had little competition in the motor industry. British companies owned the greatest share of Spanish business with nearly 20 per cent of all foreign capital investment. The United Kingdom was also the largest importer of Spanish goods, including over half of her iron ore.

Oil had now become almost as vital a commodity in war as ammunition. The US Neutrality Act of 1935 did not reflect this change, thus allowing Franco to receive 3,500,000 tons of oil on credit during the course of the war, well over double the total oil imports of the Republic. The president of the Texas Oil Company was an admirer of the fascists, and on receiving news of the rising he diverted five tankers en route for Spain to Nationalist-held ports. Since Texaco had been the principal supplier to the government, his decision was a severe blow to the Republicans. Standard Oil of New Jersey was another supplier, though on a smaller scale. The

Duchess of Atholl, one of the few British conservatives to support the Republic from the beginning, claimed that the Rio Tinto Zinc company helped finance Franco by supplying foreign exchange at over double the official rate. Later on, Ford, Studebaker and General Motors supplied 12,000 trucks to the Nationalists, nearly three times as many as the Axis powers, and the chemical giant, Dupont of Nemours, provided 40,000 bombs, sending them via Germany so as to circumvent the Neutrality Act. In 1945 the under-secretary at the Spanish foreign ministry admitted that 'without American petroleum and American trucks and American credit, we could never have won the civil war'.

Shunned by the democratic powers and the international business community, the Republic could count only on the support of Mexico and the USSR. As a result, the Nationalists' warnings of an 'international communist conspiracy' carried some conviction, even though the Comintern was purely a foreign arm of the Kremlin and thus decidedly national. After Lenin's death Trotsky's policy of worldwide revolution had been based on the premise that Russian communism could not prosper so long as it was surrounded by a hostile capitalist world. The opposing Stalinist policy of 'socialism in one country', which triumphed in 1927, implied an abstention from involvement in revolutions abroad. The Chinese communists, for example, were sacrificed to Chiang Kai-Shek's Kuomintang to further Russian interests, and Stalin gained recognition from the United States government in 1933 by promising not to indulge in subversive activities there.

For the first two weeks of the Spanish civil war, the lack of comment on events from Moscow raised alarm in foreign communist circles. Stalin was about to purge the Red Army, Trotsky's creation, and he was deeply concerned at the prospect of a foreign adventure which might provoke Hitler at such a time of Soviet weakness. But the exiled Trotsky made use of this silence to accuse Stalin of betraying the Spanish revolution and aiding the fascists. Whether or not it was Trotsky who goaded him into action, Stalin must have realized that Russian communism would lose all credibility, and probably the loyalty of European parties, if nothing was done to help the Republic. Stalin, therefore, decided to send aid to the Spanish government, but never enough for the Republic to win. In this way he would neither frighten the British government, to whom he looked as a potential ally, nor provoke the Germans. On 3 August 'popular demonstrations' and 'spontaneous indignation meetings' took place all over Russia. Factory workers made 'voluntary contributions' to help the Republic and the government sent its first, non-military supplies. Comintern officials, using false names, were also sent to Spain to make sure that the young Spanish Communist Party should not step out of line. Mexico, the other country to support the Republic, refused to join the non-intervention agreement and, despite limited resources, provided the Republicans with 20,000 rifles, ammunition and food.

The Spanish war was no longer simply an internal struggle. Spain's strategic importance, and the coincidence of the civil war with the Axis powers' preparations to test their secretly developed weaponry in Europe, ensured that the war lost its amateur character. The Nationalists were inundated with foreign advisers, observers, technical experts and combat personnel. Relations were seldom smooth, for Franco and his officers hated being indebted to foreigners, while their often arrogant German allies might perhaps have agreed with the Duke of Wellington's comment on the officers attached to his staff that 'the national weakness was boasting of Spain's greatness'. The Republic, however, was to suffer far more from its only powerful ally, Russia.

XII

SOVEREIGN STATES

The need for a formalized state structure to impress foreign governments affected the Nationalists as well as the Republic. The authoritarian nature of the Nationalist movement also made the call for a single leader inevitable. Franco had refrained from any overt manœuvring until the relief of the Alcázar became certain in late September. As with his military strategy, he did not make any political move until everything possible was in his favour.

His command of the most professional force, the Army of Africa, had made him a contender for the leadership from the start. Then the German proviso of giving military aid only to his forces greatly strengthened his claim. But Franco realized that if his long-term ambitions were to be satisfied, he needed to gain a complete moral, as well as military, ascendancy over his rivals. That he achieved with the relief of Toledo. To challenge the 'Saviour of the Alcázar' for the leadership of the Nationalist movement would have required rash courage.

The first meeting to resolve the leadership issue was held near Salamanca on 21 September on the initiative of the air force commander, General Kindelán. All the possible candidates for the leadership were present: Franco, Mola, Queipo de Llano and Cabanellas, the nominal president of the junta. The military were to take a decision on behalf of right-wing Spain. With the CEDA leader, Gil Robles, in self-imposed exile in Portugal (many Nationalists blamed the civil war on his lack of nerve), José Antonio in Alicante prison, where he was to be executed, and Calvo Sotelo dead since just before the rising, only the wishes of the monarchists and the Carlists had to be considered. Mola, Queipo and Cabanellas were all tainted with republicanism or freemasonry in varying degrees, so Franco benefited from his political inscrutability.

Kindelán, a royalist, proposed a single command with Franco as Generalíssimo. Mola, knowing that his reputation had suffered because his plan for the rising had not succeeded, gave in with enthusiastic good grace. Queipo did not allow himself to take such formalities too seriously. Only Cabanellas dissented. Six days later Toledo fell. Kindelán, believing that Franco would restore Alfonso to his throne, helped with the preparations for 28 September, when the 'Saviour of the Alcázar' was to return to

117

Salamanca to be accepted as supreme commander by the other generals.

The most active supporter of Franco behind the scenes was his brother, Nicolás. He arranged for a mixed guard of Falangists and Carlists to hail his brother as chief when all the generals came together in Salamanca. Then, by secretly changing the text of the decree, he made Franco 'Head of the Spanish State', not simply head of the government for the duration of the civil war. Cabanellas had objected to giving Franco both political and military command, but Nicolás' action presented the generals with a *fait accompli*. To protest against the decree once it had been made public would have looked like treason to the Nationalist cause.

Once Franco was the *Caudillo*, he never allowed opposition to develop. His speeches skilfully selected compatible aspects of the rival Nationalist ideologies. He affected an intensity of religious feeling to woo the Carlists and the church. The Falangist slogan, *'Una Patria, Un Estado, Un Caudillo'*, was converted to *'Una Patria: España. Un Caudillo: Franco'*. Historical parallels were drawn with the first *Reconquista*. This safely inspired the appropriate image in the appropriate mind. For the Falangists, it was the birth of the nation. For the Carlists and the Alphonsine monarchists it represented the establishment of a royal Catholic dictatorship; for the church the age of ecclesiastical supremacy, and for landowners the foundation of their wealth and power. Franco was very different from Mussolini and Hitler. He was a cunning opportunist who did not, despite his rhetoric, suffer from grandiose visions of racial or national destiny.

Franco's new position was given a boost on the day after the Salamanca meeting. The recently completed Nationalist cruiser, *Canarias*, came round from the Caudillo's birthplace, El Ferrol, to attack Republican warships off Gibraltar. She manged to sink the destroyer, *Almirante Fernández*, and force the others to seek shelter in Cartagena harbour. The blockade of the straits was now finished and Moroccan reinforcements could be brought across without diverting aircraft from bombing raids.

In the Republican zone Giral's government had resigned on 4 September. It had never been able to reflect the reality of the situation, let alone win enough support to influence it. All the political parties recognized that there was only one man able to gain the trust of the revolutionary committees. Largo Caballero was enjoying a great wave of popularity after his visits to the militia positions in the Guadarrama mountains. Even Prieto, the middle-class social democrat, recognized that his great rival, the obstinate, often blinkered proletarian, was the only suitable successor to Giral. Both Prieto and the communists wanted to maintain the liberal façade as far as possible but Largo Caballero wanted a coalition which was preponderantly socialist. He felt strongly that he had been exploited by the liberals in the first Republican government to restrain the mass of his union members.

The new government was presented as symbolizing unity against the common enemy since it brought together the liberal centre and the revolutionary left into one administration. It marked the first and most important move towards the progressive recuperation of power from local committees. Faced with the Nationalist successes, it was a development which even the anarchists found difficult to challenge. Nevertheless, the Republic was still far from that middle-class state which the communists attempted to portray. Their leaders, La Pasionaria and Jesús Hernández, insisted that Spain was experiencing a 'bourgeois democratic revolution' and that they were 'motivated exclusively by the desire to defend the democratic Republic established on 14 April 1931'.

President Azaña, kept on as a figurehead of liberal parliamentarianism, objected to the inclusion of communists in the government. But Azaña was increasingly isolated and Largo's will prevailed. The two communist ministers accepted their posts only after instructions to do so from Moscow. Jesús Hernández became minister of education and Vicente Uribe was given the agriculture portfolio; Alvarez del Vayo, whom Largo did not yet know to be a communist supporter, was made foreign minister.

Largo's government also included three of his left socialist supporters and Prieto with two of his social-democrat followers, one of whom, the future prime minister, Juan Negrín, was made minister of finance. Largo kept the ministry of war for himself and gave Prieto the air force and the navy. There were also two Republican Left ministers (one of whom was José Giral), one Catalan Esquerra, one Basque nationalist, and two representatives of the centrist Republican Union.

Largo had invited his old rivals, the anarchists, to join the governing coalition to broaden the representation of the anti-Nationalist groups. The anarchists made the counter-proposal (which was not accepted) of a National Defence Council with Largo as president, five CNT members, five from the UGT, four liberal republicans and no communists. Such a structure was no more than a euphemism for government, and thus a sop to their conscience. They had tacitly admitted the necessity of central coordination and collaboration in conventional war. No anarchists, however, joined Largo's government.

The committees started to be given new names and, although most of the original delegates stayed on, they gradually submitted to control from above. A new form of political parity also crept into the municipal councils which replaced the local committees. This distorted their reflection of local political strengths, especially in Catalonia, and assisted the communists, who gained more representation than the actual size of their following justified.

In Valencia the Popular Executive Committee, which had so contemptuously waved aside Martínez Barrio's delegation from the previous Madrid government, acknowledged the new one on 8 September. The effective administration in Catalonia, the Central Committee of the Anti-Fascist Militias, merged with the *Generalidad* at the end of September. This marked the first outright acceptance of government by the anarchists. They compromised their principles because they knew that the Madrid government would otherwise continue to starve their self-managed collectives of credits and currency for raw materials.

The POUM had been the most outspoken critic of the CNT leadership's refusal of power in Catalonia; this was partly because it advocated an authoritarian route to the new society, but mainly because it was more aware of the Stalinist threat than the Catalonian anarchists, who could not imagine themselves being challenged in Barcelona. Andrés Nin, the POUM leader, had lived long enough in Russia to appreciate how the infiltration of key posts made the size of the Communist Party's following almost irrelevant. From the Catalan nationalists' point of view, Companys' moderate policy was starting to prove its effectiveness. The anarchists might call the Catalan government, which they had joined, the Regional Defence Committee, but what mattered was that three of them were now members of it. Taradellas of the Esquerra was prime minister with three other Catalanists in his cabinet. Andrés Nin was councillor of justice and Juan Comorera, of the communist PSUC, was councillor of public works.

By the end of September the Defence Council of Aragon was the only major non-governmental organization in the southern part of Republican territory which retained control over its own area. This anarchist creation was under heavy pressure from the communists' campaign for centralized control. By October its committee acknowledged that it would have to make concessions in order to survive. Popular Front parties were brought into the council and Joaquín Ascaso made a successful diplomatic visit to Madrid. Mutual recognition was agreed upon without compromises that appeared to be too damaging, but it later became clear that the central government and the communists had no intention of allowing the Aragonese council to remain in existence any longer than necessary.

Largo Caballero did not realize at this stage that he was being used to re-establish central state power by the liberals, social democrats and communists. After his resentment over the way he was led to participate in the 1931–33 administration, this is surprising, but he felt that this time his position as prime minister would enable him to control the government machine. It was not until November that he started to realize that he had reloaded what Lenin called 'the pistol of the state', and that others were waiting to take it from him.

One of the arguments for centralization was that evidence of a stable, authoritative government in Madrid might persuade the British and French governments to change their policy on arms sales. This hope was dashed when the reality of non-intervention became clear. The first interventionist states, Germany and Italy, had initially given the non-intervention plan a very cool reception. But then they realized the potential advantage. Ciano soon agreed to the policy in general, but insisted that it should cover every facet, even 'propaganda aid'. Italy and Germany would then be able to accuse Russia of violating the agreement, and so justify their interventionist activities. The Germans agreed to the pact in principle, but argued that it would require a blockade to be enforced. The Soviet government, eager not to be out-manœuvred, followed similar tactics by insisting that Portugal must be disciplined. Portugal was to become Stalin's whipping-boy on the Non-Intervention Committee, since attacking the dictators was too risky for his tastes.

There seems to be little doubt that the French government had been sincere in its original intentions. The same cannot be said of Eden. His later realization, that the ambitions of the Axis were only encouraged by appeasement, tends to obscure his conduct in 1936. It was hypocritical to duck responsibility by saying that 'the Spaniards would not feel any gratitude to those who had intervened', when the British government failed to act impartially while maintaining its pretensions to being the 'international policeman'.

Moreover, Eden's argument that supplying the Republic with arms would make Hitler aid Franco was already shown to be fallacious. Even the Nationalist recruitment of Riffian mercenaries, which contravened the Algeciras agreement of 1912 establishing the Spanish protectorate, was ignored. And the Republican government was so concerned not to upset the French and British empires that it neither granted Morocco its independence, nor made serious attempts to stir up anti-colonial feelings there.

Meetings of the Non-Intervention Committee began in London on 8 September, after numerous delays, caused mainly by Germany's refusal to participate until a crash-landed Junkers 52 was returned by the Republic. The committee was organized by the British Foreign Office in London. Lord Plymouth was chairman and the rest of the committee consisted of the ambassadors of the signatory nations, which included every European country except Switzerland. Eden reported that 'the lengthy meetings continued ... Accusations were met with flat denials and the results of both were sterile.' He noted that in October 'the Russians were openly sending supplies to Spain and the evidence we had at this time was more specific against them than against the dictators in Rome and Berlin'. Yet in Geneva at the end of September he had recorded that Alvarez del Vayo, the Republic's foreign minister, 'left with me documents and photographs to prove the extent to which Hitler and Mussolini were violating the agreement'. Even the German *chargé d'affaires* was concerned at the way Wehrmacht uniforms were being cheered on the streets of Seville. And considering the sympathies of the Royal Navy in Gibraltar, it was perhaps not surprising that a blind eye had been turned on the streams of Junkers and Savoias over Gibraltar which were ferrying the Army of Africa between Tetuán and Seville. The American ambassador to Spain, Claude Bowers, later condemned the whole procedure. 'Each movement of the Non-Intervention Committee has been made to serve the cause of the Rebellion ... This Committee was the most cynical and lamentably dishonest group that history has known.'

SOVIET ADVISERS AND THE INTERNATIONAL BRIGADES

During October 1936 the Nationalists concentrated their best forces on the renewed attack towards the capital from the south-west. Their relentless advance made it look as if the Spanish Republic was mortally stricken, but the defence of Madrid was rapidly to become a rallying call throughout Europe to all those who feared and hated the triumphant forces of 'international fascism'. The communist slogan that 'Madrid will be the grave of fascism' was powerfully emotive, and the battle for the capital was to help the party to power. From 30,000 in the early summer of 1936 the Communist Party was to have a quarter of a million members by the end of the year, and nearly 400,000 by the next summer. Added to that were 350,000 members of the United Socialist Youth, although a considerable duplication of membership must be presumed. (It is important to note, however, that over 60 per cent of communist recruits could not be described as working class.)

Russian military aid and Comintern agents were on their way, though some agents, such as Codovilla, the architect of the Socialist Youth take-over, had been there since before the war. Marcel Rosenberg, the Soviet ambassador, arrived in Madrid at the end of August. The major diplomatic appointment in Barcelona was Antonov-Ovseyenko, the veteran Bolshevik who had commanded the assault on the Winter Palace in 1917. Rosenberg accumulated a large staff. The head military adviser was General Berzin (cover-name 'Grishin'), while the military mission was led by General Goriev. General Smushkevich ('Douglas') was air force adviser and Kuznetsov ('Kolya') naval attaché. (Most Russian and Comintern personnel in Spain used a *nom de guerre*.) The Comintern also sent its own staff. Palmiro Togliatti ('Ercole' or 'Alfredo'), the leader of the Italian party in exile, became the chief adviser to the Spanish Communist Party (there is doubt as to his date of arrival). The Hungarian, Erno Gerö ('Pedro'), played a similar role with the PSUC in Catalonia. Other important figures included the writer, Ilya Ehrenburg, and *Pravda* correspondent, Koltsov, who acted as Stalin's agent to spy on the others. Most ominous of all was the arrival of Alexander Orlov (whose real name was Nikolsky), the NKVD officer who was to take charge of the secret police.

Russian supplies were to be manipulated in such a way as to force the

Republican government to follow Soviet policy. In order to exercise the power of a monopoly supplier, Soviet officials did their utmost to sabotage other arms deals which the Republic tried to arrange. At a lower level pressure was later exerted in such a way that only communist formations received air and tank support, new weapons and, in some cases, even ammunition and medical treatment. Regimental commanders were sometimes forced to become Communist Party members simply to ensure that their men could fight.

The advisers, especially the tank commander, General Pavlov ('Pablo'), and the senior air force officer made the decisions, and often did not even inform their Spanish colleagues. Prieto laughed about his hollow power as air minister. He was not sure which airfields were being used, let alone the number of aircraft available. His colleague, Araquistain, commented that the real air minister was the Russian General 'Douglas'. Like the Germans, the Russians were also to use Spain as a testing-ground for their aircraft and pilots. The Soviet military advisers were ordered to stay 'out of range of artillery fire', so that captured Russian officers could never be paraded in front of the Non-Intervention Committee. The Russians also managed to camouflage the number of Red Army personnel in Spain. It has usually been accepted that fewer than 1,000 served at any one time, although more recent research indicates a total exceeding 4,000. The concealment was achieved partly by having Red Army members serve as volunteers in the International Brigades. Such well-known commanders as Kléber, Gal, Čopić and Walter were the obvious examples, and the Polish Dombrowski battalion had a core of Red Army cadres.

The most important aspect of Russo-Spanish Republican relations was the despatch of about 70 per cent of Spain's gold reserves to Russia for safe-keeping. (Most of the rest had already been sent to France.) Spain had the fourth largest reserves in the world (worth nearly $800 million) as a result of the trade boom during the First World War. With Madrid now threatened and the Republican government's need to buy arms, the idea of a 'current account in gold' in Moscow was suggested to Negrín by Stashevsky. This Russian economics expert (officially Antonov-Ovseyenko's adviser) had been told to win the finance minister's confidence. He is then said to have selected him as the future prime minister in case Largo Caballero became uncooperative.

On 13 September Largo and Negrín persuaded the cabinet to agree to the removal of the gold reserves 'to the place he (the finance minister) believes to be the safest'. Two days later the first consignment left for Cartagena, accompanied by Orlov's NKVD officials and guarded by Negrín's *carabineros*. Negrín had given Orlov false papers in the name of Mr Blackstone, representing the Bank of America. After defecting to the United States, Orlov told a Senate Committee of their anxiety at that time: 'If the anarchists intercepted my men, Russians, with truckloads of Spanish gold, they would kill my men, and it would be a tremendous political scandal all over the world, and it might even create an internal revolution.' But by the 21st 10,000 cases had been moved safely into the naval arsenal. Even Prieto, the naval minister, was not informed. On 15 October Largo agreed with Rosenberg that the gold's exact value should be determined at the moment of its arrival at the People's Commissariat of Finances in

Moscow. When the bullion arrived in Odessa on 25 October, the whole area was sealed off while senior NKVD officers carted the half-a-billion dollars' worth of gold to an armoured train. According to the agreement, the Spanish government could re-export the gold whenever it wanted. Orlov later recounted, however, that on its arrival in Moscow, Stalin was said to have remarked that 'the Spaniards will never see their gold again, just as one cannot see one's own ears'. Illusions of Russian philanthropy must have been shaken when $80,000 (at 1936 value) was charged for transporting the gold, another $70,000 for repacking and storing it, and $174,000 a year for guarding it in their own treasury. When news of the transfer leaked on 9 October, the Republican peseta, no longer backed by readily available bullion, fell sharply on the foreign exchange. (Together with the military situation this event contributed to the halving in value of the Republican peseta between the beginning of October and the beginning of December.) As a result, Russian military material cost the Republic much more. The rise in the cost of imports in general was to be exceptionally damaging to the economy, contributing largely, for one thing, to rampant inflation. The Russians, of course, maintained that their assistance was selfless. But Manuel Tagüeña, later one of the Spanish communist commanders, recorded that 'they sent us the new weaponry which needed to be tried out, but also all that was surplus in their depots'. The surplus included some nineteenth-century guns which the Spaniards nicknamed 'the battery of Catherine II'. 'It would be interesting to know', Tagüeña wrote, 'at what figure these museum cannons were priced on the arms sales sheet.'

Stalin gave the order to aid the Republic on 26 August and the Comintern began to galvanize its European subsidiaries into activity. The head of its European section, based in Paris, was Willi Muenzenburg, a highly successful publicist and organizer. International Red Help, which was already in existence, started fund-raising drives and collections. The International Committee for Aid to the Spanish People was set up, and many other front organizations were formed. The communists were remarkably effective in uniting liberals and socialists on common platforms, while quietly controlling the proceedings in the background.

The most famous achievement of the Comintern was the International Brigades. Maurice Thorez, the head of the French Communist Party, apparently suggested the idea originally. Planning started at the end of September. The basic tactic was to use communist exiles from fascism, nazism and the other right-wing dictatorships in Europe. There already existed in Spain the Thaelmann *centuria*, headed by Hans Beimler, a leading German revolutionary after the First World War, who had recently escaped from Dachau. Many other left-wingers and liberals had also arrived in Barcelona of their own accord. It has been estimated that about 5,000 foreigners fought for the Spanish Republic outside the International Brigades.

The importance of a 'non-sectarian' line was emphasized by Communist Party organizers, who declared that the International Brigades consisted of a broad grouping of spontaneous, democratic, anti-fascist volunteers. Esmond Romilly, Winston Churchill's nephew, who joined up, reported that French communists were rebuked for crying 'Vive les Soviets!' The

Communist Party in each country was set recruitment targets. It is almost certain that they were given instructions to hold back their best militants, as they were too important to be wasted in fighting. Altogether nearly 35,000 foreigners served in the International Brigades during the course of the civil war, although there were never more than 18,000 foreigners in the Brigades' strength at any one time. By the middle of 1938 they had declined to nearly half that number.

French volunteers provided the largest national group – almost 10,000 – but their contingent diminished rapidly later. The Poles and German-Austrians contributed about 5,000 men each, the Italians about 3,000, the United States slightly fewer than 3,000, the British just over 2,000, and the Yugoslavs and Czechs about 1,500 each. There were also Scandinavians, Belgians, Dutch, Irish, Cubans and Mexicans. In all, there were volunteers from 53 countries.

With right-wing dictatorships forming a belt from Hamburg to Taranto, it required careful organization to bring the East Europeans to Spain. Poles in exile from their country's military regime started to arrive in Paris, together with Hungarians fleeing from Admiral Horthy's dictatorship and Rumanians escaping from the Iron Guard. Yugoslavs avoiding the royalist police came along Tito's 'secret railway'. Even White Russians, hoping that service with the Brigades would allow them to return home, joined the mass of East European exiles. Volunteers from North America did not arrive until much later. The first detachment of them left New York on Christmas Day, and the Lincoln battalion first saw action at the Jarama in February 1937.

The story of the International Brigades later became distorted in many ways, not simply from the propaganda motive of exaggerating their role out of all proportion to that of Spanish formations. The impression has been created, especially in Great Britain and America, that they consisted of middle-class intellectuals and ideological Beau Gestes. This came about partly because the intellectual minority was news-worthy and partly because they were articulate and had a ready access to publishers afterwards. In addition, when these idealists from comfortable backgrounds became disillusioned by the reality of communism, they helped contribute to the establishment's most heart-warming theme: rebellious youth recognizing the error of its ways.

Almost 80 per cent of the volunteers from Great Britain were manual workers who either left their jobs or were unemployed. Photographs of them show scrubbed faces with self-conscious expressions, short hair, cloth caps clutched in hand and Sunday suits with boots. Some of them were glad to escape the apathy of unemployment, others had already been fighting Moseley's fascists in street-battles, as their French equivalents had fought *Action Française* and the *Croix de Feu*. But most had little notion of what warfare really meant. Slightly over half of them were Communist Party members. Jason Gurney of the British battalion described the drawing power of the Party in the 1930s: 'Its real genius was to provide a world where lost and lonely people could feel important.' Interminable, deeply serious meetings at branch level gave members a feeling of being involved in 'the march of History'. Yet all the time they were made eager to have the responsibility and effort of original thought taken from them. Slogans

in 'pidgin agit-prop', as Victor Serge termed it, became an inwardly sooth-
ing mantra despite the outward protest. George Orwell later attacked the
left's intellectual dishonesty in the apparently effortless switch from pacif-
ism to 'romantic warmongering':

> Here were the very people who for twenty years had hooted and jeered
> at the 'glory' of war, atrocity stories, at patriotism, even at physical
> courage, coming out with stuff that with the alteration of a few names
> would have fitted into the *Daily Mail* of 1918. The same people who
> in 1933 sniggered pityingly if you said that in certain circumstances
> you would fight for your country, in 1937 were denouncing you as a
> Trotskyist-Fascist if you suggested that the stories in *New Masses*
> about freshly wounded men clamouring to get back into the fighting
> might be exaggerated.

In their own countries some young middle-class idealists were ill at ease
with workers, and perhaps wary of the way their earnest social pot-holing
could risk derision. Like Marx before them, they had often despaired of
England's 'bourgeois' proletariat. The Spanish proletariat, on the other
hand, had never respected or aped their social superiors. Even in the
eighteenth century, foreign travellers were amazed at the cavalier way
Spanish servants and labourers treated their aristocracy. Also, the fact
that the Andalucian peasant had never been crushed by the seizure of the
common land or contained by religion, meant that the Spanish working
class could be romanticized in a way which their own working class seemed
to thwart. Consequently, the Spanish conflict offered Anglo-Saxon intellectuals a breath of pure and uncloseted emotion in comparison to the
suffocating complacency at home. Middle-class guilt feelings and an urge
to sublimate a privileged identity in the mass struggle made many of these
intellectuals ideal recruits for communist authority.

There were, perhaps, many volunteers who went to Spain partly in
search of excitement, but the selflessness of the International Brigaders'
motives cannot be doubted. They saw fascism as an international threat,
and the Brigades appeared to offer the best way of fighting it. Spain was
seen as the battleground which would decide the future. This belief was
maintained long afterwards, so that even to this day there are those who
argue that a Republican victory would have prevented the Second World
War.

Paris was the marshalling yard for volunteers of all nationalities. The
secret networks directed them there from eastern, central and south-eastern
Europe. From the north, British workers without passports crossed the
channel on excursion tickets. On arrival at the Gare du Nord, left-wing
taxi drivers drove them to the reception centres in the 9th Arrondissement.
Almost every day, young men, brown paper parcels under their arms,
could be seen waiting for the Perpignan train at the Gare d'Austerlitz,
conspicuously trying to look inconspicuous. Once safely on the train, they
would fraternize with those whose glances they had just been avoiding so
studiously. Wine was passed round, food shared, and the Internationale
sung endlessly. The two principal routes were either to Marseilles, where
they were smuggled onto ships for Barcelona or Valencia, or else to
Perpignan and then over the Pyrenees at night. Some anarchists, who still

controlled the Pyrenean frontier, wanted to turn them back. Their argument was that weapons were needed, not men, but their main fear was that a communist-controlled 'Foreign Legion' was being built up to crush them later. In the fields peasants straightened up to watch the young foreigners pass, singing, in their trains or lorries. The reaction to them was warmest in the towns, where most of the population, especially the children, cheered them and gave the clenched-fist salute. In Barcelona the welcome was unstinted despite the misgivings of the libertarian movement.

The base selected for the International Brigades was Albacete, which had been recaptured from the civil guard after the rising. The barracks where many of the Nationalist defenders had been killed was used as the induction centre. It was in a disgusting state until a party of German communists cleaned it out thoroughly. Hygiene was a problem, especially for those who were weakened by the malnutrition of unemployment. Certainly the rations of beans in oil contributed to the dysentery suffered by the British working-class volunteers who, like the Canadians and Americans, were unused to foreign food. As soon as they arrived, the German communists put up a large slogan in their quarters proclaiming 'we exalt discipline', while the French posted precautions against venereal disease. (With the lack of antibiotics, the latter was to take almost as heavy a toll as in the militias.)

At Albacete the Brigaders were given their initial indoctrination and issued with 'uniforms' – usually either woolly Alpine hats or khaki berets, ski jerkins, breeches, long thick socks and ill-fitting boots. Some found themselves in army surplus uniforms from the First World War, and the Americans later turned up almost entirely kitted out as 'doughboys'. It was rare to find anything that fitted satisfactorily. Senior Party cadres and commissars were conspicuously different. They favoured black leather jackets, dark-blue berets, and a Sam Browne belt with a heavy 9 mm automatic pistol. This last item was the great status symbol of the Party functionary.

The recruits were lined up on the parade ground for an address by André Marty, the Brigades' controller who had earlier brought the French volunteers over the border during the fighting at Irún. Marty, a squat man, with white moustache, drooping jowl and outsize beret, had made his name as a signals operator in the 1919 mutiny of the French Black Sea fleet. The heroic legend woven around him in Party mythology made him one of the most powerful figures in the Comintern. Almost nobody dared challenge his authority. At that time he was starting to develop a conspiracy complex that rivalled Stalin's. Influenced by the show trials in Moscow, he became convinced that 'Fascist-Trotskyist' spies were everywhere, and that it was his duty to exterminate them. Marty later admitted that he had ordered the shooting of about 500 Brigaders, nearly one-tenth of the total killed in the war. Many claim that Marty's figure is modest. The Brigades' military commander was General 'Kléber' (alias Lazar Stern), a grey-haired, Hungarian Jew and veteran soldier, who was later to be shot on Stalin's orders.

The parade ground at Albacete was used for military drill, after which battalion commissars gave the volunteers long lectures on 'why we are fighting'. These talks were followed by group discussions, used by the commissars to introduce 'ideas' which were then 'discussed and voted upon democratically'. In this manner the International Brigades followed the 5th Regiment in introducing the saluting of officers. 'A salute is a sign that a comrade who has been an egocentric individualist in private life has adjusted to the collective way of getting things done. A salute is proof that our Brigade is on its way from being a collection of well-meaning amateurs to a precision implement for eliminating fascists.'

Such meetings and 'democratic procedure' provided tempting targets for the iconoclasts to mock, but these light-hearted jokers were marked down by the commissars. They were likely to be the first suspected of 'Trotskyist-Fascist leanings'. Other sceptics, especially the old sweats from the Great War, were bitterly critical of the 'training'. Most of the volunteers were very unfit, as well as ignorant of the most elementary military skills. As one of the veterans remarked, they were not preparing to go over the top with *Das Kapital* in their hands.

Marty told the volunteers that 'when the first International Brigade goes into action, they will be properly trained men with good rifles, a well-equipped corps'. This was all part of the Party's myth of the professional, when in fact sheer courage, bolstered by the belief that the world depended on them, had to make up for appalling deficiencies in the Brigaders' basic training. Men who were to be sent against the Army of Africa had to project the aura of experts to impress the militias, but they could do little except form ranks, march and turn. Many of them had never even handled a rifle until they were on the way to the front, and the few Great War veterans had to show them how to load their obsolete weapons of varied calibres. From a box of assorted ammunition, inexperienced soldiers had to find bullets to fit their rifles. The number of jammed weapons through wedged and separated casings was predictably high.

The militias had suffered from similar disadvantages, but they had no pretensions to being an elite force arriving in the nick of time to save the situation. Nevertheless, the foreign innocents, who felt a 'moment of awe' on being handed a rifle, had several advantages over the Spanish militia-men on first going into battle. They had a slightly greater knowledge and understanding of modern military technology, they understood the value of trenches and, most important of all, they had men in their ranks who 'had been through it before'. Spain's neutrality in the Great War made the first shock of battle much more traumatic to the militia.

32 Destruction of the women's prison in Barcelona, August 1936.

33 Anarchist feminist poster against 'moral incoherence'
of anti-fascist militia using prostitutes.

34 Militiawoman and male comrades.

35 Militias requisition tractors in Aragon to tow their artillery, August 1936.

36 POUM militia volunteers at Karl Marx barracks in Barcelona.

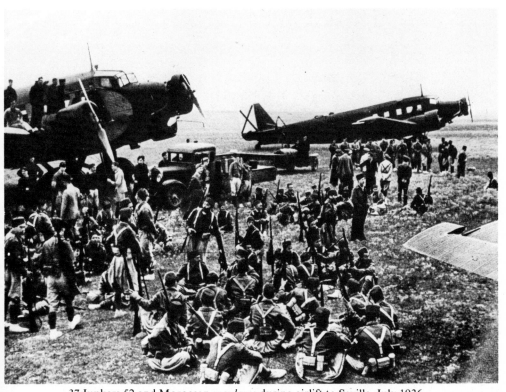

37 Junkers 52 and Moroccan *regulares* during airlift to Seville, July 1936.

38 Republican militia on the Majorcan expedition, August 1936.

39 Foreign Legion rounding up villagers during Yagüe's advance north, August 1936.
40 Right Libertarian *dinamitero* on the Aragon Front.

41 Largo Caballero visits the Guadarrama front, August 1936.

42 Toledo with the Alcázar in ruins, August 1936.

43 Militiaman shoots at pursuing legionnaires in Toledo, September 1936.

44 From the left, Moscardó, Varela and Franco after the relief of the Alcázar, September 1936.

45 Refugees sheltering in the Madrid Metro during an air raid.

46 Captain of the Russian ship *Rion* (left) welcomed in Barcelona by
Companys (centre) and Antonov-Ovseyenko (right).

47 Right Madrid crowd watches first air battles, November 1936.

48 Fighting in the Casa de Campo, Madrid, November 1936.

49 International Brigade troops in Madrid.

50 Fighting in the south west of Madrid, November 1936.

51 Buenaventura Durruti.

52 Communist poster: 'Discover and crush the fifth column without pity.'
November 1936.

53 Condor Legion officer instructs Carlists and Falangists in Avila.

54 Women in Málaga after an air raid.

55 British anti-tank section, commanded by the writer Humphrey Slater, at the battle of the Jarama, February 1937.

56 Luftwaffe pilots with their Heinkel He-45 fighter bombers.

57 Fiat-Ansaldo captured during Italian retreat on the Guadalajara front, March 1937.
59 *Overleaf* Nazi officers with Franco's Moorish bodyguard in the background.

58 General Miaja (with glasses) visits 69 Brigade at El Pardo outside Madrid.

THE BATTLE FOR MADRID

The Nationalist advance on the capital started at the end of the first week of October. The Army of Africa began a three-pronged attack: northwards from Toledo, north-eastwards along the Navalcarnero road, and eastwards from San Martín de Valdeiglesias. The left flank of the attack was strengthened by 10,000 men from Mola's army, made up of Carlist *requetés*, Falangist militia and regular soldiers. The plan was for the Nationalist forces to enter the capital on 12 October, the day of 'The Feast of the Spanish Race'. Mola had claimed that he would drink a cup of coffee that day on the Gran Vía and, although the attack on Madrid was delayed, even Franco's staff began to prepare for a triumphal entry. The seemingly inevitable capture of Madrid would not only mean a crushing psychological blow to the Republicans. It should guarantee belligerent rights, if not *de facto* recognition, from foreign powers. The crumbling of the militia in the face of the Army of Africa's advance from Seville had raised the expectations of the Nationalists and their backers enormously. Reports were sent to Germany that Madrid had no food reserves, no anti-aircraft defences and no fortifications. The militia were badly armed with old rifles of varying calibres, and they had few machine-guns which worked. The Republican fighters and bombers, consisting mainly of French Dewoitines and Potez, were no match for the Heinkels and Fiats.

The Nationalist command structure for the assault on Madrid was complex. Mola had the official command, probably a cautious move on Franco's part, and Colonel Varela was in command of the colonial troops. Yagüe was back with the Army of Africa, but in a subordinate position. After Navalcarnero on the north-east axis had fallen, Illescas on the Toledo road was occupied on 19 October. Torrejón, also on the Toledo road and some 30 kilometres (19 miles) from the capital was taken several days later. The Nationalists were not alone in believing that Madrid would fall to them rapidly. Foreign journalists and diplomats were sure that the advance of the Army of Africa, backed by squadrons of the Luftwaffe and Italian air force, could not be stopped. The Republic's administration seemed paralysed by a strange mixture of frantic activity and inertia. Many blamed 'sabotage by reactionary civil servants', but, however true, such charges only diverted attention from the government's inefficiency.

In the second half of October Largo Caballero began to issue decrees extending mobilization in an effort to improve Madrid's defences; yet for much of the capital's population the war still seemed remote. Militiamen, criticized for being on 'excessive guard duty' in the capital rather than at the front, tended to ignore official communiqués. Nor could the prime minister himself forget old rivalries. He refused to assign UGT construction workers to the digging of trenches in case they defected to the CNT. And yet the speed of the Nationalist advance was such, that on 18 October, when Largo had tried to telephone the Republican commander in Illescas, he had found himself talking to the Nationalist commander General Varela who had just occupied the town.

Of the government decrees issued at this time, the one to have the most far-reaching effect announced the establishment of 'mixed brigades'. Although this was not implemented immediately, except on the Madrid front, it marked the first major step away from militia columns towards a formalized army. The columns were to be split into battalions, and then three of these militia units were to be formed into a brigade along with one regular battalion and supporting artillery.

It was optimistic of the government to start talking of battalions and brigades when its forces were being eroded during the retreat into the capital. Concentrated artillery bombardments, or air attacks from the Heinkel 51s and Fiat fighters, totally demoralized the militias. Regular officers, too, were known to panic merely at the sound of aero engines. It is often forgotten that the Spanish metropolitan army had no battle experience, and the majority of its officers had not handled troops even on manœuvres. This lack of training, as much as the instinctive dislike which many of them felt for the militia system, contributed to the chaotic retreat of the Republican forces from Estremadura. As headquarters' staff frequently retreated without attempting to warn their forward units, it was not surprising that militia groups, feeling abandoned, should make a run for it before they were cut off. In fact, with communications virtually non-existent, a formalized command structure could not have co-ordinated the different sectors, even if it had been run efficiently. For most of the time the commanders had been issuing orders which bore no relation to the situation which existed on the ground, so they were usually ignored. Matters were made worse by petty jealousies. Cipriano Mera commented that 'if the war we were experiencing had not been so tragic, we would have been doubled up in laughter seeing how these military chiefs attacked each other for personal reasons, and out of professional pride; and yet they were the most valiant and loyal to the Republican cause.'

At the beginning of November Largo Caballero again asked the anarchists to join the government, since they constituted the largest group involved in the fight against the Nationalists. The other Popular Front parties supported this attempt to end the anti-state within the state. The only prominent dissenter was President Azaña, whose intense dislike of the anarchists appears to have dated from the Casas Viejas incident, the event which had led to the fall of his first government.

Once again CNT-FAI leaders were faced with a fundamental dilemma. They believed the state could not change its nature, whatever the politics of its leaders; yet they were extremely worried by evidence of the Russians' power and the increase in communist strength. Federica Montseny, an FAI intellectual, later explained to the American historian, Burnett Bolloten: 'At that time we only saw the reality of the situation created for us: the communists in the government and ourselves outside, the manifold possibilities, and all our achievements endangered.' The CNT-FAI asked for five ministries including those of finance and war so as to protect themselves in the two areas where they felt most vulnerable. They settled, however, for four minor posts: health, which had previously only been a director-generalship, justice, industry and commerce. The 'purists' were persuaded to accept this compromise by the 'reformist' syndicalists, such as Horacio Prieto, the secretary of the CNT National Committee, Juan Peiró, the new ministry of industry, and Juan López, who took the ministry of commerce. Federica Montseny cast aside misgivings and the warnings of her father, to become Spain's first woman minister. García Oliver proved, not surprisingly, to be an unconventional minister of justice. Legal fees were abolished and all criminal dossiers destroyed.

The CNT-FAI leaders had only just taken up their posts when, on the morning of 6 November, Largo Caballero called a cabinet meeting and stated that the government must move to Valencia. Azaña had already abandoned the capital without warning and most ministers, especially Largo and Prieto, were convinced that Madrid would fall immediately. It was argued in cabinet that, if they were captured, the Republic would have no legal leadership, and the rebels would instantly achieve international recognition. (In fact the fall of the capital alone would have had much the same result, and Barajas aerodrome to the east was not threatened if they had wanted to escape at the last moment.) The new CNT-FAI ministers opposed this plan strenuously, saying that the government should not abandon the defenders. But the anarchists were alone in their objections and it was decided that the capital would be ruled by a junta in the absence of the administration.

General Pozas, the former commander of the civil guard and soon a Communist Party member, was given command of the Army of the Centre, while General Miaja was to lead the junta in charge of the capital. The orders to these two generals were put in the wrong envelopes, but luckily they opened them immediately instead of waiting as ordered. Pozas alleged that Miaja nearly wept with rage at what he saw as an attempt to sacrifice him in Madrid.

Meanwhile, on the night of 6 November the government loaded its files on to an enormous convoy of lorries which set off for Valencia. Fears that the Valencia road might be cut at any moment by a Nationalist thrust were misplaced; instead the convoy was stopped by CNT militia at Tarrancón. For desertion in the face of the enemy, the anarchists arrested Alvarez del Vayo, the foreign minister, General Pozas, Juan López, their own CNT minister, and General Asensio, the under-secretary of war, who was reputed to have discriminated against anarcho-syndicalist militia. They also stopped the Soviet ambassador to tell him what they thought of communism. Eventually Horacio Prieto of the CNT National Committee persuaded the militia to let the convoy pass.

The effect of the government's flight from Madrid was remarkable. The anarchist attitude immmediately changed to 'Long live Madrid without government!', and the cry was echoed by others as a new feeling came over the capital. The sense of urgency which had marked the early days of the rising returned. The communists called for the formation of local committees, the very bodies which they had resolutely opposed before. The establishment of the Madrid junta was, in itself, a step back towards the fragmentation of power which had occurred in July. Slogans which would have been taboo only a few days before were now on the lips of every cadre. The gut instinct of defending the city against 'the fascists and their Moors' stirred the population. The parallel with the defence of Petrograd against the Whites in the Russian Civil War was repeatedly drawn and cinemas showed films like *Sailors of Kronstadt* and *Battleship Potemkin*. The communist deputy, La Pasionaria, was tireless in her exhortations to resistance, both on the radio and at mass rallies.

As in Barcelona in July, the mass decision to defend Madrid inspired mass bravery. The terror and loathing which the colonial troops aroused in the *madrileños* helped turn panic into a spirit of fierce resistance. In the Plaza de Atocha a large placard warned: 'In Badajoz the fascists shot 2,000. If Madrid falls they will shoot half the city.' Chains of women and children passed rocks and stones for the construction of barricades. Trenches were dug on the threatened western flank of the city. Houses in the south-west suburb of Carabanchel were prepared for a street-by-street defence.

At this moment of crisis, when the fighting reached the southern suburbs, there was a mass mobilization. Metal workers created the slogan, 'Every union syndicate a militia, every union member a militiaman.' The UGT and CNT syndicates formed themselves into battalions of railwaymen, barbers and tailors. There was a battalion of schoolmasters and a graphic arts battalion. Transport and buildings were requisitioned and, as in Barcelona, the Ritz hotel was turned into a canteen for the homeless and refugees. The junta itself took over the palace of Juan March, where typists worked in the ballroom under huge chandeliers, which jangled ominously once the air raids and shelling started.

Miaja's junta was a strange mixture. Nearly all the members were young and energetic, several being still in their twenties; as a result they were known as 'Miaja's infant guard'. On the other hand, the old general, myopic, loquacious and incapable of staying with a subject, was no revolutionary. In fact, he had been a member of the *Unión Militar Española*, which played an important part in the early planning for the rising. However, he craved popularity and was easily flattered. The communists promoted him as the hero of Madrid, giving him an idealized treatment in their press throughout the world. Miaja was thrilled and even became a Party member to repay the compliment, though joining as many political organizations as possible seemed to be his major indulgence. Azaña laughed at Miaja's 'communism', remembering that the general had told him only four years previously that socialists should be shot.

A chill warning of future developments came with Rosenberg's veto of any POUM representation on the junta, which ignored the principle of political parity which had so benefited the communists. He made it clear that there would be no Russian weapons if the 'Trotskyists' were included. (Andrés Nin had, in fact, broken with Trotsky, who was critical of the

POUM, but Nin remained an anti-Stalinist.) 'Public order' in Madrid was to take on a frightening aspect; Orlov, the NKVD chief, remained in the capital after all the other non-military Russian personnel had left. The situation was worsened by Mola's use of the phrase, 'fifth column', to describe the Nationalist supporters in Madrid. Not surprisingly this ill-judged remark greatly increased the fear of treachery from within. The civil guard, now the Republican Guard, was ruthlessly purged. This drastic act was encouraged by memories of their revolt at Badajoz on Yagüe's approach. The *asaltos* were treated in a similar manner and sent down to Valencia. The communist 5th Regiment took control of the vast majority of security operations, and the security delegate, Santiago Carrillo, presided over a spate of arrests and summary executions which may have exceeded those of July and August. There is no doubt that there were many Nationalist supporters in Madrid, but the overwhelming majority of attacks attributed to the fifth column came from a frightened population mistaking the direction of machine-gun fire or confusing artillery shells with 'grenades dropped from windows'.

It is difficult to know whether the junta authorities acted out of genuine fear of a 'stab in the back', or whether they purposely exaggerated incidents in order to justify the security forces' ruthless methods. Spy mania was at its height, and the telephones were cut off to prevent Nationalist sympathizers from telephoning intelligence to the Army of Africa in the suburbs. The activities, real and imagined, of the fifth column could not, however, justify the decision to evacuate and then shoot 1,029 inmates of the Model Prison, most of whom were leading Nationalist supporters. It is not known for sure whether this order was given by Carrillo's assistant, José Cazorla, or by Koltsov, the *Pravda* correspondent and special envoy, who declared that 'such important elements must not fall into fascist hands'. Immediate and outspoken condemnation of the killings came from Melchor Rodríguez, the anarchist director of prisons newly appointed by Juan García Oliver, but few others dared to criticize the communists at such a critical moment. It has been said that this 'firm' policy stopped a fifth column revolt within the city. But although the Nationalist faction was large, there is little evidence that they were sufficiently armed for such a role.

Meanwhile, militia units were falling back into the capital, exhausted and demoralized. Some had fled openly, even seizing ambulances to get away from the Moors, but others were fighting back with a dogged courage which slowed the Nationalist advance considerably. In fact, it would appear that the militia collapse was exaggerated by newsmen who saw only those who were fleeing. On 4 November Getafe and its aerodrome had been captured, prompting Varela to tell journalists that they could 'announce to the world that Madrid will be captured this week'. To the west Brunete had been taken two days before. The Nationalists were already organizing food convoys so as to be able to feed the population once they entered the city. Even the cautious Franco felt the outcome was virtually certain, so certain, indeed, that he decided to allow Republican troops a line of escape so that they were not forced to fight by being cornered. As a result, no push was made towards Vallecas to cut the Valencia road. It was a decision the Nationalists greatly regretted later.

In spite of the Republicans' retreat, there had been a major development to improve the morale of the militias. Russian aid purchased with the gold reserves was starting to arrive. Maisky, the Russian ambassador in London, and thus representative on the Non-Intervention Committee, had declared on 28 October that his country felt itself no more bound by the agreement than Germany, Italy or Portugal. The next day 15 Russian T-26 tanks spearheaded an assault with 5th Regiment troops under Líster. Attacking from the direction of Aranjuez they scattered Colonel Monasterio's cavalry detachments at Seseña. The infantry could not keep up, so the tanks reached Parla on the Madrid–Toledo road alone. There they were repulsed when a detachment of the Foreign Legion managed to set several of them on fire with hastily improvised petrol bombs.

The first batch of Russian aid, which arrived in October, included 42 Illyushin 15 (Chato) biplane fighters, and 31 Illyushin 16 (Rata) monoplane fighters. On 29 October a squadron of Katiuska fast bombers, which had just arrived, raided Seville, and on 3 November, Russian Chato fighters were seen over Madrid. A day later they dispersed a formation of Fiat fighters and proved superior to the Heinkel 51s. The streets of Madrid were thronged with crowds staring up into the skies and cheering whenever an aircraft was hit; it was always assumed to be an enemy. The arrival of this modern Russian weaponry, especially the tanks and the stubby I-16 Rata monoplane, made the Nazis decide to increase their aid. With Franco's agreement it was organized within an independent German command and named the Condor Legion.

Having advanced the last few kilometres to the south-western outskirts of the city during the first week of November, Varela began to make probing attacks from the west. That side of Madrid had no suburb buffer because the old royal hunting ground of the Casa de Campo stretched down to the River Manzanares. Madrid's centre and key buildings all lay within a kilometre of this exposed triangle, bound by the Corunna road running north-west, and the Estremadura road stretching to the south-west. On the north of the wedge lay the new university city with its widely spaced modern blocks. Varela wanted to make a left-flanking attack round the northern tip of the Casa de Campo, in the area of the San Fernando bridge, but Franco insisted on an assault due west, hoping thereby to reduce street-fighting to a minimum. Nationalist troops were clearly superior in open country while the majority of their casualties, especially among the *regulares*, had been sustained in house clearing. Franco also ordered a diversionary feint on the southern suburb of Carabanchel to draw off as many defenders as possible.

The thrust from the Casa de Campo would be mounted on a front only one kilometre wide. Castejón's column was to head for the University City, Asensio's force was to advance in the centre and Delgado's, on the right, towards the North Station. They would be backed by Italian light armour and Panzer Mark Is under von Thoma. The major assault was scheduled for 7 November, but the obstinate resistance of militia groups forced the Nationalists to postpone it a day.

Miaja had established his military headquarters in the finance ministry on 6 November, the day the government left. His chief-of-staff was Colonel Vicente Rojo, a conscientious, professional officer. Neither of them, however, knew what forces were under their command, nor even who was on the staff. Many officers had taken advantage of the confusion to flee the city, and some of them, including the chief of operations, had joined the Nationalists. Even Miaja's orders from the central government were contradictory, for he was told to hold Madrid at any cost and also given detailed instructions for retreat.

General Goriev, the man said by many to be the real commander in Madrid, was also established in the ministry. One of his officers, Colonel Voronov, controlled the artillery, although few batteries had any shells because of incompetence at the ministry of war. He and his Spanish counterpart established their observation post at the top of the Telefónica, a building which later attracted more Nationalist artillery fire than any other. Ironically, this skyscraper belonging to ITT became the symbol of

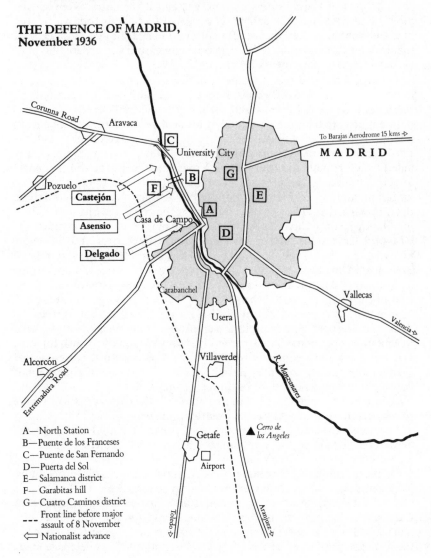

THE DEFENCE OF MADRID,
November 1936

Corunna Road
Aravaca
To Barajas Aerodrome 15 kms ⊳
C
University City
MADRID
Pozuelo
B
G
F
Castejón
E
A
Asensio
Casa de Campo
D
Delgado
Carabanchel
Vallecas
Usera
Valencia ⊳
R. Manzanares
Alcorcón
Villaverde
Estremadura Road
Cerro de
los Angeles
A—North Station
Getafe
B—Puente de los Franceses
C—Puente de San Fernando
D—Puerta del Sol
Airport
E— Salamanca district
F— Garabitas hill
G—Cuatro Caminos district
- - - Front line before major
assault of 8 November
⟸ Nationalist advance
Toledo ⊳
Aranjuez ⊳

left-wing resistance during the course of the battle. Downstairs its chairman, Sosthenes Benn, entertained journalists with brandy while awaiting the arrival of General Franco. And according to Hitler's interpreter, Paul Schmidt, he had prepared a banquet to greet the conquerors.

The international press was already describing 'the last hours of Madrid'. Several French journalists even sent details of the capital's capture so as to beat their rivals to the story. Portuguese radio gave vivid details of General Franco's triumphal entry, mounted on a white charger, and telegrams congratulating him from the Austrian and Guatemalan governments were delivered to General Miaja instead. The Nationalists and their allies simply did not consider that their success was in doubt. According to the *Daily Telegraph* correspondent, Carlist *requetés* were hurried forward so that Spanish Catholic troops were present at the entry. Reprisal tribunals and civil guard detachments allocated to each district waited behind the front line. Even the usually cautious General Franco had declared that he would attend mass in Madrid on 7 November and ordered his staff to make travel arrangements for church leaders.

The world awaited the outcome of 'a decisive battle' between progress and reaction, or between civilization and red barbarism, depending on one's point of view. Liberals and the left everywhere believed that international fascism had to be defeated at Madrid before Europe fell beneath a totalitarian ice age, while conservatives felt it to be the chance to halt the tide of communism. At this crucial moment the defenders were greatly aided by a fortunate discovery. On 7 November the day before the major attack, a militia detachment searched the body of a Nationalist officer in an Italian tank which had been knocked out. In his jacket they found the operational orders. The plan was to 'occupy the zone between, and including, the University City and the Plaza de España, which will constitute the base of departure for further advances into the interior of Madrid'. Now knowing that the assault on Carabanchel was only a feint, the Republican general staff switched the bulk of its forces to the Casa de Campo sector and prepared defensive positions for the next morning. Non-militia members of the UGT organized themselves at their *casas del pueblo* and CNT members at their *ateneos libertarios* before going to the front as reserves. They and everyone else, including the refugees from the south-west, were to wait in batches immediately behind the front line, ready to dash forward and take over the weapon of anyone killed. The reassuring presence of such a mass of comrades may have been like an injection of courage, but that night inexperienced sentries on their own took fright at shadows and opened fire. This inevitably led to fusilades into the dark across the whole sector, resulting in a wastage of ammunition. Any indiscriminate firing was serious as there were apparently fewer than 10 rounds per rifle; the departing officials of the war ministry had not left word of where the ammunition reserves were kept.

On the morning of 8 November Varela's three main assault forces under Yagüe attacked out of the cover provided by the low trees on the Casa de Campo. At the same time Barrón and Tella's smaller columns moved on Carabanchel in their diversionary attack. Being forewarned, Miaja had maintained only about 12,000 of his 40,000 strong force in Carabanchel; the rest were positioned opposite the Casa de Campo. This heterogeneous mass of militia, including a women's battalion at the Puente de Segovia, mixed with *carabineros* and regular soldiers, and backed by totally un-trained volunteers, was twice the size of their opponents. But that does not belittle their achievement that day, considering the difference in armament and experience. Probably less than half of the Republicans had been involved in earlier fighting and had only learnt how to operate the bolt and aim a rifle the evening before. Many still had no idea of how to clear a stoppage, an operation difficult enough for steady fingers. Nevertheless, the Nationalist assault columns were held at the western edge of the city that day, a victory of great psychological importance. The Army of Africa no longer appeared invincible. Republican spirits were further raised by the deployment that evening in the Casa de Campo sector of the first of the International Brigades.

The arrival of XI International Brigade, commanded by General Kléber, had a powerful effect on the population of Madrid. It was generally regarded as the best of the Brigades. Its steadiness, ammunition-discipline and trench-digging was to have a good influence on the militias. As the 1,900 foreigners marched up the Gran Vía in well-drilled step, the *madrileños* cheered them with cries of *'Viva los rusos!'*, on the mistaken assumption that they were the infantry counterpart of the fighter aircraft. An English Brigader described the scene. 'It was a brave sight. It had all the glamour and excitement that governments can use to make men forsake their homes and die on foreign soil ... but it was *ours!*'

The determination and almost suicidal bravery of XI International, especially the Germans, cannot be doubted, but the exploitation of their devotion was particularly unpleasant. Madrid was to be the Communist Party's victory alone. Communist troops under the Italian commissar, Luigi Longo, had tried to stop Major Palacios with two battalions of volunteers and a battery of Vickers 105 mm field guns from reaching the capital the day before the XI International Brigade arrived. They forced their way through, nevertheless, and were welcomed by General Miaja and Colonel Rojo just before the Brigaders arrived. Just after dawn on the next morning, these two battalions counter-atracked over the San Fernando bridge on the Nationalist left flank in the Casa de Campo, losing nearly half their men and retaking the north-eastern part lost on the previous day. But nothing was heard of this in the outside world, nor were other militia actions reported. It was forgotten that the Brigaders had not arrived in time to affect the fighting on the 8th and that they only represented 5 per cent of the Republican forces. So successful was Comintern propaganda that Sir Henry Chilton, the British ambassador, was convinced that there were only foreigners defending Madrid. Meanwhile, the Nationalists also exaggerated the Brigaders' importance, so as to justify their own failure and emphasize the 'threat of International Communism'.

Having been severely checked on the west flank, Varela switched his attack on 9 November towards Carabanchel. Fierce house-to-house fight-ing ensued in this working-class suburb, where the militias, fighting on familiar ground, not only held back the *regulares*, but inflicted heavy casualties. That evening, two kilometres to the north, XI International Brigade suffered severe losses when forcing the Nationalists to retreat a few hundred metres in the central part of the Casa de Campo. The fierce fighting continued in Carabanchel over the next few days, then on 12 November General Miaja (or more probably General Goriev), concerned that the Nationalists might thrust through to cut off the Valencia road, diverted XII International Brigade and four Spanish brigades to attack the important hill, Cerro de los Angeles. This second International Brigade had received even less training than the first and, despite the Great War veterans in their ranks, the attack collapsed in chaos. Much of this was due to language and communication problems, but the fact remains that the Brigaders were no more skilful at mounting attacks than the militias.

At this stage the anarchist leader, Buenaventura Durruti, arrived with more than 4,000 men from the Aragon front. He had been persuaded to go to Madrid by Federica Montseny, who was representing the government in Valencia. At a meeting with García Oliver at Madrid CNT headquarters, Cipriano Mera, the delegate-general of their militia battalions, warned Durruti against attempting a frontal attack on the Casa de Campo, even though the anarchists had become alarmed at the influence the communists were achieving through the International Brigades. Durruti insisted that he had no option but to counter-attack from the University City in the direction of the Casa de Velazquez. The assault took place on the morning of the 17th, but the covering artillery and air support he had been promised failed to materialize. (Whether that was through oversight or intention, anarchist suspicions of communist tactics were greatly increased.) Durruti's men, who had shown such reckless bravery in the Barcelona fighting, broke back to their start-line when they met a concentrated artillery barrage and heavy machine-gun fire, neither of which they had experienced before.

Two days later the Nationalists attacked with the support of heavy artillery, and Asensio's column found a gap in the Republican line. As a result the Nationalists were able to establish a bridgehead deep in the University City. The legionnaires and *regulares* held on despite furious attacks from XI International Brigade and other units in that sector, which was to become the most bitterly contested stretch of territory in the whole front.

During this fighting Durruti was mortally wounded. A rumour was soon started, that he had been shot by one of his own men who objected to his severe discipline. In fact the anarchists, for reasons of morale and propaganda, claimed that he had been killed by a sniper's bullet when it had really been an accident. The cocking handle of a companion's *'naranjero'* machine pistol caught on a car door, firing a bullet into his chest. Durruti was without doubt the most popular anarchist leader. He had been an unrelenting rebel throughout his life and had earned the reputation of a revolutionary Robin Hood. His funeral in Barcelona was the greatest scene of mass mourning ever witnessed in Spain, with half a million people in the procession alone. His reputation was so great, not just among anarchists, that attempts were made after his death to claim his allegiance. The Falange said that, like his two brothers, he was a Falangist sympathizer at heart, while the communists felt certain that he was on the way to joining them.

The Nationalist's failure to break through on 19 November made Franco change his strategy. He could not risk any more of his best troops in fruitless assaults now that a quick victory looked much more difficult. So, for the first time in history, a capital city came under intense air as well as artillery bombardment. All residential areas except the fashionable Salamanca district were bombed in an attempt to break the morale of the civilian population. The Italians and the Luftwaffe conducted a methodical experiment in psychological warfare with their Savoia 81s and Junkers 52s. The bombing did not, however, break morale as intended; on the contrary, it increased the defiance of the population. In London Prince Bismarck derided British fear of air attacks 'since you see what little harm they have done in Madrid'.

After the statement that the Salamanca district would be spared, the whole area became packed to overflowing and the streets became virtually impassable. Meanwhile, in a remarkably effective operation, the UGT reorganized the transfer of Madrid's most essential industries to unused Metro tunnels. The air raids destroyed thousands of buildings in Madrid, from slum dwellings to the Palacio de Liria belonging to the Duke of Alba. Alba, in his bitter charges accusing the Republic of responsibility for the damage, did not seem to find it incongruous that the Nationalist crusade was destroying its own capital with foreign bombers, but then Franco had already declared: 'I will destroy Madrid rather than leave it to the Marxists.'

The reversion to local committees was proving of great value. Despite an evacuation programme, refugees still crammed the city (its million inhabitants had been increased by half), only such a system could have helped both them and those made homeless by the bombing. The committees supervised the construction of shelters, commandeered empty apartments and organized essential supplies and canteens. In contrast to these efforts a black market boomed and inevitably damaged morale.

The Soviet advisers, commissars, senior officers and important party cadres had their luxurious and well-stocked base in Gaylord's hotel. The large number of visitors, fact-finding missions and committed supporters from abroad were also well looked after. Foreign journalists ('conspicuous as actresses' in Auden's phrase) suffered little. But for the majority of the population, the daily allowance was meagre. A horse or mule killed by the bombing or shell-fire would be stripped to its skeleton by housewives, while starving dogs hovered round. One International Brigader recorded that a militiaman, having shot a stray which was lapping at the brains of a dead man, shrugged apologetically and explained that dogs were acquiring a taste for human flesh. Cats and rats were also used as food, if only to improve the thin lentil soup. The killing of one bird in the Madrid zoo was not provoked by hunger, however, but by the way the wretched creature learned to imitate the whistle of incoming shells.

Even with the intense air attacks of 19–23 November life was almost normal. People went to work each day, and the trams still ran, even though their tracks had to be repaired continually. The underground was, of course, safer, though people joked that at least the tram had to stop before the front line, whereas on the metro you might come up behind it on the far side.

These communication systems provided supply lines to the forces. Reinforcements and supplies could be moved rapidly over the relatively short distances involved. Hot food for the front-line troops was far easier to provide than in normal defensive positions, and the troops themselves could be relieved frequently, or even visited at the front.

The troops, and particularly the International Brigades, were visited in their trenches by the large numbers of foreigners brought to Madrid by the siege. These groups included journalists and a few war tourists, as well as politically committed supporters of the Republic. Some of the visitors were there for 'pseudo-military excitement' as one International Brigader described it. On visits to the front line they would often borrow a rifle or even a machine-gun to fire off a few rounds at the Nationalist lines. Ernest Hemingway was a good example of the genre and, much as the men may have liked seeing new faces, especially famous ones, they became less enthusiastic when the thrill seekers prompted enemy bombardments.

By the end of November the struggle for Madrid had settled into a cold, hungry siege, punctuated by bombardment, air raids and the occasional flare-up. In Carabanchel, where the front line cut through the middle of streets, a strange deadly struggle continued, with sniping, flame-thrower attacks and tunnelling under houses to lay dynamite. The Carlists lost a whole company in one explosion. Nevertheless, the enthusiastic commitment of Madrid's population diminished as the immediate danger receded. This was accompanied by the gradual replacement of the committees by centralized control. The activities of the communist secret police continued even after the danger was past, which also damaged morale. Anarchist militiamen clashed violently with communist authorities and attempts were made to censor the anarchist press. It was the beginning of a process which led to a major explosion in May of the next year, the start of a virtual civil war within the civil war.

At this time the communists made their first open move against the POUM, as mutual accusations between the Marxist rivals increased. The POUM had outraged the communists on 15 November, when its newspaper, *La Batalla*, analysed Russian policy too accurately. 'Stalin's concern', the article said, 'is not really the fate of the Spanish and international proletariat, but the protection of the Soviet government in accordance with the policy of pacts made by certain others.' Antonov-Ovseyenko immediately accused *La Batalla* of having 'sold out to international fascism', and with the great increase in direct Russian control, the Party line in Spain began to reflect the witchhunt for Trotskyists in the Soviet Union. Having kept them off the Madrid junta, the communists now stopped pay and supplies to the small POUM force on the Madrid front, the immediate threat to the capital having receded. The POUM militia in the region thus had no option but to disband, and its members joined either UGT or CNT units.

The capital was saved and political passions aroused through much of the world, but it had certainly not proved 'the grave of fascism' as the communist slogan had hoped. The battle of Madrid only marked a change in the war in the way defeat turned into a temporary stalemate.

THE METAMORPHOSIS OF THE WAR

History is never tidy. A new pattern of conventional slogging began near Madrid in December 1936, although the last of the militia defeats, in the pattern of the previous summer, did not take place until February 1937, in the brief Málaga campaign. Franco became trapped in an unimaginative strategy. The enormous expectations aroused in October led to Nationalist efforts remaining concentrated on the capital. Since Varela's attacks had been checked and bombing had not broken the morale of the city, the only option left on the central front was to encircle Madrid from a flank, and at least cut off water supplies and electricity from the Sierra de Guadarrama.

With the front running eastwards to the capital and then south to Aranjuez, the Nationalists had the advantage of internal lines for concentrating offensives. Also, with the central front curling back round the Sierra de Guadarrama and across the province of Guadalajara, there was the possibility of striking down at the Valencia road, as well as attacking it from across the River Jarama on the Madrid–Toledo sector. Between the end of November 1936 and March 1937 the Nationalists mounted three major offensives to encircle Madrid; then in July the Republic tried to relieve the pressure on Madrid with the Brunete offensive.

On 29 November 1936 Varela launched the first of a series of attacks on the Corunna road to the north-west of Madrid. The intention was to achieve a breakthrough towards the sierra, before swinging right to the north of the capital. This first attack, mounted with some 3,000 Legion and Moroccan troops, backed by tanks, artillery and Junkers 52 bombers, was directed against the Pozuelo sector. The Republican brigade retreated in disorder, but the line was re-established by a counter-attack backed by T-26s. Both sides then redeployed so as to reinforce their fronts to the west of Madrid.

On the Nationalist side General Orgaz was put in charge of the central front, where a renewed offensive began on 16 December, after a 48-hour delay due to weather conditions. Varela retained the field command with 17,000 men divided into four columns. The first objective, after a heavy bombardment with 155 mm artillery, was the village of Boadilla del Monte, some 15 kilometres (9 miles) west of Madrid. It was captured that night, and the general staff in Madrid, realizing that they faced a major offensive rather than a diversion, sent XI and XII International Brigades, backed by some of Pavlov's T-26 tanks. The XI Brigade counter-attacked at Boadilla, only to find themselves virtually cut off in the village. The Nationalists withdrew to take advantage of such a clearly defined artillery target, and attacked again with their infantry. The International Brigades established defensive positions within the thick walls of country houses belonging to rich *madrileños*. They resisted desperately and on 19 December the slaughter was enormous on both sides. The next day Orgaz halted the offensive, having only gained a few kilometres. He lacked reserves and the Republicans enjoyed numerical superiority.

When Nationalist reinforcements arrived towards the end of December, Orgaz prepared to relaunch his unimaginative offensive along the same axis. During the breathing space the Republican general staff had redeployed their units in the Pozuelo–Brunete sector in a very unco-ordinated manner and without attending to the supply of ammunition. When the Nationalist offensive was relaunched on 3 January, the Republican right flank fell back in disorder. At first the Republican troops on the left managed to hold Pozuelo, in a battle 'which was the most complete chaos'. Koltsov said that 'despite all their heroism, our units suffered from the confusion, stupidity, and perhaps treason in headquarters'. Varela then concentrated most of his eight batteries of 105 and 155 mm artillery, together with his tanks and available air power on the *pueblo*. The Republican defence collapsed and the retreat of Modesto's formation, based on the former 5th Regiment, was virtually a rout. General Miaja gave 10 Brigade the task of disarming all those who fled. The only mitigating factor was the destruction of two companies of German light tanks with the 37 mm guns of Russian armoured cars.

Many Republic units and groups were broken in the retreat, losing all sense of direction in the thick fog. The ammunition supply was appalling. On average only a handful of rounds per man remained while some battalions had run out altogether. The fault lay partly with Miaja and his staff for reacting so slowly to the problem, but mainly with Largo Caballero and officers in the ministry of war in Valencia. Largo replied to Miaja's request for more ammunition with the accusation that he was simply trying to cover up his responsibility for the defeat.

While the whole Republican sector looked as if it were about to collapse, Miaja placed machine-guns at crossroads on the way to Madrid to stop desertion. He ordered in XII International and Líster's Brigade. In addition XIV International Brigade was brought all the way round from the Córdoba front. On 7 January Kléber ordered the Thaelmann battalion to hold the enemy near Las Rozas, telling them 'not to retreat a single centimetre under any circumstances'. In a stand of sacrificial bravery they followed his order to the letter. Only 35 men survived.

When the reinforcements arrived, the front line was eventually stabilized. Both sides were exhausted, and by mid-January the battle was over, the opposing armies having established themselves in defensive positions. The Nationalists had overrun the Corunna road from the edge of Madrid to almost a third of the way to San Lorenzo del Escorial, but the Republic had prevented any encirclement of Madrid from the west flank. Each had suffered around 15,000 casualties in the process.

It is important at this point to understand what fighting in the field was like for the militiamen who had now become part of the Popular Army. The majority were industrial workers who had little experience of the country. Even those who had done military service knew few of the old campaigner's tricks for making life more bearable in general and more durable in battle. Their columns and new 'mixed brigades' were marched or driven out of Madrid in commandeered trucks. Maps were so scarce that they were seldom available at company level and few could read them properly when they were issued. Once at the position which they had been ordered to defend, the soldiers, equipped with little more than a rifle, ammunition pouches and a blanket, started to dig trenches with bayonets and bare hands. They did not bother with latrines, since that would only have meant more digging in the stony Spanish earth and visiting them involved a dangerous journey. In most cases they simply used their trenches, a practice which horrified International Brigaders, accustomed to the First World War idea of digging everything into the ground.

The Castilian winter is renowned for the cold winds coming down off the sierras, and the militias froze in their trenches, often having little more to wear than their boiler suits and rope-soled canvas *alpargatas*, or sandals, which rotted quickly. With mud everywhere it was impossible to keep clean, owing to the lack of water tankers to bring up fresh water and the general scarcity of soap.

In theory each battalion had a machine-gun company in addition to its three rifle companies, but only the International Brigades or picked communist formations had anything approaching the full establishment. Automatic weapons were the key to repulsing frontal attacks, and the Popular Army's lack of them, and of experienced operators, put it at a grave disadvantage. The Moroccan *regulares* became well known as the most effective machine-gunners in the war in addition to their other remarkable ability to use dead ground. The barren terrain in which they had fought the Spanish so successfully in the colonial wars had taught them to take maximum advantage of the slightest fold in the ground. Not only did this reduce their casualties enormously, but together with their reputation for knife-work, it inspired a tremendous fear in Republican troops. Their skill often enabled them to creep in between carelessly sited positions and take the defenders by surprise.

The Nationalist generals, most of whom proved as rigidly conventional as their Republican counterparts, did not make full use of the *regulares*. The majority of the fighting was limited to set-piece offensives, which were often assaults across an open no-man's land, with attack followed by counter-attack. The only discernible difference from First World War tactics was the growing co-ordination between infantry and armour, together with the integration of artillery and air bombardment. This development, however, was almost entirely restricted to the Nationalist side and their Condor Legion advisers.

The new breed of Republican commander emerging at this time was young, aggressive, ruthless and personally brave, but as utterly conventional and unimaginative as the old officers of the metropolitan army. The outstanding examples of this type, such as Modesto and Líster, were communists from the 5th Regiment. Some, like Tagüeña, became communists in the early months of the war, having started in Socialist Youth battalions which had affiliated to the 5th Regiment during the fighting in the sierra the previous summer. Their rigidly traditional approach to tactics and their military formality were strongly influenced by Stalinist orthodoxy. The purging of Marshal Tukhachevsky and his supporters who advocated the new approach to armoured warfare returned communist military theory to the political safety of obsolete tactics. In Russia shoulder-board epaulettes for officers and saluting had been reintroduced, and the 5th Regiment followed suit. The officers of XI International Brigade had even carried swords when it marched up the Gran Vía on 8 November. The exhortation of the new Republican brigades may have been in revolutionary language, but the manœuvring was Tsarist.

After the battle of the Corunna Road Kléber left for Moscow in the company of André Marty, having been relieved of his command. It has been said that jealous Spanish communists made him the scapegoat for the Pozuelo collapse, while others, such as Borkenau, believed that Miaja resented Kléber rivalling him as the hero of Madrid. Whatever the explanation, Kléber had become much less flamboyant when he returned to Spain in June to command a division. Despite the idealized portraits of many foreign journalists, who 'played him up sensationally' as one of them admitted, Kléber never really exceeded the level of a tough First World War commander who was unsparing with the lives of his men.

In between the two parts of the Corunna Road offensive, the Republicans had fought an unsuccessful action in the south when Queipo de Llano's forces advanced to capture the rich olive-growing area of Andújar. It was a singularly inauspicious start for the new XIV International Brigade under General 'Walter', a Polish communist. This brigade included the French Marseillaise battalion, which had an English company. The main action, around a village called Lopera just after Christmas, became famous for the death of the two English communist poets, John Cornford and Ralph Fox, and for a frightening foretaste of International Brigade justice.

The XIV International Brigade was virtually untrained. Like the militia in similar circumstances, most of them turned and ran on being surprised by machine-gun fire. The commanding officer of the Marseillaise battalion, Major Gaston Delasalle, was arrested and accused, not only of incompetence and cowardice, but also of being a 'fascist spy'. He was found guilty by a court martial hastily gathered by André Marty. Ilya Ehrenburg later described Marty as speaking, and occasionally acting, 'like a mentally sick man', and Gustav Regler remarked that Marty preferred to shoot anyone on suspicion, rather than waste time with what he called 'petit bourgeois indecision'. Some Brigaders, however, admired him greatly. 'A true revolutionary,' Sommerfield called him, 'compounded of patience, granite firmness, and absolute unswerving determination.' Tom Wintringham, who later commanded the British battalion, described the proceedings as 'a thoroughly fair court martial'. The interpreter present at the trial described Delasalle's fate. 'He was found guilty, and one comrade just went up behind him and shot him through the head.'

The Nationalists and their Axis backers began to adjust themselves to a protracted war. Hitler was not surprised by the turn of events, informed as he was by accurate assessments from Voelckers, the German *chargé d'affaires.* He was also unperturbed by pessimistic reports from his ambassador, von Faupel, and the Condor Legion commander, von Sperrle, because a long war suited his purposes better. Mussolini, on the other hand, was eager to win military glory in Europe, but his mood fluctuated wildly according to the performance of his troops.

The most urgent task facing Franco's staff was to create a trained army of sufficient size. German assistance in this task was almost as important as their combat contribution. One Wehrmacht officer claimed that 'German soldiers carrying out their duties in exemplary fashion, and in most difficult circumstances, performed discreetly, but effectively, their task of forming the new Spanish army'. The Falangist militia trained by Condor Legion officers at Cáceres in Estremadura bore little resemblance to the gangs of *señoritos* involved in the summer fighting. The Carlist *requetés*, the Nationalists' most effective troops after the Army of Africa, now numbered about 60,000. At least half of them came from Navarre, which led to the Carlist claim that 'Navarre had saved Spain'. This arrogance, combined with open contempt for the Castilian church, which they thought corrupt and pharisaical, did not make them popular with their allies. The famed discipline of the *requetés* derived, not from strong respect for hierarchy, but from the self-discipline of the hill farmer. (Their leader, Fal Conde, exaggerated when he described Carlism as a movement guided from below, but it was a uniquely populist form of royalism.) Their medieval crusading faith made them fearless. Colonel Rada described his *requetés* as men 'with faith in victory, with faith in God; one hand holding a grenade, the other a rosary'.

In early December 1936 the Carlist war council decided to establish a 'Royal Military Academy' to ensure a supply of trained Carlist officers. Franco, jealous of their strength, declared that such an unauthorized move would be considered an act against the Nationalist movement. The war council backed down, and Fal Conde went into exile in Portugal. The Caudillo followed up this victory with a decree which subordinated all political militias to direct army command.

By the end of 1936 the Nationalist army approached 200,000 men, with over half this figure made up by the Carlist and Falangist forces. The Army of Africa was increased to over 60,000 men by early 1937, chiefly as a result of intense recruiting in the Rif. Foreign volunteers also joined the Legion. The largest group was Portuguese, and consisted of about 12,000 men known as the *Viriatos*. There was also a detachment of right-wing French volunteers and 600 Irish blue-shirts under General O'Duffy, but their contribution can be ignored, as they were withdrawn after only one action in which they found themselves attacked by their own side.

In January Franco set up a joint German–Italian general staff as a result of increasing criticism from his allies over the way the war was being conducted. He simply intended it as a sop so as to be able to request more military aid, and implicate his advisers in the responsibility of any reverse.

The Nationalists' most valuable assistance undoubtedly came from the increased German contribution. The Nazi government had reacted quickly in early November to the appearance of Russian weaponry. Hitler evidently did not realize that Stalin was afraid of provoking him and that he was unwilling to let Spanish affairs embarrass Russian foreign policy.

The first contingents of the Condor Legion arrived in Spain in mid-November. General von Sperrle was the commander and Colonel von Richthofen (a cousin of the Red Baron) his second-in-command. They were both Luftwaffe officers, a reflection of the emphasis being placed on the air force. German air power in Spain grew to four fighter squadrons of Heinkel 51 biplanes (to be replaced with Messerschmitt 109s in the early summer of 1937) and four squadrons of Junkers 52 bombers. Other aircraft were sent out later; all the important machines used by the Luftwaffe at the beginning of the Second World War were tested in Spain.

The Wehrmacht reinforcements came under von Thoma's command and included anti-tank and heavy machine-gun detachments, artillery, and the equivalent of two tank battalions. In support there were 20 mm flak batteries and 88 mm anti-aircraft guns. The signals corps, too, was helped with equipment and training. There was a large contingent of engineers and civilian instructors, who later included Gestapo 'advisers', as well as a naval advisory staff, based on the pocket battleships *Deutschland* and *Admiral Scheer*, both of which stayed in western Mediterranean waters. The Condor Legion's total strength was to vary between 5,000 and 10,000 men.

The great increase in Italian aid followed the secret pact signed by Franco on 26 November at Salamanca. The Caudillo agreed to Mussolini's Mediterranean policy in return for military aid 'to restore political and social order in the country'. During the first months of the war the Italian pilots flying the Savoia 81s and Fiat fighters had in theory been attached to the Spanish Foreign Legion, whose uniform they wore. But in his desire for glory Mussolini now wanted an independent command and recognizable Italian formations in the land battles. As a result the CTV (Corps of Volunteer Troops) was organized. Its commander, General Mario Roatta, formerly of Italian military intelligence, had been Admiral Canaris' counterpart. Roatta had already been to Spain at the beginning of the war with the German liaison officer, Colonel Warlimont.

The Italian infantry sent to Spain consisted mainly of fascist militia, many of whom had been drafted or shanghaied. Having been told that they were going to Abyssinia, they arrived in Spain in mid-winter wearing tropical uniforms. The CTV's strength later reached a total of about 50,000 men, but many Spaniards were transferred to their formations and fought under Italian officers. The number of Fiat Ansaldo miniature tanks was greatly increased, but these were little better than closed-in bren-gun carriers. Italian field guns were of good quality, though old, but then artillery has always been the strongest section of Italian military industry. The 'Legionary Air Force', so called to sum up images of imperial Rome, was increased to some 5,000 men. Many more Fiat fighters and Savoia bombers were also sent. Their principal base was Majorca, from where they could attack shipping and, in Ciano's words, 'terrorize Valencia and Barcelona'. This reorganization left Franco's air force commander, General Kindelán, in a similar position to his Republican counterpart, Hidalgo de Cisneros, who, even after he became a communist, was lucky if the Russian General Douglas told him what was happening.

The Málaga campaign, the Italian CTV's first action in Spain, took place while the opposing armies in the Madrid region were preparing for the next round. The southern extremity of the Republican zone was no more than a long strip between sea and mountain, stretching from Motril to within 50 kilometres (30 miles) of Gibraltar. Only the overriding priority given to the assault on Madrid had delayed the Nationalists from attacking it earlier. Quiepo de Llano had grown particularly impatient at what he regarded as a continuing insult to his control of Andalucia. The Nationalist field command was given to a Bourbon prince, Colonel the Duke of Seville. Franco asked Roatta to join this offensive with his 10,000 Fascist militia-men and the Legionary Air Force in close support. It was a clever move, since victory was certain, and Mussolini would therefore be encouraged to continue his aid at a time when he had suddenly become worried about international opinion.

If any campaign was fated to be lost by the Republic it was this one. The terrain and the elongated sector meant that the Nationalists could cut it almost wherever and whenever they wanted. The state of the defence was pitiful, for Málaga had led a revolutionary existence cut off from the reality of the war. Within the town there was strong antagonism between the communists and the CNT, while in the countryside the predominantly anarchist peasants were immersed in their collectives. The mountain range provided a most dangerous sense of security.

The Republican forces consisted of only about 12,000 militiamen, a third of whom had no rifles. There was little ammunition even for those who were armed. This state of affairs was largely the result of the deliberate neglect of the government, which disliked the continuing independence of the province. Largo Caballero is reputed to have said 'not a round more for Málaga'. The performance of Colonel Villalba, the commander, more-over, was unimpressive, although there was probably little he could have done.

The Duke of Seville's offensive began slowly in mid-January with the capture of small pieces of territory. The first major section to be captured was the extreme south-west, including Marbella. Then a small force from Granada occupied a chunk of territory to the north-east of Málaga, endan-gering its communication with Motril, which lay at the exit of the bottle-neck. Yet the attack on Málaga itself in the first week of February still came as a surprise. The Duke of Seville's force advanced up the coast, rolling back the militia detachments with ease; the blackshirt militia under Roatta cut down to the sea; and the Granada force pushed further towards the coast road, although they left this escape route open so as not to provoke resistance. Within three days the Nationalist and Italian forces had entered the outskirts of Málaga, after a naval bombardment by units of the Nation-alist fleet, backed by the *Admiral Graf Spee*. The Republican warships at Cartagena never even left port.

Descriptions of the fleeing civilians and exhausted militiamen along the coast are harrowing. Crazed mothers nursed dead babies and the old and weak died by the roadside. It seemed to Arthur Koestler and Sir Peter Chalmers-Mitchell as if only a few solitary figures were left in the aban-doned landscape of the city. Smoke drifted upwards from houses ruined in the shelling. In the shock of defeat odd militiamen waited apathetically to be put up against a wall. The Nationalist revenge in Málaga was perhaps the most horrific of the war, judging by the British consul's report of

20,000 executions between 1937 and 1944. The prime minister inherited by King Juan Carlos from General Franco in 1975 was, as Hugh Thomas pointed out, the Nationalist prosecutor in Málaga, Carlos Arias Navarro.

The transformation of the militia columns into a formalized army started in earnest in December 1936, and at the beginning of 1937 Republican forces totalled about 320,000 men, although only about half this number were at the various fronts at any one time. These forces were split among the central and southern zone with about 130,000, the three northern zones (Euzkadi, Santander and the Asturias) with over 100,000 and Aragon with about 30,000. The remaining 80,000 or so in rearguard areas included the *asaltos*, the National Republican Guard, formed from loyal civil guards, the *carabinero* frontier police, and the MVR, the Militias of Rearguard Vigilance, which were a government incorporation of irregular forces. The *carabineros* came under Negrín, the minister of finance, who built them up as a personal force to about 40,000 strong. The main reason for lack of precision in army figures is inaccurate reporting, both of ration returns (minor and major frauds were carried out by staff and quartermasters) and of unit strengths (commanding officers sometimes adjusted the figures for personal and political reasons).

These greatly increased figures were achieved mainly by increasing the call-up of the classes of 1933, '34 and '35. It is impossible to gauge what proportion of the intake was prompted by idealism, circumstances, or even hunger, for the rations were considerably better than those which the civilian population enjoyed. An English International Brigader in hospital later observed that the 'local people were so desperate they'd eat what we'd left even if it had been chewed'. Meanwhile, with a mixture of encouragement, manipulation and blackmail, the militias were forced into the command structure already prepared on paper. Columns were turned into battalions and brigades during the winter of 1936. In the spring of 1937 divisions and even army corps started to be formed.

The other development which went ahead rapidly was the practice of attaching commissars to every brigade and battalion headquarters. The commissars' official role was to watch over regular commanders and look after the welfare of the troops. However, Alvarez del Vayo, the foreign minister and secret communist supporter, persuaded Largo Caballero to make him commissar-general, and with his assistance the communists managed to control this powerful branch. By the spring 125 out of 168 battalion commissars were from the Party itself (PCE and PSUC) or from the Joint Socialist Youth.

The *Generalidad* in Catalonia followed the policy of the central government, but at the same time it tried to establish the eastern forces as an independent Catalan army. This was an ambitious policy, intensely disliked by the central government. The communists refrained from criticizing the *Generalidad*, since their policy was to aid Companys' assertion of state power at the expense of the anarchists. Once that was close to being achieved, they would use their Catalan PSUC to help bring the *Generalidad* under central government control.

The militia columns on the Aragon front were reorganized into six under-strength divisions without going through the brigade stage. The conduct of the war on this front, particularly the lack of action, soon became a major cause of tension between the anarchists and the communists. It is true that once the possibility of recapturing the key towns of Saragossa, Teruel and Huesca had diminished, lethargy seemed to descend on the Catalonian militias. Nevertheless, the communist charges (such as the football matches with the enemy, which Hemingway accepted as gospel) were often inaccurate and misleading. They made sure that none of the new equipment went to the Aragon front, certainly no aircraft or tanks, which were reserved for their own troops and were, therefore, concentrated around Madrid. Nor was the numerical superiority of the Republican militias on the Aragon front nearly so high as the communists claimed, for the Nationalists had about 20,000 men between Teruel and the Pyrenees. In addition, some of the best Catalonian troops were helping on the Madrid front, and many of those left behind were armed only with shot-guns. Under such conditions it was unrealistic to expect conventional offensives to be mounted, particularly since XIII International Brigade failed in seven attacks on Teruel.

Even so, anarchist inactivity in a region which they had promised to turn into 'the Spanish Ukraine' was remarkable. Nothing was done by the CNT–FAI leadership to organize guerrilla groups and prosecute a Makhnovista-style campaign, which would have avoided the military conventions which they detested. It is surprising that a man such as García Oliver, who was energetic and imaginative, did not realize that extending enemy forces over wide areas through vigorous guerrilla campaigns would be far less costly in human lives than the slaughter into which they were being inexorably drawn. The Nationalists did not have the troops to fight both an anti-guerrilla campaign in their rear areas and a conventional war at the front. There were, it is true, many guerrilla groups behind enemy lines. But, as will be seen later, a considerable proportion of them were simply refugees from the Nationalist execution squads trying to survive. Nevertheless, there was active resistance in Galicia, León, Estremadura, and Andalucia, where an irregular brigade under the Granadine cabinet-maker Maroto operated.

In a letter to Largo Caballero in December 1936 Stalin advocated the formation of detachments behind enemy lines. Later on, Orlov, who had been a partisan organizer in the Russian civil war, was put in charge of this project along with his secret police responsibilities. After the war he claimed to have trained 1,600 guerrillas in his schools and put 14,000 'regulars' in the field, but the latter figure is probably a gross exaggeration.

The conversion of militia forces into the Popular Army was known as 'militarization' and it was not a smooth process. Those anarchists, *POUM-istas* and left socialists, who defended the militia system on the basis of principle, often refused to see that it could not answer the needs of the situation. A 'military machine' can be defeated only by a better machine or by the sabotage tactics of irregular warfare. The militia fell between the two roles. Their improvisation had been a revolutionary necessity, not a military virtue, and as a force to resist a relatively sophisticated enemy they were utterly obsolete.

The theory used to justify the militia system depended almost entirely on morale, which is only one part in the military mix, and the most vulnerable of all. There were too many anarchists who allowed morale to serve as a substitute for practicality, who did not replace the discipline they rejected with self-discipline and who sometimes let their beliefs degenerate into an ideological justification of inefficiency. But there were others, like Cipriano Mera, who realized that they were now committed to a course of action, which they had to pursue even if it conflicted with their ideals. More and more anarchists came to accept this during the autumn and winter of 1936. They were alarmed by the increase in communist power, but they knew that they faced a war of survival.

There were two main stumbling blocks in the process of militarization. One was the principle of 'unified command', which worried the anarchists and the POUM because they feared the communists, even though they came to recognize its necessity in conventional war. The other was the imposition of traditional military discipline. The POUM wanted soldiers' councils like those formed in the Russian revolution, an idea which horrified the communists, while the anarchists were split among themselves. Mera emphasized on several occasions that the instinct of self-preservation had proved itself too strong to be controlled solely by individual willpower in the unnatural atmosphere of the 'noise of artillery, the rattle of machine-guns, and the whistle of bombs'. On the other hand, one militia representative said that 'if the success of the war depends on there being a man armed with a pistol behind every seven or eight comrades, we can state right away that we've lost'. Others, such as one Iberia column delegate, did not object to discipline of itself: 'We accept an iron discipline; we'll shoot those who leave the front; we accept a single command structure; but we don't accept that someone sitting behind a table will command us while avoiding the danger.'

The anarchists' beliefs usually made them extremely reluctant to accept any form of command, which of course made them vulnerable. (This was not new; in 1917 Trotsky became head of the Petrograd soviet when Voline refused the post on the grounds of anarchist principle.)

The conflicts between the anarchists and the military hierarchy were solved by a series of compromises. Saluting, the formal term of address and officers from outside were rejected by the anarchists, and delegates they had already elected were confirmed with the equivalent rank. (As only regular officers could become colonels, militia column commanders remained majors.) The problem over pay differentials was usually solved by officers contributing everything they earned above a militiaman's wage to the CNT war fund. Collado of the Durruti column described the compromise as 'not militarization, but a military type of structure'.

It was inevitable that many people were forced to alter their attitudes in the winter of 1936. In less than six months an attempted *coup d'état* had turned, first into a full-scale civil war, and then into a world war by proxy. On 31 December 1936 Nationalist artillery opposite Madrid rang in the new year by dropping 12 shells into the Puerta del Sol on the stroke of midnight. The Caudillo was said to have been angered by this unprofessional levity. Nevertheless, even such a career-minded general as Franco could not have liked the words of Captain von Goss of the Condor Legion: 'No longer in the spring of 1937 could one talk merely of the *Spanish* war. It had become a real war.'

THE JARAMA AND GUADALAJARA OFFENSIVES

In the second half of January 1937, immediately after the bloody stalemate of the Corunna Road, Franco started to plan yet another operation against Madrid. The stubborn side to his character would not let go the idea of taking the capital before spring, but, although his strategy of a pincer attack to the east of Madrid was sound, he did not follow it.

The front ran southwards from Madrid along the line of the road to Aranjuez, and a new offensive was planned in the centre of this sector, thrusting north-eastwards across the River Jarama to cut the Valencia road. This was to be accompanied by an attack of the Italian CTV under Roatta, which would strike down towards Guadalajara from the northern part of the Nationalist zone. These two assaults did not coincide because the bad weather in January had delayed the Italian troops involved in the Málaga campaign, so that they had no chance of being in position by the first week of February. But Mola and Franco decided to launch the Jarama offensive without waiting.

Franco was slow in appreciating how the war had changed in the last few months and that his best troops could not put the Republican forces to flight as they had done in the previous autumn. It was no longer a war of rapid manœuvre, but of head-on slogging, and as a result the advantage of his troops' fieldcraft and tactical skill was greatly reduced. Even the increase in air and artillery support was not enough to ensure victory, especially since the Russian Rata made the Heinkel 51 obsolete. Delivery of the new Messerschmitt 109 to the Condor Legion was accelerated, but the first models did not arrive until March. In any case, the Republican forces were already better prepared to survive air or artillery bombardment.

General Mola was in supreme command, General Orgaz the commander of the front and once again Varela was the field commander. He had five brigades of six battalions each, with a further 11 battalions in reserve, totalling some 25,000 men. They were backed by two German heavy machine-gun battalions, von Thoma's tanks, six batteries of 155 mm artillery, and the 88 mm guns of the Condor Legion which were to be battle-tested for the first time. Colonel García Escámez commanded the brigade on the right flank, by Ciempozuelos near Aranjuez. Colonel Rada was on

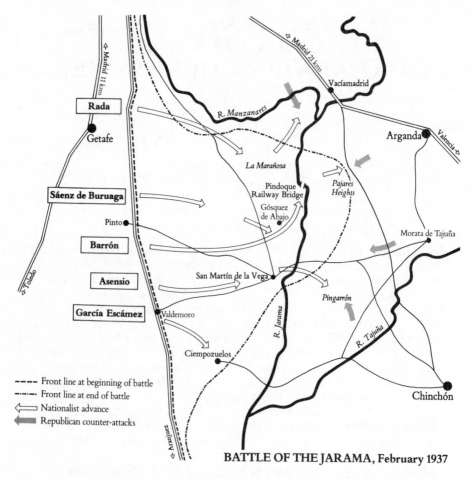

BATTLE OF THE JARAMA, February 1937

---- Front line at beginning of battle
----- Front line at end of battle
⇐ Nationalist advance
⬅ Republican counter-attacks

the left or northern flank which was bounded by the River Manzanares as
it flows eastwards to join the Jarama. In the centre were the brigades of
Asensio, Barrón and Sáenz de Buruaga with an axis of advance towards
Arganda. The majority of the troops were Moroccan *regulares* and legionnaires. Rada also had a Carlist regiment, and Barrón 10 squadrons of
cavalry.

The Republican general staff were also planning an offensive in this
sector, but jealousies between General Miaja in Madrid and General Pozas
commanding the Army of the Centre had held it up. Even so, the Republic
mustered some 50 battalions in the area, making the opposing infantry
forces roughly level.

When heavy rain stopped on 5 Febuary, Mola gave the order for the
attack to begin the next morning. On the left Rada's force assaulted La
Marañosa, a hill almost 700 metres (2,300 ft) high which was defended to
the end by two Republican battalions. Five kilometres (3 miles) to the
south, Sáenz de Buruaga's brigade took the hamlet of Gózquez de Abajo,
only one kilometre short of the River Jarama. Asensio's brigade thrust
eastwards from Valdemoro and overran San Martín de la Vega, while

152

García Escámez's force captured Ciempozuelos after heavy fighting in which the defending 18 Brigade lost 1,300 men. By the morning of the 8th the Nationalists controlled most of the west bank of the Jarama, and on the following day Rada's men occupied the high ground in the loop formed by the confluence of the Manzanares and the Jarama opposite Vaciamadrid. Varela's strategy was correct in allocating the Rada and García Escámez brigades to secure his flanks, but the remaining three columns in the centre proved too small a force to ensure a breakthrough.

The Nationalist offensive was held up for the next two days because heavy rain had made the Jarama unfordable. On 11 February at first light, Moroccan troops from Barrón's brigade knifed the French sentries of the André Marty battalion (XIV International Brigade) who were guarding the Pindoque railway bridge between Vaciamadrid and San Martín de la Vega. The bridge had been prepared for demolition and the charges were detonated just after its capture, but the metal construction, which was similar to a Bailey bridge, went up in the air a few feet, and came down to rest again. Barrón's brigade, followed by Sáenz de Buruaga's troops, crossed rapidly, but they were then held up for some time by heavy fire from the Garibaldi battalion on high ground above it. Later in the day 25 T-26s counter-attacked twice, but each time they were driven back by the Nationalist 155 mm batteries on La Marañosa. Downstream, Asensio's *regulares* captured the bridge at San Martín de la Vega in a similar attack at dawn the next morning, despite Varela's order to wait until the other bridgehead was established. His brigade then swung south-east towards the high ground at Pingarrón, which like other key features in the area had not been prepared for defence.

General Pozas, the Republican commander of the Army of the Centre, had immediately hurried to Arganda to organize a counter-attack. Matters were not helped by his squabble with Miaja, whose chief-of-staff, Colonel Casado, described their differences as 'fundamentally childish'. Miaja refused to send the five brigades he had available to join the battle unless he was given command of the front. He had his way, but by then the Nationalists were across the river in strength, despite air attacks against the two crossing points, in which the Chato fighter squadrons suffered heavy losses from the Condor Legion's 88 mm guns.

On 12 February Asensio's troops captured the commanding feature of Pingarrón, while to the north XI International and 17 Brigade just held on at Pajares. The newly formed XV International Brigade was thrown into the breach on the San Martín–Morata road to face Sáenz de Buruaga's troops. They consisted of a British battalion, commanded by Tom Wintringham, the Dimitrov battalion and a Franco–Belgian battalion. The American battalion was being hurried through induction at Albacete to be ready to reinforce them.

The British bore the brunt of the attack on the south of the road and lost over half their men in capturing, and then defending, 'Suicide Hill'. The French '6th of February' battalion on their right was forced back, without warning, allowing the British machine-gun company to be captured by a group of *regulares* from the exposed flank. 'Suicide Hill' could be held no longer, and the whole brigade had to fall back. But a breakthrough in the centre had been prevented, because the Nationalists believed

Republican forces to be much stronger than they were, and did not discover the weakness on XV International Brigade's southern flank.

Meanwhile, on its right flank, the brigade's own Dimitrov battalion of Balkan exiles and the reformed Thaelmann battalion of XI International held off an equally severe attack. Very heavy casualties were inflicted on the *regulares* until the old Colt machine-guns jammed. In the rolling hills and olive groves to the east of the Jarama between Pajares and Pingarrón, attack followed attack throughout 13 February, as Varela became desperate to achieve his breakthrough. Eventually the Edgar André battalion of XI International Brigade was forced back as a result of fire from a Condor Legion machine-gun battalion and 155 mm bombardment from La Marañosa. The shell-fire also destroyed brigade headquarters, and cut all field telephone lines to the rear. Barrón's column took advantage of this gap at Pajares, and his attack turned the right flank of XV International Brigade. Since the other Nationalist formations had already been fought to a standstill, Barrón's troops pushed on alone towards Arganda on the Valencia road. The front was on the point of disintegrating on the night of the 13th, as XI International Brigade and its flanking formations fell back trying to re-establish a line. Varela was worried by the fact that Barrón's brigade was exposed, so he ordered him to halt until the other columns could protect his flanks. It was to be the furthest limit of their advance, for the next day 50 of Pavlov's T-26s counter-attacked in what could best be described as a confused charge of mechanized heavy cavalry. Although not a success in itself, this attack gave the Republicans enough time to bring forward reserve units to consolidate the centre of the sector.

Mola was by now extremely concerned at the way the offensive had halted. He, too, was obsessed with the idea of Madrid, and he had persuaded Franco to let him commit the last six battalions in reserve, but these units could not even replace the losses which the columns had suffered. Both sides had fought to a temporary standstill. Front-line troops had suffered fearful casualties in charges of hopeless bravery. And, because the intensity of the fighting had often prevented the arrival of rations, both sides were weakened by hunger. The Republican general staff had reacted so slowly to the crisis that fresh units were not in position to take advantage of the Nationalists' exhaustion by counter-attacking. The only reinforcement available at this point was XIV International Brigade, which consolidated the centre of the sector between Arganda and Morata.

On 15 February Franco ordered Orgaz to continue the advance, despite Nationalist losses. It was an obstinate and unjustifiable decision, since the Italian forces were regrouping for transfer to the Guadalajara front. Any further push should have at least been co-ordinated with their offensive. The Nationalists lost more of their best troops for an insignificant gain in ground. Also, on the same day, Miaja's control over the front came officially into effect. With Colonel Rojo he reorganized the Republican formations into four divisions. On 17 February the Republican forces went on to the offensive. Líster's 11 Division moved on Pingarrón in a frontal attack which brought appalling casualties; 70 Brigade, attached from Mera's 14 Division, lost 1,100 men, over half its strength. On the same day Modesto's division crossed the Manzanares from the north to attack La Marañosa, which was defended by Rada's Carlists. A communist battalion called the 'Grey Wolves of La Pasionaria' was shot to pieces in a doomed attack over a long stretch of open ground. Peter Kemp, an English volunteer serving as a Carlist subaltern, records how his aim was not helped by their chaplain screaming in his ear to shoot more of the atheist rabble.

The only effective part of the Republican counter-attack forced Barrón's brigade back to the Chinchón–Madrid road. Little then happened for the next 10 days, until General Gal threw his newly formed division into an impossible attack on Pingarrón. His orders stated that it 'must be taken at any cost', and he persisted with the attack even though the air and tank support, which had been promised, never arrived. Once again both Brigaders and Spanish troops were paying for the deficiencies of their commanders and staff.

The tight political control of ambitious commissars made propaganda motives interfere with military sense. There were a few extremely competent officers, like the French Colonel Putz, or the English Major Nathan (who was not promoted because he refused to become a Party member), but most senior officers bluffed their way through, relying on rigid discipline. Often their decisions resulted in massive casualties for little purpose. Their bravely dramatic orders like 'stand and die' or 'not a centimetre's retreat', when ammunition was exhausted, sounded well in the propaganda accounts, but it was not the staff who suffered from them. One of the most tragic episodes involved the men of the Lincoln battalion, who had arrived in the middle of February fresh in their 'doughboy' uniforms. They were put under the command of an English charlatan who pretended to have been an officer in the 11th Hussars. He ordered them into attack after attack, losing 120 men out of 500. The Americans mutinied, nearly lynched the Walter Mitty character who had been imposed on them, and refused to go back into the line until they could elect their own commander. Soon after these last attacks at the end of February, the front stabilized, because both sides were now completely exhausted. The Valencia road had not been cut, and the Nationalists had suffered heavy losses among their best troops. (It would seem that casualties were roughly equal on both sides, although estimates varied from 6,000 up to 20,000.)

The battle of Jarama had seen the beginning of close liaison between air and ground forces. The Nationalists used the Condor Legion Junkers 52 to counter the T-26 attack on the Pindoque bridge and Modesto's advance on La Marañosa. The Republican air force managed to maintain an effective umbrella for most of the early days of the battle, but after 13 February their supremacy was challenged by the Fiat CR 32s of the Nationalists, which engaged the Chatos in a large-scale dogfight over Arganda. Five days later the 'Blue Patrol' Fiat group, led by the Nationalist ace, Morato, was transferred to the front. Together with Fiats of the Legionary Air Force they inflicted heavy losses on a Republican group comprising a Chato squadron with a flight of American volunteers, a Russian Chato squadron, and a Russian Rata squadron. It would appear that the Russian pilots were ordered to act with great caution as a result of this engagement.

After digging in, this second stalemate became a monotonous existence in the damp olive groves. It was a life of rain-filled trenches, congealed stew, occasional deaths from odd bursts of firing, and useless attempts to get rid of lice in the seams of clothes. The commissars attempted to keep up morale with organized political 'discussions', and by distributing pamphlets or Party newspapers. The lack of fighting also brought to the International Brigades at the front such diversely famous visitors as Stephen Spender, Henri Cartier-Bresson, Professor J. B. S. Haldane and Errol Flynn.

The events of recent months, especially the fall of Málaga, provoked dissension within the government over the handling of the war. The communists led a determined attack on General Asensio Torrado, the undersecretary of war, whose conduct Largo Caballero had successfully defended against criticism the previous October. (Earlier the communists had tried to flatter Asensio Torrado as the 'hero of the democratic republic', but he rejected their advances and took measures against them, such as insisting on an inquiry into irregularities in their 5th Regiment's accounts and trying to stop their infiltration of the *asaltos*.) Alvarez del Vayo openly supported the communist ministers, thus finally ending his friendship with the prime minister. The anarchist ministers did nothing to help the general because they felt he had consistently discriminated against their troops; the republicans and right socialists also disliked him, mainly because of Largo's obsessive reaction to any criticism of his chosen subordinate. The general was finally removed on 21 February. His place was filled by the socialist, Carlos de Baráibar, a close colleague of Largo Caballero. The communists were disappointed not to have one of their own men appointed.

The political in-fighting over Asensio Torrado at Valencia came immediately after the power struggle already mentioned between Miaja and Pozas. Having increased his responsibilities to include both the Jarama and Guadalajara fronts, Miaja was to have overall command during the largest battles of the first year of the civil war, including the only Republican victory, Guadalajara.

Franco's decision to continue with the second half of the pincer operation was as unjustifiable as launching the Jarama offensive on its own. Varela's troops were supposed to recommence their advance, but the Nationalist forces on the Jarama front were incapable of recreating any momentum. It may be that Franco continued with the operation in response to the misplaced optimism of the Italians after the Málaga walkover. The advance was to be almost entirely an Italian affair.

General Roatta now had some 35,000 men in General Coppi's Black Flames, General Nuvolini's Black Arrows, General Rossi's *Dio lo vuole* Division, and General Bergonzoli's *Littorio* Division. The last had regular officers and conscripts; the other formations contained fascist militia. This force of motorized infantry was supported by four companies of Fiat Ansaldo miniature tanks, 160 field guns, and four squadrons of Fiat CR 32 fighters, which poor visibility and water-logged airfields were to render virtually non-operational. Mussolini's appetite for military victory pushed on the officers commanding these 'involuntary volunteers' whom he had now managed to have concentrated in an independent command.

The Republican general staff appears to have been aware of the growing threat to the Guadalajara sector on the Madrid–Saragossa road, but only one company of T-26 tanks was sent to reinforce the thinly spread and inexperienced 12 Division under Colonel Lacalle. On 8 March, at first

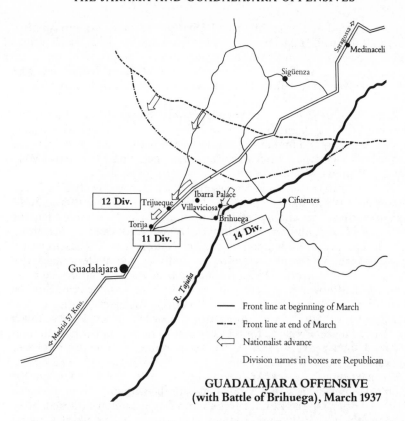

GUADALAJARA OFFENSIVE
(with Battle of Brihuega), March 1937

light, Coppi's motorized Black Flames Division, led by armoured cars and
Fiat Ansaldos, smashed straight through the Republican lines in the
schwerpunkt manner. On their right the 2nd Brigade of the Soria Division
commanded by the recently promoted Alcázar defender, General Moscardó,
also broke the Republican front, but they were on foot and soon fell
behind. During that day fog and sleet reduced visibility down to 100 metres
(110 yards) in places. Bad weather continued on the 9th and the Italians
allowed their attack to slow down while they widened the breach in the
Republican front. Then that night they stopped to rest because their men
were cold and tired (many of their militia were still in tropical uniforms).
This break in the momentum of the attack was incompatible with *blitzkrieg*
tactics and was all the more serious since there was no co-ordinated attack
on the Jarama front. English and French strategists (with the notable
exceptions of Liddell Hart and Charles de Gaulle) were to point to the
Guadalajara offensive as proof that an armoured thrust was a worthless
strategy. The Germans, on the other hand, knew that it had not been
followed properly and that the Italian forces were ill-trained for such a
manœuvre in the first place.

Reacting more rapidly to the threat than they had at the Jarama, Miaja
and Rojo rushed in reinforcements and reorganized the command structure. Colonel Jurado was ordered to form IV Corps based on Guadalajara.
Under his command he had Líster's division astride the main Madrid-

157

Saragossa road at Torija, Mera's 14 Division on the right, opposite Brihuega, and Lacalle's 12 Division on the left. Colonel Lacalle was furious at being passed over in favour of Jurado, but few people were impressed by this professional officer. The Russian adviser, Colonel Rodimstev, who visited the front just before the offensive began, was horrified by what he saw.

After three days of battle, Lacalle claimed he was ill and the Italian communist, Nino Nanetti, was given his command. There was a large degree of foreign communist control at headquarters and Jurado's staff was closely supervised by Russian advisers, including Meretskov, Malinovsky, Rodimstev and Voronov.

On 10 February the Black Flames and Black Arrows reached Brihuega almost unopposed and occupied the old walled town. In the afternoon the Italian Garibaldi battalion of XII International Brigade was moved up the road from Torija, and one of their patrols came across an advance group of their fellow countryment fighting for the Nationalists. The fascist patrol spoke to them, and went back to report that they had made contact with elements of the Littorio Division which was advancing astride the main road. Soon afterwards a fascist column led by Fiat Ansaldos came up the road from Brihuega assuming the way to Torija was open. An Italian civil war then began, later concentrating around a nearby country house called the Ibarra Palace. Prepared for the propaganda opportunity, the communists used loudspeakers to urge the fascist militia to join their brother workers.

The next day the Black Arrows pushed Líster's troops back down the main road, but the advance was halted with the help of tank support just short of Torija. On the 12th the Republican forces counter-attacked. They were greatly aided by having a concrete runway at Albacete, where General Douglas directed operations. Nearly 100 Chato and Rata fighters, as well as two squadrons of Katiuska bombers, harried the Italians while they were pushed back in the centre by counter-attacks supported by Pavlov's T-26 tanks and some of the faster BT-5s. The Legionary Air Force Fiats could not get off the ground to support them because of water-logged runways, and the Italian forces withdrew down the Saragossa road and back into Brihuega. General Roatta then proceeded to change the positions of his motorized divisions, a complicated manœuvre which resulted in many vehicles becoming stuck in the heavy mud, where they were easy targets for the strafing fighters.

The next day, 13 February, IV Corps started to prepare for a major counter-offensive, while the Republic's representatives protested to the League of Nations and the Non-Intervention Committee with documentary proof from prisoners of the presence of Italian formations. The Republican plan was straightforward. Líster's division and all available tanks were to be concentrated on the Saragossa road, while Mera's 14 Division was to cross the River Tajuña from the south-east bank and assault Brihuega. Franco's chief of operations, Colonel Barroso, warned the Italians that Republican forces might attack their flank in this way, but he was ignored. Nevertheless, Mera's preparations for the offensive were not without problems. He had placed a battalion of *carabineros* by the river to guard a small bridge prepared for demolition by his *dinamiteros*, in case the enemy made a further attempt to advance, but their commanding officer blew it up despite his orders. A serious setback was avoided only because Mera was helped by local CNT members acting as spies and scouts who were able to advise him of the best places to throw a pontoon bridge across the swollen river. At dawn on the morning of 18 February his division crossed the pontoon bridge and occupied the heights above Brihuega. Heavy sleet shielded them from the enemy's view, but it also caused the general offensive to be delayed. Mera had no alternative but to keep the division lying in the wet with instructions not to fire and hope that the Italians would not discover them. The weather did not start to clear until after midday; only then did the Chato and Katiuska squadrons become operational.

At the beginning of the afternoon Jurado gave the order to attack. Líster's division moved up the main road behind the T-26s. His troops were facing Bergonzoli's Littorio Division of regular troops, which was undoubtedly the best of the Italian formations. On the Republican right flank Mera's division had nearly managed to surround Brihuega when the enemy fled in panic. Total disaster for the Italians was prevented by the fall of darkness, by the Littorio Division's well-conducted retreat on the main road, and by the CTV's wealth of transport. Even so, the campaign cost them around 5,000 men and a considerable quantity of material.

Being the only clear Republican victory of the war, the 'Battle of Brihuega' became a propaganda trophy. The communists claimed that the town was captured by El Campesino's brigade, and even added several anecdotal touches. In fact El Campesino arrived alone at dusk on a motorcycle and was fired at by outlying pickets of 14 Division. He raced back to report that the town was still in enemy hands. Considering that Líster's division was supposed to be advancing up the Saragossa road, El Campesino had no official reason for being anywhere near Brihuega. The communist version of events was dropped in later years after he was disgraced during his Russian exile and sent to a labour camp.

Since Moscardó's troops had suffered very few casualties, Franco's officers refused to see the engagement as a Nationalist defeat. They were scathing about their allies' performance, and composed a song ending 'the retreat was a dreadful thing; one Italian even arrived in Badajoz'. The failure of the Guadalajara offensive was excellent for Republican morale, but it was not the turning-point which the Republic and its supporters abroad tried to portray. The only certain consequence was that Franco had to abandon his obsession with entering Madrid quickly and adopt a long-term strategy. After the heavy casualties suffered at the Jarama, German advisers were able to argue more strongly for a programme of reducing vulnerable Republican territories first. The most attractive target was undoubtedly the industrial and mining region of the north.

XVII

THE WAR IN THE NORTH

The beleaguered northern zone of Republican territory had been left untouched by the centralization carried out by Largo Caballero's government. The councils of Asturias and Santander still reflected the union-based organization which followed the rising, while the Basques regarded themselves as autonomous allies of the Republic. Although Basque volunteer units had fought at Oviedo, and Asturian and Santanderino militia helped in Vizcaya, the northern regions were not united, except in their objection to a centralized Republican command. The Basques, in particular, rejected the idea that the 'Army of Euzkadi' should simply be part of the Army of the North, commanded ultimately from Valencia. Largo agreed to this without telling General Llano de la Encomienda, the army commander.

On 1 October 1936 the statute of Basque autonomy had come before the Cortes sitting in Valencia. It took effect four days later. On 7 October the municipal councillors of the region met under the oak tree of Guernica, 'the sacred city of the Basques', in accordance with their ancient customs. The purpose of this meeting was to elect a president. The proceedings had been kept secret in case of air attack, and this small country town to the east of Bilbao was unmolested as José Antonio Aguirre swore his oath in the Basque language.

Afterwards he named his government, which included four members of the Basque Nationalist Party, three socialists, two republicans, a communist and a member of the social-democratic Basque Action. The Basque Nationalist Party, or PNV, whose motto was 'God and our old laws', controlled the ministries of defence, finance, justice and the interior. The minister of the interior was a young aristocrat, Telesforo Monzón, who some 40 years later became the leader of *Herri Batasuna*, the political front of the ETA guerrilla organization. His first move was to disband the civil guard and the *asaltos*. Then he started to recruit his new police force among Basque-speaking supporters. They were heavily armed, selected for their height, and dressed in shiny, leather uniforms. This elite corps, the *Ertzana*, under the sole control of the PNV, was hardly reassuring to some of their left-wing allies, particularly the anarcho-syndicalist CNT.

Friction, however, came less from political than military differences.

The CNT had shown in its furious assaults on the rebel-held buildings in San Sebastián during the rising, in its burning of Irún when it was almost surrounded by the Nationalists and later in its intention to lay waste to San Sebastián before Mola's troops occupied it, that it wished to fight a war to the finish. The CNT stated openly its preference for dying in the ruins rather than submitting to Franquist rule. The Basques, in line with the character of a mountain people, were content simply to defend themselves when directly attacked. They even had their symbolic Maloto tree on the border marking the point beyond which their forces should never advance. The Basque nationalists made it clear from the beginning of the civil war that, apart from their anti-fascist feelings, they were on the side of the Republic because it promised them autonomy. They proudly proclaimed their Catholic faith and attacked the anti-clericalism in other parts of Republican territory. Nevertheless, their resistance to the military rising was supported by the great majority of their priests in spite of the unqualified backing of the Vatican and the Spanish church for General Franco.

The Basque nationalists also pretended that there were no class divisions in Euzkadi. This had been true of the agricultural side of Basque life, where feudalism had only existed in southern Navarre. But the seafaring side was scarcely classless, and then, in the nineteenth century, industrialization attracted cheap labour from Castile, Galicia and Asturias. It was from this non-Basque workforce that the membership of the socialist UGT, the CNT and the Communist Party was largely recruited (indigenous workers were represented by the STV, Solidarity of Basque Workers).

The left believed fervently that the Nationalists must be defeated. The Basque nationalists, on the other hand, seemed to know in their hearts that the Republicans would be defeated. Many of their leaders had been brought up by English nannies (Castilian families tended to have *fräuleins*) and educated in England. It may be that they learned the idea of being good losers from the English. At any rate, they treated their prisoners extremely well, sending many to France for release in the hope that this might induce the enemy to be a good winner. To paraphrase Bosquet, it was admirable, but it was not the Spanish civil war. The Nationalists made no reciprocal gestures to this attempt at 'humanizing the war', as Manuel de Irujo, the Basque minister in the central government called it. They merely stepped up their campaign of hate, using such self-contradictory phrases as 'soviet-separatists' to describe the Basques. Having the Catholic Basques as enemies was an embarrassment to the Nationalist crusade and Franco was later to attack 'these christian democrats, less christian than democrat, who, infected by a destructive liberalism, did not manage to understand this sublime page of religious persecution in Spain which, with its thousands of martyrs, is the most glorious the Church has suffered'. The archbishop of Burgos called Basque priests 'the dross of the Spanish clergy, in the pay of the reds'. The professor of moral theology at Salamanca, having described 'the armed rising against the Popular Front' as 'the most holy war in history', said 'all who positively oppose the National government in present circumstances, trying to weaken its strength or diminish its power or obstruct its role, should be considered as traitors to the fatherland, infidels to religion and criminals to humanity'. Cardinal Archbishop Gomá accused the Basque clergy of taking part in the fighting.

Even though most modern military chaplains carry sidearms to protect the wounded, it would appear that only a few, if any, Basque priests were given a pistol, and there is no evidence that they used them. The primate also chose to overlook the fanatical Carlist chaplains on his own side. Many of these *requeté* almoners, purple tassles hanging from their large red berets, were in the tradition of the ferocious nineteenth-century Carlist priest, Santa Cruz, who used to absolve his prisoners *en masse* before shooting them. It was the Navarrese Carlists who were chosen as the main instrument to reduce their Basque neighbours in the spring of 1937.

There had been two major areas of action on the northern front during the winter. The fierce siege of Oviedo continued and a Basque offensive was mounted against Villarreal on 30 November 1936, when General Llano de la Encomienda secretly assembled 19 infantry battalions, six batteries of artillery and some armoured vehicles.

A breakthrough to capture Vitoria might have been achieved if they had not been spotted by a Nationalist reconnaissance aircraft from Burgos. The Nationalists counter-attack prevented the capture of Villarreal, but the Basques were left in control of the three mountains, Maroto, Albertia and Jacinto, whose peaks they proceeded to fortify. Establishing uncamouflaged defensive positions on peaks was to be one of their most serious mistakes. The Basques did not appreciate the ground-attack capabilities of fighters or the effects of bombing.

The isolated northern zone was the logical military target for the Nationalists after four unsuccessful attempts to cut short the war by capturing Madrid. The German advisers put strong pressure on Franco to change his strategy; not only would a longer war help Hitler's plans in central Europe, but they were also interested in obtaining the steel and coal of the Cantabrian coastal region for their accelerating armaments programme. In any case, Franco could not muster sufficient troops to mount a decisive offensive around the capital where the Republic had the advantage of interior lines as well as numbers. The only way to improve the ratio of forces was to crush a weaker sector first in order to release troops for the tougher objectives in the centre. As both the Aragon and Andalucian fronts could be reinforced by the Republicans fairly rapidly, the northern zone was the obvious choice.

To resist this threat, the Basque nationalists and their left-wing allies had raised some 46 battalions, of which about half were Basque militia, the Euzko-Gudaroztea, the rest UGT, CNT, communist or republican units. (Many Basques were shocked by the idea of women fighting in some of the left-wing ranks.) These formations were reinforced by 10 battalions from Asturias and Santander who did not get on well with the local population. The general staff under Llano de la Encomienda consisted of professional officers, none of whom seem to have been either energetic or efficient. The greatest liability, however, was the shortage of weapons.

At the beginning of the war Telesforo Monzón's trip to Barcelona had produced only limited supplies. Other means had to be used. The gold reserves in the Bank of Spain were seized. Weapons were purchased abroad, or even stolen, and smuggled back by fishing vessels through the Nationalist blockade or brought on English ships. Some larger ships still managed to get through in the late autumn after the Republican battleship

Jaime I had left the area. One of these was the Russian *A. Andreu*, which brought the Basques two squadrons of Chatos, 30 tanks (T-26 and Renaults) and 14 Russian armoured cars with 37 mm cannon. Food was also a major worry with seldom more than two weeks' supply. The monotonous and sparse diet of chickpeas was all that separated the Basques from starvation. There were few cats left alive in the Basque country and ingenious methods of catching seagulls were tried.

The Nationalist naval force off the Cantabrian coast consisted of the battleship *España*, the cruiser *Almirante Cervera* and the destroyer *Velasco*. The Basques had only an ancient destroyer and two scarcely serviceable submarines. They, therefore, improvised by mounting 101 mm guns from the battleship *Jaime I* on four deep-sea fishing vessels.

On 5 March the Nationalist cruiser *Canarias* was spotted off the mouth of the River Nervión with a small vessel which she had captured. Basque 105 mm and 155 mm shore batteries opened fire immediately to drive her off; they knew that armed trawlers, escorting a boat from Bayonne, were due. When they appeared out of the mist, the *Canarias* left her prize to engage them. One of the trawlers, the *Bizkaya*, nipped round the *Canarias* and made off with her prize while the other two replied to her 8-inch guns with their much smaller armament. The *Guipuzkoa* caught fire and had to make for the shelter of the shore batteries, but the crew of the *Nabara* continued the attack and fought into the night until all ammunition was used and the trawler sunk. This incident, reminiscent of Tennyson's *The Revenge*, was commemorated in an epic poem by Cecil Day-Lewis.

In mid-March the Nationalist commanding general, Emilio Mola, issued his preliminary orders for the campaign. His chief-of-staff, Colonel Vigón,

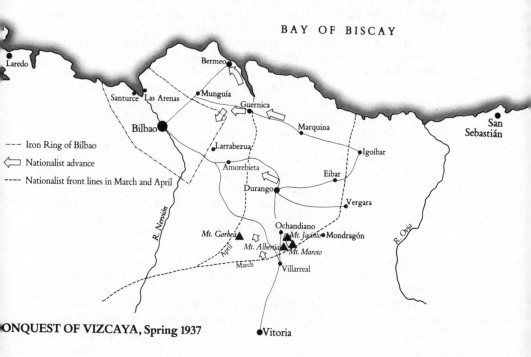

BAY OF BISCAY

---- Iron Ring of Bilbao

⇐ Nationalist advance

---- Nationalist front lines in March and April

ONQUEST OF VIZCAYA, Spring 1937

was the most capable planner in the Nationalist army and one of the few senior officers to be respected by his German colleagues. However, even Vigón could do little to overcome Mola's excessive caution.

The Nationalist force was based on the Navarre Division of four Carlist brigades. In addition, there was the Black Arrows Division with 8,000 Spanish infantry commanded by Italian officers and supported by Fiat Ansaldos. In this mountainous region, however, the Condor Legion was to prove the Nationalists' biggest advantage. Mola realized that the thin coastal strip allowed the defenders little warning of raids, while the terrain greatly restricted their choice of airfields from which defending fighters could be scrambled. The Basques had only a minute fighter force, so the Condor Legion was able to risk using obsolete Heinkel 51s as ground-attack aircraft while waiting for more of the new Messerschmitts to arrive.

The Condor Legion fighter wing was concentrated at Vitoria, the bomber squadrons at Burgos. General Sperrle stayed with Franco's GHQ at Salamanca leaving Colonel Wolfgang von Richthofen as the operational commander of the strike forces. On the northern front these consisted of three squadrons of Junkers 52 bombers, an 'experimental squadron' of Heinkel 111 medium bombers, three squadrons of Heinkel 51 fighters and half a squadron of Messerschmitt 109s. The Italian Legionary Air Force also flew missions in support of troop attacks, with Savoia Marchetti 81s and 79s as well as their CR 32 fighters.

After issuing his ultimatum that 'if submission is not immediate I will raze Vizcaya to the ground', Mola ordered an advance from the south-east. The offensive opened on 31 March with an assault on the three mountains – Albertia, Maroto and Jacinto – which had been taken by the Basques in the Villarreal offensive the previous year. The Nationalists showed in this first day that they meant to make use of their crushing superiority in the air. The town of Durango, behind the front line, was bombed in relays by the heavy Junkers 52s. It had no air defences nor any form of military presence. A church was bombed during the celebration of mass, killing 14 nuns, the officiating priest and most of the congregation. Heinkel 51 fighters then strafed fleeing civilians. Altogether, some 250 non-combatants died in the attack. The objective of the raid appears to have been to block the roads through the town with rubble, though that does not explain the activities of the fighters. General Queipo de Llano stated on Seville radio that 'our planes bombed military objectives in Durango, and later communists and socialists locked up the priests and nuns, shooting without pity and burning the churches'.

The other objectives that day included the three mountains, and bombing raids were combined with an artillery barrage just before the Navarrese troops went into the attack. The Basque militiamen, known as *gudaris*, hardly knew what had hit them before they were overrun by red-bereted Carlists screaming their war cry of *'¡Viva Cristo Rey!'* Reserves could not be brought up because of air strikes on all communications leading to the front. The artillery barrage had also cut field telephone wires from the forward positions.

The Basque counter-attack on Mount Gorbea was successful, and they were to hold it for another eight weeks, thus securing their extreme right flank. But two other mountains were lost the next day, while the air attacks on and around the town of Ochandiano smashed a hole in the front. The *gudaris* were demoralized by this overwhelming air power. They could fight back against the fierceness of a Carlist infantry attack, but they lacked both anti-aircraft guns and fighter cover. Twenty battalions lacked proper automatic weapons and some units' machine-gun companies had only a handful of machine pistols.

The Nationalist offensive paused on 4 April, despite protests from the Condor Legion that the opportunities created were not being followed up. Bad weather then grounded Nationalist aircraft and the Basques were given a chance to reorganize their defences. On 6 April the Nationalists announced a blockade of Republican ports on the Cantabrian coast. The same day the Nationalist cruiser *Almirante Cervera*, with the moral support of the pocket battleship *Admiral Graf Spee* in the background, stopped a British merchantman. However, HMS *Blanche* and HMS *Brazen* of the British destroyer flotilla assigned to the Bay of Biscay raced up, and the cargo ship was allowed into Bilbao.

Baldwin's government was alarmed that Anglo-Basque trade might force Great Britain to take sides in Spain. It did not wish to recognize either the Nationalists or the Republicans as belligerents, because that meant allowing them to stop and search British ships en route to Spanish ports. Nevertheless, in the light of subsequent events it is difficult to credit the cabinet or its advisers with impartiality. Admiral Lord Chatfield, the First Sea Lord, was an admirer of General Franco and his officers in the Bay of Biscay had an undoubted sympathy for their Nationalist counterparts. Sir Henry Chilton, the ambassador at Hendaye, who still had the ear of the Foreign Office though he was not on the scene, acted as a mouthpiece for the Nationalists. Chatfield and Chilton informed the British Government that the blockade of Bilbao was effective because the Nationalists had mined the mouth of the River Nervión, and would shell British ships if they did not stop. Although no unit of the Royal Navy had been near the area in question for months, the Basques' assurances that all mines had been cleared were ignored. The Royal Navy flotilla was ordered by London to instruct all British vessels in the Biscay area en route to Bilbao to wait in the French port of St Jean de Luz until further notice. As if to mitigate any damage to British prestige caused by this implicit support of the Nationalists, the battle-cruiser HMS *Hood* was ordered to Basque waters from Gibraltar.

The Royal Navy's view of the blockade's effectiveness led to furious scenes in the House of Commons. There were only four Nationalist ships watching 200 miles of coast and the Basque shore batteries controlled an area beyond the three-mile limit. The government was taken aback at the onslaught it received but Sir Samuel Hoare, the First Lord of the Admiralty, was dishonest about the mines in the Nervión, for his source of information was the Nationalist navy.

On 20 April the *Seven Seas Spray*, a small British merchantman which had decided to ignore all Royal Navy instructions and warnings, arrived off Bilbao from St Juan de Luz. There were neither Nationalist warships nor mines; only an ecstatic welcome from the population of Bilbao awaited them. The British government and the Admiralty were totally discredited. Other vessels waiting near the French Basque coast immediately set out for Spain. One of them was stopped ten miles from Bilbao by the cruiser *Almirante Cervera*. The merchantman radioed for help and this time the Royal Navy, in the form of HMS *Hood*, had to take a firm line with the Nationalists. In the Basques' view it was poetic justice that the battleship *España* struck a Nationalist mine off Santander nine days later and sank.

The Basques could not now be starved into collapse, but the fighting which had begun again on 20 April was going badly for them. The combination of Nationalist air power, the fighting qualities of the Carlist troops, and Republican units pulling out of line without warning brought the front close to collapse. Chaos was increased by the slowness and incompetence of the general staff. Its chief, Colonel Montaud, was notorious for his defeatism, and the regular officers were widely criticized for 'their civil service mentality'. The situation was so bad that Aguirre tried to intervene. Luckily for the Basques, Mola's cautious advance failed to take full advantage of the Republican disarray. During 25 April many of the demoralized troops from Marquina fell back on Guernica, which lay some 10 kilometres (6 miles) behind the lines.

On the next day, Monday the 26th, at 4.30 in the afternoon, the main church bell in Guernica rang to warn of air attack. It was market day and, although farmers had been turned back at the edge of the town, many had still come in with their cattle and sheep. The refugees from the advancing troops together with the town's population went down into the cellars which had been designated as *'refugios'*. A single Heinkel 111 bomber of the Condor Legion's 'experimental squadron' arrived over the town, dropped its load on the centre, and then disappeared. Most people came out of their shelters, many going to help the injured. Fifteen minutes later the full squadron flew over, dropping various sizes of bombs. People who rushed back into the shelters were choked by smoke and dust. They then became alarmed as it was evident that the cellars were not strong enough to withstand the heavier bombs. A stampede into the fields around the town began, then the Heinkel 51 fighter squadrons swept over strafing and grenading men, women and children, as well as nuns from the hospital and even the livestock. The major part of the attack had not even started.

At 5.15 the heavy sound of aero-engines was heard. The soldiers immediately identified them as 'trams', the nickname for the ponderous Junkers 52. Three squadrons from Burgos carpet-bombed the town systematically in 20-minute relays for two-and-a-half hours. (Carpet bombing had just been invented by the Condor Legion when attacking the Republican positions around Oviedo.) Their loads were made up of small and medium bombs, as well as 500 kg bombs, anti-personnel twenty-pounders, and incendiaries. The incendiaries were sprinkled down from the Junkers in two-pound aluminium tubes like metallic confetti. Eyewitnesses described the resulting scenes in terms of hell and the apocalypse. Whole families were buried in the ruins of their houses or crushed in the *refugios*; cattle and sheep, blazing with thermite and white phosphorus, ran crazily between the burning buildings until they died. Blackened humans staggered blindly through the flames, smoke and dust, while others scrabbled in the rubble, hoping to dig out friends and relatives. Approximately a third of the town's population were casualties – 1,654 killed and 889 wounded. Those hurrying towards the town from Bilbao had their original disbelief at the news changed by the orange-red sky in the distance. The parliament buildings and the oak tree were found to be untouched because they had been just outside the flight path which the pilots had followed so rigidly. The rest of Guernica was a burnt skeleton.

As with the account of Durango, the Nationalists set out to reverse the story. Using the precedent of Irún, they said that the town had been destroyed by its defenders as they withdrew; Queipo de Llano specified Asturian *dinamiteros*. Franco's GHQ issued a statement on 29 April. 'We wish to tell the world, loudly and clearly, a little about the burning of Guernica. Guernica was destroyed by fire and gasoline. The red hordes in the criminal service of Aguirre burnt it to ruins. The fire took place yesterday and Aguirre, since he is a common criminal, has uttered the infamous lie of attributing this atrocity to our noble and heroic air force.' The Spanish church backed this story completely, and its professor of theology in Rome went so far as to declare that 'the truth is there is not a single German in Spain. Franco only needs Spanish soldiers which are second to none in the world.' It was a version which even Franco's most fervent supporters abroad had difficulty in sustaining.

Condor Legion veterans were later to claim that their squadrons were really trying to bomb the Renteria bridge just outside Guernica, but that strong winds blew their loads onto the town. The bridge was never hit, there was virtually no wind, the Junkers were flying abreast and not in line, and anti-personnel bombs, incendiaries and machine-guns are not effective against stone bridges. According to von Richthofen's diary, the attack had been planned jointly with the Nationalists. Mola's chief-of-staff, Colonel Vigón, agreed to the target the day before the raid and again a few hours before it. No Nationalist officer mentioned the importance of Guernica in Basque life and history, but, even if they had, the plan would not have been changed. One intention of the raid may have been to block the roads, as at Durango, but everything else points to a major experiment in the effects of aerial terrorism.

As the retreat continued in this sector there were several brave and effective rearguard actions. At Guernica the communist Rosa Luxembourg battalion under Cristóbal held back the Nationalists for a time, despite the extraordinary incompetence of their formation commander, Colonel Yartz, who appears to have been incapable of reading a map. Then on 1 May, as the withdrawal steadied, the 8th UGT battalion laid a highly successful trap at Bermeo, on the coast, putting 4,000 men of the Black Arrows and their Fiat Ansaldos to flight. For the Army of Euzkadi, though, it was now necessary to start retreating to the 'Iron Ring' round Bilbao. This defence-works, with a perimeter of some 80 kilometres (50 miles), had been started the previous winter. With 15,000 men working on it as well as civilian contracting companies who installed concrete strong-points, it was wrongly compared to the Maginot Line. It had no depth – in many places nothing more than a single line of trenches – and it was incomplete. There was no attempt at concealment and the officer in charge, Major Goicoechea, had gone over to the Nationalists with its detailed plans.

The Italians were increasing the size of their forces in the north and the Nationalists' four Navarrese brigades were each brought up almost to divisional strength. The Republicans, meanwhile, raised more *gudari*, UGT, CNT and communist battalions and brought in Asturian and San-tanderino reinforcements. The Valencia government tried to help by sending aircraft via France, but the Non-Intervention Committee frustrated it on two occasions. That the non-intervention policy was effective only on the French frontier increased Republican bitterness greatly. It was thought too dangerous to fly the aircraft straight to Bilbao and risk arriving with little fuel and no protection against Nationalist fighters. There were now only six Chatos left in the Basque country and, although their pilots had managed to shoot down the first two Dornier 17s to arrive in Spain, morale seemed to sink after the ace, Felipe del Río, was killed.

Relations between the Basques and the Valencia government became strained by misunderstandings. Aguirre's government was often suspected of trying to arrange a separate peace, while many Basques felt that elements in the Valencia administration were actively trying to stop assistance being sent. The Republic was, in fact, well aware that the conquest of the north would not only give the Nationalists vital industries, but also release large numbers of enemy troops for deployment in the centre. They therefore planned to launch two attacks in May, the Huesca offensive and the attack down the Sierra de Guadarrama towards Segovia. Neither of these attempts, however, forced the Nationalists to divert troops from the northern front.

On 22 May the 4th Navarre Brigade reached the eastern side of the Iron Ring. The Nationalists' progress was slower as the Basques and their allies were now fighting more effectively and seemed less affected by air attack. They were beginning to fire back, a tactic which, even if not successful, kept the Fiat and the Heinkel fighters at more of a distance. (Almost a third of the Fiats destroyed in action during the war were brought down as a result of small arms fire.)

Some of the incompetent senior officers had also been replaced. But Aguirre's attempts to animate the army staff during the campaign had done little to improve the situation. His interference stopped when Llano de la Encomienda was replaced by General Gámir Ulíbarri, a Basque regular officer sent from Valencia. Some new brigade and divisional commanders were also appointed, such as the remarkable mechanic, Belderrain, who had organized the effective defence of the Inchortas, Cristóbal, the communist smuggler, and the French Colonel Putz from the International Brigades. On the other hand, the Russian General Goriev stayed on despite his unimpressive performance.

A change in the Nationalist command was at the same time made necessary by the death of General Mola, in an air crash, on 3 June. His death could be described as a setback for the Basques, because his caution, which so exasperated the Germans, had saved them at critical moments. On the Nationalist side there were many who suspected that the Caudillo or his supporters were somehow involved, but the suspicion was almost certainly groundless. It was, of course, remembered that Franco's other great rival, Sanjurjo, had died in similar circumstances, but air crashes were frequent and accounted for nearly as many lost machines as enemy action.

Mola's place was filled by General Dávila, who was also methodical, but far more stable than his predecessor. Dávila rearranged his forces, ordering the assault on the Iron Ring to begin on 12 June. Major Goicoechea's plans, confirmed by air reconnaissance, pinpointed the weakest spot in the defence line. Heavy artillery and air bombardment was followed by a swift attack via dead ground. There was no depth to the defences and the whole sector crumbled rather than be attacked from behind. Nevertheless, it was certainly not a rout. Many units held their ground with great bravery and slowed the advance.

In Bilbao the Basque government decided to evacuate the city after agonized discussions. The Basque nationalist leaders also decided that the steel works and war industries should not be destroyed (their allies were horrified when they found this out later). The coast road to the west was soon packed with refugees and, although only a small part consisted of Santanderino units heading for home, the whole mass was strafed by Heinkel fighter squadrons. A junta of defence under Leizaola, the minister of justice, stayed in the city, while the government withdrew towards Santander. Other Basque leaders and senior officers fled on ships leaving the harbour.

The Republican forces were assigned new positions along the line of the River Nervión, which curves around Bilbao to the east. With the imminent arrival of the Nationalist forces, the Nationalist fifth column in Arenas, on the east of the river's mouth, started shooting into the streets in their excitement. The anarchist Malatesta battalion, positioned on the other side of the river, stormed across and dealt with them rapidly. Their final action before withdrawing was to set fire to the church. The commander knew that its priest was a Nationalist sympathizer; he was his brother.

The city was under continual artillery bombardment. Eventually the Republican forces had to withdraw because they were threatened on their southern flank, where troops under the Italian commissar, Nino Nanetti, had withdrawn without blowing the bridge behind them. The fifth column-ists in the city had another shock when they gathered in the main square with monarchist flags to greet the Carlist troops. A Basque tank suddenly appeared round the corner, fired at some flags hanging from balconies and disappeared. The cheers for the Nationalists when they arrived sounded hollow in the half-empty city.

The Nationalist casualties for the campaign were high – about 30,000 – but the proportion of fatalities was low. The Basques and their allies suffered only slightly more in total, but their death rate was nearly a third, mainly due to air attacks. The Basque army had operated in a markedly different way from the Republican army in the centre. There was far less waste of men's lives through futile counter-attacks over open ground.

Summary court martials were held in the newly conquered territory, and thousands, including many priests, were sentenced to prison. There were, however, fewer executions than usual, because of the strength of feeling that Guernica had provoked abroad. Nothing, however, stopped the con-querors' resolution to crush every aspect of Basque nationalism. The Basque flag, the *ikurriña*, was outlawed, and use of the Basque language suppressed. Threatening notices were displayed: 'If you are Spanish, speak Spanish.' Regionalist feelings in any form were portrayed as the cancer of the Spanish body politic.

169

The units which retreated along the coast to Santander were demoralized. They knew that it was only a matter of time before Santander and the Asturias fell as well. They were at least given a chance to reorganize, when the Nationalist advance was delayed by the major Republican offensive at Brunete in the Madrid sector on 6 July. Once this had been repulsed, General Dávila redeployed his troops. They included six Carlist brigades under General Solchaga, the Italian force now commanded by General Bastico, which comprised Bergonzoli's Littorio Division, the March 23rd Division, the Black Flames and the mixed Black Arrows. The air support consisted of more than 200 planes, split between the Condor Legion, the Legionary Air Force and the Nationalist squadrons, which were being given the Heinkel 51s as the Messerschmitts arrived in greater numbers.

General Gámir Ulíbarri's force of some 80,000 men had not only less infantry than the Nationalists, but also only 40 operational fighters and bombers, many of which were obsolete. On the opening day of the offensive, 14 August, Solchaga's Carlist brigades attacked from the east and smashed through 54 Division. The Italians were held up by fierce resistance in the Cantabrian mountains to the south-west, but with overwhelming artillery and air support they captured the Escudo pass two days later. The three Republican divisions sent to hold the breach were not quick enough and the breakthrough was complete.

Many of the Republican formations then carried out a fighting retreat into the mountains of Asturias. The remainder were bottled up in the area of Santander and the small port of Santoña. In Santander the desperation was so great that many men sought oblivion in drink. Officers organized parties of soldiers to go round destroying the wine stocks. The general staff arranged to escape in ships, but the small boats were swamped by panic-stricken men and many capsized. The 122nd and 136th battalions tried to organize a defence, but apathy seemed to take over once the last chance of escape had gone. They waited for the Nationalists and their firing squads. Since about 3,000 Nationalist supporters had been killed in the previous year, mainly on the orders of the socialist Colonel Neila, little mercy was expected.

In Santoña the Basques arranged surrender terms for their *gudaris* with the Italian commander of the Black Arrows, Colonel Farina. Apparently, these had already been discussed in Rome between Count Ciano and Basque PNV representatives, who felt that the Valencia government had let them down badly. It was agreed that there would be no reprisals, and that no Basque soldier would be forced to fight on the Nationalist side. Spanish officers announced immediately that this agreement was invalid and Basque soldiers were taken off British ships in the port at gunpoint. Summary trials followed and a large proportion of the officers and many soldiers were executed. It was this dishonouring of the articles of surrender which the Basque ETA guerrillas advanced in later years as a reason why the Republic of Euzkadi was still at war with the Franquist state.

Mussolini and Count Ciano were overjoyed at this 'great victory'. Ciano wanted 'flags and guns captured from the Basques. I envy the French their Invalides and the Germans their Military Museums. A flag taken from the enemy is worth more than any picture.' They felt that their decision to keep Italian troops in Spain after the débâcle of Brihuega had been vindicated. Their jubilation was premature, however, for approximately half of the Republican forces had pulled back into the Asturian mountains, where there was to be a much tougher campaign lasting until the end of October, followed by a further five months of ferocious guerrilla warfare. Franco was not able to bring down the Army of the North as quickly as he had hoped.

The relative speed of the Nationalists' victory in the Basque campaign was due to the Condor Legion's contribution. The Nazi government did not delay in taking payment. German engineers moved into the factories and steel mills which the Basque nationalists had refused to destroy and most of the industrial production went to Germany to pay the Luftwaffe's expenses for destroying the region. Franco, on the other hand, had to wait longer for his benefits, though he knew that the reduction of the north would eventually give him infantry parity in the centre and south. Combined with his increasing superiority in air and artillery support, it would ensure ultimate victory, unless a European conflict broke out first. The war was now little more than straight pounding, and he could pound the hardest, for this campaign had shown that his allies possessed far better means of delivering high explosive than his enemies' allies.

THE PROPAGANDA WAR

History is usually written by the winners, but in the case of the Spanish civil war it has mostly been written on behalf of the losers. This development was of course decisively influenced by the subsequent defeat of the Nationalists' Axis allies. At the time, however, the Republic may have won many battles for international public opinion, but the Nationalists won the war by concentrating on a select and powerful audience in Britain and the United States. They played on the fear of communism in an appeal to conservative and religious feelings, and their sympathizers' mistrust of the Republic was only confirmed by Russian military aid.

The Nationalists argued that they represented the cause of Christianity, order and Western civilization against 'Asiatic Communism'. To bolster this version of events, they alleged that the communists had planned a revolution with 150,000 shock troops and 100,000 reserves in 1936, a coup which the Nationalist rising had pre-empted. After their setback at Madrid, they also alleged that 500,000 foreign communist troops were helping the Republic. They declared that the election results of February 1936 were invalid, even though CEDA and monarchist leaders had accepted the results at the time. They exaggerated the degree of disorder in the spring of 1936 as further justification of their rebellion. They concentrated on presenting life in the Republican zone as a perpetual massacre of priests, nuns and innocents, accompanied by a frenzied destruction of churches and works of art.

The basis of the Republican government's case was that it had been elected legally in February 1936 and was then attacked by reactionary generals aided by the Axis dictatorships. Thus the Republic represented the cause of democracy, freedom and enlightenment against fascism. (In later years supporters of the Republic held that the Spanish conflict represented the start of the Second World War. The Franquists, on the other hand, said it was simply the prelude to a third world war between Western civilization and communism, and that any Nazi or fascist aid they received was incidental.)

The Republic's foreign propaganda emphasized that their government was the only legal and democratic one in Spain. This was of course true when put against the illegality and authoritarianism of their opponents' conduct. But liberal and left-of-centre politicians had hardly respected their own constitution at times, and the rising of October 1934, in which Azaña, Prieto and Largo Caballero had participated, undermined the Republican case against the rebels. Nor was their argument helped when the Cortes was reduced to a symbolic body with no control over the government. Then, during the second half of 1937 and 1938, the administration of Juan Negrín developed marked authoritarian tendencies. Criticism of the prime minister and the Communist Party virtually became an act of treason.

The Republic's need to convince the outside world of the justice of its cause was greatly increased by the effects of British foreign policy. In addition, the already strained political atmosphere of the 1930s and the internationalized aspect of the civil war made foreign opinion seem of paramount importance to the outcome. The Spanish workers and peasants believed, with innocent earnestness, that if the situation were explained abroad, Western governments must come to their aid against the Axis dictatorships. Foreign visitors were asked how it was possible that in a democracy like America, where the majority of the population supported the Republic (over 70 per cent according to opinion polls), the government refused it arms for self-defence. Republican leaders were much more aware of the reasons for the actions of Western governments, but even they were wrong in believing that the British and French governments would eventually be forced to accept that their interests lay in a strong anti-Axis policy before it was too late.

Under such circumstances it was inevitable that journalists and famous writers should be courted by the Republic. There was a great deal of ground to be made up after the first reports of the 'red massacres', and the tide started to turn in the Republic's favour only in November 1936 with the bombing of working-class areas and the San Carlos hospital during the battle for Madrid. Five months later the destruction of Guernica gave the Republic its greatest victory in the propaganda war, particularly since the Basques were conservative and Catholics. The non-interventionist policy of Western governments, however, remained unaffected.

In July 1936 the Catholic press abroad sprang to the support of the Nationalist rising and castigated the anti-clericalism of the Republic, the desecration of churches and the killing of priests. The most sensational accusation was the raping of nuns, a similar fabrication dating back to the Middle Ages, when it was used to justify the slaughter of Jews. Two unsubstantiated incidents became the basis for a general campaign of astonishing virulence. The Nationalists were on firmer ground when they condemned the murder of priests, and they were supported by the Pope who declared the priests to be martyrs. On 1 July 1937 Cardinal Gomá issued an open letter to 'the Bishops of the whole World' calling for church support of the Nationalist cause, a letter in which he stated, somewhat defensively, that the war was 'not a crusade, but a political and social war with repercussions of a religious nature'. This was in contrast to the statement of the Archbishop of Valencia a month earlier that 'the war has been called by the Holy Heart of Jesus and this Adorable Heart has given power to the arms of Franco's soldiers'. In addition, the Bishop of Segovia had said that the war was 'a hundred times more important and holy than the *Reconquista*' and the Bishop of Pamplona called it the 'loftiest crusade that the centuries have ever seen ... a crusade in which divine intervention on our side is evident'. Leaflets with photo-montages of Christ flanked by Generals Mola and Franco were issued to Nationalist troops.

The political role of the church was ignored when the religious victims were made into martyrs, although some Catholic writers abroad made the connexion. One was François Mauriac, who turned against the Nationalists after a Nationalist officer told him that it was more practical to shoot the enemy wounded rather than cure them for execution later. 'For millions of Spaniards', Mauriac wrote to Ramón Serrano Súñer (Franco's brother-in-law and political adviser), 'Christianity and fascism have become intermingled, and they cannot hate one without hating the other.' Mauriac defended his fellow-Catholic writer, Jacques Maritain, when the pro-Nazi Serrano Súñer derided him as 'a converted Jew'. The publication in 1938 of Georges Bernanos' book, *Les Grandes Cimetières Sous La Lune*, which described the Nationalist terror on Majorca, greatly strengthened the liberal Catholic reaction against the church's official support for Franco.

In the United States the Catholic lobby was very powerful. Luis Bolín recounted that a young Irishwoman, Aileen O'Brien, 'spoke on the telephone to every Catholic bishop in the United States and begged them to request their parish priests to ask all members of their congregations to telegraph in protest to President Roosevelt'. As a result of her efforts, Bolín claimed, more than a million telegrams were received at the White House and a shipment of munitions for the Republic was stopped. The power of the pro-Nationalist lobby was best demonstrated in May 1938. A group led by the ambassador to Great Britain, Joseph Kennedy, managed to frighten Congressmen who depended on the Catholic vote into opposing the repeal of the arms embargo. They did so even though no more than 20 per cent of the country and 40 per cent of Catholics supported the Nationalists.

Nevertheless, in 1937 the Nationalists began to complain that they were losing the battle for international public opinion. There were several factors operating against them. First, there was a fundamental difference of attitude between the opposing military commands in their dealings with the press. The Nationalists often regarded journalists as potential spies and allowed them very little free movement, especially when they might witness a mopping-up episode. As a result their correspondents could not compete in the 'din of battle' personal accounts so beloved by the profession. Also, not all the Nationalist press officers were as articulate and urbane as Luis Bolín. One of his successors, Count de Alba de Yeltes, proudly announced to an English visitor that 'on the day the civil war broke out, he lined up the labourers on his estate, selected six of them and shot them in front of the others – "*pour encourager les autres*, you understand"'.

A modern public realtions officers would blanch at some of the extraordinary speeches of General Millán Astray, the founder of the Foreign Legion, who had been so mutilated in the colonial wars. 'The gallant Moors,' he once proclaimed, 'although they wrecked my body only yesterday, today deserve the gratitude of my soul, for they are fighting for Spain against the Spaniards . . . I mean the bad Spaniards . . . because they are giving their lives in defence of Spain's sacred religion, as is proved by their attending field mass, escorting the Caudillo, and pinning holy medallions and sacred hearts to their burnooses.' Franco, of course, avoided such indelicate contradictions when he spoke of 'the Crusade'.

There was also one technical factor which undoubtedly told against the Nationalist version of events for much of the war. The overseas cableheads were in Republican territory, so that journalists in that zone usually had their copy printed first. The accounts from Nationalist Spain were, therefore, often out of date. Nevertheless, the Nationalists had won the first round for several reasons. There were very few journalists representing foreign newspapers on its territory during the first days of rearguard slaughter, while Barcelona and Madrid had attracted vast numbers, so that the initial killings on Republican territory were reported the most rapidly. The other key point for the early reports was Gibraltar, where many upper-class refugees were arriving, especially from Málaga. On 21 August 1936 the *New York Herald Tribune* reporter, Robert Neville, wrote: 'In Gibraltar I found to my surprise that most of the newspapermen had been sending only "horror" stories. They do not seem to be awake to the terrible international implications in this situation.' Sensational accounts sold newspapers, but the initial 'white terror' just to the north in Andalucia was reported only by one or two correspondents, one of them Bertrand de Jouvenal of *Paris Soir*. This can be explained in part by the fact that most journalists were incapable of understanding the peasants who had fled from the Army of Africa, whereas middle- and upper-class Spaniards were more likely to speak a foreign language. However, there can also be little doubt about journalistic or editorial bias.

The battle-lines of the war in Spain were rapidly taken up in France, Great Britain and the United States. A foretaste of the propaganda struggle came in Great Britain just before the rising, when reports appeared claiming that Calvo Sotelo's eyes had been dug out with daggers, a story to which even Spanish right-wing papers had not given credence. The Republic was supported by the *News Chronicle* and the *Manchester Guardian*, *The Times* and *Telegraph* remained more or less neutral, while the rest supported the Nationalists. Immediate sympathizers with the rising were the *Observer*, whose editor, Garvin, was a great admirer of Mussolini, and the Northcliffe press, which had backed Moseley's British Union of Fascists. Its *Daily Mail* correspondent, Harold Cardozo, was accordingly accredited to the Nationalist forces. The practice of a newspaper sending a reporter to the side it supported became customary. In fact, Kim Philby, already a secret communist, developed a conservative image as *The Times* correspondent with the Nationalists. An exception in the early days was another secret communist agent, the writer Arthur Koestler. Although representing the left-wing *News Chronicle*, he started with the Nationalists in Seville, but had to escape when seen by a German journalist called Strindberg, who knew he was a communist. Luis Bolín, the Nationalist press officer, was too late to arrest him as a spy. Koestler returned to Republican territory, but Bolín caught up with him at the fall of Málaga, and only pressure from the British and American press saved him from execution.

In the majority of cases the correspondent reflected, or adapted himself to, the political stance of his paper. As a result, Richard Ford's comment of 1846 was equally true 90 years later: 'The public at home are much pleased by the perusal of "authentic" accounts from Spain itself which tally with their own preconceived ideas of the land.' At the beginning of the war correspondents were rushed to Spain, regardless of whether they spoke the language or understood the country's politics. But then even a respected expert like Professor Allison-Peers was unable to differentiate the parties of the left accurately and attributed the peasant troubles in Andalucia to agitators who were profiting from improved communications. The ideas that Latin people had 'violence in the blood' and that military dictatorships were natural to them were reflected in the shorthand of headlines. As always, the pressure of space and journalistic simplification to make accounts easy to digest distorted the issues.

Newspapermen were as much affected by the emotions of the time as anybody else. Many became resolute, and often uncritical, champions of the Republic after experiencing the siege of Madrid. Their commitment affected their coverage of later issues, such as the Communist Party's manœuvring for control. The ideals of the anti-fascist cause anaesthetized many of them to aspects of the war which proved uncomfortable. It was a difficult atmosphere in which to retain objectivity.

There were also various types of censorship and pressure which affected the accounts printed at home. These ranged from propaganda-oriented briefings from government press officers and Republican censorship through to the political or commercial prejudices of the editor. At the end of the war Herbert Matthews of the *New York Times* was told by his editor not to 'send in any sentimental stuff about the refugee camps'. In 1937 Dawson, the editor of *The Times*, blocked some of Steer's accounts from the Basque country because he did not want to upset the Germans. On 3 May, a week after Steer's report on Guernica, he wrote that he had 'done the impossible night after night to keep the paper from hurting their susceptibilities'. The most famous dispute was the one between Louis Delaprée and his editor on the right-wing *Paris Soir*. Shortly before his death (he was flying back to France when his plane was shot down), Delaprée complained that his reports were suppressed. He finished his last despatch by observing bitterly that 'the massacre of a hundred Spanish children is less interesting than a sigh from Mrs Simpson'.

Republican propaganda was often little different from its Nationalist counterpart. Both sides seized upon isolated incidents to make general points. The Republicans spread horror stories of Moorish *regulares* chopping off the hands of children who clenched their fists, in case they were making the left-wing salute. They also recounted secular miracles, like the Nationalist bombs which did not go off because they contained messages of solidarity from foreign workers instead of explosive. There were undoubtedly cases of sabotage by munitions workers, but the exaggeration of Republican propaganda developed such addiction to misplaced hope that it became a major liability. Colonel Casado argued with justification that it was a major contribution to the Republicans' defeat. Once the government had excited wild optimism over an offensive, it became virtually impossible to admit failure and this led to the loss of vast quantities of men and material in the defence of useless gains.

The major problem of the Republican government was the need to provide two incompatible versions of events simultaneously. The account for external consumption was designed to convince the French, British and United States governments that the Republic was a liberal property-owning democracy, while domestic communiqués tried to persuade the workers that they were still defending a social revolution. Censorship came under Alvarez del Vayo's control. The aide responsbile for English-speaking journalists stated that he 'was instructed not to send out one word about this revolution in the economic system of loyalist Spain, nor are any correspondents in Valencia permitted to write freely of the revolution that has taken place'.

The Spanish civil war engaged the commitment of artists and intellectuals on an unprecedented scale, the overwhelming majority of them on the side of the Republic. The conflict had the fascination of an epic drama involving the basic forces of humanity. Yet they did not just adopt the role of passionate observers. The slaughter of the First World War had undermined the moral basis of art's detachment from politics and made 'art for art's sake' seem a privileged impertinence. Socialist realism took this to its logical extreme by subordinating all forms of expression to the cause of the proletariat. The support given by intellectuals to the Republican cause was usually moral rather than practical, although a few writers, including André Malraux, George Orwell and John Cornford, fought, and others, like Hemingway, John Dos Passos, W. H. Auden, Bernanos, Stephen Spender and Antoine de Saint-Exupéry, spent varying amounts of time in Spain.

A number of writers were to have their idealism seriously undermined by the events they witnessed. Simone Weil, who supported the anarchists, was distressed by killings in eastern Spain. She was particularly affected when a fifteen-year-old Falangist prisoner was captured on the Aragon front and shot after Durruti spent an hour with the boy trying to persuade him to change his politics and giving him until the next day to decide. Auden, who had written an enthusiastic description of the social revolution at the end of 1936, returned from Spain after service with an ambulance unit saying little, but evidently disillusioned. Stephen Spender, shaken by the executions in the International Brigades, left the Communist Party soon afterwards.

Not all writers were pro-Republican. Evelyn Waugh, having said that he would support Franco if he were a Spaniard, then emphasized: 'I am not a Fascist, nor shall I become one unless it were the only alternative to Marxism. It is mischievous to suggest that such a choice is imminent.' Ezra Pound replied that 'Spain is an emotional luxury to a gang of sap-headed dilettantes', Hilaire Belloc, a supporter of the Nationalist, had already described the struggle as 'a trial of strength between Jewish Communism and our traditional Christian civilization'. The majority of those questioned in Europe and America declared their opposition to Franco in varying forms. Samuel Beckett replied 'UPTHEREPUBLIC!' In the United States William Faulkner and John Steinbeck simply declared their hatred for fascism, while others qualified their position by supporting a particular faction on the Republican side. Aldous Huxley specified his opposition to communism and sympathy for anarchism (which led Nancy Cunard in her survey for the *Left Review* to mark him as a neutral). Other supporters of the CNT–FAI included John Dos Passos, B. Traven and Herbert Read.

Nothing, however, could match the intellectual mobilization for which the Communist Party aimed. In the 1930s the Communist Party succeeded in attracting to its cause many writers, particularly poets, who included Miguel Hernández and Rafael Alberti, Stephen Spender, Cecil Day-Lewis, Hugh MacDiarmid and Pablo Nerauda. The most famous writer to support the Republic, and lend his weight to the campaign which the communists organized so effectively, was Ernest Hemingway. Nevertheless, the two sides to his character are of great interest when seen against the conflict of political forces within Republican Spain. Hemingway was an individualist who believed in discipline for everybody else. He supported communist broadsides against the anarchists, but backed their methods only because he thought them necessary to win the war. 'I like the communists when they're soldiers,' he remarked to a friend in 1938. 'When they're priests, I hate them.' The communists did not realize, when they accorded him such special attention, that his deep and genuine hatred of fascism did not mean that he admired them out of any political conviction. Even so, the brutal way in which Hemingway informed Dos Passos of the communists' secret execution of José Robles (Dos Passos' great friend) ended their association. Hemingway found fault with Dos Passos for supporting the anarchists and for not being 'regular enough in his attitude towards the commissars'.

It is difficult to ascertain how much Hemingway was influenced by the privileged information he received from senior party cadres and Russian advisers. Being taken seriously by experts distorted his vision. It made him prepared to sign moral blank cheques on behalf of the Republic. Hence his absurd statements that 'Brihuega will take its place in military history with the other decisive battles of the world', and that the Republic was 'licking the rebels', as if the fight was also between Yankees and Southern slave owners. The American civil war haunts his major work, *For Whom the Bell Tolls*. This novel, written just after the Republic's defeat, reveals both a lingering admiration for communist professionals and yet also the author's libertarianism. Its hero, Robert Jordan, one of Hemingway's self-images, asks, 'Was there ever a people whose leaders were as truly their enemies as this one?'

While the Republic won the propaganda battle, greatly helped by Comintern efforts, the communists were winning the conflict on the left. The Bolshevik coup in Russia had given them the unique position of 'controlling the only beacon of revolutionary hope' in the world. Bertrand Russell remarked that any resistance or objection 'was condemned as treachery to the cause of the proletariat. Anarchist and syndicalist criticisms were forgotten or ignored, and by exalting State Socialism, it became possible to retain the faith that one great country had realized the aspirations of the pioneers.' The triangular nature of the civil war in Spain could, in fact, be said to echo the Kronstadt rising against the Bolshevik dictatorship in 1921. Three years later, when Emma Goldman condemned the communist regime vehemently at a dinner of 250 left-wing intellectuals, held to welcome her to London, Russell was the only person to support her. The rest sat in shocked and embarrassed silence. Yet even Russell wrote soon afterwards that he was 'not prepared to advocate any alternative government in Russia'.

Less than a month after the outbreak of the Spanish civil war, the first of the major show trials began in Moscow. Victor Serge, speaking against them in Paris, was heckled by a communist worker: 'Traitor! Fascist! Nothing you can do will stop the Soviet Union from remaining the fatherland of the oppressed!' Apart from rare exceptions, like the poet, André Breton, socialists dared not speak out because 'the interest of the Popular Front demanded the humouring of the communists'. André Gide prepared a statement, but when Ilya Ehrenburg heard of it, he organized communist militiamen on the Madrid front to send telegrams begging him not to publish a 'mortal blow' against them. Gide was appalled: 'what a flood of abuse I'm going to face! And there will be militiamen in Spain who believe that I am actually a traitor!' In Spain the POUM's *La Batalla* published critical accounts of the trials, thus greatly increasing the enmity the communists felt for their Marxist rivals. Even CNT leaders tried to prevent their press from attacking Stalin's liquidations at a time when Russian arms were so desperately needed. The blind, short-term reaction of Western governments and their weakness in the face of Hitler and Mussolini gave the Comintern an apparent monopoly of resistance to fascism.

All this time, the Republic suffered from its dependence on Soviet supplies, which confirmed the fears and prejudices of the minority to whom Nationalist propaganda was addressed. In 1938 Churchill said of Neville Chamberlain that 'nothing has strengthened the Prime Minister's hold upon well-to-do society more remarkably than the belief that he is friendly to General Franco and the Nationalist cause in Spain'. This section of the population cannot have made up much more than 20 per cent of the total, yet it would appear that it had far more influence over British, and therefore Western, policy towards Spain than the large majority who supported the Republic. On this basis, the communists' role on behalf of the Republic probably helped the Nationalists become the effective winners of the propaganda war. Appeasement and the Western boycott of the Republic greatly strengthened the power of the Comintern, which was able to present itself as the only effective force to combat fascism. It is a lesson which has still not been learnt in the post-war era. Another is the way that mass self-deception is simply a sedative prescribed by leaders who cannot face reality themselves. And as the Spanish civil war proved, the first casualty of war is not truth, but its source: the conscience and integrity of the individual.

DISSIDENTS AND HERETICS

The failure of four attempts on Madrid in five months did not only strain Franco's relations with his German and Italian allies. It also provoked rumblings of discontent within the Nationalist coalition. The Carlists had not forgotten Franco's strong reaction to their attempt to maintain the independence of their *requeté* formations, and Falangist 'old shirts' shared their dead leader's fears that the army would annex them, even though they had grown from 30,000 to more than a million members in a year.

Franco kept himself well informed of developments within these two important parties. He was not unduly worried, because the Nationalist alliance wanted a single leader and he had no effective rival. The main Carlist leader, Fal Conde, was exiled in Portugal, and the Count of Rod-ezno, who remained, was far more amenable. The continued suppression of any announcement of José Antonio's execution at Alicante by the Republicans encouraged wishful rumours amongst the Falange that he was still alive, which prevented the appointment of a permanent replacement. The German ambassador, von Faupel, commented in a report to the Wilhelmstrasse that Franco was a chief without a party and the Falange a party without a chief. In addition, the Falange was still weakened by the potential split which came from the inherent contradiction in José Antonio's philosophy: socialist aspirations had been swamped by reactionary nationalism. José Antonio could be quoted by the proletarian 'old shirts', led by the provincial chief, Manuel Hedilla, to show that the 'socialist' aspect of their movement was fundamental. At the same time the *señorito* wing, which was growing more powerful than the 'old shirts', could point to other statements to show that recreating 'traditional Spain' was upper most in the mind of José Antonio.

It was the latter group, the modern reactionaries, who contacted the Carlists during the winter of 1936 for secret talks about an alliance, while the proletarian elements, led by Hedilla, opposed such a move. Franco heard privately of these discussions, which went on throughout February, and although they came to nothing, he saw that trouble was more likely to come from Falangist ranks than from the Carlists, who were disciplined fighters uninterested in political intrigue. The Falange had many units of their German-trained militia at the front, but the bulk of their strength was devoted to the para-military and social roles which they had assumed in the rear areas. The violent *limpieza*, or ideological cleansing, continued with little respite, but there were still many Falangists left with plenty of time for political manœuvring.

Hedilla had been the Falangist chief in Santander, and he was lucky to be in Corunna when the rising began in the north, for his home town was held for the Republic. In Corunna he played an important role, both in bringing the well-armed Falange to help the rebels secure the town and in conducting the subsequent repression, which was among the worst in Spain. Yet this former mechanic soon became the most outspoken critic of indiscriminate Nationalist killing on the grounds that it alienated the proletariat from their cause. On Christmas Eve 1936 he told the Falange not to persecute the poor simply for having voted for the left 'out of hunger or despair. We all know that in many towns there were – and are – right-wingers who are worse than the reds ... Let there only be one nobility: that of work! Let there only be one class: that of Spaniards! The bosses of industry and banking, and of town and country, should disappear! The idle should be wiped out!' Such statements made Hedilla and the left-wing veterans highly suspect in the eyes of the Spanish right. Many army officers saw them as little better than 'reds'. Only Yagüe was a committed left-Falangist amongst senior officers. The *señorito* wing, on the other hand, with its power base in Andalucia, was more favourably regarded by the traditional power base which the Nationalist movement represent. It attracted to its ranks the professional middle classes who wanted to run a corporate state unfettered by any unproductive ideology.

During the winter of 1936 von Faupel, the German ambassador, had started to cultivate the admiration which the 'old shirts' held for the Nazis. It seems that he was trying to curry favour at home, not acting on orders. He encouraged Hedilla to resist the middle-class take-over of the Falange and advised Franco that the Nationalists could win the war only if they introduced social reform. Nevertheless, he wrote to the Wilhelmstrasse that if a clash occurred between Franco and the Falange 'we are in agreement with the Italians that despite our sympathy for the Falange and its healthy tendencies, we must support Franco at all costs'. Franco tolerated his allies' interference in military affairs because he had no choice, but he would not brook their involvement in the political future of Spain. He demanded von Faupel's replacement, even though he had not been involved in any attempt to change the Nationalist leadership.

In mid-April the *señorito* wing seized Falange headquarters in Salamanca in a move to oust the leftists, but, having recaptured the building with assistance from Falangist militia, Hedilla set out to arrest his opponents. A gun battle broke out in the Plaza Mayor and the civil guard had to be sent in to restore order. Arrests were made and Hedilla was fortunate to have stayed clear of the disturbance. On 18 April he arranged a meeting of the Falange council at which he was elected leader. He thought his triumph was complete when Franco congratulated him and brought him on to the balcony so that they would be cheered together by the crowd. The wily Caudillo made his move the next evening. The Falange, the Carlists, the Alphonsine monarchist *Renovación Española*, and the remnants of other right-wing groups, like the CEDA's Popular Action, were amalgamated into one party by decree. The party was to be called the *Falange Española Tradicionalista y de las JONS* (The Traditionalist Spanish Falange and the National Syndicalist Offensive Juntas). As the choice of name indicated, the Carlists came off worst in this forced union, but, as Franco had calculated, they were more obedient and less politically minded. The new uniform consisted of the Falangist blue shirt and the Carlist red beret. The fascist salute was officially adopted. The Caudillo was proclaimed chief of the new party and his brother-in-law, Ramón Serrano Súñer, was appointed executive head. (This produced a new Spanish word, *cuñadismo*, meaning 'brother-in-lawism', as a variant on nepotism.) Serrano Súñer, who began his career as a lawyer, had become a vice-president of the CEDA, and then moved towards the Falange in the spring of 1936. He was captured in Madrid after the rising and held in the Model Prison, where he witnessed the killings in revenge for the news of Badajoz. This experience made him one of the most intransigent advocates of the *limpieza* when he escaped from the hospital and reached Nationalist territory in February 1937.

The suddenness of Franco's coup increased its effect, and since he had no potential challenger the risk was minimal. By the time the announcement had been fully appreciated, anyone who wanted to object only exposed himself to the charge of treachery towards the Nationalist movement. Hedilla, somewhat unimaginatively, believed that he could maintain a position of power as the head of the Falange and guarantee its independence. He was arrested at the end of April, after sounding out supporters, and condemned to death for 'conspiring against the security of the state'; however, the sentence was commuted. The new puppet council appointed by Franco was no longer challenged, after the rest of the Falange was rapidly brought into line by dismissals and about 80 imprisonments.

As commander of the most important formation in the Nationalist army, the Army of Africa, Franco had started his climb to leadership from an advanced position. He had no effective rival and the very nature of the Nationalist movement begged a single, disciplined command. As a result he had achieved supreme power in two well-timed stages: September 1936, and April 1937. With the first he became *de jure* leader; with the second, suppressing all potential opposition, *de facto* dictator.

A power struggle had also begun in Republican territory during the winter of 1936 and the spring of 1937, although the winners, the communists, were never to achieve the same degree of power as Franco. They started from a very restricted base and their policies were resisted throughout by one of the major components of the Republican alliance, the anarchists. However great their control of the army and war materials, they could not take on the umbrella role which the army easily assumed in Nationalist territory. Stalin wanted to be able to control events in the Republic so as to prevent any embarrassment to his foreign policy, which was dominated more by a fear of Germany than by a desire to expand the frontiers of communism. The Russian attempt to woo Britain into an anti-Nazi pact meant that communist power had to be hidden.

The splits in the Republican camp grew rapidly in the early spring of 1937. The social democrats, or right socialists, like Prieto and Negrín, together with the liberal republicans and the Communist Party, asserted that the war could be won only by rigid discipline and central control.

The left socialists, anarchists and POUM claimed that the suppression of the revolutionary spirit countered everything for which they were fighting. Nevertheless, the majority in their ranks accepted, however reluctantly, that conventional organization was necessary in conventional war. Thus the explosion of May 1937 in Barcelona sprang more from deep distrust of communist motives behind the campaign for centralized power, than from any premeditated resistance to the process itself.

The communists' first objectives were the police and the army. They cultivated officers, most of whom were already impressed by the Party's discipline, with plans to reconstitute a formal army. They sought out the ambitious, presenting themselves as the experts of power. Being the supreme statists, Lenin's followers understood the mechanism of bureaucracy best of all. Stalin had demonstrated what could be achieved by placing a few picked men in key posts. In the army the communists managed to have Antonio Cordón appointed to control pay, discipline, supply and personnel in the war ministry. There was little competition for a post which was usually despised by regular soldiers. They also sounded out senior officers, and removed those who were obviously unsympathetic, like Colonel Segismundo Casado, the chief of operations of the general staff, after he complained openly at the diversion of supplies to the 5th Regiment. His replacement was a Party supporter, as were other officers whom Largo Cabellero thought were loyal to him, including even his own ADC. Every time there was a shake-up after a defeat, more and more vital posts in the army were taken over by communist appointees. General Krivitsky, the Soviet intelligence chief for western Europe, claimed that 90 per cent of the most important administrative and command posts were held by officers who acknowledged allegiance to the Communist Party. Casado estimated the proportion at about 70 per cent.

The communists also set up a police school in Madrid, where students who refused Party membership were failed. The secret police were taken over by Orlov and his NKVD agents in the late autumn of 1936, and it soon became the communists' most feared weapon. Even Wenceslao Carillo, the director general of security, found himself powerless against them. Many of the Spaniards who were recruited for this work could hardly be described as 'anti-fascist', but they were given Party cards nevertheless. When the first Soviet ambassador, Rosenberg, made his comment about scum always coming to the top in revolutions, he failed to add that much of it was creamed off into the secret police afterwards. Meanwhile, the campaign to win over the para-military forces like the *asaltos* was helped by Margarita Nelken, a socialist member of the Cortes and another secret communist. It was against this effort that General Asensio Torrado objected, earning the Party's bitter enmity for the first time.

The communist attack on Asensio Torrado was launched in January 1937 by Marcel Rosenberg, who had been acting 'like a Russian viceroy in Spain', telling the prime minister which officers to promote and which to dismiss. Largo Caballero lost his temper on this occasion, but his position was already being eroded. He could no longer disguise from himself that his close friend, Alvarez del Vayo, the foreign minister, was an active Party supporter. The communist Enrique Castro described their attitude to the foreign minister, saying 'he is a fool, but more or less useful'. The irony of the affair was that on 21 February, while the communists were still calling for Asensio Torrado to be shot, Rosenberg was recalled to Moscow, where he was executed soon afterwards in the purges. Although Rosenberg's successor, Gaikins, played a less dominant role, he continued to urge the fusion of the socialist and communist parties, a step to which Largo Caballero was now completely opposed. Strong-arm tactics became less necessary at such a high level, because the Party controlled most of the bureaucracy. The Soviet military advisers, nevertheless, continued to exert pressure by saying to any Spanish officer who objected to their plans that they ought to ask their government whether Soviet assistance was still required. Such activity took place despite the famous letter from Stalin, Molotov and Voroshilov to Caballero on 21 December 1936, which stated that the Russians had been 'categorically ordered [to] keep strictly to the functions of an adviser, and an adviser alone'.

Communist control of the Republican administration increased greatly during the winter, and by early March 1937 only Largo Caballero and his supporters, the anarchists and the POUM, were prepared to resist further increases in the Party's power. Isolated republican liberals and professional army officers were also alarmed at the direction events were taking, but they had neither the strength nor the organization to be effective. The prime minister was caught up in a net which was bewildering and infuriating for an unimaginative old unionist. He could not reveal the dangerous extent of communist infiltration, because to do so would confirm British prejudices, which up till then had been unjustified.

On 17 April Largo stopped Alvarez del Vayo increasing the establishment of commissars from one per battalion to one per company. The communists had invested a great deal of care and effort into this department of the army and they reacted angrily at being thwarted. Their press asked 'who can feel hostile to this corps of heroes? Only the declared enemies of the people.' Once hailed as 'the Spanish Lenin', Largo was now, by implication at least, a 'declared enemy of the people'. La Pasionaria gave a remarkable example of what Orwell later called double-speak. According to her, restricting the commissars would 'mean leaving our soldiers at the mercy of officers, who could at a moment disfigure the character of our army by returning to the old days of barrack discipline'. Yet the Communist Party was the chief advocate of drill, saluting, and privileges for officers.

Largo Caballero soon realized that he had few allies on whom he could rely, because the right-wing socialists, like Prieto and Negrín, and the liberal republicans were working closely with the communists for the centralization of power. The various sections of opinion within the socialist party began to polarize, either for or against collaboration with the communists. The *Negrinistas* followed the finance minister's virtually unqualified support for the communists. Prieto and his associates regarded communist policies as necessary for the conduct of the war, but he started to have private doubts in mid-1937 and then moved to outright opposition during the course of 1938. The *Caballeristas*, backed by peasants and part of the Socialist Youth, had abandoned their original enthusiasm for fusing with the Communist Party and now led the resistance to communist manœuvrings in the UGT and the Joint Socialist Youth. They were joined by the Asturian UGT, which had previously followed Prieto. Besteiro, meanwhile, stayed clear of involvement, but later in the year he started to distrust Negrín's ambition, and finished by taking part in the anti-communist coup of 1939.

The liberal politicians of Martínez Barrio's Republican Union and Azaña's Republican Left Party followed a course which was broadly similar to that of Prieto. They had been exasperated to see centralized military planning sacrificed to Catalan and Basque separatism or revolutionary self-management. They also backed Negrín's policy of taking advantage of the collectives' lack of capital so as to bring them under government control with a programme of nationalization.

Lacking the support of the liberals and social democrats, Largo had to look to the four CNT-FAI ministers to help him resist the communists. He began, therefore, to support his old rivals, the anarchists, in their struggle to maintain the integrity of their military formations. In the movement towards mixed brigades the previous winter, the communists had made a great show of breaking up their so-called 5th Regiment (which was the equivalent of three divisions by then) as an example to the other militias. This, in fact, was what they had been planning to do since its inception, for the 5th Regiment was intended to provide nuclei of trained cadres, with which to achieve control of the conventional army. The anarchists had steadfastly refused to follow such urgings and had warned that any attempt to impose communist officers on them would be met by force. This attitude was justified after the war by García Pradas, who said that 'thanks to our attitude it was possible for us to maintain until the very end those forces with which we were able to crush the Communist Party in March 1939'.

The tension between the communists on the one hand, and the anarchists, POUM and sections of other parties, particularly *Caballerista* socialists, on the other, grew in the army, the rear areas and the government during the first quarter of 1937. There were still anarchists who were convinced that Durruti had been murdered by the communists, and if communist-controlled artillery or aircraft bombarded other units by mistake, many believed it to be intentional. Similar feelings were prompted when promised tank, artillery or air support failed to arrive, even though this happened to communist units as well. If an attack was ordered over a large stretch of open ground covered by enemy machine-gun fire, anarchist suspicions were aroused if the officer who gave the order was a communist, even though communist formations, in particular the International Brigades, frequently suffered even more in the futile slaughter caused by useless attacks. Meanwhile, if any non-communist officer queried the wisdom or necessity of sacrificing his men, he received the retort that to question orders was to want to lose the war.

Tremendous resentment was also caused by the communists' habit of reserving the best weapons, transport, equipment, rations and medical care, as well as air, tanks and artillery support, for their own troops. The appropriation of supplies covered all sources and not just material purchased from Russia with the gold reserves. The greatest anger aroused among the troops of other political tendencies was caused by the frequency with which their men were seized by communist police on trumped-up charges. Soon after the battle of Brihuega, Antonio Verardini, the chief-of-staff of Mera's 14 Division, went to Madrid on a 24-hour leave. There he was arrested on the orders of Cazorla, the communist councillor of public order, and accused of espionage and treason. As soon as Mera found out he left for the capital with Sanz, the commander of 70 Brigade, and a lorry-load of heavily armed soldiers. On his arrival he told General Miaja that, if Verardini was not freed by the communists, his men would free him by force. Miaja obtained his release immediately. Mera was to return to Madrid on a similar mission when the communist persecution of the POUM reached its height. On the second occasion he had heard that Mika Etchebehere, the woman militia commander, had been arrested for 'disaffection to the Republic'. It was only by seeing the director general of security that he obtained her release and had her brought to his head-quarters so that she could not be snatched again.

About 80 anarchists were shot by communist police in Madrid during the spring, provoking many reprisals in return. The scandal with the most far-reaching effects was revealed when the CNT published accusations by the delegate for prisons, Melchor Rodríguez, who had already attacked the communists' mass shooting of prisoners in November. Rodríguez revealed that José Cazorla had set up secret prisons, where socialists, republicans and anarchists who had been marked down by the communists were taken, often to be tortured or shot. Other victims included defendants released by the Popular Tribunals whom the communists still thought guilty. A sub-sequent inquiry revealed that these allegations were justified, and Largo Caballero seized the opportunity to dissolve the communist-dominated junta of defence, thus restoring the capital to the control of the Valencia government. The socialist newspapers followed with accounts of similar prisons elsewhere, but there was little that Largo could do to restrict Orlov's NKVD men, know in Russia as 'the unsheathed sword of the Revolution'. Borkenau observed a change in the type of person whose life was at risk in Republican territory: 'In August [1936] it was the man who, through his social status, was an adversary of the lower classes. In February [1937] it was the man who, through his opinions was not even an adversary, but a critic of the official policy of the Communist Party.'

The communists' opponents had reason to be distrustful. Within a month of the start of the war, Jesús Hernández declared to a French news-paper that they would 'make short work of the anarchists after the defeat of Franco'. The self-managed collectives were attacked by José Díaz as 'tantamount to aiding the enemy'. Through most of the winter a barrage of abuse continued in the communist press, led by *Mundo Obrero* which attacked the CNT-FAI and the POUM as 'wreckers' or 'saboteurs' and referred darkly to 'the efforts of the fascists, Trotskyists and some anarcho-syndicalists to rupture the People's Front'. The anti-Stalinist POUM counter-attacked in *La Batalla*, their newspaper, especially by condemning the Moscow show trials, but the CNT-FAI leadership re-strained their own press in order not to put arms deliveries at risk.

In January 1937 Santiago Carrillo appealed to the anarchists: 'All we ask of them is that on their part they should abandon their sectarian prejudices, that they should not regard us as passing friends of today, and enemies of tomorrow, but as as friends today, tomorrow and always.' It is hardly surprising that the anarchists, hearing this language, remembered the Russian civil war and Lenin's treachery in the Ukraine. The Russians in Spain pretended to make up to anarchist ministers, and Rosenberg even suggested to Federica Montseny that she should to go Moscow, where 'Comrade Stalin' would receive her 'like a little queen'. He also offered to look after her daughter. 'When I heard these suggestions,' she said later, 'the blood froze in my veins.'

Anarchists began to question the wisdom of continued participation in the central government. Their units had in most cases not received the weapons and supplies promised them on accepting incorporation into the Popular Army, while the central government was trying to dismantle the self-managed collectives. The most searching criticism of the CNT-FAI leadership's decision to enter the government came from the veteran French anarchist, Sebastian Faure, who had invented the word 'libertarian'. He insisted that, if it was right to discard opposition to the concept of the state out of temporary necessity, then it could not be a valid principle. There was, of course, point to Faure's remark. The previous autumn the anarchist leaders had refused to join the government because 'the "worker-state" signals the beginning of a new political slavery'. But when they did finally join Largo's government, in November 1936, the anarchist press defended the decision in a manner which suggested that black had suddenly become white.

The process of demoralization and confusion in anarchist ranks was accompanied by a decline in their strength and influence. The CNT retained its pre-war members, but many of those who had joined in the summer of 1936 switched to the growing communist camp. The CNT still claimed to have nearly two million members, but the true figure was probably no more than one-and-a-half million. The focal point for frustration was Barcelona, where anarchists now reflected bitterly over having refused Companys' offer of total control in July 1936. From being in a position then to insist on the exclusion of the communist PSUC from the *Generalidad*, the CNT and the PSUC now had only four seats each. Companys' unofficial alliance with the communists was intended to strengthen the *Generalidad*'s power. Yet, he was particularly concerned at the loss of membership of his Esquerra party to the PSUC.

The change of atmosphere in Barcelona was remarked upon by observers who returned after a year's absence. The camaraderie and the optimism were gone. Nightclubs and expensive restaurants supplied by the black market had re-opened, while the bread queues started at four in the morning. The anarchists blamed the food crisis on Juan Comorera, the communist PSUC leader who was the *Generalidad* councillor in charge. Comorera had disbanded the food committees, which the CNT set up in July 1936, and ended bread rationing. The food distribution committees had certainly had their deficiencies, but these were overshadowed by the hoarding and profiteering which followed their abolition. Angry scenes outside shops were frequent, and even when there was no trouble, the *asaltos* often rode their horses into the bread queues or dispersed the women with blows from rifle butts.

There had been many more serious developments to make the anarchists and the POUM feel threatened in Catalonia. In the winter the PSUC had set out to exclude the POUM from the Catalan government. The anarchists, who until then had regarded the Communist–POUM battle simply as a Marxist rivalry, began to realize that its outcome would affect them.

Tension in Catalonia began to mount rapidly at the end of April. On the 25th Negrín sent his *carabineros* to seize the frontier controls at Puigcerdá, which the CNT had run since the rising. Eight anarchists who resisted were killed. On the same day a prominent communist was found dead. The CNT promptly condemned this murder and, although it may well have been carried out by an anarchist, there were apparently grounds to suspect fellow communists after criticisms the victim had made.

Two days later the *Generalidad*'s commissioner for public order, Artemio Ayguadé, who, though a member of the Esquerra, was under strong communist influence, gave the CNT-FAI and the POUM 48 hours to surrender all their weapons. This announcement caused great alarm. The POUM was particularly worried, for it had received several warnings of communist plans for its elimination on the orders of Moscow.

On 1 May the CNT and the UGT agreed to the *Generalidad*'s request to cancel the traditional May Day celebrations because of the political tension. Nevertheless a rally was held in Valencia, at which Largo Caballero's friend, Carlos de Baraíbar, in a speech containing veiled references to the communist threat, made a strong plea for UGT-CNT unity. But this move to rally support came too late from the prime minister who had dismantled syndicalist power on the urging of the communists the previous autumn.

The clash came 48 hours later in Barcelona. The central telephone exchange, captured by the anarchists in the fighting of 19 July, was run by a CNT-UGT committee in conjunction with a delegate from the Catalan government. At three o'clock in the afternoon of 3 May the communist police chief, Rodríguez Salas, arrived at the telephone building with three truckloads of armed guards. They grabbed the sentries and disarmed them, but, as they rushed inside, they were halted by a machine-gun which was trained on them from the first floor. Warning shots were fired out of the window. News of the incident spread across the city in minutes. Asens and Eroles, the anarchist leaders of the Control Patrols, arrived rapidly to calm the situation and, although they succeeded at the telephone building, the whole of Barcelona had gone spontaneously on to a war footing. Organized by the Libertarian Youth, the 'Friends of Durruti' and the POUM youth, barricades appeared everywhere, and hidden weapons were brought out. These younger elements, exasperated with the continual concessions of the CNT-FAI leadership, wanted to turn the clock back to July of the previous year.

The anarchists demanded the withdrawal of the police from the telephone building and the resignations of Ayguadé and Salas. The *Generalidad* refused and the battle-lines were confirmed. (According to Azaña, Ayguadé made his move without informing the other members of the *Generalidad*, although Companys had been talking 'idiotically of giving battle to the anarchists, but he had neither the ways nor the means'.) The Catalan government, backed by the police and PSUC held only small parts of the centre, while the CNT controlled the rest. The castle of Montjuich, with its heavy guns dominating the city, was also held by the CNT.

Buildings were defended and barricades constructed. In some ways it seemed like a return to the previous July. Cars daubed in initials drove at full pelt to avoid sniping. Journeys were so dangerous that the CNT used a couple of its improvised armoured vehicles. The *asaltos* attempted to take several buildings and were in turn attacked by groups of anarchists or *POUMistas*. Intermittent firing over the rooftops, or from sandbagged balconies, echoed across the city. The atmosphere of rumour and uncertainty is best described in Orwell's *Homage to Catalonia*.

The anarchist ministers, Juan García Oliver and Federica Montseny, flew in from Valencia after broadcasting an appeal for a ceasefire. This helped Jover and Vivancos, the commanders of the anarchist 25 and 26 Division on the Aragon front, who were having great difficulty preventing men from marching on Barcelona. The news of the communist move on the telephone building had triggered as strong a reaction at the front as in Barcelona itself. Nevertheless, no anarchist troops or members of the POUM's 29 Division went beyond Barbastro, and the front was not left bare as the communists claimed later.

The POUM was frustrated at being unable to make any move without the assurance of anarchist support. They stood little chance against the Stalinists on their own. Their leaders approached the CNT–FAI and suggested that communist power in Catalonia should be smashed while they still had the opportunity. The anarchist leaders rejected the idea, mainly because they felt committed by their participation in government, but also because they believed that an alliance with Largo Caballero and the non-communist majority of the UGT was the only effective brake on the Soviet-backed threat. But at a time when even those who had been in politics all their lives were being manipulated, their few months' experience of government left them mere children in such matters against the communists.

García Oliver and Federica Montseny went to the *Generalidad* hoping to find a solution, but the dismissal of Ayguadé and Rodríguez Salas was resisted by Companys and Tarradellas. Companys was utterly demoralized because Comorera of the PSUC persuaded him that he had no option but to surrender control of public order to the central government. A compromise solution was reached on 5 May by which a new government would be formed excluding Ayguadé. Other events were, however, to maintain the tension, of which the greatest was the discovery of the bodies of some anti-communists. The Italian anarchist, Camillo Berneri (the professor of philosophy at Florence University until Mussolini's rise to power) had been taken with his colleague, Barbieri, and shot in the back of the head. Among the other bodies found were those of Francisco Ferrer, the grandson of the educationalist executed in 1909, and Domingo Ascaso, the brother of the anarchist hero who was killed during the rising. Presumably in reprisal for these killings the communist UGT leader, Antonio Sesé, was assassinated in his car en route to the *Generalidad*.

Largo Caballero found himself in a difficult position. He needed the CNT, yet events in Barcelona were giving ammunition to the communists. He felt there was no alternative but to agree to the transfer of *asalto* reinforcements from the Jarama front. In addition Prieto despatched two destroyers packed with para-military forces from Valencia. Meanwhile, in other parts of Catalonia and Aragon the communists had taken advantage of events to broaden their offensive by seizing the telephone buildings in

Tarragona, Tolosa and many smaller towns. All these attempts were resisted and developed into street fighting, causing the *asalto* column which was heading for Barcelona from the Jarama to stop in Tarragona and crush resistance there.

The reinforcements which arrived in Barcelona increased the government's forces towards the level of the rebel troops the previous July, but they had even less hope of taking the city. The anarchists had an overwhelming numerical superiority, holding almost 90 per cent of Barcelona and its suburbs, as well as the heavy guns of Montjuich. These overwhelming advantages were not used because the CNT-FAI knew that further fighting would lead to a full civil war within the civil war, in which they would be cast as traitors, even if the Nationalists were unable to take advantage of the situation.

In the afternoon of Thursday, 6 May, the CNT-FAI proposed an armistice. They offered to pull down all barricades and return to work immediately, providing that the *asaltos* withdrew at the same time and there were no reprisals. No answer was received until 5.15 the next morning, when the *Generalidad* agreed to the terms. The CNT broadcast the news and, despite one outbreak of firing, the barricades started to be dismantled later in the day. However, the PSUC and the *asaltos* did not honour the agreement. They stayed in their positions in the centre and seized individuals or small groups, whom they arrested or whose CNT membership cards they tore up. The libertarians had scarely even won a Pyrrhic victory. Companys repudiated Rodríguez Salas' attempted seizure of the telephone building and removed Ayguadé from the government, but in fact both the libertarian movement and Companys suffered a defeat, while communists had also gained the lever they wanted against Largo Caballero. Their press began to work itself up into a high pitch of indignation over 'the May Days of Barcelona'.

The 'fascist plot' and 'anarcho-Trotskyist putsch' theories, which the Comintern spread throughout the world, were crude extensions of the mentality of the Moscow show trials. The Soviet advisers tried to use them as the basis for mounting similar spectacles in Spain. No evidence supported the communist interpretation of events, other than Franco's boast to von Faupel that Nationalist agents were responsible. But then any agent would be quick to claim responsibility for such events and Franco obviously wanted to impress his German allies.

On the other hand, the communists' opponents portrayed the move against the telephone building as a carefully planned provocation to give the communists the excuse to crush their enemies. It is a reasonable hypothesis, and there are isolated pieces of evidence pointing to a general preparation for such a move. (One of the sinister aspects was the role of Rodríguez Salas' Comintern controller, Erno Gerö, who later played a key role in the suppression of the Hungarian uprising of 1956.) Nevertheless, if it had been a case of calculated provocation, the communists would have had troops in the vicinity ready to crush the reaction and then pose as saviours of the Republic. (According to Companys there were only about 2,000 armed police in Barcelona on 3 May.) On balance, it would appear that their move on the telephone building was simply a further step in their progressive campaign to whittle away elements of opposition whenever an opportunity presented itself. Yet even though the communists probably did not plan the confrontation, they made the most of the opportunity. It has been noted, for example, that the majority of those found shot in the head were outspoken critics of the show trials in Moscow. The casualty rate of about 500 dead to 1,000 wounded is unusual, and very different from the fighting of the previous July.

The Barcelona events and their outcome could only strengthen the communists at the anarchists' expense. The CNT radio and press were heavily censored, as were POUM newspapers, and they were unable to reply to the barrage of communist innuendo and accusation. The very brazenness of the lies had an initial effect of disorienting people. They were tempted to believe what they heard on the grounds that nobody would dare to invent such allegations. Jesús Hernández, the communist minister, who turned against the Party after the war, said with some exaggeration 'if we were to decide to show that Largo Caballero, or Prieto, or Azaña, or Durruti were responsible for our defeats, half a million men, tens of newspapers, millions of demonstrators, and hundreds of orators would establish as gospel the evil doing of these citizens with such conviction and persistence that in a fortnight all Spain would agree with us'. However, several of the Spanish communist leaders were uneasy at the brash tactics insisted upon by their Soviet and Comintern advisers. La Pasionaria realized that such methods were 'premature' in Spain, where the communists did not have a total control of the media.

On 9 May just after the ceasefire, José Díaz of the Party's central committee advanced their strategy of deposing Largo Caballero and dealing ruthlessly with the POUM. 'The fifth column has been unmasked,' he declaimed, 'we need to destroy it ... Some call themselves Trotskyists, which is the name used by many disguised fascists who use revolutionary language in order to sow confusion. I therefore ask: If everyone knows this, if the government knows it, then why does it not treat them like fascists and exterminate them pitilessly? ... It was Trotsky himself who directed the gang of criminals that derailed trains in the Soviet Union, carried out acts of sabotage in the large factories, and did everything possible to discover military secrets with the object of handing them over to Hitler and the Japanese imperialists. And, in view of the fact that all this was revealed during the trial ...' With these words the communists revealed their plans for a spectacular arraignment of the POUM. A renewed attack on the POUM by Trotsky's Fourth International was, of course, ignored by the Stalinists who were determined that their label should stick.

At a cabinet meeting on 15 May (two days before measures introduced by Largo against communist infiltration of the commissar department became effective) the communist minister, Uribe, demanded on Moscow's orders that the POUM be suppressed and its leaders arrested. Largo Caballero refused, saying that he would not outlaw a working-class party against whom nothing had been proved. The anarchist ministers backed him and proceeded to charge the communists with provoking the events in Barcelona. Uribe and Hernández walked out, followed by the right socialists, Prieto and Negrín, the Basque nationalist, Irujo, Alvarez del Vayo and Giral. Largo was left with the four anarchist ministers and two of his old socialist colleagues. Azaña was warned by Giral on 7 May that the social democrats and liberals would back the communists at the next cabinet meeting. They took this decision partly because they identified with the communist policy of increased central government power and partly because they felt that any other course would put the Republic's arms supply at risk. Prieto insisted that as the coalition was broken, Largo Caballero must consult the president, but Azaña wished to avoid any complications. He told Largo to carry on so that continuity of planning might be maintained on the Estremadura offensive which had been projected for the middle of the month. The anarchist press joined their leaders in supporting Largo Caballero and his 'firm and just attitude which we all praise'. But without Soviet approval of the government, there would be no arms. Largo had not appreciated his growing isolation. He knew about Alvarez del Vayo; he may well have suspected Negrín; but, although he had quarrelled frequently with Prieto, he never expected him to come out on the communists' side. (Prieto, later virulently anti-communist, of course denied any collusion after the war, but it is hard to credit.)

The Comintern's switch to the Popular Front, or 'Trojan Horse', strategy in 1934 now appeared to have triumphed. By flattering liberals and social democrats, while appealing to their governmental instincts, the communists had reached a position where they could destroy their enemies one at a time (the 'salami tactic' as it was later called). The centrist politicians' key role in helping to reload 'the pistol of the state' for the communists' use did no more than reserve them the last place in the firing line. Stefanov, the Bulgarian Comintern delegate, remarked about Prieto to a colleague: 'For us, as you well know, there are neither friends nor enemies; there are persons who serve and persons who do not.' Valentín González, the communist commander 'El Campesino', expressed his surprise in later years that intelligent men had been taken in by such transparent manœuvres. It is more likely, however, that they believed themselves capable of stopping the communists later, much as the conservatives and the army officers in Germany had believed they could make use of Hitler.

The governing system of the Republic had become what Negrín and the communists described as 'controlled democracy'. This basically meant government from above in which the leaders of the main parties negotiated the distribution of ministries. Normal political life and argument was made difficult under war conditions and contact between leaders and party members was severely restricted. Azaña complained at the lack of internal debate and its result: 'The newspapers seem to be written by the same person, and they don't print anything more than diatribes against "international fascism" and assurances of victory.' The infrequent proceedings of the Cortes were no more than the trappings of democracy. Only the surviving members from the Popular Front parties remained to take part in its cosmetic role.

When, on 14 May, Azaña asked Largo Caballero to continue as prime minister, Largo realized that he would not be able to form another administration with the existing distribution of ministries. He therefore returned to the idea of a basically syndical government. This was similar to the National Defence Council which the anarchists had proposed the previous September, with Largo at its head and the bulk of the ministries split between the UGT and the CNT. Largo had resurrected the idea in Feb-

60 The war in the north – Carlist *requetés* are blessed by a chaplain before battle.

61 General Mola and the press near Durango, April 1937.

62 Republican naval gun crew.

63 Colonel von Richthofen with Nationalist and Condor Legion officers.

64 Durango after the Condor Legion attack of 31 March 1937.

65 Republican horse-artillery crossing a bridge.

66 Rata fighter, intended as Basque reinforcement, crash-landed in France, May 1937.

67 Nationalist armour entering Bilbao welcomed by sympathizers, June 1937.

68 Joris Ivens filming *Spanish Earth*.

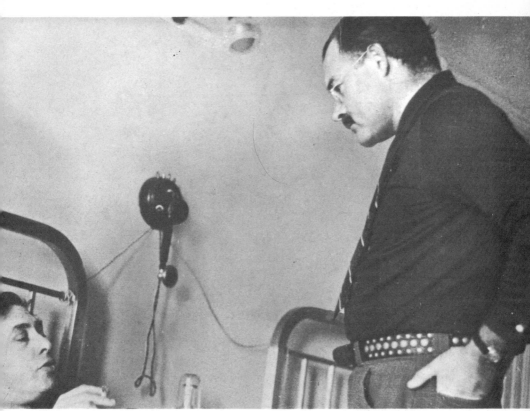

69 Ernest Hemingway visits Ilya Ehrenburg in hospital.

70 André Malraux.

71 Paul Robeson with American International Brigaders in **Madrid.**

72 General Orgaz fails to appreciate a Falangist priest addressing him as 'Comrade General'.

73 Franco (saluting), Serrano Súñer behind him and Yagüe (in glasses) to his right.

75 El Campesino making a speech.

76 García Oliver broadcasts appeal for a ceasefire during the May days of Barcelona.
74 *Left* Young libertarians shot by communists during May events in Catalonia.

77 A Republican attack in the sierra.

78 General Pozas and communists take over Catalan Council of Defence, May 1937.

79 Republican soldiers and T-26 tanks during the battle of Brunete, July 1937.

80 Garibaldi battalion of XII International Brigade in the Sierra de Guadarrama.

81 French merchant vessel *El Djem* sunk off Valencia by the Italians.

82 International Brigade machine-gunners dug in during the battle of Brunete, July 1936.

83 British communist leader Harry Pollitt addressing British battalion.

84 The communist commanders Enrique Líster (left) and Juan Modesto.

85 Funeral after the *Deutschland* bombing (29 May 1937) with British escort in Gibraltar.

86 Low cartoon: 'The question of Franco's existence'. 29 July 1937.

87 Two of the fast BT-5 tanks lost by Líster at Fuentes del Ebro at the end of August 1937.

88 Fighting in Belchite at the end of August 1937.

89 Republican disciplinary camp run by the communists.

90 CNT soldiers reading their newspaper *Solidaridad Obrera* at the front.

ruary, when he first became alarmed at the growth of communist influence. Azaña had then angrily rejected the proposal. The Russian supply of arms made the proposal impracticable. Largo was therefore allowed to continue only if he resigned as war minister. This Largo refused to do, believing that his presence at the war ministry was the last barrier to a communist coup. The communists, meanwhile, had approached Negrín and obtained his agreement to be the next prime minister. (Krivitsky claims that this had first been prepared the previous autumn by Stashevsky. The other important communist renegade, Hernández, asserts that the decision was taken at a Politburo meeting early in March when foreign communists including Marty, Togaliatti, Gerö and Codovilla outnumbered PCE members.) Prieto and the liberal republicans agreed with their choice, and Juan Negrín formed his administration on 27 May.

Negrín tends to be portrayed either as a puppet of Moscow or else as a man who, recognizing necessity, tried to ride the communist tiger for the benefit of the Spanish Republic. Both interpretations are misleading. Negrín was born into a rich, upper-middle-class family in the Canary Islands. He does not appear to have held strong political opinions in his youth. He was, however, convinced of his own abilities, and there are signs that he felt unsatisfied with the seemingly effortless success of his medical career, which led to his becoming professor of physiology at Madrid university at a young age. He soon started to dabble in politics, and his talents were undoubtedly greater than those of the professionals. Like many men who are conscious of their ability, he showed himself to be a firm believer in hierarchy, an authoritarian with few scruples who knew what was best for others. Not surprisingly he soon acquired a strong taste for power, once it was offered to him. In his case it appeared to run parallel to gross tastes for food and sex rather than act as a substitute.

Negrín's credentials and his 'iron hand' were applauded by official circles in London and Washington. His cabinet contained only two communists, both with minor ministries, while the former prime minister, Giral, was foreign minister, Irujo, the Basque conservative, minister of justice, Prieto minister of national defence, and another social democrat, Zugazagoitia, minister of the interior. Yet this government, which was welcomed by Churchill for its 'law-and-order stance' and toughness towards the communists and anarchists, was to leave the NKVD-controlled secret police unhindered in its persecution of persons who opposed the Moscow line and to sacrifice the POUM to Stalin in order to maintain arms supplies.

On its first day, Negrín's government agreed to the closing of the POUM's *La Batalla* newspaper. Soviet and Comintern advisers were under great pressure to achieve results quickly. Lt-Colonel Antonio Ortega, the new communist director general of security, took his orders from Orlov, not Zugazagoitia, the minister of the interior. On 16 June, when the POUM was declared illegal, the communists turned its headquarters in Barcelona into a prison for 'Trotskyists'. The commander of 29 Division, Colonel Rovira, was summoned to army headquarters and arrested. The POUM leaders who could be located, including Andrés Nin, were also arrested. The wives of those who could not be found were taken in their place. The communists then put their important prisoners in secret cells to obtain confessions. These actions were given a veneer of legality by the retroactive decree on 23 June creating Tribunals of Espionage and High Treason.

Despite pressure inside Republican Spain and demands from abroad, the government did nothing when the communists denied any knowledge of Nin's whereabouts. Jesús Hernández gave one version of his fate:

> Nin was not giving in. He was resisting until he fainted. His inquisitors were getting impatient. They decided to abandon the 'dry' method. Then the blood flowed, the skin peeled off, muscles torn, physical suffering pushed to the limits of human endurance. Nin resisted the cruel pain of the most refined tortures. In a few days his face was a shapeless mass of flesh.

Nin consistently refused to confess to treason and Orlov gave up. A detachment of German communists from the International Brigades was organized to dress up as a special 'Gestapo commando team'. This group then faked a rescue, leaving behind ponderous clues such as German banknotes. Nin was killed that night and buried secretly, or else, according to two other accounts, he was put in a crate and then shipped to the Soviet Union. His bravery undermined the show-trial programme in Spain, thus saving his fellow POUM leaders. Many Soviet advisers were recalled to Moscow and a number of them were liquidated.

Distanced by time from the atmosphere of the Moscow show trials or Spain in 1937, it is difficult for us to understand how anyone could believe the accusations laid against the POUM. Having stated that 'fascist planes were going to be sent to the assistance of the putschists' and that the POUM made a 'non-aggression pact' with the Nationalists, the communists claimed that 'the Trotskyists were obliged to retreat before the overwhelming forces of the Catalan working class'. Then 'a great wave of popular indignation swept through Barcelona and the entire people demanded justice.' The POUM were accused of acting as fascist *agents provocateurs* and spies. They were accused of planning the assassinations of Prieto and the foreign communist, General Walter, 'one of the most popular commanders of the Spanish People's Army'. (The linking of social democrat and communist in this context was presumably calculated.) José Díaz, the Party's secretary-general, claimed, before any trial took place, that the charges were proved: 'Let the firing squad do its work and make an end of traitors and terrorists.' The Party's last word on the disappearance of Nin was that he was 'taken away by friends. They had every reason for wanting to get him away before his examination, which would have inevitably revealed a mass of further incriminating evidence.'

Negrín seemed content to accept the communist version of Nin's disappearance, though Azaña was openly sceptical. The Republican government did little to stop the private communist executions of *POUMistas* and their foreign sympathizers in Spain. A kidnapping was usually followed by intense interrogation, torture in their secret prisons and an anonymous death. The 'disciplined machine' had taken over, but its vaunted efficiency was of little use without the energy of popular support to drive it. For many, there seemed to be few ideals left to defend. The anarchist theorist, Abad de Santillán, remarked, 'Whether Negrín won with his communist cohorts, or Franco won with his Italians and Germans, the results would be the same for us.'

THE BRUNETE OFFENSIVE AND THE MEDITERRANEAN

In the wake of the events of May, the communists began to control all the forces in Catalonia and Aragon. General Pozas took over the *Generalidad*'s Council of Defence and set out to reorganize its six divisions into the Army of the East. Eventually this was to include the disbandment of the POUM's 29 Division, whose men had to seek shelter from the communist secret police by joining anarchist formations. Pozas also made plans for an offensive against the town of Huesca, almost as if to confirm the implied communist claim that only they could animate the Aragon front. However, this attempt to take pressure off the northern zone tended to give substance to some of their opponents' complaints. General Lukács, who commanded the attack, had not improved their weapons and the artillery and tank support was negligible. Air support did arrive, but only after a vigorous Nationalist reaction. The offensive failed and Lukács was killed by a shell. Distrust was increased by the fact that almost all the casualties were from CNT units. The enemy was found to be waiting for them, but there is no evidence to suggest that this was anything other than coincidence. Security before operations was notoriously bad, although the constant flood of rumours tended to confuse enemy intelligence.

The other offensive to help relieve the pressure on the Basque front took place in the Sierra de Guadarrama, from Navalcarnero down towards Segovia, on 30 May. (Hemingway used this battle as the background in *For Whom the Bell Tolls*.) The operation, involving mostly communist formations, had full artillery and air support, although Pavlov's tanks were of little use in the pine forest and scrub oak on the steep slopes. The main force was grouped around 35 Division commandered by the Polish General 'Walter' (alias Swierczewski). The overall commander was Colonel Moriones of I Corps. The Nationalist response, directed by Varela and backed by fighter squadrons from Avila, recaptured the Cabeza Grande mountain and the whole of Walter's advance on La Granja was threatened. This action saw the first outward sign of protest in the International Brigades against the way in which they were often sacrificed to little purpose. In addition, the Republican air force and the Russian pilots were criticized by their fellow communists on the ground in an unprecedented way. They had apparently shown little taste for the battle, while the

Nationalist Fiat squadrons were said to have fought bravely and skilfully. According to Franco's air force commander, General Kindelán, the sierra offensive retarded the fall of Vizcaya by two weeks, because he had to transfer aircraft, but the Republican operation was just as much a failure as the one at Huesca.

Largo Caballero's general staff advisers had begun to plan a much larger offensive in Estremadura during April while the Nationalists were advancing in Vizcaya. The idea of a major attack in the west to split the Nationalist zone in two came originally from General Asensio Torrado before he was ousted in February. The intention was to avoid the cycle of battles round Madrid, which ended in fruitless blood baths. There were several reasons for choosing the west instead of New Castile. The Nationalist troops in the area were thinly spread, inexperienced and less well equipped than in the centre. Franco would also find it more difficult to bring in reinforcements, due to the nature of the road and rail networks. In addition left-wing guerrillas were already operating behind Nationalist lines in Estremadura, although their effectiveness was probably overestimated. Advocates of the plan were probably over-optimistic in their belief that it could lead to the conquest of the south-west.

The arguments against the project were the difficulty of achieving surprise after moving the necessary quantity of troops to the area, the difficulties presented by long supply lines and the danger of taking the best formations away from Madrid. Nevertheless, the proposed Estremadura offensive was likely to be more effective than an operation in the centre, where the Nationalists could rapidly redeploy their forces and bring the Condor Legion back to Avila.

The Soviet advisers and senior communist officers opposed the Estremadura plan, mainly for political reasons. They wanted the next offensive to take place in the western Madrid sector, next to the area of the battle of Corunna road. They were still obsessed with the fight for the capital, as Franco had been until only a short time before. The communists had invested much effort and many of their men in the defence of Madrid. It was the centre piece of their international propaganda campaign.

The dispute over the Estremadura offensive also marked the first reaction of regular officers against communist control. Some of those who had at first welcomed communist ideas on discipline now started to suspect that the communists were perhaps more interested in extending their control than in winning the war. They were dismayed by the complete misrepresentation of events for propaganda purposes and alarmed at the vitriolic campaigns against officers like General Asensio Torrado, who had dared to criticize the Party's manipulation of military supplies.

Largo Caballero and the officers who planned the Estremadura offensive soon found that they faced both a Soviet refusal to commit tank and air support as well as General Miaja's pointed failure to obey orders to transfer formations from his command. Largo's fall in May and Negrín's accession greatly increased the communists' control of military affairs. Prieto, the new defence minister controlling all three services, still believed in collaborating with them closely. It was not until his experience of communist command in this next great battle that he began to change his attitude.

BATTLE OF BRUNETE, July 1937

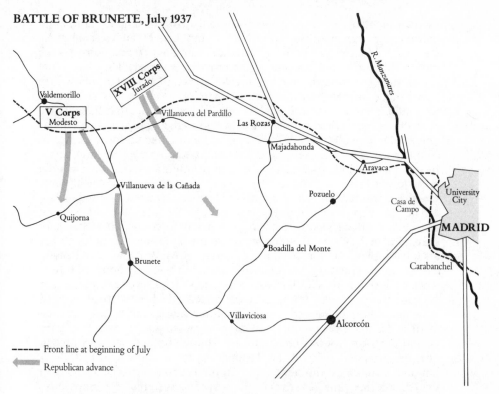

- - - - - Front line at beginning of July

⬅ Republican advance

The sector which the communists had chosen for their alternative to Largo's project was 10 Division's front opposite Brunete, a village some 30 kilometres (19 miles) to the west of Madrid. The composition of the attacking force, together with the commitment of every available tank, field gun and plane to support it, emphasized that the Brunete offesive was to be the Party's demonstration of strength. All five International Brigades and the communists' best-known formations were given the key roles, and every important officer had a Soviet adviser at his elbow. Miaja was overall commander. Under him were Modesto's V Corps on the right with Líster's 11 Division, El Campesino's 46 Divison, and Walter's 35 Division; Jurado's XVIII Corps on the left with 10, 15 and 34 Division (Jurado, the only non-communist senior commander, became ill and was replaced by Colonel Casado during the battle); and a forward reserve of Kléber's 45 Division and Durán's 69 Division. In support Miaja could count on 129 tanks, 43 other armoured vehichles, 217 field guns, 50 bombers and 90 fighters. It was by far the largest concentration of strength yet seen in the war.

Nevertheless it concealed crucial weaknesses. The Popular Army supply services were not used to coping with such large numbers, and the Segovia offensive had shown up the bad communications between commanders as well as their lack of initiative. This last defect, which was to prove so serious in the Brunete offensive, is usually attributed to a fear of making independent decisions among Party members. This caution may seem surprising in aggressive 30-year-olds like Modesto and Líster. Yet, among this new breed of formation commander, only Modesto and El Campesino had seen service in Morocco as NCOs, and Líster had received some training in Moscow. Their first experience of military command had come during the sierra engagements of the previous summer. They had often shown themselves daring and resourceful at battalion level, but now they commanded formations with anything up to 30 battalions and had to cope with unfamiliar staff procedures. Azaña disliked the fact that these 'crude guerrillas', 'improvised people, without knowledge', pushed aside regular officers. Despite all their efforts, they could 'not make up for their lack of competence'. But if the new leaders of the Popular Army were intimidated by their responsibilities or conscious of their limitations, they certainly did not allow it to show. As with the International Brigades at the Jarama, ignorance was hidden behind a bluff confidence sustained by discipline.

The plan was to smash southwards through the weak Nationalist front line, then south-eastwards to cut off the enemy forces on the west side of the capital in the Casa de Campo sector. At the same time a complementary assault was planned from the southern suburbs of Madrid towards Alcorcón to form a pincer action. The offensive started in the early hours of 6 July, when 34 Division from XVIII Corps attacked Villanueva de la Cañada. The Nationalist resistance was unexpectedly fierce, and when the troops seemed reluctant to keep going into the assault, Miaja gave orders to 'take Cañada at all costs, and if the infantry will not go forward place a battery of guns behind our own troops to make them'. Though outnumbered by nine to one, the defenders held off the Republicans for a whole day. Líster's 11 Division swung past this action and captured Brunete on the morning of the 7th, but then failed to advance. He was concerned that El Campesino's 46 Division had failed to crush the Falangist battalion defending Quijorna to his right rear. (A similar hold-up due to a brave defence occurred on XVIII Corp's left flank at Villanueva del Pardillo.) Instead of advancing while the way ahead lay open, Líster and his Russian adviser, Rodimstev, ordered their troops to dig in just south of Brunete, where they waited for El Campesino's troops to finish off the Falangists in Quijorna. That took three days, and by then Varela, the Nationalist commander, had brought in Sáenz de Buruaga's 150 Division to attack between Brunete and Quijorna. This threat was met by Walter's 35 Division, which filled the gap between Líster and El Campesino.

While Líster waited, the major thrust of the offensive was made towards Boadilla del Monte by Gal's 15 Division from XVIII Corps. On its line of advance lay a low ridge which the International Bridgaders called Mosquito hill because of the sound of bullets. It was to become as horrific a memory as Suicide Hill at the Jarama. With the momentum of the attack dissipated because of two tiny pockets of resistance, and the tanks misused as self-propelled artillery, the Nationalists were given the time they needed to recover.

Varela, the Nationalist commander, brought in Barrón's 13 Division within 24 hours of the beginning of the offensive and 150 Division on 8 July. On the next day, the 9th, Assensio concentrated his forces in front of Boadilla, towards which the Republican 15 Divison was advancing. He managed to block their attack in a battle which cost both sides heavily. On the 10th the Nationalists counter-attacked with their 10 and 150 Division, opposite V Corps south-west of Brunete-Quijorna. Varela had thus achieved the first step of halting the offensive and, as Franco was not satisfied simply to contain the advance, he waited for reinforcements from other fronts before launching a major counter. Franco's obstinate insistence that the Republicans should not be allowed to hold any captured territory, however unimportant, helped the Republicans to achieve their objective of draining pressure away from the northern front. Dávila was ordered to divert two double-strength Carlist brigades, and the Condor Legion was brought down to Avila and Talavera airfields.

The most important and flexible reinforcement for the Nationalist troops was their air support, which took full advantage of the targets presented by eight divisions blocked in less than 200 square kilometres (75 square miles) of Castilian plain. The exposed T-26s were attacked first, and by 11 July, only two days after the Nationalist air force began its full sortie rhythm, the Republicans were left with only 38 operational armoured vehicles, a quarter of what they had started with five days before. The Nationalist squadrons of Junkers 52s and Heinkel 45s, now flown by Spanish pilots, and the Fiat fighters were committed first. The Condor Legion was reluctant to risk its aircraft, because of the Chato and Rata squadrons which the Republic had allocated to the front, but when the Russian and Republican pilots failed to provide an effective fighter umbrella for their troops, the Luftwaffe changed its mind. Once having decided to participate, it did not spare its aircrew. Sorties were made throughout the day and even into the night with the Heinkel 111 experimental squadron and Junkers 52s. (Three of the latter were shot down by Russian Rata pilots in what was claimed to be the first examples of aerial night-fighting.) The Messerschmitt 109s, which had been used very cautiously on the Vizcaya front, were fully engaged on the Brunete sector after 12 July. They immediately showed that the Chato biplane stood little chance against them. Even the fast Rata was outclassed.

Meanwhile, on the ground, Miaja's staff had failed to foresee all the problems of ammunition and water re-supply. The 'monk-brown' Castilian plain in July was scorched and bare. Even the River Guadarrama had dried up, and tank crews became speechless with thirst in their oven-like conditions. The infantry could only dig shell-scrapes in the sandy earth to protect themselves against machine-gun fire or bombs. For camouflage and shade there was only shrivelled scrub. The whole area was littered with swollen, black corpses, putrefying in the sun, despite the brave work of stretcher bearers, who suffered a higher casualty rate than the infantry in that landscape.

Líster's failure to advance, and the blocking of XVIII Corps near Mosquito Hill on the south-east part of the salient, meant that only a few kilometres had been gained since the first 24 hours of the offensive. The Nationalists' counter-attacks built up gradually. Asensio's division, which had fought off four furious assaults on Boadilla, turned to the offensive on 11 July. The next day, 4 and 5 Navarrese Brigades and 108 (Galician) Division joined in, forcing the Republican forces onto the defensive. Fierce fighting continued for the next week with little result. On the 18th the Nationalists tried to break the stalemate by attacking simultaneously on all sides. They finally succeeded in forcing the Republican troops to retreat on 24 July and recaptured most of the lost territory including Brunete. The Republic ended up with a total gain of less than 50 square kilometres (20 square miles) at the cost of some 25,000 casualties, 80 per cent of their armoured force, and more than a third of the aircraft allotted to the front. The Nationalists suffered about 17,000 casualties and a lower death rate. Their losses in material were small in comparison to the disaster which their opponents sustained, particularly at a time when the blockade of Republican ports had become increasingly effective.

The communists declared Brunete a victory. XV International Brigade was told that 'it completely vindicated the active war-policy, which the Negrín government was elected to enforce, as contrasted with the laissez-faire conduct of Largo Caballero, and impressed the outside world with the promise the newly reorganized Republican Army held for the future'. The premature and wildly exaggerated claims about the operation's success in the first two days had forced Miaja and his staff to persist at horrendous cost rather than admit failure. The communists defended the operational plan furiously, but such a concentration of slow-moving forces on a re-stricted front enabled the Nationalists to profit from the vastly superior ground-attack potential of their combined air forces. With both Avila and Talavera airfields less than 30 minutes' flying time from Brunete they were able to establish a bombing shuttle and fighter sortie rhythm, which the advocates of the Republican offensive must have seriously underestimated.

The Republican forces suffered badly from their communications, as they did in all the battles in which field telephone-lines were cut by shellfire and runners shot down in the open. Such conditions were perilous for an army which allowed its formation commanders so little initiative. The Nationalists, on the other hand, met the offensive with instinctive reactions at all levels of command and did not wait for orders when it was im-possible to consult superior officers. Nor did they blindly follow instruc-tions when a change in circumstances on the ground showed them to be inadequate.

Republican commanders, on the other hand, often misled headquarters. For example, El Campesino grossly exagerrated enemy casualties in Qui-jorna when it finally fell, so as to justify his previous lack of success. Líster quadrupled the number of defenders of Brunete in his report, then pro-ceeded to claim that his forces had reached Navalcarnero, some 12 kilo-metres ($7\frac{1}{2}$ miles) beyond where they were dug in. (The Communist Party history of the war published in 1971 stands by this account.) Later in the battle when Mera's 14 Division was brought in to replace 11 Division at Brunete, even Líster was not aware that the village had been recaptured by *regulares*, and Miaja's chief-of-staff, Colonel Matallana, thought Líster's men still held the high ground several kilometres beyond. Prieto, who was present in army headquarters when Mera pointed out how his orders were no longer accurate, stormed out angrily at Miaja's excuse of being de-ceived. The consequent attempt by Modesto, the commander of V Corps, to blame the loss of Brunete on 14 Division so as to protect the reputation of the most famous communist formation, was not therefore lost on the defence minister.

Brunete marked an important stage in the growing dissatisfaction within the International Brigades. The men of XIII International refused to go back into the line after unnecessary losses and even set off for Madrid before being surrounded by *asaltos* and armoured cars. There was also a revolt in the American Lincoln battalion and a successful mutiny in the British battalion against the hated General Gal. The Brigade cavalry squadrons were used almost exclusively throughout the battle for rounding up those who retreated without orders. In V Corps Modesto ordered that 'machine-guns shall be placed behind the front line with orders to open fire on any individual or group which tries to abandon their post on any pretext'. Morale was badly damaged by the heavy casualties, which included such popular figures as George Nathan, especially since the majority of the Republicans must have suspected that the slaughter was futile.

The Republic's first major offensive had ended in a severe setback, despite its very limited success in taking pressure off the northern zone. The damage to morale, the loss of so many experienced soldiers at a time when the Nationalists were in sight of numerical parity, and the catastrophic loss of material were not compensated by the month's delay in the Nationalists' northern campaign which the offensive had achieved. But although the 'active war-policy' of Negrín's government had not started auspiciously, the new prime minister hoped that his cabinet's moderate and disciplined image would succeed in persuading the Western governments to change their policy towards Spain. He did manage to impress Eden and Churchill, but the former had scarcely six months left before his resignation in protest at Chamberlain's policy, and the latter remained 'in the wilderness' until over a year after the end of the civil war.

The civil war had now lasted for a year. The British government had kept France in the non-interventionist camp by working on the French fears of isolation in the face of Hitler. As Eden's assistant, Viscount Cranborne, stated later to the House of Commons, 'The last word in French policy is always said in London. This was proved over the reoccupation of the Rhineland, over the *Anschluss*, and over the Sudeten-land. In each case France said "Never", but Britain thought otherwise. So today, if Britain tells France to "pay" in Spain and in Africa, she will "pay". At the bottom of the question of war or peace is a problem of British internal politics.' The diplomatic charade of non-intervention received a severe shock on 23 March 1937, when Count Grandi, the Italian ambassador, openly admitted to the Non-Intervention Committee that there were Italian forces in Spain and asserted that none of them would be withdrawn until the war was won. Even so German and Italian intervention continued to be 'unrecognized'. The only practical step taken had been a measure on foreign enlistments, which meant that each of the signatories passed laws preventing private citizens from volunteering. This, of course, affected those trying to join the International Brigades, while the Axis powers' contribution of military units was ignored. In addition, the only effective control on importing war material proved to be the Pyrenean frontier, so again only the Republic suffered.

The isolationism of the United States helped the Nationalists, who were aided by many influential sympathizers in Washington. The government had tacitly upheld the non-intervention policy from the beginning. At the end of 1936, when aircraft were to be shipped to Republican Spain by a private company, Roosevelt introduced legislation to prevent it. Nevertheless, the cargo left on board the *Mar Cantábrico* just a few hours before the law took effect. This Spanish merchantman took on more material in Mexico, and then, disguised as British, made for Basque waters. The deception was no use, for the Nationalist cruiser *Canarias* put to sea from El Ferrol on 4 March to await it. The *Mar Cantábrico* was captured on 8 March and all the Spanish seamen were executed. It is still not known who warned the Nationalists of its route.

On 20 April the Non-Intervention Committee introduced its scheme to patrol ports and frontiers. Naval patrols furnished by Great Britain, France, Germany and Italy watched the coasts. The uselessness of the scheme was shown by the fact that not a single breach of the agreement was reported by the time it collapsed in the autumn. The incident with the greatest potential danger in this period occurred on 29 May, when the port of Palma was attacked by Russian-piloted bombers from Valencia. In their raid, which was principally directed against the cruiser *Baleares*, two direct hits were made on the German battleship *Deutschland*, killing 31 sailors and wounding 74. Hitler, on hearing the news, worked himself up into a fit of terrifying proportions. He ordered units of the German navy, including the *Admiral Scheer*, to bombard the undefended town of Almería in reprisal. Prieto wanted the Republican air force to attack all German warships in reply. The communists were greatly alarmed and radioed Moscow for instructions. Stalin, not unexpectedly, was entirely opposed to Prieto's suggestion, since provocation of Hitler alarmed him more than anything else. It was later rumoured that orders had been given to liquidate Prieto if he persisted.

Germany threatened to withdraw from the Non-Intervention Committee. Neville Chamberlain, who had become prime minister on 17 May, tried to soothe the Fuehrer with 'definite and considered' attempts to improve Anglo-German relations. The Germans, realizing that they could take further advantage of the situation, claimed on 15 June that their cruiser *Leipzig* had been attacked off Oran by an unidentified submarine. They used this as their justification for withdrawing from the naval patrol.

The German and Italian policy on Spain was as closely co-ordinated as that of England and France. Having recognized the Burgos regime in the previous November, they recommended that belligerent rights should be granted to both sides so that non-intervention controls should no longer be needed. The British were opposed to the granting of belligerent rights, which would mean interference with British shipping. The French government (now led by Camille Chautemps, but still containing Blum and Delbos), knew that Nationalist naval power, with covert help from Italian submarines, could blockade the Republic into surrender. The British government suggested a compromise formula which involved granting belligerent rights only when foreign troops had been withdrawn. This was then amended to 'substantial reductions', which led to haggling over figures and percentages.

During the summer the Italians began a random campaign of maritime attacks from Majorca, with 'Legionary' submarines and bombers. In August alone they sank 200,000 tons of shipping bound for Republican Spain, including eight British and 18 other neutral merchantmen. On 23 August

Ciano made notes of a visit from the British *chargé d'affaires* in Rome: 'Ingram made a friendly *démarche* about the torpedo attacks in the Mediterranean. I replied quite brazenly. He went away almost satisfied.' On the 31st the Italian submarine *Iride* fired torpedoes at the British destroyer HMS *Havock*. On 3 September Ciano wrote: 'Full orchestra – France, Russia, Britain. The theme – piracy in the Mediterranean. Guilty – the Fascists. The Duce is very calm. He looks in the direction of London and he doesn't believe that the English want a collision with us.' It was not surprising that Mussolini could perceive this. Lord Perth, the British ambassador, was later described by Ciano as 'a genuine convert', a man who had 'come to understand and even to love Fascism'. Chamberlain, ignoring Eden's advice, wrote to Mussolini directly in the friendliest terms, thinking he could woo him away from Hitler. Meanwhile, he had instructed Perth to start working towards a Treaty of Friendship with Mussolini. He was also to use as a personal envoy his sister-in-law, Lady Chamberlain, who proudly wore fascist badges and insignia.

There were the beginnings of a small group in the Conservative Party and its supporters who were sensitive to the dangers of Chamberlain's policy. Harold Nicolson, who was one of them, agreed with Duff Cooper that 'the second German war began in July 1936, when the Germans started with their intervention in Spain'. He went on to say that 'the propertied classes in this country with their insane pro-Franco business have placed us in a very dangerous position'. The only area where the Conservative government was prepared to display a semblance of firmness was in the Mediterranean, the sealane to the Empire. It was simply concerned that Axis bases should not exist on Spanish territory once the civil war was over. The French initiated the only active diplomatic step to enforce non-intervention.

Delbos decided that the submarine attacks had to be stopped. He called a conference at Nyon at the beginning of September to discuss the situation in the Mediterranean. Italy and Germany refused to attend, the Nazi government claiming that the *Leipzig* incident had still not been resolved, the Italians protesting at the Soviet Union's direct accusation of continued submarine attacks. The British and French governments 'regretted this decision', adding that they would keep the Axis powers informed of what happened. Meanwhile, Neurath warned Ciano that British naval intelligence had intercepted signals traffic between Italian submarines. Knowing there was little to fear, Ciano replied that they would be more careful in future. The Nyon conference decided with remarkable speed that any submerged submarines located near a torpedoing incident would be attacked by the naval forces of the signatories. Nothing, however, was said of air or surface attacks. That had to be added later at the League of Nations in Geneva. The British then proceeded to make such large provisos in an attempt to persuade the Italians to join the agreement that the whole exercise was rendered virtually worthless. Mussolini boasted to Hitler that he would still continue his 'torpedoing operations'.

At the League of Nations that autumn, Eden tried to justify the non-intervention policy by claiming, untruthfully, that it had reduced the inflow of foreign forces. The British government also tried to prevent the Spanish Republic from publishing details of Italian intervention. Eden admitted that 'it would be idle to deny that there have been wide breaches of the agreement', but he went on to recommend the maintenance of the non-intervention agreement because 'a leaky dam may yet serve its purpose'. For the Nationalists it was, of course, no barrier at all and never had been. Eventually, the League decided that if it 'cannot be made to work in the near future, the members of the League will consider ending the policy of non-intervention'. The Spanish Republican representative asked for a more precise definition of 'the near future'. The French foreign minister, Delbos, hoped it meant not more than ten days, and the British representative replied 'probably an earlier date than the Spanish delegate thinks'. The near future had still not arrived 18 months later when the Spanish Republic ceased to exist.

THE WAR IN ARAGON
AND THE CONSOLIDATION OF
COMMUNIST POWER

After the failure of the Brunete offensive in July, the Republican general staff finally admitted that nothing could be achieved by major operations in the central region. But even though another attack on such a massive scale could not be considered after their losses in material, a further effort to help Santander and Asturias was urgently required. If the Republican forces in the north could hold out until the winter snows blocked the passes of the Cordillera Cantábrica, Franco would not be able to bring down his Navarrese, Galician and Italian troops (which would bring him numerical parity) or the major part of his air power before the late spring of 1938.

The Aragon front was chosen for the next Republican attack. The reasons for deciding on the east rather than the south-west were primarily political. The communists and their senior supporters in the army could not select Estremadura, because it would be a virtual admission that the Brunete strategy had been wrong and Largo Caballero's project right. General Rojo, the chief-of-staff, never resisted their direction of military affairs. Communist influence had promoted him from major in less than six months. The major reason, however, for switching the emphasis of the war to the east was the intention of Negrín's government and the communists to establish complete control over Catalonia and Aragon. In the wake of the May events in Barcelona, the central government had taken over responsibility for public order in Catalonia, dissolved the *Generalidad's* Council of Defence, which had been run by the anarchists since its inception, and appointed General Pozas to command the newly designated Army of the East. This represented the first stage in ending the *Generalidad's* independence and anarchist power in Catalonia. The next stage in reasserting central government control was to be the crushing of the Council of Aragon by bringing in communist troops and placing the three anarchist divisions under overall communist command. The composition of Republican forces in the east was changed radically in the summer of 1937. Before Brunete the only communist formation in the region had been the PSUC's 27 (Carlos Marx) Division, but during the last days of July and the first part of August, all the elite communist formations were transferred from the central front: Kléber's 45 Division, Modesto's V Corps (including Líster's 11 Division, Walter's 35 Division and El Campesino's

46 Division). For the first time the anarchists were threatened in their 'Spanish Ukraine'. The true outcome of the May events was now becoming clear.

At the end of July, after the battle of Brunete, the communists launched a propaganda offensive against the Council of Aragon's president, Joaquín Ascaso, who was a controversial and flamboyant figure. The communists accused him of acting like a Mafia chieftain. His libertarian supporters, on the other hand, defended him vigorously when he was accused of smuggling jewellery out of the country. Ferocious attacks were made on the system of self-managed agricultural collectives in the main Party newspapers *Mundo Obrero* and *Frentre Rojo*, because it ran counter to the 'controlled democracy' which Negrín and the communists advocated.

At the end of July the *carabineros*, which Negrín had built up when finance minister, were used to harass the collectives by confiscating their produce. Then, on 11 August, the central government dissolved the Council of Aragon by decree while its members were gathering in the last of the harvest. The anarchist 25, 26 and 28 Divisions were kept occupied at the front and cut off from news of what was happening, so that Líster's 11 Division, backed by 27 and 30 Division, could be sent against the anarchist and joint CNT–UGT collectives. These 'manœuvres', as they were officially described, involved mass arrests and the forcible disbandment of the Council of Aragon along with all its component organizations. CNT offices were seized and destroyed, and the collectives' machinery, transport, tools and seed grain were given to the small proprietors whom the communists had encouraged to resist inducements to work the land communally.

The anarchist members of the Council were the first to be arrested, and they were fortunate not to have been shot out of hand. The communists counted on arranging a spectacular trial for Ascaso, but he had to be released a month later when they could produce no evidence. (La Pasionaria tried to revive the accusations in 1968, saying that Ascaso had fled to South America where he was living in luxury on his booty. He was, in fact, still working as a servant in a hotel in Venezuela.)

The justification for this operation (whose 'very harsh measures' shocked even some Party members) was that, as all the collectives had been established by force, Líster was merely liberating the peasants. There had undoubtedly been pressure, and no doubt force was used on some occasions in the fervour after the rising. But the very fact that every village was a mixture of collectivists and individualists shows that peasants had not been forced into communal farming at the point of a gun. It is estimated that there were about 300,000 people belonging to the collectives and 150,000 individualists. Perhaps the most eloquent testimony against the communists is the number of collectives which managed to re-establish themselves after Líster's forces had left. Meanwhile, the degree to which food production was disrupted and permanently damaged became a matter for bitter debate. José Silva, the head of the Institute of Agrarian Reform, later embarrassed his colleagues considerably, when he admitted that the operation had been 'a very grave mistake'.

The exact part in these events played by the non-communist members of Negrín's government, especially Prieto, is the subject of dispute. Negrín himself backed the communist action without reservation, while the liberals and the other right socialists continued to support measures which destroyed 'cantonalism' and increased centralized power. Prieto, the minister of defence, and Zugazagoitia, the minister of the interior, certainly gave instructions for the dismantling of the Council of Aragon, and were prepared to use force if necessary. But Prieto denied Líster's claim that he was given *carte blanche* to destroy the collectives as well.

The events in Aragon also caused the rift between the CNT leadership and its mass membership to widen. The weakness of the CNT leaders in their refusal to condemn Líster's action outright provoked much frustration and anger. The only attempt to restrain the communist action came from Mariano Vázquez, the CNT secretary-general, who asked Prieto to transfer Mera's division to Aragon immediately. But he was satisfied by the minister of defence's reply that he had already reprimanded Líster. (Vázquez, a 'reformist' syndicalist and the chief advocate within the CNT of complete obedience to government orders, was a great admirer of Negrín, who in fact despised him.) The CNT leaders claimed that they had prevented death sentences from being carried out by the special communist military tribunals, but the prospect of three anarchist divisions turning their guns against Líster's troops probably weighed more with the communists. Besides, the protests of the CNT officials were in vain when El Campesino's division later carried out a similar disbandment of collectives in La Mancha and New Castile.

The officers of the three anarchist divisions had great difficulty in preventing sub-units, and even battalions, from pulling out of line to attack the communist troops to their rear. General Pozas, however, had foreseen this eventuality. The offensive planned to take pressure off the north was also made to serve the purpose of suppressing another flare-up in the Republic's own civil war.

Apart from reducing pressure on Santander (which in fact fell on 24 August, the day the offensive was launched), the principal objective was the city of Saragossa. The recapture of this regional capital offered more than just symbolic significance. It was also the communications centre of the whole Aragon front. The first year of the war in this part of Spain had emphasized that the possession of a key town was of far greater importance than the control of wide areas of open countryside. The Nationalists had only 51, 52 and 105 Divisions spread across the 300 kilometres (185 miles) of front, with the majority of their troops concentrated in towns.

General Pozas and his chief-of-staff, Antonio Cordón, set up their headquarters at Bujaraloz. Their plan was to break through at seven different points on the central 100-kilometre (60-mile) stretch between Zuera and Belchite. The object of splitting their attacking forces was to divide any Nationalist counter-attack and to offer fewer targets for bombing and strafing shuttles than at Brunete. On the north flank 27 Division would attack Zuera before swinging left on Saragossa itself. In the right centre Kléber's 45 Division was to attack south-eastwards from the Sierra de Alcubierre towards Saragossa. Meanwhile, the main weight of the offensive was concentrated up the south side of the Ebro valley. 25 Division was to cross the river from the north bank to prevent reinforcements from Saragossa coming to aid the forward towns of Quinto, Codo and Belchite.

Then Líster's 11 Division would thrust along the southern bank towards Saragossa, spearheaded by nearly all the T-26 and BT-5 tanks allocated to the offensive. The majority of the 200 Republican aircraft on the front were also reserved for the Ebro valley attack. They greatly outnumbered the Nationalists' obsolete Heinkel 46 light bombers and Heinkel 51 fighters.

The Republic thus had overwhelming local superiority on the ground and in the air, and Modesto's general order for attack made the whole operation sound like a foregone conclusion. He emphasized that the enemy's front was 'guarded by a few troops of poor quality' and that 'there are few reserves in Saragossa'. Modesto seemed to be more interested in making certain that Líster's division, helped by its tanks, would have the glory of entering Saragossa first, than in considering alternatives should the operation not turn out to be the walkover he assumed it would be. It was only six weeks since Brunete, but Modesto appears to have forgotten what happened there, unless he believed the propaganda which had turned defeat into a victory.

In the event the Nationalist defenders turned out to be even more tenacious than at Brunete. The Republican commanders became obsessed with reducing pockets of resistance, when they should have left them to be contained by the reserves while the attacking force concentrated on the main objective. The small town of Belchite had only a few hundred men, yet their bravery managed to tie down half of Modesto's V Corps. They fought on for 13 days, even though their water supply was cut, and the stench of rotting corpses was at times enough to make their attackers wear gasmasks. Quinto had been taken on the fourth day of the offensive, but the village of Codo was held by three companies of Carlists against two brigades. These delays, and the failure of 27 Division and 45 Division in their respective attacks to the north, gave the Nationalists time to throw in Barrón's 13 Division and Sáenz de Buruaga's 150 Division, just as they had at Brunete. The well-defended strongpoints on which so many lives and hours were wasted did not hold enough men to have threatened Modesto's rear. The Republic's ponderous attack won 10 kilometres (6 miles) at heavy cost, but failed utterly in its attempt on Saragossa and attracted only part of the Nationalist air force away from the north. The most serious Republican losses in material were once again in armour. Líster lost nearly all the fast BT-5 tanks in Fuentes del Ebro. Even Modesto turned against him, and a quarrel between the two most important field commanders continued for the rest of the war. Prieto was furious at the handling of the battle, and his bitter criticism aroused the Party's anger against him. Along with a growing number of senior officers, he had begun to recognize that communist direction of the war effort was destroying the Popular Army with prestige operations which it could not afford. The Aragon offensive had come too late to help Santander. Nor did it delay the start of the third and final stage of the war in the north. Well aware of the importance of reducing the remaining Asturian territory before winter set in, General Dávila redeployed his forces rapidly to continue the advance westwards from Santander.

The Council of Asturias, based at the port of Gijón, had declared itself independent from the Valencia government at the end of August. General

Gámir Ulíbarri was replaced by Colonel Prada, who took command of the remnants of the northern army – about 40,000 men. The Republic's pocket of territory was about 90 kilometres (55 miles) deep from Gijón and 120 kilometres (75 miles) wide, with the Nationalist salient to the besieged town of Oviedo stuck into its west flank.

Dávila's attack on this last piece of Republican resistance in the north came from the east and south-east. His force was at least twice the size of the Republicans' and included six Carlist brigades, three Galician divisions under Aranda, and the Italian CTV. Nevertheless, the advance, which began on 1 September, averaged less than a kilometre a day, even with the Nationalists' crushing air superiority. The Picos de Europa on the east, and the Cordillera Cantábrica continuing along their southern flank, gave the Republican defenders excellent terrain to hold back the enemy and they did so with remarkable bravery. Passes such as El Mazuco were lost and then recaptured at bayonet point. It has been said that they fought so desperately only because the Nationalist blockade gave them no hope of escape, but this can never have been more than one factor. When most of the senior officers managed to escape in small boats, the rank-and-file fought even more fiercely.

Dávila's two main groups started to make headway only in mid-October, when all available air power was concentrated on achieving a breakthrough. His third column, which had slowly advanced northwards up the Léon–Oviedo road, was held at the Pajares pass over the Cordillera. But the defenders there were outflanked when the breakthrough finally came at Campo de Caso. The collapse was then rapid and Gijón was taken on 21 October. Nevertheless, guerrilla warfare continued in the Cordillera for another six months, tying down considerable bodies of Nationalist troops.

The real effects of the conquest of the north were not to become apparent until the new year, when the Nationalists started to deploy the Carlist formations, the Italian corps and Aranda's Galician troops in the southern zone. The considerable growth in Nationalist manpower at this time was assisted by drafting prisoners from the northern campaign into their infantry units as well as labour battalions. This manner of increasing their forces was not very successful, because a large proportion deserted as soon as they reached the front line. There were at least two cases of rebellion caused by left-wingers in their ranks. At Saragossa anarchists drafted into the Foreign Legion started a revolt and attempted to release their comrades from prison. And 200 sailors in El Ferrol, chiefly on the *España*, had been discovered preparing a mutiny during the previous winter. In both cases all those involved were executed. There were also cases of sabotage in the air force which led to crashes and other incidents which the Nationalists kept quiet.

Meanwhile in Republican Spain the autumn of 1937 witnessed the continued decline of anarchist power, the isolation of the Catalan nationalists, discord in socialist ranks, and the development of the secret police. Negrín's government presided over these developments, and as a result of communist power the repression of dissenters was far greater than it had been during Primo de Rivera's dictatorship. The prime minister's pretended ignorance of secret-police activities was unconvincing, while, as Hugh Thomas has pointed out, his attempt to restrict political activity through censorship, banning and arrests was parallel to Franco's establishment of a state machine where ideological divergence was also contained. Nevertheless, most of the Republic's supporters abroad who had defended the Republic's cause on the grounds of liberty and democracy made no protest at these developments.

The need to collaborate with the Russians, together with the seriousness of the military situation, was later used by Negrín's supporters to justify the actions of his administration. But it was Negrín who had persuaded Largo Caballero to send the gold reserves to Moscow, so he bore a major responsibility for the Republic's subservience to Stalin in the first place. Yet during his administration the flow of Russian military aid decreased dramatically. This was partly the result of the Nationalists' naval blockade, but it was also a consequence of Stalin's increasing desire to extricate himself from Spain when he realized that the British and French governments were not going to challenge the Axis. Paradoxically, Stalin's unease was probably increased by Negrín's obvious hope that the Republic would be saved by a European war.

President Azaña encouraged the prime minister's dictatorial rule in the early days of his administration, but his attitude was to change when he came to understand Negrín's character better. Both men disliked Companys, and Azaña supported Negrín's plans to bring Catalonia under central government control. The president still resented Companys' initial success in increasing the *Generalidad*'s independence during the turmoil of the previous summer. The reduction of Catalonia's identity was both symbolized and effected by moving the Republic's government from Valencia to Barcelona, and Negrín took every opportunity to emphasize Companys' reduced status.

Meanwhile, Largo Caballero had realized after his fall from power that the socialist party and the UGT were in an even worse state than he imagined. He still had his loyal supporters, especially the inner circle of Luis Araquistain, Carlos de Baráibar and Wenceslao Carrillo (the father of Santiago Carrillo). But many right socialists, a powerful faction within the UGT, and the majority of the Joint Socialist Youth were collaborating closely with the communists. Many responded to their call for unification. A joint newspaper, *Verdad* (meaning 'truth' and presumably intended as a Spanish *Pravda*), had been founded in Valencia. It was the first to praise the socialists in Jaén, who had established their own party of socialist-communist unification called the PSU (United Socialist Party). The PSOE newspaper, *El Socialista*, and even Largo's *Claridad*, had already been taken over by the pro-communist wing of the party. But the most disturbing event for Largo came at the end of September, when his supporters were disqualified from voting at the national plenum of the UGT. Nevertheless, many pro-communist socialists still hung back from the fateful step of outright union with the PCE. Largo Caballero's speech on 17 October (the first he had been allowed to make since May) explained the fall of his government and gave strong warnings of the dangers the party faced. Largo did not, however, recover any power, for he was kept off the executive committee, and his supporters on it remained in a minority.

Probably the most ominous of all the developments in Republican territory at this time was the rationalization of the security services into the SIM, *Servicio de Investigación Militar*. Prieto was the architect of this restructuring to increase central control, but the communists promptly seized it for their own use. Prieto believed that the fragmented growth of counter-espionage organizations was uncontrolled and inefficient. One intelligence chief complained that 'everyone in our rearguard carried on counter-espionage'. Independent services with their own networks of agents were run by the army, the Directorate General of Security, the *carabineros*, the foreign ministry, the *Generalidad* and the Basque government in exile (now based in Barcelona). Even the International Brigades had their own NKVD-run branch of heretic hunters based at Albacete. The new department was out of its creator's control as soon as it was constituted in August, since the communists had started to infiltrate and control the police and security services in the autumn of 1936.

The SIM was later described as 'the Russian syphilis' by the German writer, Gustav Regler, who served in the International Brigades. This particular variety of the disease can, of course, be ascribed to Russian carriers, but one cannot say that, if Orlov and his NKVD men had not come to Spain, nothing of the sort would have happened. If Russian communism appeared to its critics as Tsarism with a proletarian face, then Spanish communism, with its power base in New Castile, seemed to them to be growing into a Marxist variation of Philip II's integrated state based on the army. The SIM resembled the Inquisition and the commissars the church.

SIM officers included both unquestioningly loyal Party members and the ambitious. Its unchallenged power attracted opportunists of every sort to its ranks. Even its former civil guard commander, Colonel Uribarri, escaped abroad with several million pesetas. The core of executive officers then created a network of agents through bribery and blackmail. They even managed to plant their organization in resolutely anti-communist formations as a result of their control of transfer and promotion. For example, a nineteen-year-old rifleman in 119 Brigade was suborned and then promoted overnight to become the SIM chief of the whole formation with a greater power of life and death than its commander.

It is difficult to know the total number of agents employed by the SIM. There were said to have been 6,000 in Madrid alone, and its official payroll was 22 million pesetas. Its 13 sections covered every facet of civilian and military life and its agents were present in every district and command. There was a separate espionage section operating in Nationalist territory, called the SIEP (*Servicio de Investigación Especial Periférica*). The most feared section was the 13th, otherwise known as the Special Brigade, which was responsible for interrogation. When its infamous reputation became known abroad, it simply changed its name. The government insisted that it had been disbanded, but in fact there was an increase in the number of its victims who 'crossed over to the enemy' (the euphemism for death under torture or secret execution).

The SIM's interrogation methods evolved beyond beatings with rubber piping, hot and cold water treatment, splinters inserted under nails, and mock executions which had been carried out in the early days. The Soviet advisers made the procedures more scientific. Cell floors were specially constructed with the sharp corners of bricks pointing upward so that the naked prisoners were in constant pain. Strange metallic sounds, colours, lights and sloping floors were used as disorientation and sensory-deprivation techniques. If these failed, or if the interrogators were in a hurry, there was always the 'electric chair' and the 'noise box' but they risked sending prisoners mad too quickly.

There are no reliable estimates of the total number of SIM prisoners, nor of the proportions, though it seems fairly certain that there were more Republicans than Nationalists. It was alleged that any critic of Russian military incompetence, such as foreign volunteer pilots, was as likely to find himself accused of treason as a person who opposed the communists on ideological grounds. Meanwhile, in public, the new military tribunals tried 'fifth columnists' (a term which had been extended to include any opponents of the communist line). The Basque minister of Justice, Manuel de Irujo, resigned his post in protest at their rigged proceedings, but he still kept his seat in the cabinet. Negrín simply dismissed critical accounts of SIM activity as enemy propaganda.

The communists had been remarkably successful in creating a large degree of control over the government, the bureaucracy and the machinery of public order, while retaining a token presence of only two minor ministries in the cabinet – a requirement of Russian foreign policy. They had made themselves indispensable to the centrist politicians who had wanted to restore state power and who were now too involved in the process to protest. Nevertheless, a reaction against communist power was starting to develop, especially within the army.

In the autumn of 1937 communist propaganda was making great claims about the progress of the Popular Army. It is true that there had been improvements at unit level. But few commanders or staff officers had displayed competence or tactical sense, and the supply organization was still corrupt and inefficient. Above all, damage to morale had been increased by events behind the lines.

Communist preferment and proselytizing at the front had reached such levels that former communist supporters among the regular officers were horrified. Prieto was shaken when he heard that non-communist wounded were often refused medical aid. Battalion commanders who refused invitations to join the Party found weapon replacements, rations or even their men's pay cut off. Those who succumbed were given priority over non-communists. They were promoted and their reputations were boosted in despatches and press accounts. Co-operation was withheld from even the most senior non-communist officers. Colonel Casado, when in command of the Army of Andalucia, was not allowed to know the location of airfields, or availability of aircraft on his front. Commissars given recruitment targets to fulfil by the Party hierarchy went to any lengths to achieve them. Prieto later stated that socialists in communist units who refused to join the Party were frequently shot on false charges such as cowardice or desertion. After Brunete 250 men from El Campesino's division sought protection in the ranks of Mera's 14 Division because of the treatment they had suffered for not becoming communists. Mera refused to return them when El Campesino arrived in a fury at his headquarters. General Miaja, though officially a communist, backed him against a Party member.

Perhaps the most dramatic deterioration in morale after mid-1937 occurred in the ranks of the International Brigades, who had just been officially incorporated into the Spanish Republican army. There had always been non-communists in their ranks who refused to swallow the Party line, but now even committed communists were questioning their position. At the beginning of 1937 the Irish had nearly mutinied, after the Lopera débâcle, when they were prevented at the last moment from forming their own company. The American mutiny at the Jarama in the early spring had been successful, though that was seen as an aberration which had been put right. The Italians from the Garibaldi battalion deserted to join the liberal and anarchist Giustizia e Libertà column. During the Segovia offensive XIV International Brigade had refused to continue useless frontal attacks on La Granja, and foreigners in a Brigade penal battalion mutinied when ordered to shoot deserters.

The anger at futile slaughter was accompanied by a growing unease at the existence of 're-education' camps, run by Russian officers and guarded by Spanish communists armed with the latest automatic rifles and dum-dum bullets. At these camps labour was organized on a Stakhanovite basis, with food distribution linked to the achieving or exceeding of work norms. The prisoners were mostly those who wanted to return home for various reasons and had been refused. (It was not known until later that several Brigaders in this category were locked up in mental hospitals.) Then, at Brunete, there were multiple outbursts of pent-up frustration and bitterness at the slaughter resulting from the ineptness of senior officers. Wally Tapsell, of the British battalion, outraged by Colonel Gal's stupidity and carelessness with men's lives, said that he was not 'fit to command a troop of Brownies, let alone a People's Army'. Gal wanted to have him executed on the spot, but Tapsell had the rifles of the battalion to back him. A French unit also revolted during the Brunete offensive and, when Colonel Krieger ordered them back into the line, their officers refused. Krieger shot one of them himself, the battalion mutinied and Spanish communist troops had to disarm them before they could be marched off for 're-education'.

The persistent trouble in the Brigades also stemmed from the fact that the volunteers, to whom no length of service had ever been mentioned, assumed that they were free to leave after a certain time. Their passports had been taken away on enlistment. Krivitsky claimed that these were sent to Moscow by diplomatic bag for use by NKVD agents abroad. Brigade leaders who became so alarmed by the stories of unrest filtering home imposed increasingly stringent measures of discipline. Letters were censored and anyone who criticized the competence of the Party leadership faced prison camps, or even firing squads. Leave was often cancelled, and some volunteers who, without authorization, took a few of the days owing to them, were shot for desertion when they returned to their unit. The feeling of being trapped by an organization with which they had lost sympathy made a few volunteers even cross the lines to the Nationalists. Others tried such unoriginal devices as putting a bullet through their own foot when cleaning a rifle (10 volunteers were executed for self-inflicted wounds).

Comintern organizers were becoming disturbed, for accounts of conditions in the Brigades had started to stem the flow of volunteers from abroad. Fresh volunteers were shocked by the cynicism of the veterans, who laughed at the idealism of newcomers while remembering their own with bitterness. Some of the new arrivals at Albacete were literally shang-haied. Foreign specialists, or mechanics who had agreed to come for a specific purpose only, found themselves pressganged and threatened with the penalty for desertion if they refused. Even sailors on shore-leave from foreign merchantmen in Republican ports found themselves seized as 'deserters' from the Brigades and sent to Albacete under guard.

The greatest jolt to the attitudes of those in the International Brigades was the persecution of the POUM. The Party's version of what happened was so obviously dishonest that only those terrified of the truth could believe it. This mentality was perhaps best revealed by one Brigader, who asserted that 'the institution of compulsory political discussions once a day ordered from above is evidence that we are being treated more seriously than usual'. The majority, however, realizing that they had been duped, resented the insult to their intelligence. They had to hold their tongues while in Spain so as to avoid the attentions of the SIM. Then, when they did reach home they usually remained silent, rather than undermine the Republican cause as a whole. Those, who, like Orwell, spoke out, found the doors of left-wing publishers closed to them; these uncritical supporters of the Republic were forced to justify the Moscow line. Nevertheless, the attempt to export the show-trial mentality to Spain ignored the fact that, however authoritarian Negrín's government might be, it was not totalitar-ian. As a result, that sealed maze of distorting mirrors which had replaced reality in the Soviet Union could not be duplicated in Spain.

By 1937 there were many reasons to be a communist, and within the membership of the Party five main categories may be discerned: the con-vinced member who believed that only the Communist Party could help the international proletariat; the republican who simply believed that communist direction of the war-effort was vital for military victory and the restoration of the governmental system; the careerist who saw that the Party's power offered the surest means of advancement; the businessman or small landowner who wanted protection against collectivization; and finally those secret Nationalist supporters who wanted the safety of a Party membership card. Those belonging to the second category, such as Prieto, started to wonder during 1937 if they had been right. The loyalty of the opportunists depended simply on the continuance of the Party's power *per se*. The Spanish communists' ambitions were, however, fettered by Soviet policy, which required Party control to be covert.

THE WINTER FIGHTING OF TERUEL AND THE NATIONALIST DRIVE FOR THE SEA

By the end of 1937 a marked shift of strength to the Nationalists was apparent. The reduction of the northern zone had proved to be the essential intermediate step if they were to be assured of victory. For the first time in the war they equalled the Republicans in manpower under arms (around 700,000), and the scales were to continue moving further in their favour. The conquest of the Cantabrian coast had not only released troops for redeployment in the centre; it had also yielded vital industrial prizes to the Nationalists. The most important were the arms factories in the Basque country, the heavy industry of Bilbao, and the coal and iron ore of the northern regions (though much of the latter was taken in payment by Germany). The other prize of conquest, apart from war material, had been 100,000 prisoners of war, of whom over half were formed into forced labour battalions and another 30,000 drafted into Nationalist units.

The Nationalist army was reorganized into separate formations, some to garrison fronts, some to make up an offensive Army of Manœuvre. The defensive forces included Moscardó's V Corps in Aragon, Queipo de Llano's Army of the South with II and III Corps, and General Saliquet's Army of the Centre with I Corps on the Madrid front and VII Corps on the Guadarrama front. The offensive formations of the Army of Manœuvre included Yagüe's Army Corps of Morocco, with most of the Legion and *regulares* in Barrón's 13 Division and Sáenz de Buruaga's 150 Division, Solchaga's Army Corps of Navarre with the Carlist *requetés*, Varela's Army Corps of Castile, and the Army Corps of Galicia under Aranda. After the fall of Asturias the Italian CTV, now under General Berti, was moved to a reserve role in Aragon.

The Republican general staff and the Soviet advisers refused to admit that their ponderously conventional offensives were gradually destroying their army and the Republic's ability to resist. They would not see that the only hope lay in continuing regular defence combined with unconventional guerrilla attacks in the enemy rear and rapid raids at as many points as possible along the enemy's weakly held fronts. At the very least this would have severely hindered the Nationalists' ability to concentrate their best troops in their new Army of Manœuvre. Most important of all, it would not have presented large formations of Republican troops to the

Nationalists' superior artillery and air power. A blend of conventional and unconventional warfare would have been the most efficient, and least costly, method of maintaining Republican resistance until the European war broke out. Nevertheless, the pattern of set-piece offensives continued until the Republic's military strength was finally exhausted on the Ebro in the autumn of 1938. Propaganda considerations still determined these prestige operations, and the principle of the 'unified command' was vigorously maintained by the communists, the government and regular officers, even though it had become a bureaucratic tourniquet. In addition, the Popular Army was projected at home and abroad as the orthodox army of an orthodox state, and it therefore used the most orthodox tactics.

The inflexibility of Republican strategy became even more serious at the end of 1937, when the Nationalist air support was increased. Spanish pilots took over the older German aircraft, especially the Junkers 52s, and four Nationalist fighter squadrons were now equipped with Fiats. (The fighter squadrons had nine aircraft each, and the bomber squadrons twelve.) The Italian Legionary air force had nine Fiat squadrons and three bomber squadrons on the Spanish mainland, apart from those based on Majorca. The Condor Legion replaced the Junkers 52 with the Heinkel 111 entirely. In addition, it had a reconnaissance squadron of Dornier 17s, two squadrons of Messerschmitt 109s, and two with the old Heinkel 51. All told, the Nationalists and their allies deployed nearly 400 aircraft.

The Republican air force was inferior in numbers and in quality after its losses in the north and at Brunete. The Nationalists' main fighter, the Fiat, had shown itself to be rugged and highly manœuvrable, while the Messerschmitt was unbeatable if handled properly. Finally, Republican pilots, especially the Russians, did not seem prepared to take the same risks in aerial combat as the Nationalists. Rata squadrons sometimes fled from the determined attack of a few Fiats.

The Soviets were handing over more and more machines to Spanish pilots who arrived back from training in Russia. Two of the Rata squadrons were now entirely Spanish, while the four Chato squadrons had Spanish pilots. These biplanes were being manufactured at Sabadell-Reus, near Barcelona, but the replacement of Ratas was limited by the increasingly effective blockade in the Mediterranean. (The Nationalists' cruiser *Baleares* had sunk a whole convoy from Russia on 7 September.) The Republicans did, however, receive a consignment of 31 Katiuska bombers bringing their bomber force up to four squadrons of Natashas and four of Katiuskas.

The Republic's only aerial success had come during an intense series of strikes each side was making against its opponent's airfields. On 15 October during a further unsuccessful offensive on Saragossa, Republican fighters and bombers attacked the Nationalist airfield near Saragossa, wiping out almost all the aircraft at dispersal. As a defensive measure against counter-strikes the Republican air force made great use of dummy aircraft, and switched their machines from one airfield to another.

Having crushed the northern zone, Franco felt justified at mounting another offensive on Madrid at the end of 1937. His new strength more than compensated for the Republic's advantage of having interior lines in this region. The Nationalist Army of Manœuvre was deployed behind the

Aragon front for an assault south-westwards down the Saragossa–Madrid road which the Italians had used as their centreline on Guadalajara in March. Varela's Army Corps of Castile was on the left, the Italian CTV in the centre, the Army Corps of Morocco on the right, the Condor Legion and the Legionary Air Force in support and the Army Corps of Galicia and Navarre in reserve.

The threatened sector of the Guadalajara front was held by the Republic's IV Corps, now commanded by Cipriano Mera. As had happened before the battle of Brihuega, Mera was helped by fellow anarchists who crossed the lines into enemy territory gathering intelligence. This time the information was far more valuable. Nationalist sources later said that Mera himself had crossed, disguised as a shepherd, and had read the operational plans in their headquarters. In fact, as Mera himself recounts, the spying mission was suggested and carried out by a young anarchist called Dolda who did not go near their headquarters. Reports from CNT members in Nationalist Aragon, whom he visited secretly, warned of major troop concentrations from Saragossa to Calatayud. Dolda's return via Medinaceli confirmed his hunch that the Nationalists were preparing for the biggest offensive yet and that it was to be directed at the Guadalajara sector. Dolda was back through the lines by 30 November. He briefed Mera, who in turn informed Miaja. Rojo then shelved his plans for an Estremadura offensive, and an attack to disrupt the Nationalist operation was examined. The town of Teruel was chosen for a pre-emptive strike because it formed the corner where the Aragon front turned back north-westwards to run through the province of Guadalajara.

The assault on the Teruel front was launched on 15 December. The force carrying out the operation was based on General Hernández Saravia's Army of the Levant. Bolstered by troops from the Republic's Army of Manœuvre, it totalled nearly 100,000 men, including reserves. The armour was spread out between formations according to the ineffective French tactic which the Republic usually followed. Winter conditions were, however, to make this weakness almost irrelevant.

The provincial capital of Teruel, a gloomy town in bleak terrain, was famous for its cold in winter. It was snowing on the 15th, when the Republican offensive against this exposed promontory of Nationalist territory was launched. The Republican forces achieved complete surprise, partly as a result of the weather, more by foregoing any preliminary bombardment. XXII and XVIII Corps thrust through the weak lines and by-passed the town on each side to join at San Blas the next morning. Once Teruel was completely cut off, these formations established a front before trying to deal with the town's defenders.

The Nationalist high command was disconcerted by this pre-emptive attack and Franco was unsure whether to continue with the Guadalajara offensive as the German and Italian advisers urged. For the moment, he brought up three divisions to fill the breach at the corner of the two fronts, while the Condor Legion and Legionary Air Force were asked to fly missions in support of the beleaguered garrison. The Fiats and Heinkel 111s, however, had serious problems with the weather. For most of the following week their aircraft were grounded by bad visibility, snow-covered airfields and frozen machinery.

In the first 36 hours the Republican forces managed to take the commanding feature to the west of the town known as La Muela de Teruel. The Nationalist commander, Colonel Rey d'Harcourt, pulled all his forces back into the town. On the 23rd Franco finally decided to abandon the Guadalajara offensive and to use his Army of Manœuvre to save a minor provincial capital. It was a decision which attracted a great deal of criticism in Nationalist ranks. Franco's critics did not believe that the political importance of Teruel outweighed the military potential of the planned offensive. A Nationalist breakthrough was not certain, however, because IV Corps, assisted by all available engineer regiments, had established strong defences along the threatened sector.

The Nationalist counter-attack on the Teruel sector was slowed by the terrible weather conditions until 29 December, when the Nationalist artillery opened with their greatest bombardment. (From this point until the end of the war, Franco's artillery was capable of delivering even more explosive than his air support.) That day visibility was better. The snow storms had stopped, and the Nationalist air forces were able to operate at full strength for the first time since the attack began. More than 100 tons of bombs were dropped on Republican positions, and the Rata squadrons shied away from attacking the Fiat escort squadrons. On the ground ten Nationalist divisions attacked south-eastwards to regain their former salient. Yet, despite the overwhelming bombardment, the Republican line did not break; only a stubborn retreat began. Franco ordered Colonel Rey d'Harcourt to 'trust in Spain as Spain trusts in you' and hold out until relieved. But Teruel was no Alcázar of Toledo, and the Republicans were already in the town, working from house to house by smashing through the walls. House-clearing with grenade and bayonet is one of the most brutal and bloody forms of fighting and the civilian population suffered in the dark confusion.

On New Year's Eve there was a blizzard and the lowest temperature of the century was recorded. The aircraft could not be made operational even by using blow torches on their cylinders. Tanks and all mechanical transport froze solid. Those who tried to keep warm by drinking *aguadiente* died of cold in their sleep once the alcohol wore off. The casualties from frostbite were enormous. When Prieto visited the front, Rojo gave him details of the fierce fighting around La Muela de Teruel, which the Nationalists had reached that afternoon, but the minister of defence apparently only made scathing remarks about the inefficiency of the whole operation. San Blas was also lost that evening, before the Nationalist advance was halted by another blizzard. As soon as the weather cleared again, Rojo sent in Modesto's V Corps to prevent any further advance. The conditions for attack could hardly have been worse for both sides; silhouetted against the whiteness, dark figures lumbered through the deep snow, making easy targets.

On 6 January Colonel Rey d'Harcourt surrendered with the last of his troops. (The Nationalists were to curse him, unjustly, as a coward and a traitor, after he was taken off to prison with the local bishop.) The civilian population was evacuated at the same time, despite the weather conditions and transport problems, because another Nationalist attack was massing. Within a week it was the Republicans' turn to be besieged in the town.

The major assault on 17 January broke the line. Walter's 35 Division of International Brigades was pushed forward to retrieve the situation, but the Nationalists were still able to take La Muela de Teruel. Again the Republican line was re-formed and counter-attacks were made; but the staff was expecting far too much of the troops. The snow had prevented food supplies from getting through. Water could be obtained only by melting down snow, and there was no fuel, except in Teruel, where they could burn doors and furniture. The most serious shortage, however, was of ammunition; 46 men of 84 Brigade were summarily executed for refusing to attack with empty rifles.

On 7 February the Nationalists launched a well-organized attack at Alfambra, some 25 kilometres (15 miles) to the north of Teruel. Its purpose was to turn the Republican flank. It was directed by General Vigón and carried out by Aranda's Army Corps of Galicia and Yagüe's Army Corps of Morocco, backed by the CTV and the Army Corps of Navarre. Peter Kemp, the English volunteer now serving in the Foreign Legion, gives a vivid description of the beginning of this offensive. It was a bright, freezing dawn in the Sierra de Palomera as divisions of red-bereted Carlists and green-coated Legionnaires waited for the bombers to soften up the enemy. Only the sound of the pack-mules' accoutrements broke the silence. Then, waiting on the ridge, the Nationalist troops heard the heavy drone of the Italian bombers coming from their rear. To their sudden horror, they realized that the Savoia–Marchettis had mistaken them for the enemy. Two waves in succession bombed the rocky mountainside, despite the recognition strips and arrows laid out behind. The Nationalists' casualties, however, were much lighter than might have been expected. The operation was hardly delayed.

The attack of the Moroccan and Navarrese corps was accompanied by Monasterio's 1 Cavalry Division, which made the one great mounted charge of the war in the valley below them. The Republican troops manning this part of the front had never seen action before and they were broken immediately by the onslaught. The Nationalist formations then swung south, forcing the main Republican force to withdraw rapidly. The Republicans abandoned Teruel on 22 February, leaving behind much equipment, though they did manage to establish a holding line several kilometres back.

The weather conditions and the house-fighting had made Teruel one of the most horrific battles of the war. The Nationalists suffered over 50,000 casualties, roughly a third of them due to the cold. They lost more aircraft and pilots from crashes in the bad weather than from enemy action. The Republican casualties were even higher, probably just over 60,000. The majority of them happened after the Teruel offensive had achieved its objective of disrupting a major Nationalist operation. Lives were lost and material wasted simply because, in January, the Republican general staff tried to hold an indefensible and strategically unimportant town. Once again, obstinacy, prompted by premature propaganda claims of victory, made the Republican leaders sacrifice some of their best troops. The effect on the moral and physical state of their soldiers, and the enormous losses in material, led directly to what was probably the greatest Republican disaster of the war. Scarcely two weeks after re-occupying Teruel, the

Nationalists launched their devastating attack on Aragon.

During the spring of 1938 the Republic was to enjoy only two pieces of encouraging news. One was the opening of the French frontier to military material. The other came from an unexpected source – the navy. The Republican fleet had done little to challenge the Nationalist and Italian blockade, mainly because of the inertia and inefficiency of its ships' crews. Meanwhile, the Nationalist fleet had grown with the help of Mussolini, who sent two submarines. These were renamed the *Mola* and the *Sanjurjo*, hardly reassuring choices for traditionally superstitious submariners. In addition, seven Italian 'Legionary' submarines continued to operate throughout the Mediterranean, ready to hoist the royal Spanish flag if forced to the surface. Mussolini also gave Franco four destroyers and, later in 1938, an old cruiser, the *Taranto*.

The end of the war in the north meant that the Nationalist Mediterranean fleet was reinforced by units from the Cantabrian coast, including the cruiser, *Almirante Cervera*, and two seaplane squadrons of Heinkel 60s. One of these went to Palma, Majorca, where Admiral Francisco de Moreno had set up a blockade joint-staff headquarters with the Italian navy and air force. Palma was used as the principal Italian bomber base for attacks on shipping and Republican coastal cities, chiefly Barcelona and Valencia. The Italians dominated the partnership and the island was almost entirely under their occupation. It had been their private fief ever since the early days of the war, when a Bluebeard-like Italian Fascist calling himself the Conte Rossi terrorized the island.

It was against this formidable control of the western Mediterranean that the Republican navy took everyone by surprise in March. How large a part luck played in their success is difficult to estimate. A flotilla of torpedo boats, backed by two cruisers and nine destroyers, left Cartagena on 5 March, to strike at the Nationalist fleet in Palma. Meanwhile, a Nationalist squadron escorting a convoy from Palma was heading in their direction. It comprised three cruisers, the *Baleares*, *Canarias*, and *Almirante Cervera*, three destroyers and two minelayers. The two forces made contact just before one o'clock in the morning on 6 March. Three of the Republican destroyers sighted the *Baleares*, the flag ship, and fired salvoes of torpedoes. The Nationalist cruiser sank rapidly; Admiral Vierna was among the 726 men lost. Although this was the largest battle at sea, it did not have important results because the Nationalists soon refitted the old cruiser, *República* and renamed her the *Navarra*. Their navy was much more cautious as a result of this action, but its control of the coast was not affected. And only a few days later Heinkel bombing raids on Cartagena crippled the Republic's only capital ship, the *Jaime I*.

The news of the loss of the *Baleares* reached the Nationalist Army of Manœuvre just as it was about to launch the most devastating offensive yet seen in the war. It is not certain whether Franco decided after Teruel to give up short-cuts to victory once again, and continue with the strategy of dismantling key regions, or whether he was persuaded to take advantage of the Popular Army's weakness before it could recover from the effects of the winter battle. The opportunity of dealing the enemy's most experienced formations a further severe blow, while at the same time separating Catalonia, the main source of Republican manpower and industry, from the rest of the zone, was obviously attractive. This could then be followed by the reduction of Catalonia and the severing of the Republic from France. Without Catalan industry and supplies from abroad, the central region would fall in a short space of time. It was a less spectacular strategy than a breakthrough to Madrid, but it was more certain of success.

The Nationalists began this campaign with a major advantage. They had redeployed their formations far more rapidly than the Republican general staff thought possible. Within two weeks of the recapture of Teruel, General Dávila's chief of staff, General Vigón, had finalized his plans. The Army of Manœuvre positioned itself behind the start line, which consisted of the southern half of the central Aragon sector. Starting on the left flank, which was marked by the south bank of the Ebro, there were Yagüe's Moroccan corps, 5 Navarrese Division and 1 Cavalry Division, the Italian corps, and Aranda's Galician corps. Though warned of the threat by spies, the Republican commanders were convinced that the Guadalajara front was still the Nationalists' target. They assumed, also, that the enemy's troops must be as exhausted after Teruel as their own.

Republican territory at end of campaign

Phases of the Nationalist Reduction:
1. 9 March – 20 March
2. 22 March – 8 April
3. 30 March – 20 April
4. 6 April – July
5. End April – End June
6. 5 July – 25 July

NATIONALIST REDUCTION OF ARAGON, February-July 1938

On 9 March the most ruthlessly professional offensive of the whole war began. It was a campaign in which the co-ordinated artillery and aerial bombardment was so massive that few defenders were in a fit state even to aim a rifle by the time the infantry hit them. With 400 field guns, the Nationalist artillery now greatly outnumbered the Republican. It was also far more effectively used. The Condor Legion's air strikes, too, were incomparably more accurate than those of their opponents. This campaign saw the Junkers 87, or Stuka, in action for the first time. Luftwaffe officers in Spain claimed that it could drop its load within five metres of a target.

Those Republican defenders who endured such bombardments then had to face von Thoma's tanks. Nationalist infantry casualties were the lowest of any major offensive during the war. In fact, after many of the bombardments the Foreign Legion had little to do except bayonet the shocked survivors in their trenches.

On the first day of the offensive, Yagüe's Moroccan corps, supported by tanks, smashed through 44 Division and advanced 36 kilometres (22 miles) along the south side of the Ebro. Belchite fell to the Carlist *requetés* of the second wave on the next day, 10 March. Yagüe, meanwhile, maintained the momentum of his attack, so that any defensive line which the Republicans patched together crumbled almost as soon as it was formed. After Teruel the Republican forces were exhausted and badly equipped, (many of them had still not received proper ammunition re-supply) while the fresh troops in the front line were inexperienced conscripts. The retreat was more a rout than a withdrawal. One or two brave stands were made, but demoralization quickly set in, as the Republicans saw that they were incapable of resisting the Nationalist onslaught either on the ground or from the air. The situation was made worse by the increase of anti-communist feeling after Teruel. Almost any story of communist perfidy was believed. Non-communist units thought that their ammunition supplies were being cut off deliberately. These suspicions stemmed from isolated incidents. During the battle of Teruel, for example, part of 25 Division was refused replacement weapons and ammunition when one of their senior officers refused to join the Communist Party. There were also bitter arguments among field commanders and staff, particularly the communist officers, many of which dated from Teruel. Lister had refused to obey Rojo; El Campesino claimed that Modesto had deliberately left his division to be cut off during the withdrawal; and Modesto and Lister still hated each other, as they had done ever since the loss of tanks at Fuentes de Ebro.

Mutual recriminations became more severe during the chaos of the retreat in Aragon, when some commanders, Marty and Lister in particular, sought to justify their behaviour with wild accusations of treachery and arbitrary executions. In the first 10 days of the Aragon offensive, the Nationalists took the centre-right of the front to depths varying from 50 to 100 kilometres (30 to 60 miles). On 22 March they began their assault on the sector from the Ebro up to Huesca. Moscardó's V Corps and Solchaga's Carlist divisions pushed down south-eastwards, while Yagüe crossed the Ebro to take the retreating Republicans in their rear left flank. With the whole of central Aragon now captured, the advance to the sea was launched at the end of March.

For the Republicans it was a retreat which slowed only when the enemy paused to rest. The withdrawal of a flank formation set off a panic; in the confusion nobody seemed to warn his neighbouring unit. Rations and ammunition seldom got through. And all the time the enemy fighters harried the retreating troops like hounds. Circuses of fighters dived in turn to drop grenades and strafe the Republicans. The old fear of being cut off, which had broken the militias in the early days of the war, now affected the Popular Army. The senior communist officer, Manuel Tagüeña, reported that by 1 April 35 and 45 International Divisions near Mora del Ebro had 'completely lost all capacity to fight'. The Spanish communist leaders wanted many of the International Brigade commanders to be replaced as a result of their performance, and although Marty disagreed bitterly, he was forced to compromise by replacing General Walter and Colonel Čopić. In the first week of April the former POUM stronghold of Lérida fell to Yagüe's troops, but the Italians were held for a time by Líster's 11 Division at Tortosa, which had been reduced to rubble by bombing. Meanwhile Aranda's Galician corps, together with 4 Navarrese Division, fought on towards the coast just below the Ebro's mouth. On 15 April they took the seaside town of Vinaroz, thus establishing a corridor which separated Catalonia from the rest of Republican Spain.

It was Good Friday and Carlist *requetés* waded into the Mediterranean as if it were the River Jordan. All the Nationalist newspapers described how their commander, General Alonso Vega, knelt on the shore, dipped his fingers in the sea, and crossed himself. They thought that the end of their crusade was at hand.

UNCERTAINTY ACROSS EUROPE

During that spring of 1938, while the Nationalist Army of Manœuvre was overrunning Aragon, the Republic faced a growing economic crisis and low morale in the rear areas. There was distrust between political groups, fear of the SIM and resentment against the authoritarian nature of Negrín's government, acute food shortages, profiteering and defeatism. At the same time the population of Barcelona suffered from heavy bombing raids.

The economic crisis was influenced by the way the Republican peseta flunctuated with the military situation. From standing at 226 to the pound sterling before the Teruel offensive, it fell to between 530 and 650 to the pound in the wake of the Aragon campaign. At the outbreak of the civil war the peseta had been at 40 to the pound; so imports during 1938 were costing well over 10 times what they had cost in the summer of 1936. Meanwhile, the cost-of-living index had gone from 100 in July 1936, to 171 in May 1937, 223 in December, and 314 by May 1938. (Industrial production in Catalonia during this period declined from a base of 100 in the spring of 1936 to 73 in the following winter, and then right down to 33 in the summer of 1938.)

The greatest burden on the economy at the beginning of the war had been the militia wage bill. The rate of pay, however, was not raised from the original 10 pesetas a day, despite the high level of inflation, so that by the winter of 1936 arms purchases from abroad had become by far the greatest expenditure. Spain had no arms industry, apart from small factories in the Basque country and Asturias. It was therefore unrealistic to expect metallurgical industries in Catalonia to be able to convert themselves for war production when the expertise was lacking. In fact it was remarkable what their factories managed to improvise during the first six months of the war, when the central government, determined to take control from the CNT collectives and the *Generalidad*, refused to provide foreign exchange for the purchase of machinery from abroad. Later, when the Republic arranged for Chato fighters to be assembled at Sabadell during the naval blockade, the Russians objected to the workforce belonging to the CNT.

Every type of military equipment came from abroad and imports accounted for more than 90 per cent of the Republic's supply. In the summer of 1936 about 150 aircraft had been bought from France, and between October of that year and the end of the war, between 700 and 1,000 aircraft, about three-quarters of them fighters, were purchased from the Soviet Union. Another 150 aircraft, most of which were unarmed, were bought from other countries, including Great Britain and the United States. Russia also supplied about 1,200 armoured vehicles (of which three-quarters were T-26 and BT-5 tanks), about 1,500 field guns, 4 million shells, 15,000 machine-guns and half a million rifles. Mexico sold the Republic about 20,000 rifles and 30 field guns.

The Republic's suppliers insisted on payment in advance, especially after news of the gold transfer to Moscow leaked out. Also, as Hugh Thomas has pointed out, the Russians could cut their losses at any time, having had what amounted to advance payment in gold, whereas Germany and Italy were committed to Franco's victory if only to have their credits repaid. Although the foreign purchases of Nationalist and Republican Spain have been calculated as roughly similar ($900 million approximately), the Republic had to pay far more in real terms. The extremely vulnerable position in which the Republic found itself as a result of the non-intervention policy, together with the cost of transport and surcharges, and the number of vessels sunk by Italian and Nationalist action, must have reduced the effective value of its purchases by anything up to a half. In addition to the $500 million which the Republic paid Russia, (the Soviet Union claimed that it was still owed another $50 million after the war) and the $100 million worth of purchases made elsewhere, the Republic also had to import oil and, when its domestic production was further damaged by the loss of Aragon, more food. Chickpeas and lentils were imported mainly from Mexico, while citrus fruit from the Valencia region formed the core of Republican exports.

Food shortages were serious everywhere, but Barcelona had to cope with the refugees from Aragon, in addition to those who had come from Andalucia, Estremadura and Castile earlier in the war. The scenes of peasants from the collectives, herding in livestock and bringing their few belongings on carts as they fled from the Nationalists, were as pathetic as those in Madrid during the autumn of 1936. Food queues were worse than ever and women were killed and maimed during the bombing raids because they would not give up their places. The daily ration of 150 grammes of rice, beans or, more usually, lentils (known as Dr Negrín's little pills) could not prevent the effects of vitamin and protein deficiency among those unable to afford black-market prices. Children, especially the increasing number of war orphans (the Quakers reported that there were 25,000 in Barcelona alone), suffered from rickets.

Politicians and senior officials, however, did not seem to be losing much weight; a banquet organized in Negrín's honour in Barcelona led to angry demonstrations of protest. On the whole the troops were much better fed than the civilian population, but they were very conscious of the way their families were suffering. Inevitably they became bitter at the scandals involving theft by the staff and supply services of petrol, rations and equipment for resale on the black market.

By 1938 demoralization was particularly strong among Catalan nationalists, whose support for the Republic in 1936 had been more solid than that of the Basques. (The Catalan industrialists of the Lliga supported Franco, but they were greatly disappointed when they appreciated, eventually, the strength of his centralist beliefs.) The unity of the Catalan left, Esquerra, had been severely stretched in 1937, and by 1938 Companys was described as a broken and ignored man. The majority of the Esquerra had gravitated towards the communist insistence on discipline and respect for private property. Esquerra members had been joining the communist PSUC from the autumn of 1936 onwards, although a minority had remained distrustful of communist ambitions and centralism and had maintained good relations with the anarchists. Esquerra employers, who had looked after their workers in pre-war years, were zealously protected throughout the war. They stayed on the workers' committee for the factory at the current salary and, although their standard of living was obviously lower than what they had been accustomed to, they never risked starvation.

Inevitably, the Catalanist majority which had opted for a tacit alliance with the communists against the CNT, had felt the most betrayed when Negrín's government rapidly dismantled the *Generalidad*'s independence in the wake of the May events. They were also angry at the failure of their old trading partners, France and especially Great Britain, to help them. They became defeatist and swelled the silent Catalan centre which had disliked the Nationalists and the left equally. Most of them now longed for the end of the war, persuading themselves that the initial harshness of Franco's regime would not affect them for long.

During this period the UGT and the CNT increased their collaboration. Even in the early militia days there had been a close relationship at the front, and many of the self-managed collectives were run from the beginning with mixed memberships. The two organizations finally signed a pact in the middle of March 1938 – the last and perhaps greatest CNT concession made under the pressures of war. The agreement involved a tacit admission of the state with a programme of federal socialism. It also confirmed the steady process whereby their industrial collectives were being nationalized. Some apologists even claimed that the breach between Marx and Bakunin in the First International was now healed; in fact the deal was the work of the CNT's syndicalist wing, led by Mariano Vázquez, the secretary-general. The anarchist purists, especially the FAI, were happy to work closely with non-communist socialists, but they were not prepared to abandon their basic beliefs. Any internal dispute at this point, however, was put aside in the face of the most prolonged bombing raids of the war on civilian targets.

The bombing of Barcelona, which had begun in earnest on the last day of 1937 with Italian squadrons from Rome, was continued by the Legionary Air Force in Majorca during January. Ciano was thrilled by the account of the destruction, which he found 'so realistically horrifying'. These raids prompted both a retaliation by the Republican air force on Nationalist cities and a diplomatic attempt to have such actions suspended on both sides. The Republicans ceased their raids when Eden promised to help. It was later revealed, however, that the British had made no attempt to do anything. Mussolini halted the bombing in February, out of pique with the Nationalists for not allotting the CTV a sufficiently glorious role at Teruel. But during the advance to the sea he decided, without warning Franco, to relaunch the raids on a far more intensive scale. Ciano noted,

'Mussolini believes that these air raids are an admirable way of weakening the morale of the Reds'.

On the night of 16 March the Savoia-Marchetti squadrons from Majorca started an around-the-clock bombing relay. There were no anti-aircraft guns and Republican fighters were not scrambled from airfields in the region until the afternoon of 17 March. The casualties were about 1,000 dead and 2,000 wounded. One bomb was at first said to have struck an explosives lorry in the Gran Vía, but soon more enormous blasts indicated that the Italians were experimenting with a few giant bombs. Mussolini was greatly encouraged by the horrified international reaction. As Ciano said, 'This will send up our stock in Germany too, where they love total and ruthless war.'

At this time military activity was concentrated in the east of Spain, while the south and west were quiet. Even battle-scarred Madrid enjoyed a partial return to normal lofe. Girls travelled by tram to the front to meet their *novios* and make love in the ruins behind the trenches. The population was becoming inured to danger and death. As one of the subjects recounted in Ronald Fraser's book, *Blood of Spain*, mothers would call to their children to come indoors when the shelling began as if it were just starting to rain. People had grown accustomed to the sight of mangled bodies in the streets, and the *madrileños'* black sense of humour never seemed to fail. Brutalized by war, children played at firing squads executing 'fascists'.

Few soldiers thought of the end of the war except in the despair and panic of retreat, because the Republic's propaganda diet fed their hunger to believe in ultimate victory. The middle-class liberals and social democrats, on the other hand, were much more objective. One facet of this divide was that right-wing liberals like Martínez Barrio believed that they would suffer far more than the workers from Franco's victory. Prieto's pessimism was by now notorious, and when, as minister of defence, he told the French ambassador that the Republic had lost, he became a liability in spite of his international reputation. Prieto had hoped that the pre-emptive offensive on Teruel might lead to a negotiated peace and the ensuing débâcle left him entirely disillusioned. Like other moderates, however, whether in Spain or in the democracies, his hopes for a compromise peace with Franco were quite as deluded as the workers' anticipation of ultimate victory. The Nationalists regarded any suggestion of compromise as a betrayal of their absolutist ideals. The 'Red contagion' had to be purged as ruthlessly as any heresy had been by the Inquisition. Prieto's private overtures to the Nationalists through third parties were contemptuously rejected.

Meanwhile, his bitterness was centred on the arrogance of the communists, though he would not recognize his own responsibility for the situation. His last venture with them in the re-establishment of state power had been Líster's destruction of the collectives in Aragon; but from then on the tempo of minor and major quarrels built up rapidly. These ranged from a dispute over whether a Messerschmitt 109 captured intact should be handed to the French or to the Russians, up to the Party's continuing take-over of army commands. Prieto attacked the communists' control of his own SIM when he realized what a terrifying machine it had become, but he was too late. His measures against individuals within this state-spawned state enraged the communists and the Russian NKVD 'advisers', without lessening the secret executions and torture. The rare occasions on which the SIM was effectively challenged occurred at the front, when SIM agents seeking out dissidents were sometimes killed by 'stray bullets'.

Prieto attempted to limit communist power in the army by reducing the commissar network. He even transferred to a front-line brigade the young commissar-general of the Army of the Centre (who lived with La Pasionaria and claimed to be her lover). This order was not obeyed, but then communists in the forces and government were always told that only Party instructions counted. Prieto was also hated by the communists for revealing that the Party made money for itself out of the Republic's merchant navy, which had been reorganized through British holding companies so as to beat the blockade.

On 16 March the communist campaign against Prieto, which had been growing in their press since Teruel, came out into the open. (The most virulent articles were written by his fellow minister Hernández under a false name.) It was the morning before the major Italian air raids, and a full cabinet meeting had been called by Negrín at the Pedralbes Palace in Barcelona. The events which followed appear to have been part of a plan laid jointly by the prime minister and the communists, in order to engineer Prieto's resignation. To sack him risked jolting pro-Republican opinion in France and Great Britain. Just before the meeting, Negrín spoke to Prieto and other ministers, implying that he expected their support on peace initiatives, a course to which they agreed. But then, soon after the meeting had begun, a communist demonstration led by La Pasionaria surged up to the palace denouncing Prieto, the minister of defence, as a traitor and defeatist. Negrín proceeded to reassure them that there would be no compromise with the enemy.

For the rest of March Negrín continued to assure Prieto that he needed him in the cabinet, but not as minister of defence, because the Russians were refusing to supply more arms until he was removed. In several ways Prieto's departure resembled that of his old rival, Largo Caballero. The anarchists, while acknowledging their 'enormous ideological differences' rallied to him as they had to the former prime minister, because, as before, they feared the increased Russian power which would follow his departure. Prieto refused Negrín's offer of a minor post in the cabinet and was asked to resign.

These developments perturbed President Azaña. With increasing unease he saw Negrín embrace the communist notion of 'dictatorship under democratic rules', even though he had himself advocated it earlier. He knew, too, that the cabinet reshuffle which followed Prieto's departure was influenced by Russian foreign policy.

Stalin was alarmed by the Sino-Japanese war and by German rearmament, now that his purge of the Red Army officer corps was accelerating. His desire to arrange a pact with France and Great Britain became more urgent, and it was therefore thought to be important to conceal communist power in Spain. Jesús Hernández stepped down, reducing overt communist presence in the cabinet to one; but Negrín brought back Alvarez del Vayo as foreign minister, and gave even more posts in the army and security services to Party members.

Negrín had become minister of war in addition to being prime minister, but the new communist under-secretary, Antonio Cordón, was effectively in charge. Hernández became commissar-general and, with Prieto's departure, these two were now unchallenged. The air force and tank corps were also completely under Party control. Every military operation therefore required communist approval. Negrín also gave the communists the under-secretaryship of the navy, but the navy was one service over which they were never able to gain control. The new director-general of security was also a Party member, as was the new commander of the *carabineros*, which made communist control of the para-military corps virtually complete. The *carabineros*, which had been built up by Negrín when he was minister of finance, were now nicknamed 'The Hundred Thousand Sons of Negrín' – a laconic reference to the French army sent in 1823 to restore Ferdinand VII. Considerable resentment was caused by their receiving priority in equipment and weapons as well as being paid two-and-a-half times as much as the infantry.

The Party's control of most headquarters and the senior commissar posts ensured that scarcely any but communist newspapers reached the soldiers at the front. The Party also controlled the training establishments and personnel appointments. In the period from May to October 1938 it was alleged that 5,500 out of 7,000 promotions in the army went to communists or JSU members. They also began to dissolve the forces of rival political groups, especially anarchist divisions. Just before Prieto left the ministry of defence, the CNT-FAI complained that many of their members had been shot on trumped-up charges or assassinated at the front. But Prieto, who had received similar complaints from his own party, was powerless to intervene.

Meanwhile, the Republican formations which had been forced back to Catalonia by the Nationalists' spring campaign, needed time to regroup and rearm before they were capable of effective action. The Aragon débâcle, following swiftly behind the enormous cost of Teruel, had prevented military action for the moment. Little was done to delay the advance of the Navarrese and Moroccan corps across northern Aragon, even though the hydro-electric plants in the Pyrenees to the west of the River Segre were essential to Catalonian industry.

The most famous part of this phase would seem to provide a good illustration of the way heroes could be created for the propaganda machine. The communists claimed that one of their men, Antonio Beltrán, had led 43 Division in a heroic and brilliant rearguard action in the Pyrenees near the Valle de Arán; with his back to the French frontier he had heroically defended a pocket for several weeks before being forced to leave Spanish territory. The other version of these events is somewhat different, and the non-communists who disputed the official story were locked up. When some of his soldiers went to the ministry of defence after their return from France to complain about the inaccuracy of this account, they were arrested for desertion. According to a senior officer in the Army of the East, Beltrán allowed the Nationalist breakthrough in the first place, then withdrew to a position where the enemy would leave him alone without risk, while they went on to capture the hydro-electric plants. His final comment on this 'glorious legend' was 'that's how the history of the Spanish war is being written at the moment'.

Despite the success of the Army of Manœuvre in Aragon, the Nationalists started to experience a feeling of anti-climax in May. The shattering effect of their troops' advance had raised hopes of a quick victory, but the fulfilment of these hopes depended upon a daring stroke, and Franco was not prepared to take risks. As a result there was muted, but perceptible, disagreement within Nationalist Spain over the strategy which followed the occupation of north Aragon. Franco's critics could not understand why he had not followed the drive to the sea with an advance on Barcelona before the enemy could recover. The Republican chief-of-staff, General Rojo, later admitted that the Catalonian capital could have been taken with little difficulty, which would have shortened the war by perhaps as much as nine months.

Instead of using the Army of Manœuvre for a rapid offensive on Barcelona during April, Franco decided to continue reducing Aragon segment by segment with Valencia as the principal objective. This strategy was followed by broadening the base of the corridor to the sea on the Teruel side in May, then mounting a general attack south during June, parallel to the coast; but the Nationalist forces never regained the momentum which they had built up during March and April. Heavy rain and bad visibility limited their air support. More importantly, the Republican forces on the south of the corridor had not suffered the Aragon collapse, and they were strengthened by new material which had come across the French frontier since its opening on 17 March.

The prospect of French intervention in Catalonia, following Hitler's *Anschluss* in Austria on 9 March, was used by Franco's supporters to justify the decision to turn south on Valencia and refrain from striking at Barcelona. Yet Franco like Ribbentrop, the new German foreign minister, surely knew that Blum's government was not in a position to act. (Blum's second administration replaced Chautemp's on 10 March and only lasted until 19 April when Daladier took over.) Chamberlain had made it clear that if the Nazis were provoked by any French action over Spain, Great Britain would not intervene. In addition Franco must have known of the French general staff's opposition to intervention, partly because of their lack of sympathy for the Republic, partly because developments to the east made them alarmed at any move which might lead to a war on two fronts.

The most likely explanation for Franco's decision not to launch an immediate assault on Barcelona was pressure from his allies. Hitler was nervous of British and French reactions after his Austrian coup and he was not interested in the rapid defeat of the Republic. Not long before, he had emphasized the need to divert attention from his expansionist policies in central Europe: 'From the German point of view we are not one hundred per cent interested in a Franco victory. What does interest us is a prolongation of the war in Spain, so that tension in the Mediterranean is increased.' It has even been suggested, but not proved, that the German government supplied the Republic with arms.

Italian policy, meanwhile, toed the German line. Mussolini and Ciano were both anxious lest the dispute over the South Tyrol should antagonize Hitler too much. Ever since early February, when the Führer had dismissed ministers who advocated caution in Austria, the Italian government was aware of the aggressive new direction in German policy. In addition,

Mussolini was still unsure how far he dare antagonize Great Britain by his Mediterranean policy. His characteristic fluctuations of boldness and fear, enthusiasm and disillusionment, dominated his attitude to Spain. In many ways he was tired of the war. He had started to contemplate Albania greedily, and he complained of the lack of gratitude shown by Franco. Nevertheless, he knew that, as long as the fighting continued, he could retain his air and naval forces in the Balearics. In the event of a European war, they would greatly increase his ability to attack convoys bringing French colonial troops from North Africa.

Both Hitler's moment of doubt after the *Anschluss* and Mussolini's anxiety, which together seem to have influenced Franco's military strategy profoundly, proved to have been unjustified. Neville Chamberlain's government in 1938 took the existing policy of appeasement to lengths which made Anthony Eden resign as foreign secretary on 20 February. This event reassured the dictators that there was little to fear from the British government. Then Chamberlain's insistence on an Anglo-Italian treaty demonstrated convincingly that Axis intervention in Spain would not be challenged.

As soon as Lord Halifax succeeded Eden as foreign secretary, the arrangements for the treaty went ahead, even though more British shipping had been sunk by Italian submarines at the beginning of the month. (Eden had ordered the anti-submarine patrols to be recommenced, noting that 'the Admiralty feared that this would impair the relations which they had established with General Franco's Admiral Moreno'.) On 16 April Ciano recorded that 'at 6.30 p.m. the Pact with England was signed. Lord Perth was moved. He said to me: "You know how much I have wanted this moment to come." It is true – Perth has been a friend. Witness dozens of his reports which are in our hands.' The date of the signing had been chosen to 'please Halifax as it is his birthday. All very romantic . . .', the young fascist foreign minister added sarcastically. The part of the treaty which affected Spain most directly was the provision that Italy should be allowed to keep its troops there until the end of the war. This agreement was not referred to the signatories of the non-intervention pact, although it was deemed to be still in force. It is not surprising that even Churchill, who had supported non-intervention strongly, later described it as 'an elaborate system of official humbug' which had 'been laboriously maintained'.

The Spanish Republican government was horrified by the treaty. Two weeks after it was signed, Negrín launched a vain diplomatic offensive. He issued his 'Thirteen Points' plan for establishing what amounted to a caretaker government with free elections to follow. It was intended as a formula for peace negotiations. It is difficult to know how much Negrín seriously hoped to achieve in the way of a settlement. Ciano was convinced that 'in civil war there is no compromise', but Negrín seems to have had great confidence in his diplomatic talents.

On several occasions during 1938 Negrín tried to make peace through third parties. Like Prieto, he wanted to negotiate before the Republic's military strength weakened to such a point that no opponent would consider talking. He had the full support of Stalin, who was seeking to extricate himself from any further commitment to Republican Spain. Nothing,

231

however, came of Negrín's diplomatic efforts, since Franco would not consider compromise and the French were still guided by British policy. Negrín simply had not appreciated the shallowness of the Conservative Party's commitment to democracy abroad. Chamberlain's government was later to pressure Daladier into closing the border to arms supplies once again on 13 June. (The French foreign minister, Bonnet, was a fellow appeaser.) Lord Halifax, while protesting about a bombing raid on a civilian target in Republican Spain, emphasized that he wanted 'to avoid creating any ill-will in Germany'. The government's refusal to react to renewed Italian attacks on ships flying the British flag provoked minor revolts on its own back benches. Lord Perth immediately warned Ciano that the administration might fall and the attacks were stopped until the crisis was past. It was now obvious to the Republic that any hope of change in Anglo-French policy, which the opening of the French frontier had inspired in mid-March, was groundless, and that the policy of non-intervention would be maintained against its interests. Similarly, the hopes aroused in the first week of May that the United States would repeal the arms embargo act were dashed when Ambassador Joseph Kennedy threatened congressmen with the Catholic lobby.

Although it may have appeared to the Republic at this point that there was an international conspiracy against it, relations between the Nationalists and their allies were hardly cordial. Despite the restraint which appears to have been put on Franco in late March, both the Italian and the German advisers became impatient at the slow progress made towards Valencia in May and June. In addition, Ciano had been deeply angered by the Nationalist attitude. 'I talked to Nicholas Franco about our aid for 1938,' he recorded in his diary at the end of March. 'They want a billion lire worth of goods, payment to be mostly in kind and very problematical. We must keep our tempers. We are giving our blood for Spain – do they want more?' The Germans also worried about financial dealings with Franco, and they even suspected that he might somehow be cheating them on the mining rights he had been forced to concede in payment. Relations between the national contingents were not helped by mistakes, however genuine: Italian bombers mistook targets and Condor Legion Messerschmitts attacked Nationalist Fiats which they took for Chatos. The Italian troops were becoming very unpopular in the rear. Even officers were frequently involved in brawls with Spaniards after mutual insults. Also an increasing number of Legionaries were deserting to the enemy, and their commanders were making money on the black market. 'It seems from reports we have had', Ciano noted, 'that a bad impression is being created by the sight of Italian troops filling the cabarets and brothels in the back areas, while the Spaniards are fighting a grim battle ... The soldiers of Fascism must not, at any moment or for any reason, set an example of indifference to the struggle.'

THE BATTLE OF THE EBRO

Franco's decision not to advance eastwards on Barcelona in April, whether due primarily to pressure from his allies or to a fear of French intervention, had already attracted criticism within Nationalist ranks. This grew in volume as his alternative strategy of attacking south towards Valencia failed to satisfy the hopes which had been aroused when Carlists reached the sea at Vinaroz on 15 April. The most serious consequence of this change of strategy was that it gave the broken Republican troops from Aragon time to re-form and re-equip with material which had come over the French border since mid-March. The rugged terrain on the southern side of the corridor was far easier for the Republic to defend than the River Segre, which now marked the western front of Catalonia. Also, the troops available to Miaja, who was now supreme commander of the whole central and southern zone, were fresh and still had their equipment intact, even if they were not battle-hardened like the troops in Catalonia. In addition Miaja could bring up reinforcements rapidly from other fronts.

During May and June the Nationalists had been extending the southern side of their corridor to the sea, but the Army Corps of Castile and Galicia, together with García Valiño's formation, found it heavy going. They had few suitable airfields for providing close support, while the Republic started to deploy their new Super-Ratas, with four machine-guns and a larger engine. But these new aircraft were not to play a major role. According to Nationalist sources 'they declined to enter combat' on many occasions. At this period the Nationalists lost almost as many fighters from small-arms fire as in aerial combat, and the 'kills' claimed by Republican squadrons were totally unrealistic.

It was disconcerting for the Nationalists to find their enemy on the ground fighting more effectively than ever before, just after what they thought had been the decisive campaign of the war. The Republican defence made the most of the terrain. Yet despite the slowness of the Nationalist advance, Franco's obstinacy prevailed. Early in July he reinforced the three army corps with the Italian CTV and Solchaga's Navarrese corps. Miaja accordingly increased the Republican force defending this 90-kilometre (55-mile) front to seven army corps. The balance in forces was in fact closer than might appear, for the Nationalist formations were

233

nearer to established strength than the Republican. (Both sides operated with 12 battalions to the division, but many Republican units numbered only three or four hundred men.)

The Republican army held its ground on the right flank along the Almenara heights by the sea, where the Galician corps did not enjoy the usual support from the Condor Legion. The tension over Austria had delayed the sending of replacement aircraft, so that the Condor Legion operated with only 16 serviceable fighters until a squadron of the new Messerschmitt 109c arrived. Nevertheless, their flak batteries and 88 mm guns compensated in part, bringing down ten Republican aircraft in June alone.

At the other end of the front, the Italian corps had pushed down from Teruel with an armoured thrust led by Fiat Ansaldos. Their initial advance was rapid, but after less than 100 kilometres (60 miles) the Italian and Spanish forces came up against a previously prepared line of defence known as the XYZ line, which consisted of well-constructed positions along the Sierra de Javalambre in the west, then across the Sierra del Toro to the Sierra de Espadán by the coast. The Nationalists tried assault after assault, but even with more than 1,000 field guns and the massed bombers of the three air forces, they failed to break through. The good defence line gave the Republican troops confidence in their flanks, and as virtually every action during the civil war had shown, only air attack could break them in such circumstances.

The bitter experience of air and artillery bombardment had taught Republican troops the need for well-constructed trenches, and the infiltration of Moors who crept forward in dead ground encouraged them to select better sites. They also planned interlocking fields of fire, and positioned their machine-guns so that they covered the most likely starting points of an attack. The great advantage of prepared positions like the XYZ line was that ranges could be discovered in advance and codewords allotted to probable enemy assembly areas or key features. These fixed defences, with their field-lines buried against shellfire, also helped to prevent the panic which sometimes resulted from a breakdown in communications.

The Nationalists were shocked to find that the untried Republican divisions were able to inflict a sharp reverse without any need for the costly heroism of Modesto's troops. In fact this purely defensive operation was a much greater victory for the Republic than Guadalajara, even though it was less spectacular. With 20,000 Nationalist casualties to only 5,000 Republican, the slogan 'to resist is to win' at last had some meaning. The tragedy for the Republic was that its leaders did not learn from this battle, but continued to give priority to political and propaganda considerations over military effectiveness. The coming battle of the Ebro was to exceed even Brunete as a spectacular operation, and lead directly to the collapse of the Popular Army.

While the struggle on the front north-east of Valencia continued into July, Queipo de Llano prepared to end the inactivity in the west. His attack in Estremadura pre-empted a Republican offensive which was planned to coincide with their major attack in the east. Queipo started in the second week of July with a local offensive on the southern flank of the blunt

Republican wedge pointing at the Portuguese frontier. When this proved successful, reserve divisions from the central sectors were re-deployed to assist him. On 19 July the offensive was made general, with three divisions on the north of the wedge and five on the south. The defending troops were inexperienced, and suffered from a lack of equipment. After a week, however, the Nationalist attack eased considerably, having been downgraded again to a local offensive because the Republican army in Catalonia had just launched its great assault across the Ebro and Franco's headquarters was clamouring for every available battalion.

After the Aragon collapse in the spring, the Republican government had set out to reconstitute an army from the formations pushed back into the isolated eastern zone. They had the River Segre to the west and the Ebro to the south as reasonable defence lines behind which they could reorganize. They had the 25,000 tons of war material which came over the French frontier between March and mid-June (when the British government persuaded Daladier to close it again as an encouragement to Franco to agree to the withdrawal of foreign troops). They also had more time than they could have reasonably expected, thanks to Franco's offensive towards Valencia.

During the late spring and early summer the call-up was extended to the classes of 1925–29 and 1940–41. Twelve new divisions were formed, the conscripts ranging from 16-year-olds to middle-aged fathers and including many men who had been exempted previously because of special skills. (The veterans called the youngest recruits the *quinta del biberón*, the baby's bottle call-up.) Many drafted technicians had become available because the loss of hydro-electric plants had cut Catalonian production dramatically. Nevertheless, since there were too few rifles to go around, the government's militarization decrees seem to have had more to do with creating an impression of resolute resistance than with military requirements. The new war material was of most use to the air force, special arms and machine-gun companies. The small-arms did no more than replace those lost at Teruel or in Aragon.

After the failure of his peace overtures, Negrín, supported by the communists, felt that international attention must be aroused by a great heroic action. If it were successful, the Republic could negotiate from a position of greater strength. The military justification for the project consisted of the need to link the two Republican zones again by recovering the Nationalists' corridor to the sea. The reasoning, however, contained several basic flaws. European attention was much more preoccupied with events in the east, especially Hitler's designs on Czechoslovakia. There was no prospect of Franco changing his refusal to compromise, nor of Chamberlain coming to the diplomatic aid of the Republic. The military rationale did not appear to take into account the probability of heavy material losses and the difficulty of replacing equipment now that the French border had closed again. Finally, the likelihood that another battle involving heavy casualties would damage Republican morale irretrievably was not appreciated. Altogether it was a monumental gamble against very unfavourable odds, incompatible with Negrín's hope that the Republic would still be resisting strongly when a European war broke out.

The Army of the Ebro was specially formed for this offensive. As at

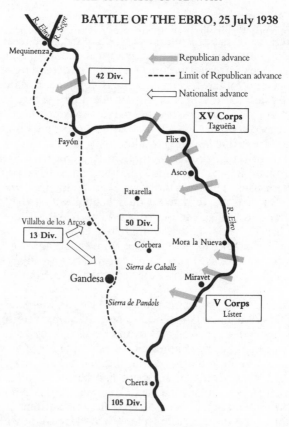

BATTLE OF THE EBRO, 25 July 1938

Brunete, its commanders and formations were predominantly communists, and it was allocated nearly all the armour, artillery and aircraft. Modesto was the army commander, and he had XVIII Corps in reserve, V Corps under Líster, and XV Corps under the 26-year-old communist, Manuel Tagüeña. His right flank was covered by XII Corps, which defended the bottom part of the River Segre from Lérida to where it joined the Ebro opposite Mequinenza. The curve of the Ebro between Fayón and Cherta was the sector chosen for the main assault, with XV Corps on the right and V Corps on the left. Two subsidiary actions were added – 42 Division crossing to the north, between Fayón and Mequinenza in order to impede a counter-attack from the right flank, and the French XIV International Brigade crossing downriver at Amposta. The total strength of the assault force was about 80,000 men. Each division in theory had 10,000 men with 5,000 rifles, 255 machine-guns, 30 mortars, four anti-tank guns, three artillery groups of nine field guns, and a battalion of engineers to organize the crossing. The greatest weakness was in artillery, as a result of losses in Aragon. The whole army had no more than 150 guns, some of which dated from the last century. In addition, the 76 mm anti-aircraft ammunition was known to be defective, although the soldiers were not told this 'for reasons of morale'.

One recent innovation was the establishment of a commando force in the so-called XIV Corps, and several of its detachments were to play an

important preparatory role by securing the crossing points and then striking inland to cause maximum disruption behind enemy lines. The crossing
of the 100-metre (330-foot) wide river was to be carried out with boats and
pontoon bridges recently purchased in France. Practising the procedures
at night contributed greatly to the initial success of the operation.

The Nationalist 50 Division responsible for the 35-kilometre (20-mile)
bulge within the loop of the Ebro reported troop movements on the far
bank. It has been said that although Yagüe had this confirmed by air
reconnaissance, he was allowed no more than Barrón's 13 Division in
reserve, and 105 Division to cover from Cherta on the southern point of
the bulge to the sea. The colonial troops in 50 Division were certainly
taken unawares. The Nationalists did not consider the Republic capable
of launching another major offensive after Aragon, especially across such
a wide river. Frequent headlines, such as 'The Reds Flee!' or 'Reds on the
run!', also made Nationalist Spain's morale particularly vulnerable to any
reverse.

On the night of 24 July commandos swam across to knife the sentries
and attach ropes for the assault boats. As soon as this was completed, they
moved on quickly to secure important cross-roads and prepare ambushes.
The regular forces started crossing in the early hours of 25 July. Just to the
north of the bulge, part of 42 Division crossed above the *pueblo* of Fayón,
nearly capturing General Yagüe by chance. XV Corps crossed the north
part of the Ebro's curve and Líster's V Corps the south-eastern part. The
attack downriver at Amposta by XIV International Brigade was repulsed
by 105 Division after only a few hours.

Within the bulge, the Republican formations advanced rapidly, capturing 4,000 men from 50 Division. The next day, however, the leading
elements of both corps came up against Barrón's division at the town of
Gandesa. Yagüe must have remembered Modesto's ponderous tactics at
Brunete and Belchite, and he had ordered forward 13 Division who held
back the enemy forces with a desperate stand. Some of its men died of
exhaustion on the 50-kilometre (30-mile) forced march to Gandesa.
General Volkmann, the new commander of the Condor Legion, who
visited Yagüe at his headquarters at this point, observed how calm he was.
He was undoubtedly the Nationalists' most capable field commander.

Franco reacted to the news of the surprise offensive with characteristic
obstinacy. He would not allow the Republic to retake territory, whatever
the cost. All available reserves were ordered to the Ebro front, and the
Condor Legion and the Nationalist air force were instructed to concentrate
on the bridges. At the same time, the Nationalists opened the dams on the
River Segre (a tactic which the Republican command does not appear to
have considered) and the resulting two-metre (6½-foot) increase in the level
of the Ebro swept away the Popular Army's pontoons. Only the heroic
efforts of the sapper battalions managed to restore communications 40
hours later. The loss of the bridges was a serious blow, since the failure of
the Republicans to break Barrón's troops round Gandesa was largely due
to the small number of tanks and field guns they had managed to get across
the river in the first phase. Nationalist bombing of the bridges was less
successful, however, and its effects were usually repaired the following
night. The half-squadron of Stukas would have been the best weapon for

this task, but the Luftwaffe was very concerned that the enemy might capture one intact (even Nationalist pilots were not allowed to examine them). In the Aragon campaign there had been little risk in using them against an enemy which was retreating so fast.

On 30 July Modesto reorganized the Gandesa sector and took personal control. But even concentrating the majority of Republican armour and more than half the artillery on one point did not break the Nationalist defence, which had by then been strengthened with reinforcements. Once again a major Republican offensive had failed to achieve its objective through lack of speed and the insistence on reducing every pocket before proceeding. On 1 August Modesto ordered the Army of the Ebro to go on to the defensive. It had lost 12,000 men in the first week.

Yagüe's delaying action gave the Nationalists time to bring down the first of eight divisions of reinforcements. They had lost only the bulge and the bridgehead occupied by 42 Division just to the north. The Republic's position, on the other hand, was even more vulnerable than at Brunete, since, with the river behind them, re-supply was far more difficult. In addition, the Nationalists soon established a crushing superiority in artillery. To make matters worse for the Republican troops, the rocky terrain made the digging of trenches virtually impossible, so that rough breastworks made out of large stones often formed their only protection.

The continuation of the battle could not be justified by Republican leaders on military grounds. The offensive, now at a standstill, had done its work in preventing the Nationalists from restarting their offensive against Valencia (though the defence of the XYZ line had broken the back of that attempt already). Any hope of recapturing the corridor to the sea was gone. Yet, instead of withdrawing in good order so as to preserve their troops and material for a more advantageous opportunity, the general staff ordered still more divisions across the Ebro. Once again, battle strategy was decided by propaganda. Having made wildly optimistic forecasts in the early days, the government feared that withdrawal would look like defeat. The only consolation, perhaps, was that Franco was obsessed with destroying the force which had taken Nationalist territory. The Army of the Ebro was thus saved the logical Nationalist counter, an attack across the Segre in the rear of its right flank.

The air battles over the Ebro sector escalated into the largest seen in the war. More than 300 aircraft were involved on 31 July. On 13 August there was a dogfight involving 100 fighters, including three Messerschmitt squadrons, the 3rd Super-Rata squadron, and a mass of Fiat and Chato biplanes. The Condor Legion's Heinkel 111s and the Nationalist Junkers 52s continued to attack the pontoon bridges occasionally, though they had mainly reverted to their usual role of 'flying artillery' against infantry positions. The air battle was an unequal fight. The Republicans' slight numerical advantage in late July was reversed to 2 : 1 against them by September.

On 6 August the bridgehead to the north of the bulge held by 42 Division was crushed. Two weeks later the Nationalists attacked the central part of the main sector after pushing Líster's corps back from Gandesa. To concentrate on this part was a surprising decision, in view of the Republican advantage of high ground in the Sierra de Pandols, but it was, perhaps, difficult to believe that any force could stand up to what Líster's troops were taking. The temperature was usually over 30° centigrade, and, as at Brunete, machine-gun teams had to urinate on their weapon during combat to cool it down. They had little water to drink and their rations did not always get through. There was very little cover, and the construction of proper defence works to withstand artillery or bombs was impossible. The shelling, strafing and bombing never seemed to stop during daylight hours, for the Republican air force provided little protection. The troops took it, the propaganda version goes, because they were disciplined anti-fascist fighters. The sceptic, on the other hand, might ponder the cold hysteria of commanders like Modesto and Líster, who were willing to shoot anyone 'who loses an inch of ground'. Their stubborn bravery, however, was more likely to have been an inarticulate expression of their hatred of the enemy.

Despite the slaughter on the Ebro front, where the Republicans lost nearly 25,000 men during the first three weeks of the battle, propaganda bulletins strove to maintain exaggerated hopes in the rear areas. Even the normally pessimistic Azaña had been greatly encouraged by the initial reports. Negrín, however, was faced with a cabinet crisis on 16 August, by the resignations of the Basque, Manuel de Irujo, and the Catalan, Jaime Ayguadé (the brother of the Artemio Ayguadé involved in the events of May 1937). Their main reasons were Negrín's dictatorial methods and the activities of the SIM; the occasion was the prime minister's insistence that all pending death sentences be carried out immediately. The censorship department tried to keep the affair quiet (even Azaña was not informed), but when news leaked out, the communists hastened to attack the two ministers for being involved in 'a separatist plot'.

Negrín appears to have been worried that Azaña would try to replace him with Prieto or Julián Besteiro, his other opponent within the socialist party. He indulged in brinkmanship by suggesting to many people that he would retire from politics, but even Companys urged him to stay. There seemed to be no alternative to Negrín's alliance with the communists while the most desperate battle of the war was in progress. The communists' control of the military which had been so greatly increased under Negrín, meant that if they were removed from power the Republic would be temporarily paralysed. Nevertheless, the Party was not prepared to leave anything to chance. The contrived leak of Negrín's impending resignation was matched by an orchestrated campaign demanding that he stay in office. There were demonstrations in Barcelona, and communist units at the front sent telegrams of support *en masse*. (Negrín used these telegrams to demonstrate to Azaña, in a veiled threat, that the army commanders were with him. Azaña described it as 'an unforgettable interview'.) The communists rejected half-measures. Tanks and troops were brought into Barcelona, while aircraft were flown low over the city in an intimidating manner. Negrín's former liberal and right-socialist allies were outraged. Prieto condemned the prime minister for 'imposing his will over the composition of the government with a military show of strength through Barcelona streets'. Their protests were too late; and, at any rate, Negrín's action was overshadowed by graver events. The appalling sacrifice on the Ebro was virtually ignored by Europe as it moved to the brink of war over Czechoslovakia in the late summer of 1938.

DEFEAT IN THE EAST

The Anglo-Italian treaty of April 1938, which signified the tacit acceptance of Italian intervention, had been a serious blow to the Republic. The Munich agreement of September was a disaster. This climax of appeasement did not only mean that British policy towards Spain would not change, it also led to Stalin's decision that Russia's only hope lay in a *rapprochement* with Hitler. This meant that Soviet support to the Republic was an embarrassment. Munich also marked the postponement of the European war on which Negrín was counting to force Great Britain and France to aid the Republic. In fact, it was rash of him to believe that even then their intervention would have been immediate. There would be little incentive for the British government to aid a severely weakened Republic at a time when all available material would be needed for its own forces. Moreover, it would have exposed Gibraltar before a programme for improving the Rock's defences had been started.

On the other hand, the Republic's other potential ally, France, was starting to resent the British government's domination of its foreign policy. The French had been forced consistently from one compromise to another, as Lord Cranborne admitted, in what they thought was the cause of democratic unity, when in fact Chamberlain was far closer to Franco, Mussolini and Hitler with his contemptuous belief in the decadence of France. Fear of their traditional German enemy, combined with resentment against the anti-French attitude prevalent in the British government, made even conservative army officers feel they should intervene in Catalonia on the Republic's behalf. But the French general staff was firmly opposed to any move which might result in a war on two fronts. It was therefore greatly relieved, during the Czechoslovakian crisis, by Franco's assurance of Spanish neutrality in the event of a European war, as well as his guarantee that Axis troops would not approach the Pyrenean frontier. Ciano was sickened by Franco's action, but the German and Italian regimes were at least assured that France as well as Great Britain would not hinder their intervention in Spain.

In fact the proceedings of the Non-Intervention Committee had never given them cause for alarm. The sittings continued as before, despite the Anglo-Italian pact in April. 'The entire negotiation in the committee', the

German representative reported, 'has something unreal about it since all participants see through the game of the other side ... The non-intervention policy is so unstable and is such an artificial creation that everyone fears to cause its collapse by a clear "no", and then have to bear the responsibility.' The plan for the withdrawal of volunteers, which the British had originated as a formula to retard the granting of belligerent rights, had been undermined in the Anglo-Italian pact. Lord Halifax had deemed a partial withdrawal of troops sufficient to satisfy the spirit of the non-intervention agreement.

Franco was unsure how to react to the revised British plan for the withdrawal of foreign forces from Spain, once it had been agreed by the committee in London on 5 July. He asked his allies for advice, and they counselled him to accept in principle, but delay in practice. On 26 July the Republican government accepted the withdrawal proposals, even though it was deeply disturbed at the prospect of the Nationalists' being awarded belligerent rights. This meant that ships flying the British flag, which included their own merchant fleet, would become liable to search, thus allowing the blockade to become completely effective. Eventually, on 16 August, Franco made his reply to Sir Robert Hodgson, who had been appointed British agent to Nationalist Spain in November 1937. He demanded belligerent rights before the British minimum figure for withdrawal of 10,000 men on each side had been reached. His attitude was almost certainly encouraged by the fact that the British had pressured the French into closing the frontier to Republican war material.

Against this background Negrín made a speech to the League of Nations on 21 September to announce the unconditional withdrawal of the International Brigades. His surprise gesture had little of the dramatic effect upon which he had counted to focus sympathy for the Republic. Concern over the Czechoslovakian crisis, which was then reaching a climax, had turned Spain into a sideshow which those in Geneva preferred to forget, since it was an embarrassing reminder of the worst aspects of international diplomacy. Ciano was perplexed by Negrín's move. 'Why are they doing this?' he asked in his diary. 'Do they feel themselves so strong?' Or is it merely a demonstration of a platonic nature? So far as we are concerned, I think this robs our partial evacuation of some of its flavour. But it has the advantage that the initiative is not made to appear ours – this would certainly have lent itself to disagreeable comments about Italian weariness, betrayal of Franco, etc.'

The Duce, on the other hand, although infuriated at times by Franco's 'serene optimism' and his 'flabby conduct of the war', offered fresh divisions. At that stage there were about 40,000 Italian troops in Spain. Eventually it was agreed that the best of them should stay and be concentrated in one over-strength division, while the rest would be repatriated. In order to make up for this withdrawal, Mussolini promised additional aircraft and artillery, which were what Franco really wanted. The Italian government was then able to point to its infantry withdrawals and insist on the implementation of the Anglo-Italian pact. Chamberlain asked for a brief delay, so that it would not look to the House of Commons, in Ciano's words, 'as if Mussolini has fixed the date'. This was necessary as Italian attacks on ships flying the British flag continued sporadically.

241

The Italian troops disembarked in Naples to an orchestrated welcome on 20 October. Lord Perth asked permission for his military attaché to witness the event, which prompted Ciano to note: 'No objection in principle on our part – so long as the thing is useful to Chamberlain for the parliamentary debates.'

Ciano had every reason to feel that he could afford to be patronizing in the wake of Munich. The prospect of a European war (which had frightened both Mussolini and Ciano despite all their bombastic statements) had receded. Mussolini claimed that 'with the conquest of Prague, we had already practically captured Barcelona'. Soviet policy towards the Republic changed from cautious support to active disengagement. The sacrifice of Czechoslovakia finally convinced Stalin that he could not count on Great Britain and France as allies against Hitler and so must cover his vulnerability by an alliance with Germany. But it would be misleading to link the fate of the Republic entirely with that of Czechoslovakia. The final destruction of the Republic's hope of survival had begun with the fighting across the Ebro, two months before the Munich agreement.

Chamberlain also felt that Munich had been a diplomatic triumph. He was so pleased with his efforts that, just before Mussolini and Ciano left Munich, he suggested 'the possibility of a Conference of Four to solve the Spanish problem'. Evidently he felt that the Spanish Republicans could be made to see reason like the Czechs, and be persuaded to sacrifice themselves in the cause of what he thought was European stability.

The late 1930s were years in which statesmen were particularly tempted to cultivate inflated ideas of their diplomatic abilities. A diplomatic coup in times of tension offers the dazzling prospect of political stardom. As Anthony Eden commented about Chamberlain. 'This is a form of adulation to which Prime Ministers must expect to be subject: it is gratifying to indulge, and hard to resist.' This observation was also true of Negrín, who, perhaps because of his undeniable talents in many fields, gravely overestimated what could be achieved by personal reputation and the power of persuasion. It is difficult otherwise to understand how he could have taken such an unjustified gamble as the Ebro offensive to serve as the backing for his diplomatic ventures.

His declaration to the League of Nations on 21 September, however, did not involve a major sacrifice for the Republic, because the foreigners serving in the ranks of the Popular Army were already considerably reduced. And if the Czechoslovakian crisis had not completely overshadowed this gesture, it would have been a well-judged propaganda move, since the press had laid a disproportionate emphasis on the International Brigades. By September 1938 there were fewer than 10,000 foreigners left in the Brigades, whose formations had been brought up to strength with Spanish battalions. The stories of communist heresy-hunting and the treatment of volunteers who wanted to leave, which had circulated in the second half of 1937, affected recruiting so seriously that the handfuls of new arrivals had done little to replace the losses suffered at Teruel and in Aragon. (The death rate amongst non-Spaniards in the International Brigades was just under 15 per cent up to the end of the Aragon campaign according to Soviet army statistics. A total casualty rate of 40 per cent is the most frequently cited.)

On the Ebro front Negrín's withdrawal plan was not passed on to the Americans, Canadians and British of XV International Brigade. They were due to attack Hill 401 the next day, and it was thought that such news might affect their performance. The foreign survivors in the Brigades were pulled out during that last week of September, then brought back to Barcelona prior to their official withdrawal, although just over half were given Spanish nationality so that they could stay on in the Popular Army. They were, mainly, the men who could only look forward to a reception by the secret police on their return home, whether in Germany, Italy, Hungary or the other dictatorships across Europe and Latin America.

André Marty, however, rewrote the last editorial of the Brigades' newspaper, *Volunteer for Liberty*, telling the 'anti-fascist fighters' to return to their home countries to lead the struggle against fascism there. In other words, only selected senior cadres would be given refuge in the USSR. Marty was also terrified that proof of his summary executions might threaten him in the future, and headquarters personnel at Albacete only just escaped with their lives in his mania to suppress the truth.

Seven weeks after their withdrawal from the front, the International Brigades assembled for a vast and dramatic farewell parade, and La Pasionaria said in her speech:

> Comrades of the International Brigade, political reasons, reasons of state, the welfare of that same cause for which you offered your blood with boundless generosity, are sending you back, some of you to your own countries, and others to forced exile. You can go proudly. You are history. You are legend. You are the heroic example of democracy's solidarity and universality. We shall not forget you, and, when the olive tree of peace puts forth its leaves again, mingled with the laurels of the Spanish Republic's victory – come back!

It was a moving occasion. Even the passionless expression on a huge portrait of the Russian leader who was secretly considering an alliance with Hitler could not belittle the emotion of internationalism which made the tears of the Brigaders and the crowd flow.

The beginning of the departure of foreign communists in the second half of 1938 did not change Party policy outwardly. The Spanish communists, however, must have been relieved that the exporters of the show-trial paranoia were returning home. The PCE leaders had on several occasions argued against the orders of Moscow, not necessarily because they disliked Russian methods, but because they considered them to be 'premature', as La Pasionaria put it. They realized that totalitarian tactics worked only if you had complete control of the army, the police, the legal system and the media, and they were embarrassed when Soviet advisers used blatantly totalitarian methods, which contradicted their own Comintern policy of reassuring the bourgeois democracies.

The trial of the POUM leaders began on 11 October, over 15 months after the disappearance of Andrés Nin. Most Spanish communists realized that, although the process set in motion had to be followed through, it was unwise to be implacable. Even so, a remarkably unsubtle case was presented. It was based on crudely forged documents linking the POUM to a Nationalist spy organization in Perpignan. The communists also prepared a reserve line by adding the events of May 1937 to their charge of high treason. They claimed that the POUM had made a 'non-aggression pact with the enemy' so that their 29 Division could participate in the Barcelona fighting. The trials ended in something of a compromise verdict. The Republic's reputation could not be dragged through the mud at such a moment, so the most outrageous charges were rejected; but the POUM's role in the events of Barcelona was used to justify imprisoning its leaders.

In Barcelona the population was by now on the edge of starvation. The ration, if obtainable, was down to about 100 grams of lentils per day as winter approached. People collapsed from hunger in the bomb-scarred streets and diseases such as scurvy increased. The propaganda broadcasts sounded increasingly hollow to their ears. They kept going only because there was no alternative. Workers weak from lack of food carried on in factories with virtually no electricity or raw materials for the same reason that the army kept fighting: it was less painful than thinking about the consequences of stopping.

On the Ebro the pattern of assault and defence, withdrawal and recapture, had not changed since the beginning of August. Apart from the dent in the centre, the line had moved back less than 10 kilometres (6 miles). Five major counter-attacks had been fought off, but still the artillery barrages and air strikes seemed to continue ceaselessly. (According to Tagüeña the telephone line between XV Corps headquarters and 45 Division had to be repaired 83 times in a morning because of shellbursts.) Republican soldiers hung pieces of wood from their necks to bite on during the bombardments. Shell-shock and battle-fatigue were far more prevalent on the Republican than on the Nationalist side.

The air battles had become totally confused. The Nationalist fighter ace, García Morato (currently with 36 victories), was shot down on 3 October for the only time in the war by one of his own novice pilots. Yet, while the Ratas, Chatos and Fiats fought individually in these hectic dogfights, risking collision as much as bullets, the Condor Legion's Messerschmitts were developing the tactic of fighting in closely co-ordinated pairs, a tactic which was to play its part in the Battle of Britain.

On the bleak terrain below, the Popular Army's reserves were almost exhausted. On 30 October the Nationalists began their major operation against the bridgehead. A devastating attack in the Sierra de Caballs was followed by a successful night attack on the Pandols heights. Then, while the retreat gathered pace on 2 November, 17 Republican fighters were destroyed, even though they had just been ordered to avoid battle with Messerschmitts and Fiats. In three days the Republican air force had lost more than a quarter of its strength. And when the south-eastern portion of the bulge was recaptured by the Nationalists during the first week of November, the Republican general staff knew that complete evacuation across the river could not be delayed. The last troops pulled back across the Ebro on 16 November under cover of a river mist. The battle had lasted 113 days. It had cost the Popular Army nearly 70,000 men and the war material on which further resistance depended.

Criticism of the Ebro campaign came primarily from the professional non-communist officers. General Gámir Ulíbarri stated that the fall of Catalonia was determined on the Ebro, and others, like the commander of the Army of the East, Colonel Perea, were scathing at the poverty of military thinking behind the operation. Once across the Ebro, the Republican forces lacked both the transport and the armour to achieve their physical objectives with sufficient speed. And once again they became embroiled in a holding battle, which gave the Nationalists time to bring in reinforcements. In addition, the whole operation repeated the cardinal error of concentrating large formations in open country against an enemy with overwhelming air and artillery superiority. Only the outstanding bravery and stamina of the Republican troops held the Nationalists for so long, inflicting almost as many casualties as they themselves received. But that was small compensation when the Republic could not afford such losses. In the ensuing slide towards defeat Negrín's supporters made out that he alone maintained the spirit of resistance of the whole Republic. This was a strange interpretation of events, which overlooked both Negrín's fundamental miscalculation on the Ebro and the way his collaboration with the communists undermined Republican unity and morale.

The onset of winter in Republican Spain was bleak. Food supplies had diminished even further, industrial production was down to about one-tenth of 1936 levels as a result of raw material shortages and the lack of electricity in Barcelona. There was little fuel for heating. Cigarettes and soap had been generally unobtainable for many months. Defeatism was rife, and even those who had, in desperation, convinced themselves that the struggle would eventually end in victory could not now avoid the truth. They realized that the next battle would be the last and faced the prospect with bitter resignation.

In late November and early December Negrín's government issued more mobilization decrees. They served little purpose because there were no spare weapons. Many of the new conscripts went home again, despite the shooting of deserters. Only a tiny proportion were caught because the administration was unable to cope with the new intake.

Even the army, where morale was usually higher than in the rearguard, looked beaten before the battle of Catalonia began, though this did not mean that they could not once again astonish the enemy with actions of brilliant and ferocious resistance. Apart from having lost some 70,000 men on the Ebro, the Republican forces in Catalonia had little material left. The Army of the Ebro and the Army of the East, with an estimated total strength of more than a quarter of a million men, were left with only 49 tanks, fewer than 100 field guns, 106 aircraft (of which only about a half were serviceable, thanks to a shortage of spare parts) and only 40,000 rifles.

THE FALL OF CATALONIA

At the beginning of December, two weeks after the last Republican units slipped back across the Ebro, the Nationalist Army of Manœuvre redeployed along the two river frontiers of the Republic's eastern zone. The Republican general staff quickly planned attacks in the west and south to divert the enemy's attention from Catalonia. On 8 December Republican forces attacked on the Córdoba–Peñarroya front towards Seville, while another effort was made on the north side of the Estremaduran front. An amphibious assault in reinforced brigade strength was also planned for the same day against the Andalucian coast near Motril, but it was called off just as the troops were ready to leave.

The Nationalist assault on the remainder of Catalonia was due to start on 10 December, but heavy rain and sleet made Franco decide to wait. He did not intend to attack unless his 'flying artillery' and close-support fighters were fully operational. His forces for this great offensive amounted to some 340,000 men, nearly 300 tanks, more than 500 aircraft and some 1,400 guns. Even though their superiority was overwhelming, the Nationalists were concerned at being halted by a fierce resistance at Barcelona. Ciano was suspicious of optimism after the disappointment which followed the Aragon campaign. 'The forthcoming attack in Catalonia may assume a decisive character,' he noted on 6 December. 'I myself am rather sceptical – that phrase has been used too often to be believed any longer.' Meanwhile, foreign statesmen like Roosevelt, who admitted that the arms embargo 'had been a grave mistake', and Churchill and Eden, who had previously held aloof in disapproval of the Republic, now realized what its extinction signified. The few democracies left on the continent included France, Switzerland, the Low Countries and Scandinavia; even the pessimists did not imagine that most of these had only 18 months left. Attempts to mediate in Spain were made by many foreign governments, but Franco rejected all approaches. The attitude of the British government left him feeling secure enough to continue to insist on belligerent rights before volunteers were withdrawn. Italian infantry he could do without, but the Condor Legion was his guarantee of victory.

The eventual outcome of the campaign was hardly in doubt, short of French intervention. Ciano warned London on 5 January (shortly after the despatch of more Italian fighters and artillery) that 'if the French move, it will be the end of non-intervention'. His fears were proved unnecessary, for Lord Halifax immediately told Paris once again that if the Axis powers were provoked over Spain, Great Britain would not help France. Franco's concern that Catalonia might declare itself independent and ask for French protection was also groundless: Negrín was almost as much of a centralist as he himself was. There was never a serious possibility of French troops being sent to intervene, despite the dramatic mutterings of those Frenchmen who felt humiliated by Chamberlain's behaviour at Munich. It was, indeed, the French government which stopped the Republic from receiving the last batch of Russian war material. This consignment had been arranged in Moscow, but the continued French closure of the border resulted in the materials being held until after the Republican forces had fallen back into France. They were then handed over to the Nationalists.

The Nationalist air forces had benefited from having more than a month to reorganize for the Catalonian campaign. Nearly 400 new Spanish pilots, fresh from flying school, were posted to the Fiat squadrons. At the same time the Condor Legion began to hand over the Messerschmitt 109b fighters to the more experienced Spanish pilots, as their own squadrons were to be re-equipped with the 109e. Another Spanish squadron was equipped with the Heinkel 112, which had been beaten by the Messerschmitt in the Luftwaffe comparison trials. The Italians were also to rush in their latest fighter, the Fiat G.50 monoplane, to be battle-tested in the closing stages, but it never saw action.

At the end of 1938 the Nationalists and their allies mustered 14 squadrons of Fiat CR 32 fighters and three squadrons of Messerschmitts with 12 aircraft each. Added to the Fiat force based in the Balearics, this gave them over 200 fighters (a total roughly equal to their combined bomber forces of Junkers 52s, Heinkel IIIs and Savoia-Marchettis). To face this force the seven Republican fighter squadrons now had far fewer Ratas than Chatos. This was because their only aircraft replacements were the Chatos manufactured at Sabadell. The 45 aircraft which they produced in the last three months of 1938 did little to make up their losses over the Ebro. The Republican forces were suffering from an acute shortage of spare parts in almost every field, and machines, weapons and vehicles were being cannibalized ruthlessly so as to ensure a bare operational presence.

The Nationalist forces for the Catalonian campaign were commanded by Dávila and consisted of six corps: on the left of the Segre front, near Andorra, there was the newly formed Army Corps of Urgel under Muñoz Grandes (who commanded the *División Azul* three years later), the Army Corps of the Maestrazgo under García Valiño and the Army Corps of Aragon under Moscardó; closer to the confluence of the Segre with the Ebro there were the 55,000 strong Italian Legionary Corps (the new name for the CTV) under Gambara, and Solchaga's Army Corps of Navarre. Yagüe's Army Corps of Morocco was concentrated on the Ebro front. The proportion of forces devoted to the Segre front showed that the Nationalist general staff had learned that it was better to attack first from the west, and only from the south-west across the Ebro once that front's defenders were outflanked. It is not difficult to detect the influence of General Vigón in this more competent planning.

Despite appeals for a Christmas truce from the Vatican, the Nationalist offensive finally started on 23 December. It was a cold clear day in contrast to the snow and rain of the previous fortnight. The Italian and Carlist formations launched an attack from their bridgehead east of the Segre at Serós, some 30 kilometres (19 miles) upstream from the Ebro. They were faced by 56 Division of *carabineros*, who, despite being the best-armed troops in the army, turned and ran immediately. The breach made the crumbling of that part of the sector inevitable and enabled the Italians and Carlists to push on towards Granadella, to the rear of the Ebro front. The Italian corps fought far more effectively than its allies or enemies had expected.

Another major assault was made on the same morning near Tremp, just short of the Pyrenees. There the Urgel and the Maestrazgo corps, backed by massive artillery support, crossed the River Flamisell, a tributary of the Segre. However, their opponents, 26 Division, the old Durruti column, maintained a 'magnificent resistance', according to General Rojo, and conceded only a small amount of ground. A breakthrough high on the west flank would have been catastrophic, but this fierce defence against heavy odds limited the advance to 'a slight bending of the line'. After five days General Vigón was forced to change the point of attack to the area of Balaguer, 30 kilometres downstream.

The real threat to Catalonia remained the thrust near the corner of the two fronts, where the Italians and the Carlists were fighting a reconstituted corps under Líster. This force, particularly 11 Division, managed to slow the Nationalists near Granadella on Christmas Day. Both they and the other formations defending the Ebro had been extremely fortunate that Yagüe's troops were held back by floodwater from the Pyrenees.

The crucial day was 3 January 1939. Yagüe's troops finally crossed the Ebro and established a bridgehead opposite Asco in the centre of the bulge which had been occupied by the Popular Army in the autumn. Solchaga's Carlists pushed forward to reach the Borjas Blancas–Montblanch road, some 50 kilometres (30 miles) behind the Ebro front. Also on that day the offensive from the Balaguer sector overran the key town of Artesa. The war in the air had also been going badly for the Republic. Nearly a whole squadron of Natashas was wiped out in one battle on Christmas Eve, and about 40 fighters were lost in the first 10 days of the campaign. Only a handful of fragmented squadrons remained. Meanwhile, the Republican general staff made another desperate attempt to distract the Nationalists. In Estremadura XII and XXII Corps attacked in the Pozoblanco sector, capturing a considerable amount of territory. But it was too little and too late. Franco was not diverted from his immediate objective of attacking Barcelona.

In the days following the Nationalist successes of 3 January, the Urgel and Maestrazgo corps increased the large dent in the middle of the Segre front, while to their south Moscardó's Aragon corps advanced from Lérida to protect the Legionary Corps' left flank as it overran Borjas Blancas. The Republic's V and XV Corps were too late to cut off the Carlists and Italians, and the northern half of the Ebro front collapsed in disorder at the threat of encirclement. It was an inglorious end for those who had endured so much for so little purpose in the Army of the Ebro.

The most dramatic move was then made by Yagüe's colonial troops, who cut straight through from their bridgehead towards Tarragona, covering 50 kilometres (30 miles) in a day with one of their famous forced marches. By the middle of January the Nationalists had captured 23,000 Republican soldiers, killed 5,000 and wounded 40,000. According to the Republican commander-in-chief, there were only 17,000 rifles left, yet more than 10 times that number of soldiers were retreating. In fact the battle of Catalonia was decided when only about a third of the territory had been taken. This time, however, Franco did not repeat the mistake of the Aragon campaign: the advance from the line of Tremp to Tarragona was continued before the enemy had a chance to recover.

The Popular Army's general staff had designated fall-back positions and defence lines, but they proved purely theoretical. Rallying calls were ignored by nearly all groups of dispirited fugitives. Calls to summon up a defence of Barcelona like that of Madrid were futile. In terms of armed troops, the odds were more than 6:1 against the Republicans, and they had little ammunition with which to defend a besieged city. More importantly, the spirit of 1936 no longer existed. In Barcelona too many people agreed with Abad de Santillán that whether the communists or the Nationalists won, the consequences would be the same. There might have been a fierce resistance had the people of Barcelona been trapped, but the escape route to the frontier was still open.

Handbills calling for resistance blew in the deserted streets along with abandoned identity papers when Companys drove around the city centre during the early hours of 26 January. It was his last view of Barcelona. The Gestapo handed him over to Franco for execution in October of the next year. There was an air of complete desolation. Food shops had been looted for provisions to last the long walk to the frontier, a journey which more than half a million people were making.

During that day the fifth column of Nationalist supporters, men and women who had stayed *incognito* for two-and-a-half years, emerged to take revenge. They were joined by elements from the leading troops of their liberating army, and it is said that as many as 10,000 people were killed in five days, even though the political prisoners of the Republic were released unharmed. Italian officers were taken aback by the cold-blooded slaughter, though Mussolini ordered that all Italians in the Republican army who were captured should be shot immediately 'as dead men tell no tales'. Yagüe's Moors, who were among the first into the city, were given several days leave to collect their 'war-tax': it made no difference whether the owners were Nationalists or Republicans. Meanwhile, the priests of Barcelona who had been tolerated by the Republic, together with those who had arrived in the baggage train of the conquerors, were busy. The military governor angrily told the Falangist leader, Dionisio Ridruejo, that he could not distribute literature to win over the workers. 'This is a city which has sinned greatly', he explained, 'and it must now be sanctified. Altars should be set up in every street of the city to say masses continually.' The Catalan language and any manifestation of Catalan culture were rigorously banned. Posters ordered everybody to 'Speak Castilian, the language of the Empire!' Bonfires were made of any books banned by the clergy or the army.

Some had stayed hidden waiting for the Nationalist troops, like Antonio Rodríguez Sastré, the chief of Republican intelligence, who had been working for Franco, and later became Juan March's lawyer. Others remained either because they felt they had nothing to fear, or because of exhaustion and apathy. There was a numb relief that it was all over, and they told themselves that nothing could be worse than recent months. For most though, the atmosphere of downfall before the arrival of the enemy contributed greatly to their panic. Prisoners, other than those left behind in Barcelona, were herded ahead of the retreating forces. A number were shot by their guards, who either lost their heads, or acted out of the bitterness of defeat. The victims included the bishop of Teruel, and Colonel Rey d'Harcourt, who had surrendered the town.

The Nationalists' rejoicings in their capture of Spain's largest city at least gave the refugees on the road to the frontier a little extra time. There was a slow progress. The queues of cars with government officials often moved no more rapidly than the limping columns of refugees on foot. It was afterwards alleged that senior officers and politicians commandeered ambulances for themselves and their belongings, while the wounded were left to walk. Many refugees died from hunger and the bitter cold.

There were only a few formations of the Popular Army left unbroken. They put up some brave, but hopeless, stands, such as the defence of Montsech, but the reason it took the Nationalists another two weeks to reach the frontier was that they, too, were exhausted from marching. The main concern of Franco's general staff was to prevent the last Republican air force squadrons from breaking back to the central zone. As a result all available fighter and bomber groups were concentrated on strikes against Republican airfields.

The French government faced a huge influx of refugees. At first it closed the border completely, partly for economic reasons, partly because of fierce objections inside the country. France already had many political exiles and prejudice against them was being inflamed by the gutter press. Daladier's suggestion of a neutral zone to house the refugees just inside Spain was rejected by Franco out of hand. The French then announced on 27 January, as the tens of thousands waiting fearfully at the border grew to several hundred thousand, that as from midnight they would allow in only civilians and wounded soldiers. Those two categories alone amounted to at least 200,000 people, but already many thousands more had started to cross the mountains illegally, despite the presence of Senegalese troops brought in to guard the border.

By 3 February Nationalist units were within 50 kilometres (30 miles) of the frontier and it was clear that the Republican troops could not delay them. They did have enough weapons, however, to fight their way to safety over the border, so that the French government had either to reinforce their border guard or let soldiers through as well as civilians. There was little choice for a government with a guilty conscience over Czechoslovakia. On 5 February it was announced that the remnants of the Popular Army could cross into France. The refugees who had entered France since mid-January now numbered more than half a million. Another 60,000 failed to make the border in time and were rounded up by the Nationalists.

The sight of these gaunt, shivering masses was often tragic and pitiful.

But many observers noted that their manner was of men and women who still refused to admit defeat. Some Republican units marched across and piled arms on French soil under the directions of the *gendarmes*, while the colonial troops from Senegal stood with rifles at the ready, not understanding the situation. A *garde mobile*, in a scene now famous, prised open the fist of a refugee to make him drop the handful of Spanish earth which he had carried into exile. The Republican diaspora had begun.

THE ANTI-COMMUNIST COUP AND THE END OF THE WAR

On 9 February, just as the Nationalists completed their occupation of Catalonia, the Republican government, forced from Barcelona into France, met briefly in Toulouse to discuss future resistance. Negrín, accompanied by Alvarez del Vayo, then managed to elude the journalists before taking a chartered Air France plane to Alicante. Only a few ministers, generals and senior officials returned to the remaining central-southern zone. Azaña was shortly to resign the presidency when Great Britain and France recognized the Franquist regime, and his successor, the leader of the Cortes, Martínez Barrio, refused to return to Spain. The constitutional basis of Negrín's government was therefore extremely questionable. General Rojo, the chief-of-staff, who said that he would 'not ask Spaniards to commit suicide', did not return either.

The senior regular officers still in the Spanish Republican zone had no illusions about their forces' capacity for resistance, even though officially they still had about half a million men under arms. Deficiencies in material and spare parts were not quite so serious as they had been in Catalonia, but the Republicans had little hope of countering the Nationalists' superiority in armour, artillery and aircraft. The last of the Russian arms were still held in France, as Daladier's government shared Chamberlain's eagerness to finish the war quickly. The Royal Navy assisted the surrender and evacuation of the Republican forces on Minorca on the condition that Franco establish a Nationalist garrison there to prevent an Italian occupation. The chief priority of Anglo-French policy was now to secure Franco's neutrality and ensure that Axis forces left Spanish territory.

Negrín assembled the senior officers of the armed forces at Los Llanos airfield, near Albacete, on 16 February. He told them that they must resist, but they disagreed. General Matallana and the army commanders underlined the deficiencies in equipment from which they suffered. Admiral Buiza stated his agreement with the fleet delegates who said that the navy must leave Spanish waters before it was bombed out of existence in harbour. The prime minister replied that they should be shot for mutiny. The chief of the air staff then said that there were fewer than three fighter and five bomber squadrons left in operation. Negrín's promise that vast quantities of war material were about to arrive fooled nobody. Only General

Miaja, the commander-in-chief, spoke out for resistance, and he, too, was soon to change his mind.

Negrín ignored the arguments of the military chiefs and said that the Republic would fight on. But his actions did not match his words. He told one delegation that there was 'no possibility of resistance' and did nothing to organize any, but all the while the official line, backed by the Spanish Communist Party, was that the struggle would continue to the end. The communists, however, had no further control over arms from Russia; their military strategy had proved a disaster, and the methods which they had used to gain power had made them more enemies than friends. More and more army regulars, who had become communists early in the war, now opposed the Party secretly. A growing number of them were convinced that the communists formed the major barrier to peace. Some went so far as to believe that the professional officer corps could arrange an agreement with their former colleagues and escape the penalties for having stayed loyal to the Republic.

It has been argued that the communists' call for continued resistance, against the advice of the senior officers and all the other political parties, was prompted by a desire to display the treachery of their critics. The Party's earlier sectarian repression could then be justified in later years. But the fact that most of the communist leaders had already prepared their departure gives the lie to subsequent claims that their heroic resistance was stabbed in the back. Azaña was scathing about those who called for a desperate defence, and yet had organized their 'aeroplanes, and accounts in Switzerland'.

The policy of Negrín's government confused everybody. Despite his call for continued resistance, he did not reconstitute his administration in either Madrid or Valencia. Instead he remained in a villa near Elda, close to the port of Alicante, and there, guarded by 300 communist commandos from XIV Corps, he planned his own exile and that of senior officials who had remained loyal to him. His peace formula had now been whittled down to three points: free elections, no foreign presence after the war, and no reprisals. The last point was the only one which the Nationalists would consider discussing, but the recently published Law of Political Responsibilities, which effectively made every Republican guilty of a crime, made it unlikely that any agreement at all could be reached.

Negrín's supporters, especially the communists, have argued that if the Republic had held out until the autumn of 1939, it would have been saved by Anglo-French intervention. But, apart from every other consideration, after the destruction of the Republic's fighting potential on the Ebro, neither Great Britain nor France could have afforded the quantity of material which such a rescue operation would have required. A neutral Spain was altogether a safer option for the British and French general staffs than an ally who needed massive support.

The capture of the Republic's industrial base of Catalonia made the Nationalist victory certain. Both the French and the British governments recognized the new Spanish government on 27 February. Marshal Pétain was nominated as France's ambassador to the Burgos administration and Daladier handed over to the Nationalists Republican war materials and gold which had been deposited in France. He also guaranteed that his government would prevent any activities directed against them from French soil. In London Chamberlain faced furious scenes in the House of Commons, but the Conservative majority supported him. The Duke of Alba was then able to take over the Spanish embassy.

The only serious argument for continuing the fight was that it was better than waiting passively for the execution squads. Lord Halifax, the British foreign secretary, was one of many who urged the Nationalists to show generosity in victory. Franco's reply was an assurance that those who had been misled would be spared. This was accepted by foreign governments, even though the Nationalists' definition of political criminality included neutrals.

Since early in the new year the greatest opposition to Negrín and the communists had been developing in the Army of the Centre. Its commander, Colonel Segismundo Casado, a cavalryman of peasant birth and austere tastes, had been one of the very few career officers to stand out against the Party from the beginning. (Casado was one of the few regular officers respected by Azaña, who knew him well.) He was sympathetic towards the anarchists and enjoyed a close rapport with Cipriano Mera, having been at his side during the tense moments before the attack on Brihuega. Mera commanded IV Corps which covered the Guadalajara and Cuenca fronts, while the other three corps commanders were communists.

On 16 February the liaison committee of the libertarian movement criticized Mera strongly for 'taking positions and making decisions on his own account'. His reply scorned the official CNT policy of collaboration with Negrín, which had merely allowed the prime minister to ignore the anarchists. The CNT leadership, with its *Negrínista* secretary-general, Mariano Vázquez, was undoubtedly out of touch with its membership. The tortuous path which had brought Mera to this point started at the Saragossa conference in the spring of 1936, where he had strongly opposed militarization, although in the autumn of the same year he had recognized its necessity for conventional warfare. His insistence on keeping politics out of his military life had earned him the dubious praise of General Goriev and the communists, but their activities in the army had now forced him to take a political stand.

Casado's plan was to organize a fighting retreat southwards and defend the area of the Cartagena naval base with 80,000 men. He hoped thereby to ensure the departure of all those who wanted to leave Spain before the Nationalist victory. Negrín was also considering evacuation plans, having realized that the continuance of organized resistance was an illusion. Neither he nor Casado, however, planned for such an enormous task.

Like other senior officers Casado believed that the Republican government's dependence on the communists had prevented the settlement of reasonable surrender terms. Nevertheless, he was not one of those who hoped to save their necks and perhaps even their military careers by a last-minute betrayal.

During the course of February, Casado became the central figure for those who opposed Negrín and the communists. Apart from anarchists and other senior officers, they included the socialist professor, Julián Besteiro, who accused Negrín of playing with Spanish lives to gratify his taste for power, General Miaja and Largo Caballero's old associate, Wenceslao

Carrillo. (Carrillo's opposition to Negrín earned him, down to the day that he died in exile, the enmity of his son, Santiago.) Liberals and UGT leaders completed the secret alliance. The communists were well aware of Casado's attitude, particularly when he closed down the Party newspaper in Madrid, and they also suspected him of negotiating privately with the Nationalists. Negrín's failure to arrest Casado is said to have stemmed from his secretly welcoming the prospect of being overthrown and thus relieved of the responsibility for defeat. On 2 March Negrín ordered Casado and Matallana to come to his retreat at Elda, where he informed them that he meant to reconstruct the army command. The two officers voiced their objections, then Casado left for Valencia to rally support. Negrín's proposal represented the equivalent of a communist *coup d'état*. Casado was to be removed from field command (though promoted to general), while Modesto was to replace Miaja, El Campesino take over the Army of Estremadura, and Líster the Army of the Levant. Other communist officers, such as Vega, Tagüeña and Francisco Galán, were appointed to commands which controlled the Republic's remaining ports. The threat of communist control of the evacuation inevitably alarmed their opponents. Casado warned that they must strike immediately; Mera stood by to take over command of the Army of the Centre.

Negrín's appointment of the communist, Francisco Galán, to the command of the Cartagena region, where the prime minister rightly suspected Admiral Buiza of being involved with Casado, triggered inter-Republican fighting. Galán's assumption of command in Cartagena on the night of 4 March was immediately followed by the revolt of military units and the fleet. The fifth column quickly took advantage of the situation and army officers joined them hoping to establish themselves in the Nationalists' good grace. A mixed body of Falangists and marines seized the radio station and signalled for assistance from the Nationalists. Then, when it looked as if the fifth column would seize the shore batteries, the operational vessels of the fleet, including three cruisers and eight destroyers, left for the open sea on Admiral Buiza's orders. However, a fresh communist division ordered in by Hernández, the commissar-general, crushed both risings on shore and manned the guns in time to sink a Nationalist warship as it arrived with a brigade of troops (in answer to the appeal for help from the fifth column). The Republican fleet would not return, and Franco contacted Ciano the next day, 6 March, with an urgent request that the Italian navy and air force should help 'in case they should try to get to Odessa'. (In the circumstances it would have been a surprising destination.) The French government, when approached, directed the squadron to their port of Bizerta on the Tunisian coast, where the crews were interned. The ships were eventually returned to the Nationalist government in line with their agreement with France.

On 5 March in Madrid Casado refused Negrín's renewed summons. That evening the National Council of Defence was set up in the Treasury building, where it was guarded by the anarchist 70 Brigade, sent by Mera. The Army of the Centre's chief commissar, Daniel Ortega, jumped out of a window at Casado's headquarters and ran off to warn his fellow communists of what was happening. That the Party refused to react appears to support the argument that its central committee regarded the coup as being of long-term propaganda benefit. (Hernández reported the Comintern delegate, Dmitri Mannilsky, as saying: 'The Casado group fell into the trap ... the Party was spared the responsibility for the final catastrophe.' Mannilsky thus implied that the appointment of the communist officers was a conscious provocation.)

Casado was president of the council, until he persuaded Miaja to take that position. Besteiro joined as foreign minister, without party affiliation, and the remaining posts were shared by anarchists, socialists and republicans. The former director of prisons, Melchor Rodríguez, was appointed mayor of Madrid. Once these positions were filled, the appointments which had triggered the revolt were declared invalid.

At midnight Casado, Besteiro and Mera made an announcement on Madrid radio. Their message was that Negrín should not be allowed to provide for the flight of a few, while telling others to resist. Casado then telephoned the prime minister to inform him of their action. The next morning communist militants were arrested wherever they were in a minority and red stars were stripped from army uniforms. Meanwhile, the last Russian advisers rapidly organized their departure, although other communists including Modesto, Líster, La Pasionaria and the senior Comintern adviser, Togliatti, waited uncertainly with Negrín at Elda. Their control had finally been challenged. They had to choose between accepting the end of their power or counter-attacking with the formations upon which they could still depend. Many of their previously assured fiefs in the army were now in doubt, since so much of their support had been conditional upon their unchallenged power. The Party leadership, together with Negrín and Alvarez del Vayo, left for the airport, because of the advance of anti-communist formations. Líster, the commander of the Army of the Levant, had only a company of troops in the immediate area on which he could count. At the airport they waited to see whether Casado would respond to an appeal to back down. Eventually, the approach of unfriendly troops made them decide to leave; only Togliatti stayed behind. But as they flew off into exile on 7 March, the communist commander of I Corps, Luis Barceló, reinforced with elements from II and III Corps, which were also under Party command, began to attack the National Council of Defence.

Barceló's troops surrounded Madrid, seized Casado's headquarters near Barajas, and shot some of his officers. The Council buildings in Madrid were still only defended by 70 Brigade, but within a few hours of the first attack part of Mera's IV Corps began to move to their relief from the east. The fighting was fierce, both in the suburbs and around the beleaguered buildings, but Barceló appears to have hesitated because the departure of his Party leaders and the lack of communication with Togliatti left him without orders. By the 10th Mera's troops had surrounded the communist forces and a ceasefire was arranged. Barceló and a handful of other communist officers were condemned by military tribunals and shot. The Party's power in the Republican zone was now crushed.

Casado and Matallana, meanwhile, had maintained their contacts with the Nationalists in the hope of finding a peace formula. There was little to encourage them. Franco insisted on unconditional surrender, and the Republican officers soon realized that they could obtain no better terms than Negrín. Casado also found that he could not carry out his plan of with-

91 General Rojo (right) and Prieto (second from right) at Teruel, January 1938.

92 The winter fighting of Teruel, December 1937.

93 Ju 87b Stukas first saw action in the Aragon campaign.

94 General Varela (left) examines captured T-26.

95 Nationalist 155mm batteries.

96 The Republican retreat near Bujaraloz in Aragon, March 1938.

97 Barcelona harbour after an air raid.

98 German Panzer Mk 1 during advance through Aragon, late spring 1938.

LA DOMENICA DEL CORRIERE

ITALIA	ESTERO		
Anno . . . . . . L. 19,–	L. 40,–		
Semestre . . . . . » 10,–	» 21,–		

Per le inserzioni rivolgersi all' Amministrazione del *Corriere della Sera* – Via Solferino, 28 - Milano.

Si pubblica a Milano ogni settimana

Supplemento illustrato del "Corriere della Sera"

Uffici del giornale:
Via Solferino, 28 - Milano

Per tutti gli articoli e illustrazioni è riservata la proprietà letteraria e artistica, secondo le leggi e i trattati internazionali.

Anno 40 – N. 18   1 Maggio 1938 - XVI   Centesimi 40 la copia

99 Lord Perth and Count Ciano signing Anglo-Italian pact on 16 April 1938.

100 Condor Legion anti-aircraft detachment with 88mm gun.

101 Republican troops cross the Ebro, July 1938.

102 Italian Nationalist troops on the advance south from Teruel, June 1938.

103 Members of the British battalion in reserve on the Ebro front, autumn 1938.

104 Republican hospital train behind the Ebro front.

105 Messerschmitt Me 109 strafing Republican trench.

106 Final International Brigade parade in Barcelona on 15 November 1938.

107 Mussolini's withdrawn 'volunteers' welcomed home in Naples.

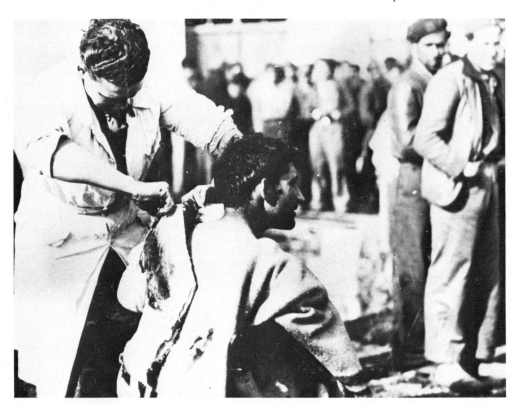

108 Wounded Republican treated during collapse of Catalonian front, January 1939.

109 Franco and staff have lunch 45 km short of Barcelona.

110 The road to the French frontier jammed by Republican refugees, late January 1939.

111 Republican vehicles at the French frontier, early February 1939.

112 Republican refugees and field guns at Le Perthus, France, early February 1939.

113 Ruins in Madrid just after the end of the war.

114 German heavy machine-gun detachment before the final advance on Madrid, March 1939.

115 Condor Legion's farewell parade in front of Franco.

116 The indoctrination of Republican orphans.

117 Nationalist children at drill.

118 Republican prisoners at Le Vernet camp in south-west France, spring 1939.

— Et maintenant, je viens "travailler" en France...

119 Right-wing French cartoon against allowing
Republican refugees to enter France.

drawal towards the south because of the panic it would trigger in the capital. Evacuation of those in most danger was the only priority left. Resistance was neither possible nor worthwhile. Even Hitler's occupation of Prague in the middle of March, much as it shook Westminster, did not make British intervention any more likely. Unfortunately, the Council of Defence had taken few practical steps to prepare for evacuation, and the contract for 150,000 tons of shipping from the Mid-Atlantic company agreed with the Negrín government was claimed to be invalid owing to lack of payment in advance. Casado seems to have placed too much reliance on Lord Halifax's unspecified offer of British help with transport, and he assumed, wrongly, that the French would assist as well. He seems to have been convinced that once he had dealt with the communists, the British and French governments would automatically become his allies.

Peace negotiations continued, but only verbal guarantees were given against political reprisals. The time-table for surrender stipulated the hand-over of Republican air squadrons on 25 March and a general surrender of the land forces two days later. Franco overruled his negotiating officers, insisting that a technical delay in surrendering the air force annulled previous agreements. The general advance on all fronts would proceed, and white flags should be shown. Some elements on the Republican side wanted to fight on when they heard of this, but it was too late to reverse the emotional process of surrender.

The Republican front lines disintegrated on 27 March in a spontaneous process, which Casado called self-demobilization. Soldiers on both sides embraced each other in relief at the ending of the war. Even relations between Republican officials and the fifth columnists who emerged to take over their administrative positions were sometimes cordial, though this friendliness was not to last. Republican troops who surrendered to Nationalist forces were ordered to pile up their arms before being herded together into bullrings or open areas surrounded by barbed-wire fences. The unsupervised threw away their rifles and either lay waiting for directions or started to trudge in the direction of home.

Meanwhile, the formations of the Army of Manœuvre continued their advance towards the principal Mediterranean ports, where between 40,000 and 80,000 people were trying to find space on ships which were leaving the country. Casado's requests for help to the French and British governments went unanswered – not that foreign assistance could have been provided in time. The loss of the fleet was bitterly felt, but even it could not have taken all those who were desperate to leave. On 29 March, at the small port of Gandía, the light cruiser HMS *Galatea* put in to collect Italian fascist prisoners as part of a pre-arranged exchange. Its captain was finally persuaded to take Colonel Casado on board along with other officials and some militiamen. Few escaped from the Mediterranean coast in those last three days. At Alicante, where up to 40,000 people were said to be thronging the port, several ships approached on 30 March, but turned away when their captains saw that they would be stormed by the multitude. A number of soldiers and civilians on the quay then committed suicide, some even using bayonets.

In Madrid, as in other cities, the flag of 'Old Spain' appeared on balconies, while fifth columnists and the fearful made fascist salutes and chanted

Nationalist slogans. In most towns the troops arrived to find the Falange already in control. The Nationalist armies occupied all their final objectives on 31 March. 'Lifting our hearts to God,' ran Pope Pius XII's message of congratulation to Franco, 'we give sincere thanks with your Excellency for the victory of Catholic Spain.' Ciano wrote in his diary that 'Madrid has fallen and with the capital all the other cities of Red Spain. It is a new formidable victory for fascism, perhaps the greatest one so far.' In London on 20 April, exactly three weeks after Franco's conquest, the Non-Intervention Committee dissolved itself at its 30th plenary session.

THE 'NEW SPAIN'

On 21 February 1939 the Fiat CR 32s of the 3rd Fighter Group flew low over Barcelona's Diagonal to celebrate the conquest of Catalonia. Their machines formed the intials of Franco's amalgam, the *Falange Española Tradicionalista*. They carried on south-westwards and off Tarragona they flew past the Nationalist flagship, the cruiser *Canarias*, from whose deck the Caudillo took the salute. It was also the day on which Franquist Spain joined the Anti-Comintern pact with Germany, Italy and Japan, though this was not made public until 26 March. In addition, on 31 March a five-year treaty was signed with Germany. The great Nationalist victory parade was held in Madrid on 19 May. Three days later the Condor Legion organized its own parade near León. The last of the Nationalists' allies finally left for home during the course of June.

Franco was undisputed master in his own house, even though he had mortgaged it heavily to gain possession. The strength of his position in Spain was guaranteed by his command of the army, but the support which his regime enjoyed was wider. Within Nationalist ranks the most powerful force for unity was the fear that the enemy might return to take revenge. This fear greatly muted internal criticism of the new regime, and the Caudillo constantly presented any form of unrest as Bolshevism. In addition the new government enjoyed the unlimited support of the church, whose influence was now raised to a level it had not enjoyed for centuries. Franquist power was also welcomed by landowners and businessmen. Nevertheless, there was to be a conflict between the ideals for which the Carlists and Falangist old-shirts had thought they were fighting and the reality of post-war Spain.

With the geographical fragmentation caused by the rising, the original executive power in Nationalist territory had been vested in rapidly created para-governmental committees. These local ruling groups covered almost every aspect of life. They were the Nationalist counterpart to the local committees which had existed in Republican Spain during the social re-volution of 1936. Their composition, which usually consisted of the most important local landowner, the priest, the senior civil guard officer, and the Falange chief, reflected the basis of the army's support. After the war they were absorbed into a monumental bureaucracy, but in their heyday they offered great opportunities to the political or religious zealot as well as to the ambitious. The 'new Spain', despite some superficial concessions to modernity, was based firmly in the traditional ruling forces of the country.

This had been confirmed in the spring of 1938 by the composition of Franco's first official administration. The monarchists, Carlists and Falangists were each given two posts to provide a balance of the coalition forces, while key appointments went to generals, such as the monarchist, Count Jordana, who became foreign minister, and General Martínez Anido, the old captain-general of Barcelona, who was made minister of public order. (The German ambassador von Faupel reported that his reign of terror was 'unbearable even to the Falange'.) The most important Falangist was the Caudillo's brother-in-law, Serrano Súñer, who was made minister of the interior.

The first task of the government was to lay a legal foundation for the new regime. Magistrates had to swear in the same breath that they would give 'unconditional support to the Caudillo of Spain, and render impartial justice'. The Nationalist labour law of March 1938 embodied the Falangist idea of 'vertical', or state-controlled, unions, but without any corresponding control over employers. The Catalan statute of autonomy was abrogated on 5 April 1938, so that the region now had 'the honour of being governed ... in accordance with the principle of the Fatherland's unity'. Other decrees that year included the censorship law of 22 April and the authorization for the return of the Jesuits on 3 May.

On 13 February 1939, just after the last pockets of Catalonia had been occupied, the Law of Political Responsibilities was published. It stated that 'all persons guilty of subversive activities from 1 October 1934 to 18 July 1936', as well as those who had then 'opposed the National Movement in fact or by grave passivity', would be tried. This represented the legal embodiment of General Mola's directive for the rising: 'Those who are not with us are against us.' It was a statement of implacable absolutes. You either supported the movement wholeheartedly, or you were guilty of 'anti-Spanishness'.

A dictatorship which placed so much emphasis on nationalism, naturally fostered xenophobia to deflect internal unrest. Franco said that Spain owed all her ordeals to that alien liberalism of the Enlightenment, which had 'arrived in Spain astride the encyclopedia'. A *cordon sanitaire* as rigorous as Stalin's was erected to keep out foreign contagion. 'Barbaric Russia' was the chief object of abuse, but it was also useful to blame France's 'decadence' on her democracy, and to point to Great Britain, Protestant and democratic, as the 'centre of the international masonic conspiracy'. When the French border was open to Republican war material in 1938, a Nationalist newspaper declared that 'those Spaniards who intend to go to France for any other reason than to spit in the faces of the French for their revolting crime, are no Spaniards'. Even the International Red Cross was distrusted as an alien, and virtually proto-communist, organization. Trivial symptoms of this phobia were the abolition of such descriptions as 'Russian salad' and the way newspapers had to refer to Leningrad as St Petersburg. As the newly renamed *Vanguardia Española* of Barcelona proclaimed, it was the duty of every Spaniard 'to think like Franco, feel like Franco, talk like Franco'. For those who did not share the National-ists' enthusiasm, the atmosphere was stifling. Hats had to be worn, in emphatic contrast to the informality of Republican Spain, and fines were imposed on men who did not wear jackets in Madrid. Everywhere the plump, complacent half-smile of Franco looked down, from hoardings in the street and from the obligatory prints in all public places. But the real watchers were the network of unofficial and secret police informers. Con-cierges would make a note of those who did not attend mass, and the *beatas* were told by their priests to look out for the devil and all his works. There was an abstract evil spirit to be exorcized which was even referred to in newspapers as the 'sixth column', a form of subversive sixth sense.

The official guardian and vehicle of Nationalist sentiment remained Franco's forced amalgamation of movements, the *Falange Española Tradi-cionalista*. This acted as an absorber of potentially dangerous energy as well as providing the political uniform for his state. Franquism was a bureaucratic machine with an ideological wardrobe patched together out of existing pieces of material. The garments of traditionalism, fascism and Catholicism could be changed round at need.

The romanticized visions of a new Spain, which had fired the Carlist and Falangists in 1936, were incompatible with the state which had developed in the course of the war. The Carlists' strength was centred on the small-holder of the Pyrenees who was inspired by a vivid picture of a golden age which had never existed. He wanted a monarch of simple tastes with no scheming courtiers to keep him from the people, 'a king who will drink from the wineskin with me'. The Carlists' rapturous welcome of the rising was prompted by the remedy it offered against modern ills, ills which they blamed on the liberals and freemasons who had defeated them in the nineteenth century. They followed their fierce priests, who uged them to save Holy Mother Church, even though they despised the corruption of the Castilian clergy. If the country was purified by the sword, they were told, everyone could return to that blessed pastoral idyll. It is not surprising that the Carlists proved to be Franco's most effective troops after the Army of Africa, nor that the bureaucracy and corruption of the Franquist state disillusioned them totally, making their subsequent decline inevitable.

Franco cleverly played off the three main forces of the movement against each other. The frustration of the monarchists was diverted against the Falangists, who in their turn attacked the monarchists as 'degenerate and reactionary' elements who 'sabotaged the national-syndicalist revolution'. Even though they had no popular base, the Alphonsine monarchists posed the greatest threat to Franco's ambitions, simply because they supported the only alternative leader for 'old Spain'. At crucial moments, when pressure for a restoration mounted, Franco would flatter the Carlist pre-tender, or give hope to the Falange that at last their dreams would be implemented. While Alfonso XIII's private property and his citizenship were restored, his son Don Juan (the present Juan Carlos' father) was kept at arms' length. The monarchists often resented the bourgeois little general's presumption. On the second anniversary of the rising Franco had proclaimed himself 'Captain-General of the Army and the Navy', a title which had been borne only by the sovereign, and later he ordered the Royal March to be played for his wife, as if she were queen. Vague promises to restore the monarchy were made whenever royalist anger needed defusing, or the Falange needed to be deflated.

Like the Carlists, the 'old shirts' of the Falange had begun the war believing that if 'Spain conquered Spain' all would be well later. Their idealistic left wing was, of course, hated by landowning monarchists. José Antonio himself (although marquis of Estella) had stated before the war that the Falange considered 'the prevailing social system to be essentially unjust'; it 'maintains vast masses on the brink of starvation and tolerates the gilded idleness of a few'. On 19 July 1936 their other leader, Onésimo Redondo, proclaimed when declaring for the rising that 'the Falange's profound preoccupation is to redeem the proletariat'. 'The capitalists and the rich', he added, 'will be traitors to the Fatherland if they continue, as they have done up to now, with their incorrigible egoism and their refusal to look about them at the trail of hunger, scarcity and pain they leave in their wake.' But socialism was swamped by patriotism, which had swept the Falange into the movement to resurrect the old social system.

Rumblings of discontent were easily contained by the regime, thanks in large measure to the support which it received from the church hierarchy. In return Spanish Catholicism gained enormous advantages. Every Spaniard was decreed to be a Catholic; divorce and civil marriage had been instantly abolished in Nationalist territory; and the penalty for abortion was made even greater than under the monarchy. The orphans of Republicans killed in the purges were forcibly baptized and given new Christian names. The church was in a position to establish a thorough control of public morals. One of their posters ordered: 'No immoral dances, no indecent frocks, no bare legs, no heathen beaches.' (The Falange, meanwhile, seized girls on the street whom they considered to be immodestly dressed and cropped their hair forcibly.)

The church was also represented on every civil committee, where few members dared disagree with a clergyman. Every prospective employee was required to have a certificate of spiritual cleanliness from his local priest. (This was the equivalent of the *harakteristika*, the certificate of political reliability in Soviet Russia.) It was unwise not to go to mass or confession, since a denunciation from a priest was virtually an accusation of treason. The church regained complete control of education, although the Falange later took over the universities. Many schools closed because all education diplomas awarded in Republican Spain were declared invalid and many Republican teachers were either shot for their suspected political sympathies or prevented from working by a clergyman's veto. One woman teacher was denounced for having attended 'mass only on Sunday and knelt only on one knee at the moment of the Host's elevation'. The school curricula were changed to put all the emphasis on religious instruction (which meant a hypnotic chanting of the catechism), the 'history of the fatherland' (which stressed the glories of the Catholic monarchs and the Empire) and 'study of the National Movement' (a panegyric to General Franco's 'liberation of Spain from communism'). Crucifixes or madonnas were placed in every classroom and singing was limited to hymns or patriotic anthems.

The only civilian organization over which the church was unable to exert control was the Falange, since Franco was content to allow the quasi-religious cult of José Antonio to develop for political reasons. Most bishops regarded the secular beatification of 'the absent' one with supreme distaste. Cardinal Segura, the controversial primate of 1931, who had returned as archbishop of Seville, banned Falangist memorials from his cathedral. The church resented a rival belief, expressed in the poet José María Pemán's statement that 'Spanish fascism will be the religion of Religion'. Nor was the hierarchy won over by such Falangist slogans as 'For God and Caesar'. Several bishops made direct or oblique criticisms of the totalitarian political state, some because they were disturbed by the use of Gestapo advisers to train the secret police, others because it was a threat to their own desire for an absolute theocracy. Some Catholic clergymen risked their lives trying to prevent remorseless and senseless executions, although there were few who opposed the regime outright, especially after the Pope had praised Franco for bringing 'honour, order, prosperity and tranquility' to Spain.

The realms of propaganda and censorship were to involve the rewriting of Lope de Vega's play *Fuenteovejuna*, because it was about a peasant uprising and therefore might have a subversive effect. This was in spite of the poet Pemán's great claim in 1936 that they were fighting for civilization in the form of Velázquez, the Escorial and Lope de Vega's plays. All dramatic works and films needed an ecclesiastical licence, and the church had the chief role in the censorship of books (a task shared by the Directorate General of Propaganda, the three service ministries, the General Staff, and the Directorate General of Moroccan affairs). Novels were usually regarded as immoral, and any book which was suspected of being disrespectful to the Catholic religion, the army, the unity of the nation, or the aims of the Nationalist crusade was automatically destroyed. The censorship of newspapers and magazines was more under the control of the military than the church, and the press law required all publications to propagate the ideals of the National movement at all times.

The role of women in Nationalist Spain reverted to what it had been in the time of the monarchy. According to the Falange, the state would only be 'strong if the woman at home is healthy, fecund, hard-working and happy'. She was therefore liberated 'from having to work outside the home', which meant that she was barred from practically all jobs except that of a domestic servant. Women without families were obliged to join one of the charity relief organizations. The Carlist Margaritas concentrated on helping the wounded and the soldiers at the front, while the Falangist *Auxilio Social* was devoted more to civilians in the rear areas. By far the larger of the two, *Auxilio Social* was largely copied from the Nazi Winter Aid. It was run by Mercedes Sanz Bachiller, the widow of Onésimo Redondo, and Pilar Primo de Rivera, José Antonio's sister. The Falange 'adopted' Republican orphans, thus making sure that they were saved the sins of 'anti-Spain'. The old were cared for, and the daughters and wives of the rich thereby gained the impression that they were helping to create a better society. The Nationalist authorities gave such schemes great encouragement, for they provided valuable propaganda. There was, however, considerable doubt about how much of the money collected so aggressively on the streets by Falangists and their youth movement, the *Flechas*, was used for charity.

Charity formed the only hope for many in the appalling conditions which Spain faced in the wake of the war. Cities and towns lay in ruins, while the country's agriculture was used to pay war debts to the Axis powers. Nevertheless, the strength of Nationalist Spain's peseta over its Republican rival during the war had rested on the likelihood of a Nationalist victory and on the economic stability promised by Nationalist labour laws. Despite a near doubling in the cost of living, workers' wages were reduced by decree to the level of 1935. All strikes had been outlawed by the Nationalists in July 1936, on penalty of execution by firing squad. In the fields a labourer knew only too well that if he protested at his conditions he risked being accused of sedition. All the agrarian reforms made under the Republic were abolished. Even the land purchased before the war was handed back to the original owners. The Nationalists, however, claimed a land reform of their own. This consisted mainly of expropriating the property of Republican sympathizers to give to their own soldiers or to reward peasants who had backed Nationalist landowners.

In Andalucia Queipo de Llano's administration had brought more land under cultivation and had even started a rice industry. Much of the olive oil from the south and the wool from the north was used to help repay Mussolini. At the same time Hitler was being paid with steel, coal, iron ore and later wolfram which was essential to his war industry. Bernhardt, the Nazi businessman from Spanish Morocco who had obtained Franco his Junkers 52 on the outbreak of the war, was in charge of all the commercial arrangements. He had convinced the German government then that it would be advantageous to have Spain as a source of raw materials. Franco had been so dependent on the Condor Legion that, in order to retain its services for the Catalonian campaign, he had signed a new agreement four days before it started. This 'Montana project' gave Germany controlling rights over five large mines in Spain and one in Spanish Morocco. Franco refused to discuss repayment of debts on the grounds that it was a 'tactless mixing of economic and idealistic considerations'. Hitler complained to Ciano that 'as a German one found oneself appearing to the Spaniards like a Jew, who wished to do business in the most sacred human values'.

The spoils of victory for 'relevant services to Spain' were to cover almost every position of power and every opportunity of gain. Monopolies were the most profitable prizes – the Caudillo's sister, for example, received the monopoly for the sale of screws to government arsenals and factories. Directorships in the major financial institutions were given especially to monarchist supporters. Four dukes, four marquis, and half a dozen counts were to benefit in this way. Profiteering was by no means restricted to the nouveaux riches: it was extraordinary how easily the old Castilian contempt for trade evaporated. Post-war fortunes came rapidly to those who were given import or manufacturing licences. The financial scandals of Franquist Spain in the 1950s and 1960s were surprising only in that they were made public.

In the most senior ranks of the army, rewards came from selling part of the soldiers' rations on the black market. Officers were given official posts from the level of civil governor down to village mayor. And to pay off non-commissioned officers after the war a vast and useless bureaucracy was created, one which stifled everything with its inefficiency and graft. A number of the hard-drinking and hard-living africanistas found it difficult to adapt to a society which was full of such pious hypocrisy.

Salvador de Madariaga, the historian and pre-war delegate to the League of Nations, observing that ministers, ambassadors and generals 'made hay while the fair weather of their offices lasted', accused the regime of having dragged the nation 'to the lowest level of public ethics it has ever known'. The victorious monarch was rewarding his knights and followers as in the first *Reconquista*, but there were no mists of time to give it a chivalric haze.

Everyone now went to church, but a truer level of devotion can perhaps best be estimated by remembering that only 14 per cent of the population had fulfilled their basic Catholic duties at Easter in 1936. After the civil war Cardinal Goma made the surprising admission to Lord Templewood, the British ambassador, that there had been no real religious revival in Spain. The defiant cry of the philosopher Unamuno, that they would conquer but not convince, must have angered the Nationalists more than anything else.

THE FATE OF THE DEFEATED AND THE GUERRILLA RESISTANCE

In a speech at Málaga soon after the last triumphal parade, Franco declared that 'the war is over, but the enemy is not dead'. It would have been unrealistic to expect the regime to make any attempt at national reconciliation, even out of self-interest. Salvador de Madariaga described the Franquist administration as an 'army of occupation which happens to be of the same nationality as the nation it occupies'. He then went on to say that it was 'a military state at war with its people. This is not just a figure of speech: it is a terse definition of the legal basis of the present Spanish state.'

The virtual fraternization between front-line troops in the last three days of March 1939 was rapidly succeeded by a relentless tide of repression and indiscriminate revenge. Franco had claimed to the German ambassador that he had a list of a million Republicans who were guilty of crimes. The most widely quoted figure for executions and political killings by the conquerors between 1939 and 1943 is nearly 200,000. Count Ciano was taken aback by the rate at which the firing squads were working when he visited Spain soon after the victory. The prison population reached a peak of 213,000 (more than 20 times the pre-war average), in addition to the penal battalions of forced labour.

During the first days of April 1939 the defeated Republican troops were herded into improvised prisons and camps – fields surrounded by hastily erected barbed wire, convents, football stadiums and bullrings. In the stadium of Puente de Vallecas the names of persons to be executed were broadcast over loudspeakers. Prisoners were forbidden to go near the top rows in case they tried to commit suicide. During the months after the Republican defeat constant identity parades were held for Nationalists seeking vengeance. On 20 November 1939, the third anniversary of José Antonio's death, 256 prisoners were shot in one session at Campo de la Bota in Barcelona. Many of the most bloodthirsty of the victors had never seen action or been in Republican hands. There were also extraordinary examples of ingratitude to those who had saved Nationalist lives. Melchor Rodríguez, the anarchist director of prisons, who had been called 'the Red Angel' by Nationalists because of his humanity, was sentenced to 20 years. Perhaps the most striking case occurred when a wife wrote in desperation to a priest whose life her husband had saved, asking him to send his evidence before her husband was condemned. The priest confirmed the account of what had happened, but he insisted that she pay for the affidavit and postage.

Some death sentences were carried out almost immediately, but many condemned men waited for months in suspense. Every day warders would read out the list, some taking pleasure in giving the first name, then pausing before the family name, to heighten the suspense. The prisoners suffered from overcrowding, malnutrition and the want of medical care. The numbers in prison only began to decline in early 1941, when the executions and transfers to penal battalions exceeded the inflow from fresh arrests.

Once the daily regime became organized in camps and prisons, punishment and indoctrination were mixed with unimaginative brutality. Prisoners were lined up in ranks and forced to sing *Cara al Sol*, the Falangist anthem, or chant Nationalist slogans while standing at the fascist salute. A Basque officer, Joseba Elosegi, recounted that a battalion commander called Losada, who was suffering from untreated gangrene in one arm, shouted *'¡Viva la Libertad!'* on one of these parades, thus assuring an immediate and less painful death. Occasionally inmates were given salted fish to eat without water, making some inexperienced prisoners go mad with thirst. The prisoners also experienced what Catholic Action called 'the great pacific battle for the re-christianization of Spain'. Compulsory classes in religious instruction and 'general culture' (a euphemism for the Nationalist version of history) were unlikely to win many converts, especially since, during confession, priests would ask persistent questions about a prisoner's activities in the war, and then pass the information on to the military tribunals. The political role of the church was also demonstrated in the way nuns served as warders to female political prisoners. At compulsory mass priests insulted their prison congregations in long tirades calling them 'red rabble, thieves, murderers, Godless men'. At Castellón de la Plana a handful of prisoners requested permission to stay in their cells rather than attend mass. They were marched there with the others, then, when they refused to kneel during the service, they were hauled out and shot in the courtyard. Father Martín Torrent, the chief prison chaplain in Barcelona, was a strong supporter of the mass executions. 'Can any greater mercy be granted', he asked, 'to a soul which has gone through life separated from God?'

The penal battalions and labour camps, with their slogan of 'redemption through work' borrowed from the Nazis, were organized on military lines and commanded by regular soldiers. There were humane older officers who did what they could to make things bearable for their prisoners; but in general the system was probably as bad as in Germany or Russia. On a ration of between 40 and 60 grams of bread a day, this vast force of slave labour was put to work on a wide variety of projects. These had included the building of fortifications in the Pyrenees and on the Moroccan border during the international tension over Czechoslovakia in mid-1938. After the civil war the labour battalions were used for clearing rubble, rebuilding towns and villages, and laying the Madrid–Burgos railway. Then the vanquished were put to work on Franco's ostentatious memorial, the Valley of the Fallen near the Escorial. A huge, underground cathedral was

267

hewn out of the rock in a manner reminiscent of a Pharoah's pyramid to serve as the burial place of both Franco and José Antonio. The Republican prisoners of war were also hired out to private contractors and local authorities. They were eventually given a nominal wage for their work, often as little as two pesetas a week after deductions.

The economic importance of this labour can hardly be overemphasized. The Franquist regime faced a deficit of 8.3 billion pesetas, a debt to Italy of 5 billion lira to be repaid by 1967, 400 million Reichsmarks to Germany and all the loan repayments to foreign banks and corporations which had given vital credits early in the war. The majority of the gold reserves were in Moscow (the French government returned £68 million worth), half the railway stock and two-thirds of motor vehicles had been destroyed, large areas of cultivated land were devastated, and many towns and hundreds of villages lay in ruins. Seven years after the end of the civil war, Lord Beveridge, the architect of the British welfare state, was secretly taken from his official programme of visits in Madrid to see the old trenches near the University city, where people still lived in holes they had dug. Nearly half the country's livestock had been killed and much of the seed grain eaten. In such a labour-intensive economy severe problems were caused by the high proportion of the active workforce who were in prison, had fled abroad or had been executed. In addition, a standing army of about 350,000 men was maintained as late as 1946. The military and security services accounted for around 30 per cent of the national budget.

The period following the civil war was one of the harshest austerity for most Spaniards, and starvation for the poor. In the most depressed areas the infant mortality rate was higher than 50 per cent, according to Abel Plenn, an attaché at the American embassy. Meanwhile, the food trains sent to Germany as part of the repayments programme carried Falangist slogans labelling the produce 'Spain's surplus for the workers of Germany'.

Most Republicans who escaped from Spain fared little better. Those who had fled to France were placed in hastily assembled camps, no more than open areas of ground surrounded by barbed wire, where they were watched by *gardes mobiles* and Senegalese troops. The *Manchester Guardian* reported that some exhausted Republican soldiers had to walk for another 26 hours without rest, or food and water. The women were taken to Le Boulou, while the first two major concentration camps, at Argèles-sur-Mer and Saint Cyprien in the Dordogne, were filled with some 70,000 men each. There were no latrines, running water, huts or any form of shelter. The inmates could only dig holes in the ground with their hands to shelter from the winds. Another dozen camps were also established at places like Cerbère, Le Perthus, Bourg-Madame, Prats-de-Mollo and Banyuls; the camps in the Pyrenees, however, were abandoned because inmates died of cold in the open.

Better conditions became available later at hutted camps like Bram near Carcassonne, which was reserved for the old who had survived, but journalists could not believe the conditions in most of the others until they saw them. Argèles was soon notorious. The French officials simply threw the food (one loaf of bread to four people per day) into the compound, as if, one witness recorded, it was corn for chickens. The medical facilities were 'reminiscent of the worst in the Crimean war', while Republican army doctors were not allowed any supplies or equipment. A few of the sick were allowed out, but for the great poet Antonio Machado it was too late.

It was soon evident that the official policy was to force the refugees back into Spain, and some 70,000 chose to risk execution or prison rather than remain. The two French prisons designated for 'incorrigibles' who protested or tried to escape were said to be worse than Dachau by people who experienced both. The right-wing sympathies of the *gardes mobiles* were well known, and the internees were totally in their power. Inmates were stripped of their possessions, with the jocular explanation that they had not passed customs.

Daladier's ministers defended the failure to prepare for the refugees on the grounds that if they had started before Catalonia had fallen, they would have been accused of sapping the morale of the Republican defenders. This was a poor excuse, yet it is too simple to condemn the French authorities for the horrific conditions of the camps and the conduct of their guards, without also appreciating the enormous problems they faced. Apart from the financial burden (around 7.5 million francs per day), they faced the violent opposition of sections of the population who were intransigently hostile to the refugees. According to some estimates there were already nearly three million foreigners in the country, and the continual influx of Spanish refugees during the war had brought an unease which the pro-Franco press played upon and exploited in every way possible. The monarchist *Action Française* asked whether France was to be 'the dunghill of the world'. There had also been rumours of a communist plot to use Republican refugees to start a revolution in southern France. Pressure was built up in a press campaign to extend the provisions of October 1937, which allowed in only those with enough money to support themselves. The pro-Franco newspapers insinuated that all Republicans were criminals, dirty and riddled with disease. Those who had slipped through the guards on the border were described as a horde of locusts, and even the most sympathetic of the French were appalled to learn that the peasants in the south-west had much of their food stolen. Weeks of actual starvation, preceded by months of hunger, had made the Spanish refugees desperate.

Whatever the French government may have been guilty of, the Soviet Union's criticisms of it were particularly unpleasant. On 2 February 1939, when 100,000 refugees had already been allowed through, *Pravda* accused the French of denying asylum. 'At the point of a bayonet', the paper declared, 'they turn back children, women, the old, and the wounded. Never has such a disgraceful scene been witnessed in history.' The Soviet Union, which had claimed to be the Spanish Republic's only true ally (while almost certainly making a handsome profit on the gold deal), gave just five million francs in refugee aid – not enough for one day's food. The USSR, having effectively failed to take in the mass of the International Brigade exiles it had called to arms, then refused all Spanish refugees except for senior party cadres. The rest were ordered to fend for themselves and return home. 'The fatherland of the oppressed' had spoken.

The British government was prepared to accept a limited number of senior officials. Other Republicans were allowed in only if a Briton stood guarantee. Not surprisingly, few of them had English friends; as a result only a couple of hundred entered. Roosevelt's administration was no more generous. Belgium accepted between two and three thousand children. Mexico declared itself prepared to allow in 50,000 political refugees without qualification, but the Mexican diplomat in charge of the operation was persuaded by the communists to give visas only to those prepared to declare their support for Negrín and state that Casado and his associates were traitors.

The communist refugees also established their power in the concentration camps by controlling food and mail distribution and by acting as prison 'trusties' for the French authorities. This did not pass unchallenged, and some old scores were settled, such as a SIM officer being buried alive. The Party also dominated SERE (Service of Emigration for Spanish Republicans), an organization which Negrín set up in March 1939 with 100 million francs of government deposits in France. Republican leaders such as General Rojo and Prieto denounced Negrín for ensuring that he and top officials close to him received large pensions out of the secret funds, while the mass were left to survive as best they could. Only a limited number of trans-Atlantic passages were provided, nothing more. Negrín had already begun to take good care of his future by renting a handsome villa in Deauville towards the end of 1938. From there Madariaga reported that '$50 million worth of jewellery as well as strong boxes packed tight with stocks and bonds' were secretly loaded on to the yacht *Vita*. But when it reached Mexico, Prieto persuaded President Cárdenas that the treasure should be seized on behalf of the Republican government-in-exile. Prieto was then backed by the permanent committee of the Cortes in Paris. JARE (Committee of Aid to Republican Spaniards) was set up by liberal republicans, socialists and anarchists as an alternative to the communist-dominated SERE.

On the outbreak of war in September 1939 the French government found that their Spanish refugee problem had its advantages. Veterans of the Popular Army were signed up for the French Foreign Legion. (One camp inmate described General Gamelin's visit of inspection like 'that of a butcher coming to visit his stock-breeding farm'.) Altogether, between 5,000 and 8,000 joined the Foreign Legion, while 10,000 went to infantry battalions, some 55,000 were drafted into labour units for improving fortifications such as the Maginot line, and another 25,000 or so were used to replace French workmen who had been mobilized. The threat of being returned to the Franquist authorities was undoubtedly a spur to enlist. In the Second World War Spanish Republicans saw action in almost every Western theatre of operations. During the fall of France English officers witnessed one Spanish labour battalion seize the weapons of a fleeing French unit and go straight into the attack against the advancing Germans. Other Republicans fought at Narvik, in the raid on Brest and in the western desert with the Long Range Desert Group and other special forces. Leclerc's 2nd Armoured Division had a large Spanish Republican contingent from the 20,000 who had been interned in North Africa. In 1944 they and other Spaniards in the British SAS Brigade fought for the liberation of France and in the advance on the Rhine. Meanwhile, on the Russian front detachments of Spanish communist partisans such as the 4th Special Service Company harassed the rear of the German army near Moscow.

The American government even made approaches to Generals Miaja and Rojo about forming a full Spanish Republican army corps to fight on the Allied side. This plan was probably stopped by the British government which was the most worried about upsetting Franco. Lord Templewood, the ambassador in Madrid, had issued urgent demands that no secret operations should be mounted in Spain by either Special Operations Executive or the Secret Intelligence Service. In May 1944 the British embassy in Madrid was greatly alarmed by reports of American arms being landed on the Andalucian coast for the anti-Franquist resistance. Churchill openly declared his opposition to helping the Republican cause. In March 1944 the Foreign Office stated that British policy towards Spain was 'based upon leaving the Spaniards to decide their own internal affairs for themselves', which was sheer sophistry considering the regime's attitude to democracy. In fact the British government regarded the restitution of the pre-1931 *status quo* as the only acceptable alternative to Franco. The Roosevelt administration, on the other hand, said that it did not wish to see the return of a society dominated by monarchy, church and landowner. This liberal attitude soon ended with the approach of the Cold War and McCarthyism.

Among the countless unsung victims of the Second World War were the 30,000 Spanish Republicans rounded up in France by the Germans and the Vichy *Milice* for slave labour in the Reich. Largo Caballero was one of them. He died in Paris just after the war from the effects of Oranienburg camp, where the vast majority of the 5,000 Spaniards died. A further 10,000 were sent to Mauthausen concentration camp marked with blue triangles, and others, such as the Catalan president, Luis Companys, Juan Péiro, the CNT minister, and Zugazagoitia, the socialist minister, were sent back to Spain where they were executed. In August 1944 the Germans are said to have returned another 14,000 Spanish Republicans before retreating, but the fate of these prisoners is not recorded.

The most important war-time role of the Spanish exiles was their contribution to the French Resistance. The first actions of these *maquisards* were carried out in south-west France during the autumn of 1940 on a spontaneous basis. This start was little more than a reaction against the threat of arrest or conscription into forced labour, but it developed into a definite movement before the war turned in the Allies' favour. Also in the autumn of 1940 some started to make their way secretly back into Spain, with the idea of joining the isolated groups in the mountains. It was thus that purely by chance, two anarchists, Ibars and Canillas, armed with a 9 mm pistol and four hand grenades each, arrived at the border station of Hendaye on 23 October. Though apparently only a short distance from where Hitler and Franco were meeting, the ranks of SS guards made any approach impossible.

During the following years Spanish Republicans provided an important element of de Gaulle's FFI (French Forces of the Interior). They also organized the 'life-line' escape routes across the Pyrenees for Allied aircrew. This clandestine traffic was enormous, although Lord Templewood's figure of 30,000 British, Commonwealth and Allied personnel is exaggerated. Basque nationalist guides led them across their sector, particularly via San Esteban in northern Navarre, and Catalan guides across the south-eastern portion of the frontier.

The guerrilla war in Spain continued, intermittently, until 1960, but it is still difficult to form an accurate assessment of its scale or effect. Both the resistance and the civil guard had reasons to exaggerate the importance of their roles, although the Nationalist regime found it embarrassing to admit to the existence of 'banditry and terrorism'. Also the secrecy of the action and its fragmentation over such a long period of time make general observations more dangerous than usual. The average life expectancy of a guerrilla was very short, perhaps even less than a year, though one leader and his group lasted eleven years. The year 1960 is cited as the end of this epoch, principally because the destruction of Francisco Sabaté's group marked the last guerrilla action of the veterans, even though one or two others were shot down on their own later. A new generation then emerged in the 1960s with the young libertarians and ETA (*Euzkadi ta Askatasuna*, Basque Homeland and Liberty). The greatest period of guerrilla activity occurred in the mid-1940s, especially when the German retreat from France enabled the Spanish Republicans in the FFI to concentrate at last on their own country. The vain hope that after the defeat of the Axis, the Allies would deal with Franco, prompted a tremendous increase in activity until 1947, when it became clear that nothing more than diplomatic sanctions would be exercised against the Franquist regime.

The guerrillas in Spain were known either as the Maquis, the 'live forces' or the 'men of the sierra'. It is important to understand the variety of motives which propelled them, if only to avoid describing them simply as heroes or villains. A majority of the 'guerrillas' were fugitives from the Nationalist *limpieza*, escapers from prison camps and penal battalions, or men avoiding conscription into the Franquist army. There were even some school-teachers who, having been refused certificates of spiritual cleanliness by their priest, faced starvation. Among those 'recruited by the repression' there were some who actively fought back; but most of them needed all their strength and wits just to survive in the mountains. They were not so much guerrillas as outlaws, men driven to stealing and therefore easily labelled as criminals by the government. In fact little had changed in the century since that remarkable English traveller, Richard Ford, observed that the Romans called the Spanish guerrillas who resisted them *latrones*, or brigands, and that Napoleon's armies called them *ladrones* because they had no uniform, 'as if the wearing of a shako given by a plundering marshal, could convert a pillager into an honest man, or the want of it could change into a thief, a noble patriot'. In Spanish history the *bandolero* and the guerrilla had always tended to overlap, because the outlaw was the only hope of retaliation against a local tyrant. This Robin Hood tradition was deep-rooted, especially in depressed rural areas. Thus, in the post-civil war period, the working class seldom looked upon the 5,000 or so 'economic coups' (varying from bank robberies to simple hold-ups) as criminal acts, because it was unusual for a real guerrilla to profit personally from them.

Those who went into the sierras with the specific intention of fighting back varied as widely in their competence and experience as in their motives. The vast majority of guerrilla leaders had been in the Popular Army and perhaps about 10 per cent of them in the Maquis in France; other groups, however, consisted of a handful of peasants with shotguns.

A group's chance of survival was minute if it did not have at least a core of experienced men. For most, a prime motive was vengeance on those responsible for the killing or raping of a member of their family, but above all they saw themselves as the common avengers against the oppressor in the old tradition.

Rather than making any rash attempt at assessing the effectiveness of the guerrilla resistance over this period, it is safer to give the official figures for the 1939–60 period. Although the statistics for some provinces are extremely doubtful, the totals probably come near the truth. There are said to have been 1,866 clashes with security forces and 535 acts of sabotage. (Assassinations and reprisal killings are not listed separately, but these actions are discussed below.) The guerrilla casualties are listed as 2,173 killed, 420 wounded, 2,346 captured, 550 surrendered, and 19,430 auxiliaries arrested. The security forces lost 307 killed and 372 wounded. This remarkable disparity in casualties (very different from what one has grown to accept in recent guerrilla wars) is due to the high proportion of fugitives as opposed to guerrillas and to the pathetic armament of most groups. Nevertheless, the civil guard commander, General Alonso Vega, said on 29 May 1955, some five years after activity had declined perceptibly, that 'communist banditry' was 'sabotaging communications, demoralizing the population, destroying our economy, breaking down our authority, and discrediting us abroad'. The term communist was used particularly to gain support in the United States, despite the decision of the Spanish Communist Party in October 1948 to abandon guerrilla resistance and infiltrate the Franquist trade-union structure instead.

The extent of guerrilla resistance varied greatly from region to region according to the suitability of the terrain and the intensity of the repression. These two factors were the major reasons for its beginning, in 1936, in the western parts of Nationalist territory: Galicia, Andalucia, and Estremadura. Guerrilla groups and fugitives sheltered in the sierras near cities where the Nationalist *limpieza* had been the most ferocious, such as Granada, Córdoba, Málaga or the Galician towns. After the massacre of the Albaicín quarter, Granada was one of the very few cities where there was an active urban guerrilla resistance. Similarly, in Aragon, the mass killings of CNT members in Saragossa and the outlying countryside forced fugitives into the hills. There, as in other parts close to the front line, the most immediate task was to organize escape lines to Republican territory for those in danger. The CNT set up SIE groups (Service of Investigation and Liaison) for this purpose and for intelligence gathering, but there was not an effective guerrilla movement, despite anarchist boasting of their 'Spanish Ukraine'. The fault lay largely with the CNT, but also with the government, which, having centralized military command, refused to give arms to independent groups.

The communists were firm believers in the value of partisans, as Stalin's letter to Largo Caballero in December 1936 emphasized, but only if they were under strict Party control. Orlov was put in charge of the programme within the SIM, which led, later, to the establishment of XIV Guerrilla Corps under Domingo Ungría. This formation was never much more than a central reservoir of a few thousand commandos, who were, in fact, used more often in a conventional role. Their best known commando actions were harassing operations from the Sierra de Espadán in the early summer of 1938, and their role in the crossing of the Ebro just afterwards.

The most effective guerrilla resistance was the irregular warfare waged in the Asturias by the remnants of the Army of the North in the winter of 1937. Even after March 1938, when the major Republican groups had been suppressed, operations such as one involving eight Nationalist battalions and 15 *tabores* of Moroccan troops were mounted against guerrilla groups totalling some thousand men. Then, after the Republican collapse at the end of March 1939, irregular resistance continued in many parts of Spain. The Franquist administration declared on 12 August that 'a period of austere sacrifices must be imposed, sacrifices which the persistence of treacherous attacks, in which the enemy is exhausting a sterile offensive, will render more severe'.

Activity then lessened as most of Europe fell under Axis control, until the battles of Stalingrad and El Alamein again aroused hopes. (The communists almost disappeared during the Nazi-Soviet pact from August 1939 until the summer of 1941.) The Allied invasion of North Africa came as a shock to Franco; it also meant that Andalucian guerrilla groups began to be supplied from French Morocco with the help of local fishing fleets. The invasion of Normandy in 1944 inevitably aroused the greatest excitement in Republican circles, and that year saw both the peak of guerrilla actions and a renewed wave of repression. According to the US embassy 433 people were shot in August and September, mainly in Madrid, Valencia and Andalucia. (The reaction of Sir Frank Roberts of the Foreign Office was: 'Do let us keep our thoughts clear ... there are no *British* grievances here – indeed quite the contrary.')

The American landings on the southern French coast on 15 August signalled the rising of the predominantly Spanish Maquis of the south-west, who hoisted the Republican tricolour on Spanish consulates in southern France. The feeling that Franco's regime would fall as soon as Germany surrendered induced even Catalan industrialists to give money to the guerrillas. The Gaullist commanders of the FFI gave the Spanish Republicans weapons and allowed them virtual control of the frontier area. Thus several thousand heavily armed *maquisards* assembled along the Pyrenean border in the early autumn.

The communists tried to resurrect the Popular Front tactic by setting up a committee of National Union, but as a result of their previous experiences, the liberal republicans, socialists and libertarians established their own ANFD (National Alliance of Democratic Forces). The Communist Party was preparing what it called *Reconquista de España*. Skeleton or phantom organizations were created *en masse* to give an impression of tremendous activity and support. In October 1944 Líster was told by Dimitrov that Stalin wanted the guerrilla war stepped up. The Party sent out directives from its headquarters in south-west France to organize fictional military formations. 'Vladimiro', who was one of the most experienced communist guerrillas, later commented scathingly on the degree to which a totally false image of a guerrilla army was created by Party cadres. Another disillusioned member, Emilio Alvarez Canosa ('Pinocho'), said that the Party regarded incursions across the border as 'purely prestige operations' and that it knew they were sending men to their death pointlessly. 'The strategy was more a programme of indoctrination,' he added. 'The Communist Party always needs lists of martyrs.'

The operation which the communists were preparing became known as the invasion of the Valle de Arán. Slightly more than 3,000 men in the so-called 204 Guerrilla Division were involved, not 15,000 as the Party later claimed. The commander, Colonel López Tovar (a communist divisional commander under Tagüeña in the battle of Catalonia), had a distinguished record in the French Resistance. But he had few Maquis veterans in his force. Most of them were totally inexperienced boys who had been hurried through one of the guerrilla training camps. The commissars, known as 'the eye of Moscow', played the same role as they had in 1936 and drilled the recruits with such inappropriate slogans as 'he who looks behind is a traitor'. This guerrilla cannon fodder was told that the Spanish people were simply awaiting their arrival to rise up *en masse*.

The objective of the 12 'brigades' was 'the liberation of Spain through guerrilla action provoking a general insurrection'. Early in October half the force advanced across the border due south towards Lérida on a centre line starting some 50 kilometres (30 miles) west of Andorra. A second wave of the other six 'brigades' occupied much of the frontier area after 17 October. There were few people left in the region because the Nationalists, anticipating what might happen, had moved most of the population. Even so, there is little to indicate that there would have been a rising. The people were too afraid of yet another wave of repression. And in spite of grandiose predictions, the partisan force was reduced to small groups of fugitives within a week.

The most remarkable aspect of the affair was the slow response of the Nationalist forces. This was either due to their insistence on using mainly the Foreign Legion and *regulares*, because they did not trust the loyalty of conscripts, or else it was a tactic to encourage as many guerrillas as possible to be drawn over the border. Nevertheless, on 31 October, General Moscardó, the captain-general of IV Military Region, was informed that 'all the red invaders of the Valle de Arán have been eliminated'.

When the Republican government-in-exile returned to France from Mexico, the formation of AFARE, the Armed Forces of the Spanish Republic, was proclaimed in January 1945 in the vain hope of boosting the official image of the émigré administration. All this time there had been the major divide between Negrín and the communists on the one hand and the liberals, socialists and libertarians on the other. There was also a major dispute over whether to continue the struggle or count on the Allied governments to bring down Franco. The moderates insisted that the democracies would come to their aid, and they stuck to this belief after the fall of Germany. Prieto eventually resigned the presidency of the PSOE in November 1950, a few months after the United States government granted Franco $62.5 million in aid. 'I am responsible', he said, 'for having induced our party to trust the governments of the democratic powers, and they did not merit this confidence, as they have begun to make clear. It is my fault that my party has been the victim of an illusion which blinded me.' Such honesty was rare among the exiled politicians, but then Prieto had also been one of the very few to make efforts on behalf of their followers. He interested himself primarily in members of his own party, particularly the

Asturian guerrillas. In January 1939, for example, he had organized a small ship from France to take 800 of them off the northern coast at the fishing harbour of Tazores. A carefully co-ordinated plan for seizing the port on the designated night went wrong when one group ran into an army patrol searching for deserters. As military reinforcements arrived, a major battle developed, and a fighting retreat was made back into the sierra. Three months later these guerrillas were to face the greatest onslaught since the previous spring, for the end of the civil war released large quantities of troops for anti-guerrilla operations. The most famous guerrilla of the area was the socialist, José Mata, who had been operating for exactly 11 years by the time he was taken off secretly by a French fishing boat in October 1948.

There was hardly a province in Spain that did not see some form of guerrilla activity. The most important regions from 1936 until the early 1950s were Andalucia, Galicia and Asturias, then Catalonia and Aragon. The type of guerrilla activity varied greatly. In Asturias the guerrillas decided not to sabotage the mines, despite the importance and vulnerability of such targets, because it would have made conditions even worse for the local population. Sabotage took many forms. In France an anarchist called Laureano Cerrado Santos, who had become a master-forger of passes and identity documents for the Resistance and Jewish fugitives from the Germans, turned to currency, intending 'to inundate the world market with thousands of millions of fake pesetas'. His operation was only partially successful. The French police, though sometimes prepared to ignore preparations for armed attacks into Spanish territory, reacted sharply to forgery. The increasingly conservative CNT-in-exile was also upset by Cerrado Santos' activities and described his methods as 'unacceptable'. Most acts of sabotage were more conventional – attacks on armouries, depots, power lines and railway track.

In the eyes of most guerrillas, their major function was to help fugitives, release prisoners and carry out reprisal killings. The prime targets were Falangists and secret policemen. In Galicia, a notorious Falangist was cornered in a café. The list of his 76 victims was read out and he was then shot. On 29 July 1939 Gabaldón, the head of the Madrid police, was shot down on the Estremadura high road, and 53 people were executed by the security forces for their alleged implication in his murder. In September 1944 the senior police officer in Granada (who was thought to have been involved in Lorca's death) was assassinated in the main street during the middle of the day. The official police record, however, states that his death occurred during an anti-guerrilla operation. Soon after the civil war had ended, the *Daily Telegraph* recounted how Serrano Súñer's fear of assassination led to his official car being 'driven over the pavement and into the rather confined hall of the Ministry, where there is just room for it, jammed against the stairs'. Lord Templewood also commented in April 1944 that, as a precaution, Franco used only the bullet-proof limousine given him by Hitler.

In the years when no help was expected from the democracies abroad, the idea that a single act might finish the regime had an inevitable appeal. The Communist Party, however, went to great lengths to condemn anarchist attempts on the life of Franco. 'The physical disappearance of the dictator', it declared, 'would not alter the correlation of forces between the social classes.' Yet ETA's assassination of Admiral Carrero Blanco was probably the most far-reaching event of the post-war years in Spain, since Franco counted on him as the guarantor of the Nationalist dictatorship.

Only a handful of attempts went beyond the planning stage. The *Brigada Política Social* found it relatively easy to infiltrate the exile organizations in Toulouse. They broke one network after another, and by 1949 they had smashed the bulk of the clandestine organizations. Their methods were taught to them by the Gestapo, under the agreement negotiated by Serrano Súñer, in September 1940. (According to Abel Plenn, he and his fellow American diplomats in 1944 were warned by their superiors 'not to show any interest' in the General Directorate of Security in the Puerta del Sol.) As a result of secret police activity, the only serious assassination attempt of the period was that organized from French territory by Cerrado Santos in September 1948. He bought a light aeroplane with his forged money, found a former Republican fighter pilot, and loaded it with abandoned German bombs at a base in the French Basque country. When Franco went on board a large launch at San Sebastián on 12 September to observe a regatta, the signal was passed to France by a waiting observer. However, by the time Cerrado Santos' plane arrived, Franco's boat was being circled by a protective fighter escort, and the attempt was aborted.

The principal anti-guerrilla force had always been the civil guard (the 'soul of Spain' as General Sanjurjo had called it, thus perhaps provoking Lorca's description, the 'soul of patent leather'). Yet several exceptionally large operations were also mounted by regular and colonial troops. In Galicia between 1946 and 1948, three *tabores* of *regulares* were added to a force of 8,000 civil guards and eight companies of *Policía Armada* in anti-guerrilla operations. The army was continually told during these years that Spain would be overrun by a communist invasion unless it maintained full vigilance in the Pyrenees. The most modern anti-guerrilla operation was that carried out by civil guards under Colonel Limia Pérez in October 1949 in the province of Granada. There the techniques of cordon and search, food-denial and speculative ambushes were put into practice. In most areas, however, the security forces were brutally unsophisticated. Potential sympathizers with the guerrilla resistance risked imprisonment, torture and execution. Mountain shepherds suffered most in this way, for they were always assumed to act as spies for the guerrillas. The helpers, or 'militia of the plain' as they were often called, had to be at least as brave as those in the mountains. An Aragonese girl was tortured so badly at the BPS Barcelona headquarters in the via Layetana that she committed suicide by cutting her jugular vein with a piece of broken glass. Many helpers died as a result of brutal interrogation methods, which prompted the name 'the rubber syndicate' to be given to the police. The Franquist version that the guerrillas were only helped out of fear is undermined by the government's own figures of nearly 20,000 arrests on this charge. Nevertheless, peasants who refused to help were undoubtedly terrorized on some occasions, but this usually happened when the guerrillas were not locals.

Once the threat of Allied intervention disappeared and the Cold War started, it became easier for the regime to convince the population that repression continued only because of futile resistance. Those guerrillas who continued to operate across the Pyrenees in the 1950s were also attacked by Republican leaders for jeopardizing the position of Spanish exiles in France. Despite this, a few groups continued to insist that the spirit of resistance had to be kept alive. Most of these groups operated in Catalonia, often from bases in the French Pyrenees. Their last clash with the security forces occurred on 3 January 1960, when Francisco Sabaté Llopart's group was surrounded by the 24th Battalion of the civil guard near Gerona after crossing the border only four days before. Sabaté broke through the cordon, but was shot in San Celoni 36 hours later. The news of his death was announced in the middle of a pop-music programme on Radio Luxembourg, and Hollywood later based a film around his exploits. For many at the time, the modern commercial flavour of this postscript symbolized the end of that age of ideology which the Spanish civil war had represented. The events of the late 1960s showed, however, that political idealism in Western society had not died.

THE LEGACY OF THE WAR

The Spanish civil war was important for more reasons than its impact on Europe or its symbolism. The collective letter to the bishops of the world organized by Cardinal Goma in June 1937 described the conflict as 'an armed plebiscite', and although that term was more accurate than many of the emotive descriptions used, it implied only the alternatives of a two-party system. Such a forced compression of the issues into a single dimension was practised by both sides. Gross simplifications were produced for propaganda purposes. The misleading impressions disseminated so powerfully at the time have been frequently reinforced since by self-justifying memoirs and official accounts. As a result the three axes of conflict (left–right, centralist–regionalist and authoritarian–libertarian) have often been crudely amalgamated, leaving the ferocity of the war partly unexplained.

   The bitterness of the Spanish conflict created the greatest impression abroad, and the stereotype assumptions of foreigners were often strengthened by the male Spaniard's own image of himself. 'I am not pretending', El Campesino said later, 'that I was not guilty of ugly things myself, or that I never caused needless sacrifice of human lives. I am a Spaniard. We look upon life as tragic. We despise death.' But violence is a distorted expression of fear. 'Eternal Spain' was terrified of modern ideas, while the centre and the left feared the reaction which they provoked. Much of the brutality can be explained by the obligation which the Spaniard felt to repress his fear. The cults of virility and death went hand in hand as the imagery of Queipo de Llano, the Falange and the Foreign Legion demonstrated. Nationalist leaders like Sanjurjo and Millán Astray revelled in the language of the stern patriarchal surgeon, whose diagnosis and proposed treatment could not be questioned by a patient who did not know what was best for him. Foreign contagions and cancers had to be cut out. National regeneration could only come through pain, in the medieval manner of trial by ordeal. One of the Nationalist poets described this purification by fire as a mortal struggle, with 'the energies of Spain at white heat in a crucible of passion, and like gold from the crucible, Spain will finally emerge, purified and without stain, in her true colours rejecting the taints artificially imposed on her'. Ideological and religious invocations made the violence abstract. There was a sweet-natured youth among

Moscardó's defenders at Toledo, who was called the Angel of the Alcázar because before firing his rifle he used to cry, 'Kill without hate!' This abstraction existed on the Republican side as well. David Antona, a CNT leader, said that 'the bullets which ended the lives of the officers at the Montaña barracks did not kill men, they killed a whole social system.'

People were encouraged to submerge their identity and individual responsibility into causes with either mystical or super-human auras. Carlist *requetés* were told that they would have a year less in purgatory for every red they killed, as if Christendom were still fighting the Moors. Inevitably, the violent reaction of the left against the superstitious bigotry and hypocrisy of the Castilian church helped a widely discredited institution to become a powerfully emotive cause on the Nationalist side. The emotions provoked by the rising, and the consequent obsession with fifth columns, often meant that revenge for the past was disguised as revolution in the Republican rear areas. The Nationalists, on the other hand, carried out indiscriminate reprisals in the belief that this would terrorize resistance into collapsing. But the archbishop of Burgos, who justified the cruelty as being ultimately less cruel because it meant a shorter war, was wrong in every sense. Neither side could be terrified into submission. Both felt that everything in which they believed, as well as their very existence, was at stake. This transmuted fear into desperate bravery.

Their fundamental opposition was polarized between class interests, whether defined in terms of the traditional order, or in terms of a just society. This clash was also shaped by the two other power conflicts, centralism against regionalism, and authority against freedom. All the reforms attempted by Azaña's two administrations were resisted implacably by the defenders of the *status quo*. Their refusal to compromise in any way with the liberals only increased the pressure from the left. The great hopes aroused amongst an underprivileged mass by the promises of the centrist politicians and by the assurances written into the constitution could not be fulfilled, because putting them into practice required revolutionary measures against property. But the hopes gave great impetus to the workers and peasants, and accelerated the circle of repression and resistance, as the right reacted with an even greater preoccupation with public order. If the landowner saw the government's role as the enforcer of respect for property, if necessary by shooting peasants who took to farming unused land, then it was understandable that he should believe, after the Popular Front victory of February 1936, that only a military dictatorship could restore the values and social system of old Spain.

The authoritarian nature of old Spain to which all Nationalist parties subscribed naturally helped Franco's efforts to take power and retain it. He also had the blessing of the church, which strongly supported the principle of disciplined hierarchy. 'God provides', the Spanish bishops stated, 'the most profound bonds holding together a well-ordered society.'

The Nationalists defended a common view of the past; the Republican coalition, in contrast, had widely different visions of the future. Hence the shifting alliances within the coalition. The liberals, who tried to re-establish centralized government in the late summer of 1936, were aided by the communists and opposed by the Catalan and Basque nationalists and the anarchists. At the same time the anarchists, the POUM and left socialists also resisted the liberal and communist attempts to limit the effects of the social revolution. The beginning of 1937 saw the Catalanists allying with the communist PSUC so as to restore the authority of the *Generalidad* and take control of anarchist-run industry. The resulting clash of May 1937 in Barcelona enabled the social democrat government of Negrín, with its communist allies, to destroy Catalan independence. However, the excesses of the communists in 1937 and 1938 led to an essentially libertarian reaction, which culminated in the new alliance of liberals, socialists and anarchists in Casado's coup of March 1939.

In the original authoritarian–libertarian split the Communist Party was the most outspoken advocate of restoring state control, and thus the natural ally of the liberal and social democrat politicians. This divide in the Republican camp tends to be neglected when everything is looked at in the misleading framework of a political spectrum running from extreme left to extreme right. Negrín recognized that the two poles in the Republican camp were the communists and the anarchists, and that the other parties' positions were forced to relate to these two. There was, in fact, an antipathy between these two extremes which probably equalled their hatred for the common enemy. While Abad de Santillán said that a communist victory would be no better than a Nationalist one, communist PSUC militants declared to the Russian writer Ilya Ehrenburg, 'rather the fascists than the anarchists'.

If the Republic had won the war, there would almost certainly have been a major struggle between the communists and the anarchists, perhaps even another civil war. The often-held assumption that the communists would have prevailed is doubtful; besides Stalin would have prevented it in his desire not to alarm Great Britain and France, nor to provoke Germany. He had already demonstrated in China that he was prepared to sacrifice local communist parties in order to further Soviet interests. Moreover, communist power in Spain grew out of emergency measures which were accepted only because of the grave military situation.

The Communist Party in Spain was in many ways the counterpart of Franco. Both were the outstanding practitioners of statecraft on their respective sides, and as a result there were a number of similarities in their methods. Both exploited the war emergency to label any opposition to their control of events as treasonable to the cause. Franco accused the conservative Basques of being 'Soviet-separatists' in the same way as the communists called the Marxist POUM 'Trotskyist-fascist'. In addition, Nationalist bureaucrats copied Stalin's tactics of turning defeated enemies into unpersons. For example, all official records of Casares Quiroga and Luis Companys, including their birth certificates, were expunged. Both Russia and Nationalist Spain defended themselves against intellectual infection from outside, and they both benefited from having the other as a prime target for propaganda.

The Nationalists professed themselves to be the defenders of European civilization against alien forces. It was natural for them to invoke the military tradition of the Castilian warrior caste, as the Nazis had the Teutonic knights, and the fascists the Roman legionaries. In contrast, the Republic's constitution had renounced war as a means of settling disputes, and the different political ideologies within the coalition rejected militarism in varying degrees. This fundamental difference in attitude between the two sides was only one of many contributions to the Nationalist victory.

The defence of Madrid, and the arrival of foreign aid to both sides, certainly marked a turning-point in the course and the manner of the war; but, although it was a major check to the Nationalists, it was not a positive victory for the Republic. The pattern and strategy which the Popular Army then assumed in the winter of 1936 was moulded more by political pressures than by military deductions. The idea that only military orthodoxy with set-piece offensives could win proved to be as grave a liability as the militias' initial belief in the triumph of morale alone. On the other hand, the Republic could not simply have abandoned orthodox warfare for unorthodox, as the conditions for a universal guerrilla war did not exist. Republican manpower strength was mainly city-based. The smallholders and hill farmers of the north were usually conservative, while only parts of New Castile and Estremadura provided good guerrilla terrain. The best-suited regions – Aragon, Asturias, Andalucia, Galicia and León – were insufficient to have stretched Nationalist forces beyond capacity. The most effective strategy for the Republic would have been a conventional defence with irregular offensives.

It is difficult to assess accurately the contribution of foreign intervention in the Spanish civil war, whether economic, diplomatic or military. The assistance varied widely in quantity and quality, and its effectiveness depended on the timing of its arrival. It could, for example, be said that 10 aircraft in August 1936 were worth 50 a year later, or that one Condor Legion bomber squadron was worth several of the Legionary Air Force.

The first, and perhaps most important, contribution was Hitler's despatch of Junkers 52s to help the Army of Africa's airlift, although it was probably not the decisive factor which Republican propaganda claimed. Of similar importance at that time was the despatch of German small-arms ammunition via Portugal to Mola's forces in Old Castile and the north-east. Then, in the late summer, the aid of Savoia Marchetti bombers and Fiat fighters speeded the Army of Africa's advance to Madrid. But the most efficient and influential foreign assistance in Spain was the Condor Legion, which ensured the Nationalist's rapid conquest of the northern zones and was of great importance in maintaining the momentum of the Aragon campaign in 1938. The Italian contribution to the Nationalist cause was enormous and more general than the German contribution. It included a major role in the Mediterranean blockade, artillery, the Savoias and Fiat CR 32s, and the CTV.

The effective results of the non-intervention policy, which prevented the Republic from purchasing arms openly, has caused much argument. The Republicans' greatest needs were aircraft and automatic weapons. French equipment was generally of poor quality and the British aircraft available at that date were nearly obsolete. Probably the only country capable of satisfying Republic aircraft needs, apart from the Soviet Union, was the United States. Roosevelt and Cordell Hull may have been influenced by the non-intervention agreement, but it was the Catholic lobby that led Congress to block arms supplies to the Republic. Thus, apart from a few aircraft purchases, Mexican rifles and ammunition, and Czechoslovakian machine-guns bought privately, it might appear that, even without the

Non-Intervention Committee, the Republic had no alternative to the Russian monopoly of arms supplies. Nevertheless, Negrín's decision to send Stalin the Republic's gold reserves was one of the most critical actions of the war. If the gold had to go abroad, Mexico would have provided a safe depository, and a secret arms trade could have been established there.

Russian military equipment was a major contribution to the Republic's survival at the end of 1936, but it cannot be said that Madrid would automatically have fallen without it. Similarly, although the arrival of the International Brigades gave an enormous boost to the defenders' morale and although these formations usually fought bravely and well, their role has been exaggerated.

All three major interventionist powers expected to benefit from testing materials, tactics and men in battle. Soviet methods remained so conventional that the Red Army learned little from the war. The cautious orthodoxy of the Russian officers was largely due to their fear of Stalin: the purge of the Red Army included many advisers from Spain. Condor Legion officers, on the other hand, regarded the war as a fascinating and important laboratory experiment: their technicians invented the napalm bomb, for example. They completely revised their attitudes towards tank design as a result of the Mark I Panzer's vulnerability to the T-26 and the 37 mm gun of the Russian armoured cars; and the development of the *schwerpunkt* armoured spearhead was helped by von Thoma's experience. The testing of the aircraft which were to play such a part in the Nazi conquest of Europe has already been emphasized. So have the tactics of terror-bombing and blocking roads with refugees. All of this contributed to the preparation of the *blitzkreig*, one of the most devastating revolutions in the history of military tactics.

The role of external powers in the Spanish civil war is not merely of European interest. In many ways the war was the prototype of more recent conflicts in the third world, as Noam Chomsky has argued in *American Power and the New Mandarins*. The colonial undertones have been widely recognized: Hugh Thomas described it as 'an imperial war carried on at home'. The role of military advisers and foreign technicians provided the fore-runner to later civil wars such as Vietnam or El Salvador.

The military developments in Spain are numerous and well recorded; but important aspects of the civilian experience also need to be remembered. On the Republican side these included the rapid advances in education and the dramatic, though short-lived, change in the role of women. The most radical social innovation was the development of self-management in industry and agriculture. In fact, the conflict is best remembered in human terms: the clash of beliefs, the ferocity, the generosity and selfishness, the hypocrisy of foreign diplomats and ministers, the betrayals and political manœuvres and, above all, the bravery and self-sacrifice.

POLITICAL PARTIES, GROUPINGS AND ORGANIZATIONS

NATIONALIST

MONARCHIST (ALFONSINE)
Acción Española
Renovación Española
The Alfonsine monarchists supported the descendants of Queen Isabella II, the daughter of Ferdinand VII, as opposed to those of his brother, Don Carlos. Thus the monarchists were those who supported Alfonso XIII and then his son Don Juan (the Count of Barcelona and the father of the present King Juan Carlos). The monarchists' importance was due to the support of conservative army officers, and the way the Bourbon king was the natural leader of 'Old Spain'. Popular support was marginal.

CARLIST
Communión Tradicionalista
Requetés (Militia)
Pelayos (Carlist youth movement)
Margaritas (Carlist womens' service)
The Carlists supported the rival claimant line of Don Carlos, standing for the idea of 'traditionalist' ultra-Catholic monarchy as opposed to Alfonsine monarchism which they felt was corrupted by nineteenth-century liberalism. The leadership, particularly the Count of Rodezno, tended to be court-orientated, while the base of mainly Navarrese smallholders was populist.

FALANGE
Falange Española de las JONS
Flechas (Falangist Youth)
Auxilio Social (Falangist womens' service)
The Falange was a small fascist-style party founded by José Antonio Primo de Rivera in 1933, which then merged in 1934 with the more proletarian JONS (Juntas de Ofensiva Nacional-Sindicalista). Perpetual tension resulted between 'modern reactionaries' who believed in the Nationalist ideals of Old Spain above everything, and the socialist wing which resented the way its anti-capitalist ideology was overridden by the modern *señoritos*. The 'left' group was even more disadvantaged by the vast influx of opportunists in 1936 and 1937. Its influence was crushed when Franco institutionalized the movement in 1937.

FALANGE ESPAÑOLA TRADICIONALISTA Y DE LAS JONS (FET)
This amalgam of the Nationalist political movements brought together the Falange and the Carlists in April 1937 with Franco as head. Their uniform was a blue shirt and red beret.

Pre-war Right
CEDA (CONFEDERACIÓN ESPAÑOLA DE DERECHAS AUTONOMAS)
Acción Popular (populist)
JAP (Juventudes de Acción Popular-Popular Action Youth)
Partido Agrario (mainly Castilian landowners)
The Spanish confederation of the Autonomous Right was a political alliance of right-wing Catholic parties, brought together under Gil Robles. It won the elections of 1933. JAP, its youth movement, joined the Falange *en masse* in the spring of 1936, when the alliance was collapsing as a political force after the Popular Front victory in February 1936.

285

RADICAL PARTY (PARTIDO REPUBLICANO RADICAL)

Led by Alejandro Lerroux, a former revolutionary and anti-cleric, who swung to the right, the party was reputed to be the most corrupt of the period. In 1933 it depended on business and landowning support. In 1934 its liberal wing broke away under Martínez Barrio to form Unión Republicana.

LLIGA CATALANA

The Catalan League was the Catalan nationalist party of the *grande bourgeoisie*, and represented the dissatisfaction of Barcelona industrialists with the centralism and taxation of Madrid.

REPUBLICAN

Popular Front Parties and Affiliated Organizations

UNIÓN REPUBLICANA

Martínez Barrio's Republican Union was a centre right party which broke away from Lerroux's Radicals (who had formed the government of 1934-5 with CEDA participation). It thus represented the right wing of the Popular Front alliance assembled for the February 1936 elections. Its support was based on liberal professions and businessmen.

IZQUIERDA REPUBLICANA

Azaña's Republican Left party came from the fusion in April 1934 of his Republican Action, Casares Quiroga's Galician autonomy party, and the Radical Socialists. Its support was based on liberal professions, small business, teachers and the lower middle class of minor officials.

ESQUERRA REPUBLICANA DE CATALUNYA

Luis Companys' Republican Left party of Catalonia was the Catalan nationalists counterpart of Azaña's party.

PSOE (PARTIDO SOCIALISTA OBRERO DE ESPAÑA)

The Spanish Socialist Worker's Party had a 'left socialist' wing which followed Largo Caballero, and a 'right socialist' wing which followed Prieto and Negrín's social democrat direction.

UGT (UNIÓN GENERAL DE TRABAJADORES)

The trade union of the socialists.

PCE (PARTIDO COMMUNISTA DE ESPAÑA)

The Spanish Communist Party switched from its 'revolutionary vanguard' tactic in 1934 in accordance with the new Comintern policy of seeking alliance with bourgeois parties in Europe against the rise of nazism and fascism. This, together with its inherent belief in centralism and authority, led to its close working relationship with 'right socialists', such as Negrín, and liberals who wanted to establish tight central government control.

JSU (JUVENTUDES SOCIALISTAS UNIFICADAS)

The United Socialist Youth was formed in the spring of 1936 by the amalgamation of the Socialist Youth and the Communist Youth, but the Socialist Youth leader, Santiago Carrillo, had already been recruited by the communists, so he was able to organize a complete take-over soon afterwards.

PSUC (PARTIDO SOCIALISTA UNIFICADO DE CATALUÑA)

The United Socialist Party of Catalonia was an amalgamation of Catalan socialist parties in the early summer of 1936 which was completely taken over by the communists.

POUM (PARTIDO OBRERO DE UNIFICACIÓN MARXISTA)

The Workers' Party of Marxist Unification was led by Andres Nin (Trotsky's former secretary from whom he had disassociated himself) and Joaquín Maurín. Its main strength lay in western Catalonia. The party was not 'Trotskyist' as the Stalinists claimed, but more left opposition communist.

Allies of the Popular Front

The Libertarian Movement (Anarchist and anarcho-syndicalist)

CNT (CONFEDERACIÓN NACIONAL DE TRABAJO)

The National Confederation of Labour, founded in 1910, was the anarcho-syndicalist trade union.

FAI (FEDERACIÓN ANARQUISTA IBERICA)

The Iberian Anarchist Federation was mainly an anarchist pressure group within the CNT

FIJL (FEDERACIÓN IBÉRICA DE JUVENTUDES LIBERTARIAS)

The Iberian Federation of Libertarian Youth.

MUJERES LIBRES

The Anarchist Feminist organization.

Basques

PNV (PARTIDO NACIONALISTA VASCA)

The Basque nationalist party of conservative Christian democrats led by Aguirre.

ANV (ACCIÓN NACIONALISTA VASCA)

Much smaller social democrat splinter from the PNV.

STV (SOLIDARITY OF BASQUE WORKERS)

Basque nationalist Catholic trade union.

CHRONOLOGY

1930 Jan. 28   General Primo de Rivera resigns.

1931 Feb.   General Berenguer replaced by Admiral Aznar.
Apr. 12   Municipal elections, monarchists defeated in major towns.
Apr. 14   Alfonso XIII leaves, Republic proclaimed.
May 7   Segura's pastoral attacking Republic.
May 10   Madrid disturbance and church burning.
Jun. 16   Army reform legislation by Azaña.
Jul. 27   CNT strike in Seville crushed with artillery.
Oct.   Legislation on church. Catholic Republicans resign and Azaña becomes prime minister.
Oct. 20   Law for the Defence of the Republic.
Nov. 19   Ex-King Alfonso condemned *in absentia*.

1932 Jan. 1   Civil guards killed by peasants of Castilblanco.
Jan.   Anarchist rising in Catalonia and CNT strikes. Jesuits dissolved and divorce law introduced.
Apr.   Cardinal Gomá appointed archbishop of Toledo.
Aug. 10   Sanjurjo's *pronunciamiento* in Seville and monarchist rising in Madrid fail.
Sep.   Catalan statute of self-government and agrarian reform legislation.

1933 Jan. 8   Casas Viejas massacre.
Apr.   Azaña's government fails in municipal elections.
Sep.   Azaña defeated. Cortes dissolved.
Oct.   José Antonio Primo de Rivera founds Falange.
Nov. 5   Vote in Basque country on statute of self-government. Navarre votes to stay out of Basque federation.
Nov. 19   Right wins general elections. Lerroux prime minister.
Dec.   Anarchist rising in Catalonia and Aragon.

1934 Feb.   Falange and JONS merge.
Mar.   General strike in Saragossa.
Mar. 31   Mussolini promises arms to Carlists.
Apr. 22   Gil Robles' CEDA organizes mass rally in Escorial.
Jun.   Agrarian strike in Andalucia and Estremadura.
Sep. 9   Covadonga rally by CEDA.
Oct. 1   Three CEDA ministers join new Lerroux government.
Oct. 6   Rising in Catalonia and Madrid easily suppressed. Rising in Asturias becomes regional civil war.

1935 Apr. 1   Gil Robles and four other CEDA ministers in new government led by Lerroux.
Oct. 29   '*Straperlo*' scandal brings down Lerroux. Alcalá Zamora refuses to call on Gil Robles. Military plotting.
Dec.   Chapaprieta government collapses. Alcalá Zamora appoints Portela Valladares.

1936 Jan. 7   Cortes dissolved.
Jan. 15   Popular Front electoral platform agreed.
Feb. 16   General Election. Popular Front narrow victory.

Feb. 26 Catalan Generalidad re-established under Companys.
Mar. Falange attacks on Socialist leaders.
Mar. 15 Falange banned, José Antonio arrested.
Mar. Army warns government about disorders.
Hitler reoccupies Rhineland.
Apr. 1 Communist and Socialist Youth merged.
Apr. 7 Alcalá Zamora deposed by Cortes.
May 10 Azaña elected president.
Capture of Addis Ababa by Italians.
May 12 Casares Quiroga appointed prime minister.
May 13 Election of Popular Front government in France. Blum to be prime minister.
Jun. Building strike in Madrid. Agrarian strikes in southern Andalucia.
Jun. 16 Calvo Sotelo speech on disorder in Cortes.
Jul. 13 Killing of Calvo Sotelo.
Jul. 17 Rising starts in Morocco.
Jul. 18 Rising starts in mainland. Casares Quiroga resigns.
Jul. 19 Rising crushed in Madrid and Barcelona. Martínez Barrio resigns. Giral premier. Orders arming of workers.
Jul. 20 Giral appeals to Blum for weapons. Franco sends emissaries to Hitler. General Sanjurjo killed in air crash on leaving Portugal for Burgos.
Jul. 27 Airlift from Morocco begins with German and Italian planes.
Aug. 8 French stop arms sales to Republican government. Start of non-intervention policy.
Aug. 14 Yagüe's colonial troops capture Badajoz.
Aug. 24 Non-intervention policy accepted in theory by Germany, Portugal and Italy.
Aug. 27 Rosenberg and other Russian officials arrive.
Sep. 3 Army of Africa captures Talavera de la Reina.
Sep. 4 Largo Caballero forms government.
Sep. 5 Beorleguí's troops capture Irún.
Sep. 6 Italian air force units arrive in Mallorca.
Sep. 7 Aguirre forms Basque government.
Sep. 9 Non-Intervention Committee (NIC) formed in London.
Sep. 13 San Sebastián occupied by Nationalists.
Sep. 26 Generalidad government formed.
Sep. 27 Capture of Toledo and relief of Alcázar by Varela's troops.
Oct. 1 Franco installed as head of government and generalissimo at Burgos. Cortes passes Basque statute.
Oct. 7 Uribe's Agrarian decree on collectives and expropriation.
Oct. 10 Popular Army decree.
Oct. 15 Commissar system established in army.
Oct 25 Spanish gold reserves reach USSR.
Oct. 28 Maisky declares to NIC that USSR will not be bound by policy.
Oct. 29 Russian aircraft and tanks appear. German and Italian bombers start raids on Madrid.
Nov. 4 Getafe falls, and Russian fighters appear over Madrid sector.
Nov. 6 Cabinet decides to leave for Madrid. Miaja's junta established.
Nov. 8 Varela's assault on north-west flank of Madrid held. XI International Brigade arrives.
Nov. 9 Varela switches attack to Carabanchel sector.
Nov. German forces reinforced and reconstituted into the Condor Legion.

(1936) Nov. 18 Germany and Italy recognize Burgos administration. Major attack on Madrid.

Nov. 20 Durruti dies from wound. José Antonio executed Alicante.

Nov. 23 Nationalist commanders call off assault on Madrid.

Dec. 13 Nationalists launch offensive on Corunna Road.

Dec. 18 First elements of Italian CTV leave Naples.

Dec. 23 Council of Aragon recognized by Valencia government.

Dec. 25 German-Japanese anti-Comintern pact.

Dec. 31 Anglo-Italian 'gentleman's agreement'.

1937 Jan. 3 Nationalists re-start Corunna road offensive, which continues until Jan. 15.

Jan. 17 Nationalist offensive on Málaga begins.

Feb. 6 Nationalists begin Jarama offensive. Continues until Feb. 28.

Feb. 8 Fall of Málaga.

Feb. 21 Gen. Asensio Torrado sacked. Largo Caballero asks for recall of Russian ambassador Rosenberg.

Mar. 8 Italian CTV starts Guadalajara offensive.

Mar. 18 Battle of Brihuega. Italian retreat.

Mar. 31 Mola's offensive in North begins.

Apr. 19 Franco merges Falange and Carlists into FET. NIC naval patrol and border watch established.

Apr. 22 Bilbao blockade broken.

Apr. 23 Dissolution of Madrid council of defence.

Apr. 26 Destruction of Guernica by Condor Legion.

May 2–6 May events in Barcelona.

May 15 Fall of Caballero government.

May 17 Negrín cabinet formed.
Neville Chamberlain becomes prime minister in UK.

May 29 *Deutschland* incident.

May 30 Republican offensive on Segovia.

Jun. 3 Mola killed in air crash.

Jun. 16 POUM leaders arrested.

Jun. 19 Fall of Bilbao to Nationalists.

Jun. 23 Germany and Italy withdraw from NIC naval patrol.

Jun. 30 Portugal ends frontier control.

Jul. 1 Collective letter from Spanish bishops.

Jul. 6 Start of Republican's Brunete offensive. Continues until Jul. 24

Jul. 12 France ends NIC frontier control.

Aug. 11 Council of Aragon dissolved by decree. Líster's 11 Division crushes agricultural collectives.

Aug. Italian submarine offensive.

Aug. 15 Prieto constitutes SIM.

Aug. 24 Santander surrounded. Republican offensive on Saragossa begins. Battle of Belchite.

Oct. 1 Split in UGT. Caballero ousted.

Oct. 7 Papal Nuncio appointed to Burgos junta.

Oct. 20 Nationalists capture Gijón.

Oct. 31 Republican government moved from Valencia to Barcelona.

Nov. 6 Italy joins anti-Comintern pact.

Nov. 16 British agent appointed to Burgos administration.

Dec. 15 Teruel offensive launched by Republic as diversion to Nationalist offensive planned on Guadalajara.

Dec. 29 Nationalist counter-attack.

1938 Jan. 30   Nationalist decree confirming Franco's powers. Burgos government constituted.

Feb. 22   Nationalists recapture Teruel after flank offensive on Alfambra.

Feb. 25   Halifax becomes British Foreign Secretary after Eden resigns.

Mar. 9   Nationalist offensive in Aragon begins. Nationalist 'Labour Charter'.

Mar. 10   *Anschluss*. Hitler marches into Austria.

Mar. 12   Blum prime minister again. French frontier opened to war materials.

Mar. 16   Intense Italian bombing raids on Barcelona. Communist demonstration to bring down Prieto.

Apr. 6   Prieto's resignation obtained by Negrín.

Apr. 15   Nationalists reach Mediterranean at Vinaroz.

Apr. 16   Anglo-Italian agreement signed.

Apr. 30   Negrín's 13 Points announced.

May–   Nationalists extend gains on southern side of corridor to sea.
Jun.

Jun. 13   Daladier closes French frontier on British pressure.

Jul. 5   Nationalist offensive towards Valencia. Withdrawal of volunteers agreed in principle by NIC.

Jul. 25   Popular Army crosses Ebro and advances on Gandesa.

Jul. 26   Republic accepts British withdrawal of volunteers proposals.

Aug. 16   Republican cabinet crisis with resignations of Ayguadé and Irujo. Negrín and communists organize show of strength in Barcelona.

Sep. 21   Negrín's speech to League of Nations announcing withdrawal of International Brigades.

Sep. 30   Munich agreement.

Oct. 11   POUM trial until Nov. 1.

Nov. 8   Republican army withdrawal across Ebro until Nov. 15

Nov. 15   Farewell parade to International Brigades in Barcelona.

Nov. 16   Anglo-Italian agreement comes into force.

Dec. 23   Nationalist assault on Catalonia begins.

1939 Jan. 3   Decisive Nationalist breakthroughs in southern Catalonia.

Jan. 15   Tarragona falls.

Jan. 26   Nationalist troops occupy Barcelona.

Feb. 1   Last meeting of Cortes at Figueras.

Feb. 5   Genoa falls to Nationalists. French government allows Republican troops to cross frontier.

Feb. 16   Negrín meets Republican military leaders at Los Llanos.

Feb. 21   Nationalist Spain signs anti-Comintern pact secretly (announced publicly Mar. 27).

Feb. 27   Britain and France recognize Burgos government.

Feb. 28   Azaña resigns presidency.

Mar. 2   Casado and Matallana summoned by Negrín to Elda.

Mar. 3   Negrín's appointments of communist officers to all key posts.

Mar. 5   Republican fleet leaves port. Valencia resists Líster. Casado's National Defence Council established in Madrid.

Mar. 10   Mera's troops surround communists in Madrid.

Mar. 15   Hitler invades Czechoslovakia.

Mar. 28   Nationalist troops enter Madrid.

Mar. 31   Nationalist troops occupy final objectives. Non-aggression pact signed with Salazar regime in Portugal. Five-year treaty of friendship signed with Germany.

(1939) Apr. 1 Franco announces end of civil war.
      Apr. 7 Italians invade Albania.
      Apr. 20 NIC dissolves itself.
      May. 19 Victory parade in Madrid.
      Aug. 23 Nazi-Soviet pact signed.
      Sep. 3 Britain and France at war with Germany.
      Sep. 4 Franco declares neutrality.

BIBLIOGRAPHY AND SOURCES

Chapter 1
Abella, Rafael *La Vida Cotidiana durante la Guerra Civil* Barcelona 1978
Basañez, Jesus *Que Dicen de los Vascos* Vol. II, Bilbao 1975
Borrow, George *The Bible in Spain* London 1947
Brenan, Gerald *The Spanish Labyrinth* Cambridge 1969
Busquets, Julio *El Militar de Carrera en España* Barcelona 1971
Carr, Raymond *Spain 1808-1939* Oxford 1968
Castillo, Michel de *Le Sortilège Espagnol* Paris 1977
Madariaga, Salvador de *Spain* London 1946
Miller, Townsend *The Castles and the Crown* London 1963
Petrie, Sir Charles *The Spanish Royal House* London 1958
Read, J. *The Catalans* London 1978
Sencourt, Robert *Spain's Uncertain Crown* London 1932
Thomas Hugh *The Spanish Civil War* London 1977

Chapter 2
Allison-Peers, E. *The Spanish Tragedy* London 1936
Bakunin, Michel *Oeuvres* Paris 1962
Berlin, Isaiah *Karl Marx* Oxford 1960
Brenan, op. cit.
Churchill, Winston *Great Contemporaries* London 1947
Ford, Richard *Gatherings from Spain* London 1970
Guerin, Daniel *L'Anarchisme* Paris 1965
Hormiga, La *Historia del Sindicalismo Español* Paris 1975
Lorenzo, C. M. *Les Anarchistes Espagnols et le Pouvoir* Paris 1969
Malefakis, Edward E. *Agrarian Reform and Peasant Revolution in Spain* Yale 1970
Maura, Miguel *Así cayó Alfonso XIII* Mexico 1962
Meaker, Gerald H. *The Revolutionary Left in Spain 1914-1923* Stanford 1974
Petrie, op. cit.
Preston, Paul *The Coming of the Spanish Civil War* London 1978
Read, op. cit.

Chapter 3
Abad de Santillan, Diego *Memorias* Barcelona 1977
Allison-Peers, op. cit.
Brenan, op. cit.
Bullejos, José *La Comintern en España* Mexico 1972
Castillo, op. cit.
Ford, op. cit.
Gil Robles, José Maria *No fue posible la Paz* Barcelona 1968
Jackson, Gabriel *The Spanish Republic and the Civil War* Princeton 1965
Langdon-Davies, John *Behind the Spanish Barricades* London 1937
Largo Caballero, F. *Mis Recuerdos* Mexico 1956
Lorenzo, op. cit.
Malefakis, op. cit.
Maura, op. cit.
Miller, op. cit.
PCE (Official History) *Guerra y Revolución* Vol. I, Moscow 1967
Payne, Stanley *The Spanish Revolution* New York 1970
Peirats, José *La CNT en la Revolución Española* Vol. I, Paris 1963
Preston, op. cit.
Sender, Ramón *The War in Spain* London 1937

Chapter 4
Abella, op. cit.
Azaña, Manuel *Obras Completas* Vol. IV, Mexico 1968
Bolin, Luis *Spain The Vital Years* London 1967

Bolloten, Burnett *The Spanish Revolution: The Left and the Struggle for Power* London 1979
Brenan, op. cit.
Bullejos, op. cit.
Crozier, Brian *Franco A Bibliographical History* London 1967
Gibson, Ian *The Assassination of Federico García Lorca* London 1979
Jackson, op. cit.
Kemp, Peter *Mine Were of Trouble* London 1957
Langdon-Davies, op. cit.
Mussolini, Benito *La Dottrina del Fascismo* Florence 1939
PCE, op. cit. Vol. I
Payne, Stanley *Falange: A History of Spanish Fascism* Stanford 1961
Peirats, op. cit. Vol. I
Preston, op. cit.
Primo de Rivera, José Antonio *Selected Writings* (Ed. Hugh Thomas), London 1972
Richards, Vernon *Lessons of the Spanish Revolution* London 1953
Sampson, Anthony *ITT, The Sovereign State* London 1973
Vanni, Ettore, *Yo, comunista en Rusia* Barcelona 1950

Chapter 5
Bahamonde, Antonio *Memoirs of a Spanish Nationalist* London 1939
Bolín, op. cit.
Broue, Pierre & Temime, Emile *The Revolution and the Civil War in Spain* London 1972
Carr, op. cit.
Cierva, Ricardo de la *Historia ilustrada de la guerra civil española* Barcelona 1970
Foltz, Charles *Masquerade in Spain* Boston 1948
Fraser, Ronald *The Blood of Spain* London 1979
Jackson, op. cit.
Kindelán, General Alfredo *Mis cuadernos de guerra* Madrid 1945
PCE, op. cit. Vol. I
Payne, Robert *The Civil War in Spain* (Anthology), New York 1962
Peinada Vallejo, J. R. *Cuando la muerte no quiere* Mexico 1967
Peirats, op. cit. Vol. I
Tagüeña, Manuel *Testimonio de dos guerras* Mexico 1973
Thomas, op. cit.

Chapter 6
Bahamonde, op. cit.
Benavides, Manuel *La Escuadra mandan los Cabos* Mexico 1944
Bolín, op. cit.
Borrow, op. cit.
Busquets, op. cit.
Cierva, op. cit.
DGFP (Documents on German Foriegn Policy 1918-1945), London 1951
Diaz de Villegas, José *Guerra de Liberación* Barcelona 1957
Eby, Cecil *The Siege of the Alcazar* New York 1967
Foltz, Charles *Masquerade in Spain* Boston 1948
Gibson, op. cit.
Ibarruri, Dolores *They shall not pass* London 1967
Jackson, op. cit.
PCE, op. cit. Vol. I
Peirats, op. cit. Vol. I
Sender, op. cit.
Thomas, op. cit.

Chapter 7
Abella, op. cit.
Basaldúa, Pedro de *En España sale el sol* Buenos Aires 1946
Bernanos, Georges *Les Grands Cimetières sous la Lune* Paris 1938
Bolín, op. cit.

Casares, Maria *Residente Privilégiée* Paris 1980
Chalmers-Mitchell, Peter *My House in Malaga* London 1938
Eby, op. cit.
Foltz, op. cit.
Fraser, op. cit.
Gibson, op. cit.
Mera, Cipriano *Guerra Exilio y Carcel* Paris 1976
Public Record Office, FO 371/39742, 9903
Saint-Exupéry, Antoine de *Terre des Hommes* Paris 1939
Spain, *The general cause, the red domination in Spain, preliminary information drawn up by the public prosecutor's office*, Madrid 1946; *2nd and 3rd Reports on Atrocities 1936* London 1937
Thomas, op. cit.
Whitaker, John T. *Prelude to War* New York 1942

Chapter 8
Abella, op. cit.
Ansaldo, J. A. *¿Para Qué?* Buenos Aires 1951
Bahamonde, op. cit.
Bolín, op. cit.
Castillo, op. cit.
Crozier, op. cit.
Fraser, op. cit.
Gibson, op. cit.
Hills, George *Franco, the Man and his Nation* London 1967
Jackson, op. cit.
Madariaga, op. cit.
Mora, Constancia de la *In Place of Splendour* New York 1939
Portillo, Luis *The Civil War in Spain* (Ed. Robert Payne), London 1963
Primo de Rivera, op. cit.
Thomas, op. cit.

Chapter 9
Abad de Santillan, Diego *Por qué perdimos la guerra* Buenos Aires 1940
Allison-Peers, E. *Catalonia Infelix* London 1937
Borkenau, Franz *The Spanish Cockpit* London 1937
Brenan, op. cit.
Fraser, op. cit.
García Oliver, Juan *De Julio a Julio* Barcelona 1937
Kaminski, H. *Ceux de Barcelone* Paris 1937
Langdon-Davies, op. cit.
Leval, Gaston, *Collectives in the Spanish Revolution* London 1975
Lorenzo, op. cit.
Malefakis, op. cit.
Mintz, Frank *L'Autogestion dans l'Espagne Revolutionnaire* Paris 1976
PCE, op. cit. Vols I & II
Peirats, op. cit. Vols I & II
Thomas, op. cit.

Chapter 10
Abad de Santillan, op. cit.
Allen, Jay, 'City of Horrors' in *Chicago Tribune* 30.8.36
Bakunin, op. cit.
Bolín, op. cit.
Bolloten, op. cit.
Borkenau, op. cit.
Busquets, op. cit.
Cardozo, Harold *March of a Nation* London 1937
Castells, Andreu *Las Brigadas Internacionales de la Guerra de España* Barcelona 1974
Castro Delgado, Enrique *Hombres made in Moscú* Barcelona 1965

Eby, op. cit. & *Between the Bullet and the Lie* New York 1969
Gerahty, Cecil *The Road to Madrid* London 1937
Kemp, op. cit.
Mera, op. cit.
PCE, op. cit, Vol. II
Peirats, op. cit. Vol. I
Southworth, H. *Mythe de la Croisade de Franco* Paris 1964
Steer, G. L. *The Tree of Gernika* London 1938
Tagüeña, op. cit.
Thomas, op. cit.

Chapter 11
Abella, op. cit.
Atholl, Katherine Duchess of *Searchlight on Spain* London 1938
Avon, The Earl of *Facing the Dictators* London 1962
Beevor, J. G. *SOE 1940-1945* London 1981
Bolín, op. cit.
Carr, E. H. *International Relations Between the Two World Wars* London 1959
Chalmers-Mitchell, op. cit.
Churchill, Winston *Step by Step* London 1939
DGFP, op. cit.
Esch, P. van der *Prelude to War: The International Repercussions of the Spanish Civil War*
    The Hague 1951
Foltz, op. cit.
Ford, op. cit.
Gathorne-Hardy, G. *A Short History of International Affairs* London 1939
International Military Tribunal *The Trial of the Major War Criminals* Nuremberg 1947-9
Jackson, op. cit.
Kirkpatrick, Ivonne *The Inner Circle* London 1958
Monelli, Paolo *Mussolini* London 1953
Thomas, op. cit.
Viñas, Angel *El Oro de Moscú* Madrid 1975

Chapter 12
Abella, op. cit.
Avon, op. cit.
Bolloten, op. cit.
Bowers, Claude *My Mission to Spain* New York 1954
Esch, op. cit.
Jackson, op. cit.
Lorenzo, op. cit.
Nin, Andrés *Los Problemas de la Revolución.Española* Paris 1971
Noriega, Fernando *Fal Conde y el Requeté* Burgos 1937
PCE, op. cit. Vol. II
Payne, Stanley *The Spanish Revolution* New York 1970
Peirats, op. cit. Vol. II
Thomas, op. cit.

Chapter 13
Araquistain, Luis *El Comunismo y la guerra de España* Carmaux 1939
Bolloten, op. cit.
Brome, Vincent *The International Brigades* London 1965
Castells, op. cit.
Cook, Judith *Apprentices of Freedom* London 1979
Gurney, Jason *Crusade in Spain* London 1974
Koltsov, M. *Diario de la Guerra de España* Paris 1963
Krivitsky, General W. *I was Stalin's Agent* London 1963
Orwell, George *Collected Essays Journalism and Letters* London 1968
PCE, op. cit. Vol. II
Payne, Stanley, op. cit.

Peirats, op. cit. Vol. II
Romilly, Esmond *Boadilla* London 1971
Sommerfield, John *Volunteer in Spain* London 1937
Tagüeña, op. cit.
Thomas, op. cit.
US Senate *Report on Scope of Soviet Activity* Washington 1954
Viñas, op. cit.

Chapter 14
Auden, W. H. 'Impressions of Valencia' in *New Statesman* 30.1.37
Azaña, op. cit.
Bolloten, op. cit.
Brome, op. cit.
Cardozo, op. cit.
Castells, op. cit.
Colodny, Robert *El Asedio de Madrid* Paris 1970
Cox, Geoffrey *The Defence of Madrid* London 1937
Gurney, op. cit.
Hills, George *The Battle for Madrid* New York 1977
Kemp, op. cit.
Koltsov, op. cit.
López Muñiz, Gregorio *La Batalla de Madrid* Madrid 1943
Lorenzo, op. cit.
Mera, op. cit.
Nicholson, Harold *Diaries and Letters 1930–1939* London 1966
PCE, op. cit. Vol. II
Schmidt, Paul *Hitler's Interpreter* London 1951
Sommerfield, op. cit.
Thomas, op. cit.
US Government *Foreign Relations of the United States 1936* Vol. II, Washington 1956

Chapter 15
Alvarez del Vayo, Julio *Freedom's Battle* London 1940
Blásquez, Martín José *I Helped Build an Army* London 1939
Bolloten, op. cit.
Brome, op. cit.
Cardozo, op. cit.
Castells, op. cit.
Chalmers-Mitchell, op. cit.
Ciano, Count Galeazzo *Diary 1937–38* London 1952
Colodny, op. cit.
Cook, op. cit.
Hemingway, Ernest *The Spanish War* London 1937
Koestler, Arthur *Spanish Testament* London 1937
Koltsov, op. cit.
López Muñiz, op. cit.
Matthews, Herbert *Two Wars and More to Come* New York 1938
Mera, op. cit.
Mintz, op. cit.
Monelli, op. cit.
Noriega, op. cit.
Orwell, George, *Homage to Catalonia* London 1938
PCE, op. cit. Vols I & II
Payne, Robert, op. cit.
Peirats, op. cit. Vol. II
Regler, Gustav *The Owl of Minerva* London 1959
Romilly, op. cit.
Thomas, op. cit.

Chapter 16
Alvarez del Vayo, op. cit.
Blásquez, op. cit.
Brome, op. cit.
Casado, Sigismundo *The Last Days of Madrid* London 1939
Castells, op. cit.
Cierva, op. cit.
Colodny, op. cit.
Commissariat XV Brigade *Book of XV International Brigade* Madrid 1938
Gurney, op. cit.
Hemingway, op. cit.
Hills, op. cit.
Kemp, op. cit.
López Muñiz, op. cit.
Malinovsky et al. *Bajo la Bandera de la España Republicana* Moscow 1965
Mera, op. cit.
PCE, op. cit. Vol. II
Regler, op. cit.
Salas Larrazábal, J.: *Air War over Spain* London 1969
Thomas, op. cit.
Wintringham, T. *English Captain* London 1939

Chapter 17
Basañez, op. cit.
Broue & Temime, op. cit.
Ciano, op. cit.
Elosegi, Joseba *Quiero Morir por Algo* Bilbao 1971
Galland, Adolf *The First and the Last* London 1957
Lizarra, A. de *Los Vascos y La Republica Española* Buenos Aires 1944
PCE, op. cit. Vols II & III
Payne, Robert, op. cit.
Salas, op. cit.
Southworth, op. cit. & *Guernica! Guernica!* Berkeley 1977
Steer, op. cit.
Thomas, Gordon & Witts, Max M. *The Day Guernica Died* London 1975
Thomas, Hugh, op. cit.

Chapter 18
Abella, op. cit.
Allison-Peers *The Spanish Tragedy* London 1936
Benson, F. R. *Writers in Arms* London 1968
Bolín, op. cit.
Bolloten, op. cit.
Campbell, Roy, *Light on a Dark Horse* London 1951
Casado, op. cit.
Chomsky, Noam *American Power and the New Mandarins* London 1969
Churchill, op. cit.
Commissariat XV Brigade, op. cit.
Cook, op. cit.
Cunard, Nancy (Ed.), 'Authors Take Sides' in *Left Review* London 1937
Donaldson, Scott *By Force of Will* New York 1977
Dos Passos, John *Journeys Between Wars* New York 1938
Foltz, op. cit.
Ford, op. cit.
Gannes, H. & Repard, T. *Spain in Revolt* London 1936
Hemingway, op. cit.
Kemp, op. cit.
Knightley, Phillip *The First Casualty* London 1975
Koestler, op. cit.
Neruda, Pablo *Memoirs* New York 1976

298

Regler, op. cit.
Russell, Bertrand *Roads to Freedom* London 1948
Serge, Victor *Memoirs of a Revolutionary* Oxford 1968
Southworth, *Mythe de la Croisade de Franco* Paris 1964
Spender, Stephen *World within Worlds* London 1951
Sperber, Murray *And I Remember Spain* (Anthology), London 1976

Fiction:
Hemingway, Ernest *For Whom the Bell Tolls* New York 1940; *Fifth Column* London 1966
Herrick, William *Hermanos!* London 1969
Malraux, André *L'Espoir* Paris 1938
Sartre, Jean-Paul *Le Mur* Paris 1939
Slater, Humphrey *The Heretics* London 1946

Chapter 19
Abad de Santillan, op. cit.
Abella, op. cit.
Azaña, op. cit.
Bolloten, op. cit.
Broue & Temime, op. cit.
Castro, op. cit.
Cattell, op. cit.
Churchill, op. cit.
Diaz, José *Tres años de lucha* Paris 1970
Garcia Pradas, José *Cómo terminó la guerra de España* Buenos Aires 1940
Gorkín, Julián *Canibales Politicos (Hitler y Stalin) en España* Mexico 1941
Hernández, Jesus *La Grande Trahison* Paris 1953
Lorenzo, op. cit.
Madariaga, op. cit.
Mera, op. cit.
Morrow, Felix *Revolution and Counter-Revolution in Spain* New York 1938
Orwell, op. cit.
PCE, op. cit. Vols II & III
Payne, Stanley, ops. cit.
Peirats, op. cit. Vol. II
Phillips, Cecil *The Spanish Pimpernel* 1960
Primo de Rivera, op. cit.
Ravines Endocio, *La Gran Estafa* Mexico 1952
Serge, op. cit.
Soria, George *Trotskyism in the Service of Franco* London 1939
Thomas, op. cit.

Chapter 20
Alvarez del Vayo, op. cit.
Avon, op. cit.
Azaña, op. cit.
Bolloten, op. cit.
Brome, op. cit.
Broue & Temime, op. cit.
Castells, op. cit.
Ciano, op. cit.
Cierva, op. cit.
Commissariat XV Brigade, op. cit.
Cook, op. cit.
Esch, op. cit.
Hills, op. cit.
Kindelán, op. cit.
Líster, Enrique *Nuestra Guerra* Paris 1966
Martínez Bande, J. M. *La ofensiva sobre Segovia y la batalla de Brunete* Madrid 1972
Mera, op. cit.
Modesto, J. *Soy del Quinto Regimiento* Paris 1969

Nicholson, op. cit.
PCE, op. cit. Vol. III
Rojo, Vicente *España Heroica* Buenos Aires 1942
Salas, op.c cit.
Thomas, op. cit.

Chapter 21
Anonymous *In Spain with the International Brigades* London 1938
Azaña, op. cit.
Brome, op. cit.
Casado, op. cit.
Castells, op. cit.
Commissariat XV Brigade, op. cit.
Líster, op. cit.
Mera, op. cit.
Mintz, op. cit.
PCE, op. cit. Vol. III
Payne, Stanley, *The Spanish Revolution* New York 1970
Peirats, op. cit. Vol. II
Pons Prades, E. *Guerrillas Españolas 1939-1960* Barcelona 1977
Prieto, Indalecio *Cómo y porqué salí del Ministerio del Defensa Nacional* Mexico 1940
Regler, op. cit.
Salas, op. cit.
Tagüeña, op. cit.
Thomas, op. cit.

Chapter 22
Brome, op. cit.
Broue & Temime, op. cit.
Castells, op. cit.
Ciano, op. cit.
Cierva, op. cit.
González, Valentín (El Campesino) *Listen Comrades* London 1952
Jackson, op. cit.
Kemp, op. cit.
Mera, op. cit.
Peirats, op. cit. Vol. III
Prieto, op. cit.
Rojo, op. cit.
Salas, op. cit.
Tagüeña, op. cit.
Thomas, op. cit.

Chapter 23
Avon, op. cit.
Azaña, op. cit.
Broue & Temime, op. cit.
Churchill, op. cit.
Ciano, op. cit.
Fraser, op. cit.
Jackson, op. cit.
Lorenzo, op. cit.
Peirats, op. cit. Vol. III
Prieto, op. cit.
Rojo, op. cit.
Salas, op. cit.
Tagüeña, op. cit.
Thomas, op. cit.
Viñas, op. cit.

Chapter 24
Abella, op. cit.
Alvarez del Vayo, op. cit.
Azaña, op. cit.
Castells, op. cit.
Fraser, op. cit.
Líster, op. cit.
Mera, op. cit.
Pérez López, F. *A Guerrilla Diary of the Spanish Civil War* London 1972
Rojo, op. cit.
Salas, op. cit.
Tagüeña, op. cit.

Chapter 25
Alvarez del Vayo, op. cit.
Avon, op. cit.
Azaña, op. cit.
Brome, op. cit.
Castells, op. cit.
Ciano, op. cit.
Cierva, op. cit.
DGFP, op. cit.
Esch, op. cit.
Fraser, op. cit.
Payne, Stanley, op. cit.
Peirats, op. cit. Vol. III
Salas, op. cit.
Soria, op. cit.
Tagüeña, op. cit.
Thomas, op. cit.

Chapter 26
Alvarez del Vayo, op. cit.
Bowyer, op. cit.
Broue, & Temime, op. cit.
Casado, op. cit.
Ciano, op. cit. & *Diaries 1939–1943* London 1948
DGFP, op. cit.
Fraser, op. cit.
Jackson, op. cit.
Líster, op. cit.
Mintz, op. cit.
Peirats, op. cit. Vol. III
Regler, op. cit.
Rojo, op. cit.
Salas, op. cit.
Tagüeña, op. cit.
Thomas, op. cit.
Wingeate-Pike David *Vae Victis! Los Republicanos españoles refugiados en Francia* Paris
    1969

Chapter 27
Alvarez del Vayo, op. cit.
Azaña, op. cit.
Casado, op. cit.
Ciano *Diaries 1939–1943* London 1948
García Pradas, op. cit.
Martínez Bande, J. M. *Los Cien Últimos Días de la Républica* Barcelona 1972
Mera, op. cit.
Peirats, op. cit. Vol. III

Salas, op. cit.
Tagüeña, op. cit.
Thomas, op. cit.

Chapter 28
Abella, op. cit.
Blaye, Eduardo de *Franco ou la Monarchie sans Roi* Paris 1974
Broue & Temime, op. cit.
Busquets, op. cit.
Castillo, op. cit.
Ciano, ops. cit.
DGFP, op. cit.
Fraser, op. cit.
Gallo, Max *Spain Under Franco* London 1973
Jackson, op. cit.
Junod, op. cit.
Lizarra, op. cit.
Madariaga, op. cit.
Plenn, Abel *Wind in the Olive Trees* New York 1946
Primo de Rivera, op. cit.
Salas, op. cit.
Southworth, op. cit.
Templewood, Viscount *Ambassador on Special Mission* London 1946
Thomas, op. cit.

Chapter 29
Aguado Sanchez, F. *El Maquis en España* Madrid 1977
Bayo Eliseo, *Los Atentados contra Franco* Barcelona 1975
Berruezo, José *Contribución a la Historia del Exilio* Mexico 1967
Ciano, *Diaries 1939–1943* London 1948
Elosegi, op. cit.
Ford, op. cit.
Gallo, op. cit.
García, Miguel *I was Franco's prisoner* London 1972
Líster, op. cit.
Madariaga, op. cit.
Pérez López, op. cit.
Plenn, op. cit.
Pons Prades, op. cit.
Public Record Office, FO 371/39742, 39703, 39675, 39741, 39704
Ruedo Iberico *España Hoy* (Anthology), Paris 1963
Sutherland, Halliday *Spanish Journey* London 1950
Tagüeña, op. cit.
Tellez, Antonio, *Sabate, Guerrilla Extraordinary* London 1974, & *Facerias* Paris 1972
Templewood, op. cit.
Thomas, op. cit.
Wingeate-Pike, op. cit.

INDEX

Numbers in *italics* refer to picture numbers.